A Bias for Hope

Books by Albert O. Hirschman

National Power and the Structure of Foreign Trade (1945)

The Strategy of Economic Development (1958)

Journeys Toward Progress: Studies of Economic Policy-Making in Latin America (1963)

Development Projects Observed (1967)

Exit, Voice, and Loyalty: Responses to Decline in Firms, Organizations, and States (1970)

A BIAS FOR HOPE

Essays on Development and Latin America

by Albert O. Hirschman

New Haven and London, Yale University Press

1971

Library of Congress catalog card number: 77–140531
ISBN: 0–300–01456–2 (cloth), 0–300–01490–2 (paper)

Designed by John O. C. McCrillis
and set in Times Roman type.
Printed in the United States of America by
The Carl Purington Rollins Printing-Office of
the Yale University Press, New Haven, Connecticut.

Distributed in Great Britain, Europe, and Africa by
Yale University Press, Ltd., London; in Canada by
McGill-Queen's University Press, Montreal; in Mexico
by Centro Interamericano de Libros Académicos,
Mexico City; in Central and South America by Kaiman
& Polon, Inc., New York City; in Australasia by
Australia and New Zealand Book Co., Pty., Ltd.,
Artarmon, New South Wales; in India by UBS Publishers'
Distributors Pvt., Ltd., Delhi; in Japan by John
Weatherhill, Inc., Tokyo.

For Katia and Alain

Contents

Preface   ix

Introduction: Political Economics and Possibilism   1

PART I   Elaborating *The Strategy of Economic
          Development*   39

1. Economics and Investment Planning: Reflections
   Based on Experience in Colombia   41
2. Economic Development, Research and
   Development, and Policy Making: Some
   Converging Views (with Charles E. Lindblom)   63
3. The Political Economy of Import-Substituting
   Industrialization in Latin America   85
4. Industrial Development in the Brazilian Northeast
   and the Tax Credit Scheme of Article 34/18   124

PART II   Addressing the Rich Countries: Critiques
          and Appeals   159

5. Primary Products and Substitutes: Should
   Technological Progress be Policed?   161
6. *Abrazo* versus Coexistence   170
7. Second Thoughts on the Alliance for Progress   175
8. Critical Comments on Foreign Aid Strategies   183
9. The Stability of Neutralism   188
10. Foreign Aid: A Critique and a Proposal
    with Richard M. Bird)   197
11. How to Divest in Latin America, and Why   225

PART III Addressing the Developing Countries:
          A Bias for Hope   253

12. Economic Policy in Underdeveloped Countries 255
13. Ideologies of Economic Development in
    Latin America   270

14. Obstacles to Development: A Classification and a
    Quasi-Vanishing Act   312
15. Underdevelopment, Obstacles to the Perception
    of Change, and Leadership   328
16. The Search for Paradigms as a Hindrance to
    Understanding   342

Index   361

Preface

In reissuing his previously published essays in book form, an author obviously hopes that the wide range of his thought as well as its essential unity will at long last be apparent to all. While this motive is both sufficient and quite honorable, it has become the custom to adduce a variety of others. I can think of three in connection with the present volume. First, after eighteen years and three books almost wholly concerned with development and Latin America, the focus of my interests may shift (as it did in my most recent book); consequently, I felt that this was a good time to assemble my shorter papers in these fields. Secondly, the seven essays published since 1965—over one-half of the book—were written so closely together in time that one often starts where the other leaves off; increasingly they became chapters of a book in formation. Finally, there is the hitherto unpublished introductory essay. It is an attempt to delineate common themes and to discover an underlying methodology and perhaps philosophy. I have been reluctant to delve into such matters, but there comes a time when one feels he ought to try. Bringing together the present group of writings supplied the indispensable stimulus.

Once assembled, the essays fell almost naturally into the three distinct parts of this volume. Within each part, they are presented in the order in which they were written. These previously published texts are reproduced here without change, except for minor corrections and deletions. In some cases, it seemed helpful to explain, in brief introductory notes, the circumstances in which a paper had been written. A few footnotes or quotations have been added where later reading has turned up additional evidence bearing on important points. Finally, a limited amount of cross-referencing has been introduced to orient the reader toward some major links between the arguments of the various essays.

One temptation I have resisted is to insert notes to the effect that I now no longer fully share this or that point of view which I put forward in papers written ten or fifteen years ago. Considering the transformation of the world and the profound change in intellectual climate that took place in the course of this period, it would be surprising and indeed shocking if the earlier papers did not contain a few passages which strike me today as quaint or even wrong. But to argue with oneself in public is to be a bore; and judgments about "continuity and change" in one's thought, like those about its quality, are best left to the reader.

A. O. H.

Cambridge, Massachusetts
September 1970

Introduction: Political Economics and Possibilism

In reflecting on the essays brought together in this volume I noted two principal common characteristics. In the first place, I frequently encounter and stress the political dimensions of economic phenomena just as I like to think in terms of development sequences in which economic and political forces interact. This focus seems to come almost naturally to me in connection with any problem I happen to be attacking and the first part of this introductory essay is an attempt at identifying the central concepts that underlie this "decentralized" activity of building bridges between economics and politics.

Another pervasive characteristic of the writings here assembled is a preoccupation with processes of social change. Understanding social change is obviously not something that can "come naturally" to anyone; one can only grope for it. Consequently the second part of this essay inquires into the nature of my own gropings.[1] It is necessarily more speculative—and, mercifully, much shorter—than the first part.

ECONOMICS AND POLITICS

If demand generated its own supply in the social sciences as it is supposed to do in the marketplace, there would exist by now a number of intellectually satisfying and empirically tested models of the social system based on the intimate interactions and interdependence of economic and political factors. In fact, of course, nothing of the sort is anywhere in sight. Economists continue to identify scientific progress with the elimination of "exogenous" forces from their constructs, while political scientists are similarly

The author is grateful to the Rockefeller Foundation which, in the summer of 1970, offered the magnificent hospitality of the Villa Serbelloni at Bellagio for the writing of this introductory essay. Its first part was presented as the Harvard Lecture at Yale University in November 1970.
1. A related attempt is in the second half of chap. 16, below.

most at ease when they have explained political events by appealing to purely political categories.[2] Where the linkage between political and economic forces is too obvious to be disregarded, both categories of scholars have held to the most primitive linkage models in which typically a phenomenon belonging to the "foreign" discipline is introduced as some sort of prerequisite—and can then promptly be forgotten as purely "domestic" or endogenous forces take over. Insofar as economists are concerned, this practice goes back to Adam Smith's dictum that "little else is requisite to carry a state to the highest degree of opulence from the lowest barbarism, but peace, easy taxes, and a tolerable administration of justice." Political scientists, from Montesquieu and Rousseau to Hayek and Holt-Turner, have similarly looked for some unique and permanent economic characteristic—a certain level and distribution of welfare, or a certain organization of economic life—which makes the emergence of some type of political organization possible, probable, or even inevitable. Once again, no allowance is made in such theories for any continuing interplay between economic and political factors.

How is it possible to overcome the parochial pride of economists and political scientists in the autonomy of their respective disciplines and to go beyond the primitivism of the briefly noted efforts at linking them? Rather than issue another clarion call for an integrated social science, I find it more useful to survey the building blocks that have already been assembled, however inadequate they may be for the construction of an imposing or systematic structure. As just noted, I have frequently turned up some mini-building-blocks of the sort, and a classification and evaluation of these finds may be helpful in bringing a more systematic search underway. The following survey will therefore be largely intro- and retrospective, but I shall make an effort both to note contributions of other writers and to introduce some new points.

2. Note, for example, the success of Samuel Huntington's explanation of political development in terms of "institutionalization" in his *Political Order in Changing Societies* (New Haven: Yale University Press, 1968).

Economic Theories of Politics

A first distinction that is not always clearly made is that between economic theories of politics and theories of political economics (or, better perhaps, theories of economics-cum-politics). The former term has come into use to designate the increasingly numerous and important contributions to political science that have been made, mostly by economists, through the application to political phenomena of modes of reasoning and analytical tools originally developed within economics. The logic of allocation of scarce resources among competing ends, of input-output relationships, and of decision making under uncertainty, to name just a few, should obviously be able to elucidate a great many areas of social and political life other than the strictly economic ones for which that logic was originally devised. Some of the better known efforts of this kind are the *Economic Theory of Democracy* by Anthony Downs and *The Logic of Collective Action* by Mancur Olson.[3] An example in the present book is the note on the "stability of neutralism" (chap. 9) where I use the apparatus in indifference and transformation curves to explain the behavior of an underdeveloped country that can choose between two aid givers and wishes both to receive aid and to maintain its independence.

Two general points can be made about these writings. First, while they may throw much new light on politics, they do not normally deal, nor do they set out to deal, with the interaction between politics and economics.[4] Secondly, there are serious pitfalls in any transfer of analytical tools and modes of reasoning developed within one discipline to another. As the economist, swollen with pride over the comparative rigor of his discipline, sets out to bring the light to his heathen colleagues in the other

3. See also the collection of articles in Bruce M. Russett, ed., *Economic Theories of International Politics* (Chicago: Markham, 1968).

4. This body of writings should therefore not be grandly designated as the "new political economy" as is done in the otherwise very useful survey article by Bruno S. Frey, "Die Ökonomische Theorie der Politik oder die neue Politische Ökonomie: Eine Übersicht," *Zeitschrift für die gesamten Staatswissenschaften* 126 (January 1970): 1–23.

social sciences, he is likely to overlook some crucial distinguishing feature of the newly invaded terrain which makes his concepts and apparatus rather less applicable and illuminating than he is wont to think. As I argue for imported ideologies, the distance between reality and intellectual schema is here likely to be both wider and more difficult to detect than was the case as long as the scheme stayed "at home."[5]

For example, Downs's assumption that parties are uniquely motivated to maximize votes is several notches more unrealistic than the one that entrepreneurs are profit maximizers; the resulting theory is therefore likely to be contradicted by the facts with special vehemence, as I have recently shown.[6]

In the case of my own study on neutralism, I became aware that the ease with which the apparatus of indifference and transformation curves could be transferred from the realm of economics to those of international relations and aid giving was deceptive: in the process, the independence of the indifference map from the production-possibility schedule, so important for the determinateness and normative significance of equilibrium, was largely lost.

The theory of public goods supplies a third example of the care that must be taken when economic concepts are transferred to the realm of politics. It is particularly striking and instructive, and I shall deal with it at somewhat greater length. One of the principal points made by the theory is that the true demand for public goods cannot be ascertained in the market or even by survey methods[7]: since the availability of public goods to an individual consumer is by definition not depleted through consumption on the part of others, each consumer is likely to understate his true preference for the public good as he hopes that others will be willing to pay for all of the supply he wishes to secure; in this manner he would

5. See below, chap. 15, pp. 335–37.

6. See Albert O. Hirschman, *Exit, Voice, and Loyalty* (Cambridge, Mass.: Harvard University Press, 1970), chap. 6.

7. See Robert Dorfman, "General Equilibrium with Public Goods" in J. Margolis and H. Guitton, eds., *Public Economics* (New York: St. Martin's Press, 1969), pp. 270–72, and James M. Buchanan, *The Demand and Supply of Public Goods* (Chicago: Rand McNally, 1968).

get a "free ride." The free rider problem has thus become a principal focus of the theory and its existence provides the basic justification for the provision of public goods by the government (and for financing through taxes).

This is all very acute and pertinent with respect to the supply of a wide variety of public services under modern conditions. Yet, if taken in the widest possible context, public goods include not only police protection, parks, and similar amenities, but public policies that are felt as right and perhaps even gratifying by large groups of citizens. Such policies could even be considered as specially pure public goods since they can be enjoyed by all citizens at the same time, whereas the capacity of parks, police protection, and the like is necessarily limited so that at some point of mass use, their consumption becomes "rival," as is always the case for private goods. Now the "production" of these public policies often requires an effort of advocacy, lobbying, and agitation on the part of the citizens, and here the free rider problem raises its head again: in normal times, with many other needs and interests claiming his time and energy, the average citizen will tend to "let George do it" even though he may be mildly or even strongly interested in the outcome. But the times, like the weather, are seldom wholly normal; on quite a few occasions, lately, they have been abnormal and "a-changin'," and astoundingly large numbers of citizens, far from attempting to get a free ride, have been taking to the streets, to the nation's capital, or to other places where they expect to exert some influence for change. In this connection, it is interesting to note that while economists keep on worrying about the free rider problem, political scientists have become increasingly concerned about the "participation explosion." The latter phenomenon is clearly the obverse of the former: in many cases the individual citizen will insist on being present in a march or demonstration, on participating in a letter-writing campaign, and perhaps even on contributing to an election campaign, although his marginal contribution to the "production" of the public policy he desires to bring about may be close to zero (if not negative at times). To justify his participation in this case, he will perhaps exaggerate to himself the likely importance of his contribution; vis-à-vis others, he may well overstate his "true" preference for the public good in question and will certainly not understate it as he is supposed to according to the theory.

Why would he act in so strange a way? Because he senses his participation not as a cost, but as a benefit, because participation in a movement to bring about a desirable public policy is (and, unfortunately, may be for a long time) the next best thing to actually having that policy. The sudden, historically so decisive outbursts of popular energies must be explained by precisely this change in sign, by the turning of what is normally sensed as a cost that is to be shirked into a benefit, a rewarding experience, and a "happiness of pursuit" in which one simply must share. The possibility of this mutation is fundamental for the understanding of political change and leadership; for achieving change often requires such a mutation and a leader is he who knows how to effect it. Yet the concept of costs turning into benefits is difficult to grasp for the economist trying to reason about "the logic of collective action" by applying tools essentially grounded in the analysis of the market economy.[8] To find someone who knew all about these matters one must go back to Rousseau, who wrote, in *The Social Contract* (bk. 3, chap. 15): "In a truly free country, the citizens . . . far from paying to be exempted from their duties,

8. See Mancur Olson, Jr., *The Logic of Collective Action* (Cambridge, Mass.: Harvard University Press, 1965). In this book, individual participation in collective action to obtain a public good is made to depend on the balancing of the private benefits to be expected from the good against the private costs of participation. At one point in the argument, Olson grants a role to "social pressures" and "social incentives" in the cost-benefit calculus: participation could occur because without it the individual would lose prestige, or the esteem and friendship of his peers (pp. 60–63). In other words, participation is always costly, but on occasion this cost is more than offset by the cost of nonparticipation. This view has much in common with the logic that shows how man always acts out of selfish motives.

In *Exit, Voice, and Loyalty*, I allowed myself to be imprisoned by the traditional notion that the use of voice is always costly. My case for the potential superiority of voice over exit would have been considerably strengthened had I realized that in certain situations the use of voice becomes acutely pleasurable and should therefore no longer be computed as a cost, but as a benefit.

would pay for the privilege of being allowed to fulfill these duties themselves."[9]

One might suggest, then, that economists setting out to elucidate political problems by wielding nothing but their own tools are likely to stumble. Fortunately, their very stumbles can turn out to be illuminating.

Political Dimensions of Economic Phenomena

In proceeding now from economic theories of politics to political economy (or political economics, or politics-cum-economics) proper, I shall stay away, for the time being, from any semblance of a general theory; rather I shall bring together numerous partial observations with the intent of learning something about the nature and structure of the interrelationship between economics and politics.

The observations I wish to relate here can be characterized as political dimensions (or side effects) of economic phenome-

9. One can also profitably go back to Pascal who was perhaps the first to note the distinction between private and public goods, in the following terms: "[Those] who have come closest to the truth have considered that the universal good which all men desire does not consist in any of the particular things which can only be possessed by a single individual. . . . they have understood that the true good must be such that all can possess it at the same time, without diminution or envy" *(Pensées,* 425). As Pascal intimates here, God is the purest public good imaginable: my possession of Him does not detract in the slightest from that of anyone else. At no point can the possession of God ever become "rival" or "exclusive." Note that for this quintessential public good the free rider problem is totally solved. The possibility of obtaining a free ride through the religious exertions of others is excluded by the personal relationship between the god-seeking individual and God. At the same time, striving for God is not sensed as a cost by the religious person particularly since there is no clear dividing line between striving and possessing, so that a free ride would not be desirable even if it were possible.

Yet, various carefully circumscribed free rides are perhaps present in the Christian religion through the concept of grace, the possibility of praying for others, and the sacrifice of Jesus. Indeed, Paul's Epistle to the Romans (5: 12–21) contrasts the free ride to salvation available to Christians through Jesus' death with the free ride to sinfulness forced on all men as a result of Adam's fall.

na. That such dimensions and side effects exist is of course no great discovery. The trouble is that the search for them has been undertaken primarily by sociologists or political scientists who have naturally focused on the most obvious, large-scale features of the economic landscape, such as economic wealth, growth, industrialization, inflation, mass unemployment, and so on. The effects of such economic macrofeatures or -events on politics are either evident and hence uninteresting, or are so complex and depend on so many other variables as to be unpredictable and inconclusive. It is for example not a very fascinating discovery that private wealth can often be translated into political power and vice versa; or that a government's public support will ordinarily be eroded by accelerated inflation or mass unemployment. On the other hand, the effect of economic growth and industrialization on, say, political stability in an underdeveloped country is quite unfathomable in the absence of detailed information about economic, social, and political conditions.

Speculation about connections between economics and politics becomes much more profitable when one focuses not on the roughest outline, but on the finer features of the economic landscape. This can of course best be done by the economist who knows about them; the trouble is that his professional interests do not ordinarily lie in this direction. At the same time, the political scientist who has the motivation to look for such connections lacks the familiarity with economic concepts and relationships that is required. Hence the field is happily left to a few mavericks like myself.

My first discovery of the "finer" kind I am talking about was made almost thirty years ago when I was examining the ways in which a country can acquire political influence through its foreign trade. It occurred to me that there is a straightforward connection between the old established economic concept of the gain from trade which country B achieves by trading with A and the influence which A can exert in B as long as the trade is foreign and is therefore subject to interruption or termination at A's will. The entire theory of the gain from trade and of its distribution became therefore relevant for an understanding of the influence and power relationships that arise out of trade.[10]

A very similar exploration of the political implications of an old established economic concept is undertaken in my most recent book. There it is shown that the famous "consumer surplus" measures not only the consumer's gain from being able to buy a product at competitive market prices, rather than at prices set by a discriminating monopolist, but also the consumer's readiness to react strongly through either "exit" or "voice" should the quality of the product deteriorate. To the extent that voice is chosen, the size of the consumer surplus can be directly related to political action which consumers are liable to engage in to resist and fight deterioration.

Or let us turn to the economic theory of customs unions. For over twenty years now, the analysis of the static economic effects of such unions has been based on the distinction, first suggested by Jacob Viner, between trade creation and trade diversion. It was shown that the trade-creating effects of a customs union had to outweigh the trade-diverting ones for the union to make a positive contribution to the efficient use of world resources. The distinction between trade creation and trade diversion is certainly not one of the more difficult ones in economics. Nevertheless, I have yet to see a political analysis of customs unions which would take advantage of the considerable value of that distinction for an appraisal of the political forces favoring or opposing a union. As a first approximation, it could be said that the political chances of the formation of a union are the exact obverse of its economic effects: the larger the trade-creating effects, that is, the greater the need to reallocate resources in the wake of tariff abolition, the greater will be the resistance to the union among the producer interests of the potential participating countries. On the other hand, trade-diverting effects imply that producers of the member countries will be able to snatch business from their competitors in nonmember countries: the trade-diverting effects will therefore

10. See my *National Power and the Structure of Foreign Trade* (Berkeley: University of California Press, 1945, rev. ed., 1969).

be highly popular with them and will provide a needed cement of interest group advocacy for the union. In the appraisal of the political appeal and feasibility of customs unions, trade creation and trade diversion thus turn out to be extremely useful categories; but the signs which they must be given there are opposite to the ones they carry in the economist's analysis of the welfare effects of customs unions.

Other dichotomies which have long been used by economists can be similarly made to yield considerable food for political thought and analysis. Attempts in this direction are made in chapter 11 with the distinction between portfolio and direct investment and in chapter 10 with that between project and program aid.[11] In the latter respect, it is pointed out that a form of aid giving such as program aid which seemed far more rational to the economist than project aid carried severe political side effects and liabilities. These are now widely recognized, but escaped detection, not only at the time when program aid was first proposed, but for a considerable period thereafter.[12]

Hidden political implications thus exist for some theoretical economic concepts, such as gain from trade and consumer surplus, and for categories originally devised for analyzing, from the economic point of view, such institutions as customs unions, international investment, or foreign aid. Further examples can be drawn from economic history. Here again it normally takes an economist or an economic historian to do the job of uncovering the political implications.[13] For the latter arise out of the char-

11. With respect to the implications of direct as opposed to portfolio investment, see also Hans O. Schmitt, "Integration and Conflict in the World Economy," *Journal of Common Market Studies* 8 (September 1969): 1–18.

12. For an early warning by a politically sophisticated economist, see Thomas C. Schelling, "American Aid and Economic Development: Some Critical Issues" in *International Stability and Progress,* American Assembly (Columbia University, 1957), p. 137.

13. The work of Barrington Moore, Jr. is an important exception to this norm. In his *Social Origins of Dictatorship and Democracy* (Boston: Beacon Press, 1966), he attributes a major role in the shaping of the political destinies of various nations to the "success or failure of the upper class

acteristic detail of economic events. This is the case, for example, for the pattern of industrialization among twentieth-century late-comers: the early stages of their industrialization are largely concerned with the production of finished consumer goods on the basis of imported machinery and intermediate goods; also, during a prolonged period, this production takes place entirely for the domestic market, to substitute previously imported commodities, with no thought of exporting. In chapter 3 it is shown that such observations on the specific differential nature of industrialization can explain much about the frequently noted lack of political assertiveness and power of the industrial bourgeoisie in the developing countries, particularly in Latin America.

When one focuses on primary production and its history in these countries, purely technical economic characteristics also turn out to be politically relevant. The wide fluctuations of coffee prices are a good example. These fluctuations have long been explained by the large number of producers, by the five-year interval between planting and full bearing of the coffee tree which means that even a strong response of producers to price changes has little immediate effect on supply, and by the tendency of the tree to yield a bumper crop at irregular intervals. But these very economic and botanical characteristics also account for the tendency of coffee growers to join together as a powerful interest group which will exert pressures on the state to undertake price support schemes in times of distress. In response to these pressures, the state can then be led to assume responsibilities with respect to the formulation and direction of national economic policy at a relatively early stage.

The low price elasticity of short-run supply characteristic of coffee has interesting further consequences for public policy

---

in taking up commercial agriculture" (p. 459). But he does not stop with this comparatively grand dichotomy and elsewhere points out the vastly different political consequences deriving from land-intensive and linkage-rich sheep raising in England, from labor-intensive grain growing in Prussia, and from the linkage-poor wine trade in France. See his chap. 1 and pp. 45–50, 460–63.

making. Once the coffee-growing country becomes ripe for industrialization, that characteristic makes it possible for the state to finance the needed infrastructure and to subsidize the nascent industries by a policy of squeezing the coffee sector by direct or indirect taxation. Such a policy would be far less successful if the to-be-squeezed primary product had a higher price elasticity of short-run supply, as is for example the case for cattle or wheat. In that case the policy might soon "kill the goose that lays the golden eggs," a phrase that has often been used to describe the ill-fated attempts of Perón to push industrialization in postwar Argentina at the expense of the agricultural sector. With respect to coffee, however, there appears the possibility of a truly dialectical sequence: first, the special production and market characteristics of coffee make for the formation of a strong pressure group of coffee growers which pushes the state into assuming responsibilities for interference with market forces. As a result, the state becomes aware of its capabilities and duties as the maker of national economic policy for development. At a later stage of growth, such a policy will require that income be redistributed away from the coffee growers and toward other sectors which need to be nurtured. And this redistribution can then be carried out with success because of the very characteristics of coffee that originally made for the vigorous and successful pressures of the coffee planters on the state.

It was necessary to show at some length the way in which political forces and relationships grow right out of specific economic situations and characteristics. For through the variety of instances surveyed, I hope to have established a double proposition. On the one hand, it appears that the number of connections between economics and politics is limited only by the ability of social scientists to detect them. On the other hand, it seems quite unlikely that there exists somewhere a master key which would bring into view the usually hidden political dimensions of economic relationships or characteristics in some more or less automatic or systematic manner. Each time, it seems to be a matter of a specific ad hoc discovery; at the same time, he who makes such a discovery increases his chances of making yet another one. For what is required is a certain turn of mind, the desire to speculate and to search in a certain direction, rather than the application of any infallible and objective technique. At most, our examples point to some practical hints or heuristic devices which might help the researcher to "catch" these elusive connections. One such device is the notion of "blessing in disguise" (or mixed blessing, i.e. curse in disguise) with which I have long been taken.[14] Frequently (but by no means unfailingly) it appears that the political dimensions takes the sign opposite to the one that attaches to the economic concept or characteristic. For example, the "gain from trade" measures also the opportunity for domination. In the same vein, the sluggish response of coffee supply to price changes and, in general, a deficient "ability to transform" which would normally be considered unfortunate characteristics by economists, turn out to be advantageous for the development of the coffee-producing country's political (and industrial) capabilities. This sort of compensatory relationship is now familiar to everyone because of the manifold noxious side effects of technical progress that have come into view. But situations in which the political side effects of economic events do not at all exhibit this contrapuntal character certainly cannot be ruled out—what has been said about late industrialization is a case in point. Here we have rather an example of a cumulative sequence à la Myrdal where an intrinsically none-too-favorable economic event—delayed industrialization—has further adverse political consequences. The notion of cumulative disequilibrium can indeed serve as another heuristic device. But there are good reasons to think that the connections between economics and politics which result from the use of this device are comparatively easy to find; therefore they are apt to be less interesting and have probably been overemphasized in what there exists of political economics today.[15]

14. See chap. 14 below, and the introduction to my *Journeys Toward Progress* (New York: Twentieth Century Fund, 1963).

15. See below, p. 33. The two heuristic devices just mentioned—the notion of blessing (or curse) in disguise and the concept of cumulative disequilibrium—do not by any means permit us to discover all the possible connections between economics and politics. A simple reason is that it is

In view of the large number of political implications of economic concepts which the politically inclined economist can uncover, I have little doubt that a similarly long list could be manufactured by the political scientist who would focus, to start with, on some political characteristic or event and would then draw attention to its economic side effects. Unfortunately, the inclination to explore such lines of causation seems to be just as weak among political scientists as it is unusual for economists to be interested in the reverse nexus. As an amateur political scientist, I shall give just one example of the potential fruitfulness of political economy speculations that would have their starting point in politics rather than in economics. One important political characteristic of some Third World societies, particularly in Africa and Asia, is the number and seriousness of cleavages along linguistic, religious, and racial-tribal lines. In comparison to Nigeria or Pakistan, countries like Colombia or even Brazil (not to speak of modern England or France) look remarkably unitary and homogeneous. Besides its many consequences for politics, the existence of such cleavages has profound implications for the appropriate strategy of economic development. For example, in countries affected by such cleavages the tolerance for income inequalities arising in the wake of development is likely to be much smaller than it is in more unitary countries. Hence, in the former, a capitalist strategy will be particularly hazardous, and may well either be abortive or lead the country straight into civil war. This is a vast topic which can only be touched upon here; it serves, however, to point up the important contribution that political scientists could make to the body of knowledge we are looking for.

Interaction between Economics and Politics

The line of inquiry outlined in the preceding section has intrinsic value since it permits political factors to permeate economic

---

impossible, in many cases, to assign an unambiguous positive or negative sign to the sociopolitical implications of an economic event or characteristic. This point is stressed and illustrated in my *Development Projects Observed* (Washington: Brookings Institution, 1967), pp. 186–88.

analysis and vice versa; it can also furnish important elements for a systematic economics-cum-politics. Without the prior accumulation of a large number of such elements, any call for a more integrated social science is bound to be futile. We even came close to describing a particular form of mutual interaction between economic and political forces in discussing the political consequences of high fluctuations in coffee prices. I probably derive special pleasure from the almost chance encounters with politics of the last section in much the same way in which I prefer the sudden, unexpected view of the main piazza one comes upon in a medieval city to the elaborate panoramic layout of later periods more given to "rational, comprehensive planning." Nevertheless, I shall now make a brief attempt to examine head-on the possible outline of general models in which economic and political forces would both be treated as endogenous variables.

Long acquired habits of thought interpose enormous obstacles to such an enterprise. The idea of a self-regulating economic system (erected on the basis of some political prerequisite such as law and order, but otherwise perfectly self-sustained) has retained a considerable grip on the economist's imagination; it has in fact been bolstered in recent years by the confection of similarly self-regulating equilibrium growth models. In such constructs, political factors and forces are wholly absent; if they play any role at all it is that of spoilers. Examples of the latter situation come easily to mind. The imposition of a price ceiling in the wake of political pressures feeding on temporary shortages and price rises makes the shortages more serious and protracted than they would be otherwise. Nationalist agitation leads to the imposition of a tariff, and a loss of welfare is the regrettable result. Lately it has been argued that the loss may not be regrettable, that the willingness to bear the loss may be explained and perhaps justified by a "taste" for economic nationalism; but since it is understood that such a taste is exceedingly odd and unenlightened this condescending "empathy" hardly changes the substance of the more old-fashioned—and more forthright—argument. The view of political factors as spoilers is bolstered by the many tales of how "controls beget more controls," how a simple political interference with economic forces will eventually make the whole system bog down in a maze of official regulations, corruption, and "perverse incentives." Clearly the construction of a model of interaction of economic and political forces will not come easily to those who have been brought up to believe that the admission of politically motivated actors into the economic arena amounts to a pact with the devil.

But economists are not alone in casting political forces in the role of spoilers. The inconclusive discussion on the relation between economic growth and political stability is instructive in this regard. The conjecture that economic growth would lead to the lowering of political tensions and to greater cohesiveness has been increasingly disputed by those who hold that growth tends to have destabilizing political effects. On the basis of the latter view it is then of some (but hardly overwhelming) interest to construct an economics-cum-politics replica of the economic demographer's "low-level-equilibrium trap": first there is economic growth, then this growth leads to adverse political developments which in turn cause economic decline so that economy and society revert to the low level from which they started out.

Such models in which economic growth either dispels or generates political storm clouds are really quite primitive. It is odd that they should have been taken so seriously and tested so doggedly when all the while a much superior construct was available: the Marxian concept of the historical process which rests on a far more realistic, if more complex, interaction between economic and political factors. If one replaces—and this does not do undue violence to Marx's thought—his "productive forces" and "relations of production" by economic and political factors, respectively, the representation of this process is somewhat as follows: at any one historical stage, the economy functions within a given political and institutional framework; on the basis of and owing to this framework, economic forces left to themselves can achieve some forward movement, but beyond a certain point further development becomes more difficult and eventually is held back by the unchanging political framework which, from a spur to progress turns into a "fetter"; at that point, political-institutional change is not only necessary to permit further advances, but is also highly likely to occur, because economic development will have generated some powerful social group with a vital stake in the needed changes.

For the economist, this vision has actually a pleasantly familiar look. It reminds him of one of the basic paradigms of his own science, namely the law of diminishing returns. It is strange that the close resemblance of this law to the Marxian concept of historical change should have been overlooked. Generations of economists have been taught that the output of any productive process will increase at a decreasing rate if the quantity of one cooperating factor of production is kept constant while that of the others is increased. Marx essentially affirmed the same relationship: the fixed factor of production causing decreasing returns was for him any given political and institutional order. In Marx's thought, this order is not subject to small incremental changes and improvements. Hence, the need for revolutionary change.

I was not aware how close I was to this generalized Marxian model of interaction between economic and political forces when I wrote in *The Strategy of Economic Development* that "nonmarket (i.e. political) forces are not necessarily less automatic than market forces"[16] and showed repeatedly how such forces are likely to arise when market mechanisms by themselves would cause shortages of social overhead capital, or would lead to regional imbalances or to other types of disequilibria which required —and were likely to entrain—the intervention of political action. Why did I fail to make the connection between one of my principal theses and Marxism? Largely, I think, because I rediscovered the possible alternation of economic and political forces in propelling societies forward in the context of processes that take place on a small scale as compared to the huge canvas on which Marx painted. But much of the fruitfulness of the Marxian scheme may well lie in applying it to slices of reality rather smaller than was intended by the master.

In any event, this is what I have been doing. An example is the

16. New Haven: Yale University Press, 1958, p. 63.

description of import-substituting industrialization in chapter 3: in combination with import controls, the existence of an over-valued exchange rate is shown to be at first a considerable help in getting the process underway in a certain political environment, but it eventually turns into a hindrance to further industrial development because it holds back both the expansion of capital goods manufacture and the achievement of a substantial volume of industrial exports. I also identify interest groups and political forces that are likely to advocate ever more powerfully the needed institutional changes.

A number of points can be made about such transpositions of the Marxian scheme to smaller-scale processes of economic-political development. In the first place, the political and institutional changes that are needed in any one of these sequences are less likely to be revolutionary than in those that interested Marx. Clearly, passing from a highly overvalued exchange rate to a slightly undervalued one is less likely to require a revolution than the transition from the capitalist to the socialist mode of production. Nevertheless, even such comparatively minor changes in institutional structure require discontinuous decisions which are often difficult and replete with political struggles and risks.

Another way in which the Marxian scheme can be usefully varied is by examining more closely the nature of political change that is supposed to resolve "contradictions" which have arisen in the preceding phase. Marx thought here in terms of revolutions that sweep away all of the institutions of whatever ancien régime needs to be done away with, and that then set up sociopolitical conditions ideal for the vigorous and unhampered unfolding of the "productive forces" during a prolonged period until such time as a new batch of contradictions emerges. Most of the time, historical reality is, of course, far less neat: sociopolitical change entrained by the contradictions is often partial, grudging, and with a lot of unfinished business left behind, so that the need for further change makes itself felt once again in fairly short order. The frequently fragmentary character of political-institutional change thus explains why the Marxian scheme is found to be so surprisingly useful on a far smaller historical scale than that for which it was conceived. This reasoning also suggests that the amplitude, length, and frequency of the interaction cycles will vary considerably over time and from country to country. One element in this variation could be the freedom different countries have to undertake large-scale political change. Untrammeled in this respect, the hegemonic powers will often go in for all-inclusive, apocalyptic, and cathartic crises that will be widely spaced in time, thereby conforming rather closely to the Marxian vision. Dependent countries, on the other hand, are kept from having their revolutions or their civil wars by some hegemonic power standing watch over them, always ready to dispatch armies or economic advisers commissioned to forestall a real crisis;[17] they must therefore introduce political change in a more stealthy and imperfect fashion[18] and are likely to exhibit more numerous interaction cycles that will revolve rapidly, so that the "next" required measure of public policy is never very far away. This is one reason why many observers of the reality of the dependent countries have found it so utterly indispensable to think systematically about the interaction of economics and politics.

A real advantage of visualizing growth processes in the manner previously outlined lies in the greater flexibility and realism with which it becomes possible to appraise economic policies and developments. No longer will one condemn any policy that is not immediately directed toward establishing the ideal tax or exchange rate system, or the most advanced agrarian reform legislation. Rather, the observer and policy maker will think in terms of sequences in the course of which a forward step in one direction will induce others, perhaps after a period of "decreasing returns" and political-action-inducing disequilibria. It is not just a matter of "[moving] the economy wherever it can be moved";[19] on the contrary, while there will be less need for trenchant statements about uniquely correct policies and absolute priorities, the policy maker will often have to engage in difficult speculations about

17. The role economic advisers play in short-circuiting crises is illustrated in my *Journeys Toward Progress*, pp. 206–10.
18. See chap. 15, pp. 333–35.
19. Chap. 2, p. 82.

what I called "efficient sequences" in the *Strategy of Economic Development:* from among the various directions in which it is possible to move, he will have to form a judgment about the one that is most likely to achieve eventually certain objectives which are not within the direct reach of policy making. It is perhaps of interest to note here that the "pure economist" who refuses ever to think in terms of certain second-best policies which, via consequential political changes, could lead indirectly to the achievement of a desired objective, has a counterpart in the revolutionary who asks for the needed political changes right away, as an absolute prerequisite to any forward movement: neither seems ever to think in terms of economics-cum-politics (or politics-post-economics) sequences.

The most difficult and critical problem in thinking about such sequences is an appraisal of the likelihood that the needed political changes will actually take place once the phase of decreasing returns to economic forces acting alone has set in or, in Marxian terms, once the productive forces have entered into sharp contradiction with the relations of production. Reflecting on the role of the bourgeoisie in the French Revolution, Marx thought he had solved the problem, insofar as the societies he analyzed were concerned, by identifying the industrial proletariat as the force that would have both the will and the power to make the socialist revolution. While in this respect his vision has turned out to be faulty, the kind of search he engaged in remains an essential part of the enterprise I am advocating here for smaller-scale sequences. There was never an intention on my part to assert that any sort of imbalance would be automatically corrected. Nor is it a question of the right size of the imbalance. The Toynbeean notion of a proper response arising directly from the challenge (provided only it is of the right size) is entirely foreign to my thinking.[20] Whenever I noted the phenomenon of economic forces alone leading to an imbalance or otherwise tension-laden or unsatisfactory state of affairs which needs to be corrected by political action, I have tried to locate specific "agents of change" which, much like Marx's

20. See also chap. 14, pp. 318–19.

industrial proletariat, would have the motivation and power to bring about that action.

Here is one example of this type of concrete search: after describing the economic forces which could make for increasing interregional disequilibrium in the course of a country's economic development, I pointed out that political counterforces might arise from the fact that "the poorer sections of the country, where careers in industry and trade are not promising, often produce, for that very reason, a majority of the country's successful politicians and thereby acquire influential spokesmen in the councils of government."[21] Similarly, in the treatment of import-substituting industrialization (chap. 3) I engage in a determined search for forces that might counteract the tendency of industrialization to bog down after the "easiest" import substitution opportunities in the last stages of production have become exhausted.

It is nevertheless tempting to inquire whether there are any general reasons to expect political actions to be forthcoming in the situations that have been described. A very general model could be derived from the observation that many actors in a society can choose, at any one point of time, to engage either in economic or in political action. It has often been noted that an industrialist, for example, has the option of spending most of his time and energy either on improving the efficiency of his production and sales organization or on lobbying in the nation's capital for special tariff protection or other legislation favoring his firm and industry. Disregarding the adverse value judgment that attaches in this example to political action, we may bring this sort of option into contact with the tendency of economic growth to run into decreasing returns when it proceeds within an unchanging institutional framework. Surely, the decreasing returns will somehow impress themselves on the consciousness of the individual economic-political actors. Once they notice that the marginal productivity of economic action is diminishing in comparison to the prospective marginal productivity of political action, there will be a tendency on their part to substitute political

21. *Strategy*, p. 193.

for economic action. Hence, it is likely that an effort to carry out the needed political changes will actually be undertaken.

This very general reasoning by no means dispenses the social scientist from engaging in a detailed search for specific "agents" or "carriers" of change. But it is useful in permitting him to get away from one feature of the Marxian system which is still very much on the—conscious or unconscious—mind of numerous contemporary writers: the obsessive search for the vanguard or spearhead of the revolution, for the one or at least the principal class or homogeneous group that can be counted on to overthrow the existing order or to effect needed changes. The model just sketched makes it quite plausible that the "decreasing returns" phenomenon will impress itself on the consciousness of a wide variety of groups and individuals; if political change comes, then, it may well result from the combined efforts of many parties rather than from the exertions of a single group. I believe that thinking about the likelihood and strategy of currently needed social and political change, in the United States and elsewhere, would considerably gain in realism if it could free itself of the notion that such change is impossible without the discovery of a single, homogeneous vanguard group.[22]

Misperception and Interaction

In the preceding treatment the emergence of "contradictions" or of "decreasing returns" has retained rather an aprioristic character. The notion has been made plausible to the economist by equating any given political framework with the existence of a factor of production in fixed supply, but I will admit that the analogy need not be wholly compelling.

22. The grip of the homogeneous vanguard-group concept is evident in the writings of otherwise highly diverse authors. Thus, Heilbroner in *The Limits of American Capitalism* (1966) and Galbraith in *The New Industrial State* (1967) look to the "scientific elites" or to the "Educational and Scientific Estate," respectively, for accomplishing the social changes they deem desirable, and New Left writers are focusing their search on youth or Blacks. See Massimo Teodori, ed., *The New Left: A Documentary History* (Indianapolis: Bobbs-Merrill, 1969), particularly the selections for chap. 16, "In Search of a Class Analysis."

Is it possible to provide a more solid foundation for the assertion that "economic forces acting alone" need to be relayed at periodic intervals by political-institutional changes? Perhaps there is really no need for an elaborate justification of this point, for it is overwhelmingly unlikely that any institutions devised by human minds will be able to accommodate indefinitely and efficiently any new economic and technological change that happens to come along. The specific reasons for which existing sociopolitical institutions are inadequate in dealing with newly arising economic forces are likely to be vastly different from one case to another, but the emergence of some such inadequacy would appear to be a remarkably safe bet. I shall nevertheless attempt to go a little farther and conclude this part of the introductory essay by pointing to one particular (and perhaps particularly interesting) class of economic-political sequences.

In market economies, the intervention of government through taxes, subsidies, and direct provision of goods and services has ordinarily been justified for cases of "market failure," the most typical of which is the presence of monopoly or of external economies and diseconomies. Government action in the economic field is thus conceived as a corrective and complement of private action. The picture that emerges from this way of looking at things is that, little by little, all the areas in which the market tends to fail will be ferreted out, and the best possible mix of market and nonmarket decision making will be approached and permanently established.

This "asymptotic" conception of the state's role is unsatisfactory because it leaves unexplained the continuous seesaw action between market and nonmarket forces which has in fact been taking place in all market economies. One way of accounting for the seesaw may be found in the notion that economic decision makers are frequently subject to misperceptions of newly emerging opportunities. Along such lines I have argued that opportunities in underdeveloped regions tend to be seriously underrated by private investors at some stage of their country's development; similarly, at some other stage, the need for continued reliance on capital from abroad will be overrated. In both cases, perception lags behind reality: the economy of the underdeveloped region and the capacity to raise industrial capital domestically have grown, but institutional inertia and past habit make it hard to take advantage of these changes or even to notice them. Decisive acts of public policy—such as the establishment of exceptional incentives for the underdeveloped region or a restrictive policy toward foreign investment—may then be necessary to acquaint economic operators with an emerging reality which they stubbornly ignore. In the case of the underdeveloped region, such acts are essentially designed to "change ingrained attitudes, both of self-deprecation within the region and of prejudices against it, its people, and resources in the rest of the country."[23]

When public policy measures are motivated by this need to change perceptions, the possibility of an optimal, once-and-for-all corrective intervention disappears. Instead, there arises the perspective of a *sequence* of interactions between market and non-market forces. For policy measures correctly designed to change expectations and perceptions will no longer be optimal once they have accomplished the mission assigned to them. In the short run, policy measures will thus have to overshoot any long-run goal. To give an example: the incentives essentially needed if misperceiving entrepreneurs are to set up their first industrial ventures in an underdeveloped region are bound to be much stronger than those that need or should prevail once a broadly based industrial establishment has come into being and entrepreneurs have been thoroughly cured of their previous misperceptions. In contrast to market failures grounded in objectively existing externalities, the presence of misperceptions therefore creates the need for a series of properly spaced corrective moves, each one requiring of course its own constellation of political pressures, alliances, and other favorable circumstances.[24]

23. Chap. 4 below, p. 154.

24. In the case just noted and in a number of others, the need for corrective public policy measures could be obviated by the timely arrival on the scene of creative Schumpeterian entrepreneurs, who are able to perceive the change in circumstances or the new opportunities that go unrecognized by their more routine-ridden and prejudiced contemporaries. My point

Moreover, the series is not necessarily convergent, for it is quite conceivable, and indeed likely, that new misperceptions arise at each successive stage. As a result, I am tempted to argue that the relentless search for permanently optimal policies and institutions which characterizes much of social science is often misdirected. In many situations, it may be possible to define optimality only with respect to the width and frequency of periodically needed reversals of policies and changes in institutions.

Let me again give an example from the area of international development policy. A discussion has long been raging about whether close contact by means of trade and capital flows with the advanced industrial countries is beneficial or harmful to the less developed countries. Some authors have been able to cite important static and dynamic, direct and indirect benefits that accrue to these countries from close contact. Others have shown that close contact had a number of exploitative, retarding, stunting, and corrupting effects on the underdeveloped countries and that spurts of development in the periphery have often been associated with periods of interruption of contact, such as world wars and depressions. To neither of these two warring parties has it apparently occurred that they may quite conceivably both be right. In order to maximize growth the developing countries could need an appropriate alternation of contact and insulation, of openness to the trade and capital of the developed countries, to be followed by a period of nationalism and withdrawnness. In the period of openness, crucial learning processes take place, but many are of the latent kind and remain unnoticed and misperceived. They come to fruition only once contact is interrupted or

---

here is precisely that in some key situations the likelihood of such a providential appearance is infinitesimal.

It should be obvious, incidentally, that misperception and underestimate of newly and gradually emerging opportunities and capabilities is no monopoly of private decision makers. Public authorities are, if anything, even more subject to the inertia that breeds misperception and that can be corrected and overcome only by incentives and ideologies which are excessive from any long-run point of view. The extremes of early laissez faire capitalism can perhaps be interpreted in this fashion.

severely restricted: the previous misperceptions are then forcibly swept away. Thus both contact and insulation have essential roles to play, one after the other.

This conclusion upsets deeply rooted modes of thought. Everywhere, not only in relation to the international economic policy of the developing countries, social scientists are looking for optimal policies and states, and that generally means that they are looking for optimal combinations of desirable, but mutually antagonistic ingredients of such states. Thus we look for the correct combination not only of contact and insulation, but of central control and decentralized initiative, of moral and material incentives, of technical progress and social justice, and so on.

It is here suggested that we devote at least a portion of our time and efforts to understanding the possible usefulness of alternation and oscillation, as opposed to optimal combination.[25] In the first place, it is possible, as in the case of contact and insulation, that certain patterns of alternation would yield results superior to the best that could be obtained by stable combination. Secondly, the focus on alternation would permit one to acquire a feeling for the right amplitudes of the many swings that do occur anyway in the real world. Finally, attention to these patterns of alternation would yield a special bonus from the point of view of this essay: it would reveal a good many sequences in which economics and politics relay each other repeatedly as principal actors.

A PASSION FOR THE POSSIBLE

The intensive practice of economics-cum-politics is no doubt a principal characteristic of the essays here collected. At the same

25. While I have only now formulated this idea as a general principle, I have long "applied" it in a variety of contexts. See *Strategy*, pp. 173–75; *Exit, Voice, and Loyalty*, pp. 124–25; and this book, chap. 12, passim, chap. 15, pp. 340–41, and chap. 16, p. 349. A similar point of view is expressed by Erik Erikson who exalts the Hindu life cycle scheme which "allows for a succession of pointedly different life styles" over "the almost vindictive monotony of Judean-Christian strictures by which we gain or forfeit salvation by the formation of one consistently virtuous character almost from the cradle to the very grave" *(Gandhi's Truth* [New York: W. W. Norton, 1969], p. 37).

time, however, these essays are pervaded by certain common feelings, beliefs, hopes, and convictions, and by the desire to persuade and to proselytize which such emotions usually inspire. I would not be true to the purpose of this introduction as proclaimed in the preface, if I did not make at least a brief attempt to talk also about these matters.

Most social scientists conceive it as their exclusive task to discover and stress regularities, stable relationships, and uniform sequences. This is obviously an essential search, one in which no thinking person can refrain from participating. But in the social sciences there is a special room for the opposite type of endeavor: to underline the multiplicity and creative disorder of the human adventure, to bring out the uniqueness of a certain occurrence, and to perceive an entirely new way of turning a historical corner.

The coexistence as equals of the two types of activities just outlined is characteristic of the social sciences. In the natural sciences the unexplained phenomenon and alertness to it are also of the greatest importance, but only as a means to an end, as the beginning of a new search for an improved general theory which would subsume the odd fact, thus overcoming its recalcitrance and destroying it in its uniqueness.* In the social sciences, on the other hand, it is not at all clear which is means and which is end: true, most social scientists behave in this respect as if they were natural scientists; but they would be more surprised than the latter and, above all, considerably distraught if their search for general laws were crowned with total success. Quite possibly, then, all the successive theories and models in the social sciences, and the immense efforts that go into them, are motivated by the noble, if unconscious, desire to demonstrate the irreducibility of the social world to general laws! In no other way would it have been possible to affirm so conclusively the social world as the realm of freedom and creativity. But by now there surely is

---

*As this book goes to press I find that I am here doing an injustice to at least one natural scientist. In his recent book, *Le Hasard et la nécessité* (Paris, Seuil, 1970), pp. 160–61, the biologist Jacques Monod argues in favor of the "disagreeable idea" that the emergence of both life and man may have resulted from unique occurrences whose a priori probabilities were close to zero.

something to be said for pursuing this theme in a less roundabout fashion.

The importance of granting equal rights of citizenship in social science to the search for general laws and to the search for uniqueness appears particularly in the analysis of social change. One way of dealing with this phenomenon is to look for "laws of change" on the basis of our understanding of past historical sequences. But the possibility of encountering genuine novelty can never be ruled out—this is indeed one of the principal lessons of the past itself. And there is a special justification for the direct search for novelty, creativity, and uniqueness: without these attributes change, at least large-scale social change, may not be possible at all. For, in the first place, the powerful social forces opposed to change will be quite proficient at blocking off those paths of change that have already been trod.[26] Secondly, revolutionaries or radical reformers are unlikely to generate the extraordinary social energy they need to achieve change unless they are exhilaratingly conscious of writing an entirely new page of human history.

I have of course not been disinterested in claiming equal rights for an approach to the social world that would stress the unique rather than the general, the unexpected rather than the expected, and the possible rather than the probable. For the fundamental bent of my writings has been to widen the limits of what is or is perceived to be possible, be it at the cost of lowering our ability, real or imaginary, to discern the probable.

The nature of these persistent widening attempts—or of what I shall call my "possibilism"[27]—varies with the public I am addressing. In putting together the essays of this volume, I found that I have been playing to two quite different galleries. The essays of part II criticize policies of the rich and powerful countries toward the developing countries and advocate substantial changes in those policies. In making my proposals, I refuse, on the one hand, to be

26. See also chap. 16 below, p. 358.
27. The meaning I am trying to bestow on this term has nothing in common with the watered-down environmental determinism for which it has stood among geographers.

"realistic" and to limit myself to strictly incremental changes. At the same time, however, these proposals are not presented as being so revolutionary or so utopian that they have no chance whatever to be adopted in the absence of prior total political change. On the contrary, I feel an obligation to make them in concrete institutional detail thereby deliberately creating the optical illusion that they could possibly be adopted tomorrow by men of good will.

This "naive" disregard of sociopolitical realities and of vested interests is precisely rooted in my possibilism: I propose fundamental changes in institutions such as international aid and investment, but I am not willing to prejudge categorically the extent, much less the modality, of the wider social and political transformations that may or may not be a prerequisite for such proposals ever being adopted. The reason for this agnosticism is in this case the observation that the constraints on policy makers are far less binding in a number of conceivable historical constellations than at "normal" times. Moreover, one important condition for such constellations to yield real change is the prior availability and discussion (followed then, of course, by contemptuous dismissal) of "radical reform" ideas that can be readily picked up when times suddenly cease to be normal.

The essays of part III deal in large measure with ideologies and concepts characteristic of the literature on economic and political development and of the intellectual climate in the developing countries. Here I have found an exceptionally good hunting ground for exaggerated notions of absolute obstacles, imaginary dilemmas, and one-way sequences. The essence of the possibilist approach consists in figuring out avenues of escape from such straitjacketing constructs in any individual case that comes up. But to go about this task efficiently it is helpful to be equipped with a few conceptual tools. In the following I shall therefore describe in general terms how I have come to practice "possibilism," how I have found it possible to increase the number of ways in which the occurrence of change can be visualized.

One handy device is, once again, the notion of blessing (or curse) in disguise. By pointing to the ways in which many presumed "obstacles" to development have in some situations turned into an asset and a spur, one obviously casts doubt on any statements about this or that "obstacle" having to be eliminated if there is to be this or that desirable development.

But the notion of "blessing in disguise" is like a label for a certain class of sense data; it has little explanatory value. An intellectually more satisfying, though more specialized, foundation for possibilism was encountered in the theory of cognitive dissonance. A group of social psychologists has shown through this theory, that changes in beliefs, attitudes, and eventually in personality can be entrained by certain actions instead of being a prerequisite to them (see chap. 14). This idea is so congenial to my thinking that I pointed to one such "inverted" sequence even before I had become acquainted with Festinger et al.: in many situations, so I argued, the Protestant ethic is not the cause of entrepreneurial behavior, but rather arises as its consequence.[28]

Similar critiques of widely accepted ideas on the one-way nature of certain sequences can now be found elsewhere in the social sciences. Take the seemingly self-evident notion that a consensus on basic values and political procedures is a precondition for the establishment of a viable democratic system. According to a recent paper which appeals to historical evidence as well as to cognitive dissonance theory, the causation has often run the other way—democracy has come into being as a result of an accidental, but prolonged standoff between forces originally quite bent on crushing each other; and what basic consensus about political decision making is later found to prevail in these cases can be shown to have been the consequence of democracy, rather than its cause.[29]

---

28. *Strategy,* pp. 185–86. Somewhat earlier, Pascal had pointed out that religious feelings can be the consequence, rather than the cause, of devotional acts, such as kneeling *(Pensées,* 233, 250).

29. Dankwart Rustow, "Transitions to Democracy: Toward a Dynamic Model," *Comparative Politics* 2 (April 1970): 337–64. This idea also is a rediscovery: Machiavelli noted in a famous passage that the "perfection" of the Roman Republic and "all the laws that were made in favor of liberty" were due to the so often lamented "disunion between the Plebs and the Senate" *(Discorsi,* bk. 1, chaps. 2 and 4).

The idea that beliefs, attitudes, and values can be refashioned and molded by more or less accidentally undertaken practice is put forward here only for the purpose of justifying the existence of alternatives to certain "orderly" sequences. There is no intention, at least on my part, to claim primacy for the inverted sequence over the orderly one. In fact, I recognize that the former can give rise to special problems and tensions in comparison to the latter (see p. 326). Moreover, I have lately come to criticize certain aspects of cognitive dissonance theory that in turn imply an excessive denial of human choice and freedom.[30] For the theory predicts that once a certain action is engaged in, beliefs will be changed to suit that action, whereupon renewed resort to the same type of action becomes more likely, leading to a further strengthening of the changed beliefs, and so forth, in a cumulative sequence. To show how it is possible to break out of such sequences is an important task of the possibilist, as will shortly be shown.

A third general foundation for possibilism is in the notion of unintended consequences of human action and in its relation to change. An episode from the recent history of Peru will serve to introduce this topic with which I shall deal at somewhat greater length.

The immediate cause of the military takeover of 1968 in that country was a public uproar over a proposed settlement of the long dispute over United States–owned petroleum interests. The expropriation of these interests by the strongly nationalistic military was a natural consequence of their seizure of power and served to justify it in the eyes of the nation. But then, in 1969, the military government struck out once again, this time at the powerful domestic "oligarchy," by expropriating the large coastal sugar plantations and in general by decreeing a far-reaching land reform. Yet, not long before, an Argentine sociologist had proved definitively, in a widely reprinted article, that the days of the progressive military coup in Latin America were gone forever! The military, he showed, had turned from being occasional, if

30. *Exit, Voice, and Loyalty,* pp. 92–96.

unreliable, innovators into staunch and cruel defenders of the socioeconomic status quo.[31]

What went wrong with this prediction in Peru's case? In the discussion of the deeper-lying causes for the actions of the Peruvian colonels and generals, two explanations recur most frequently. First, in the fifties, it was decided that the technical instruction of upper echelon officers should be supplemented by training in citizenship; as a result, a center for high military studies (CAEM —Centro de Altos Estudios Militares) was established where Peruvian anthropologists and sociologists held teaching positions and exposed the officers to modern ideas and theories of social integration and development. Secondly, these officers had conducted an antiguerrilla campaign in the early and middle sixties, during which they had efficiently destroyed the guerrilla movement; that experience, it is generally reported, was so searing for them, that they became determined to change the basic conditions which imposed such tasks upon them.

Those who supply or routinely repeat the latter explanation do so generally without realizing what a sensational and paradoxical theory they are propounding. Because this miserable century has presented psychologists with unprecedented opportunities for studying human cruelty, torture and assorted atrocities, the psychological mechanism of progressive brutalization is now well known: a person may commit his first brutality more or less by accident or on command, but then, having committed it, has to justify it to himself and in this progressive fashion he becomes ever more committed to his inhumanity—the widespread existence of this sort of cumulative movement is, alas, well established.

In the Peruvian case, on the other hand, the experience of one's own brutality appears to have produced not greater brutalization, but the determination to change the state of the world which caused the brutality in the first place—an almost miraculous conversion appears to have taken place for once among the perpetrators of cruelty. The reason may lie in the previously noted

31. José Nun, "The Middle Class Military Coup," in Claudio Veliz, ed., *The Politics of Conformity in Latin America* (London: Oxford University Press, 1967), pp. 66–118.

combination of circumstances: officers who had been taught in the CAEM that it was their mission to forge a united Peru which could be a true fatherland for all of its sons including the most miserable Indian, were suddenly placed in the position of napalming the villages of those very Indians and of killing them, as well as young poets and intellectuals from the cities who had taken seriously those very teachings. As a result, the tension between ideology and actual behavior as imposed by the environment was exceptionally wide and painful. On the other hand, the military had bred into them a high degree of confidence that the environment is subject to change at their hands. Jointly, then, that painful tension and that confidence may account for their reforming zeal, for their refusal to submit to the cumulative spiral of brutalization.

The story has several points. For example, it contains a nice instance of a blessing in disguise, a part that is played here by the thinness of the country's intellectual elite. This ordinarily much lamented characteristic of Peruvian (or Latin American) society meant that army officers, once they were to be taught sociology and political science, came (unintentionally, of course) under the influence of the very few social scientists and intellectuals whom Peru could muster and who were all strongly oriented toward fundamental changes in the status quo.

A more noteworthy lesson of the Peruvian story is that social scientists may have become overimpressed with the cumulative character of the processes they study. We are by now thoroughly conditioned to explain and anticipate cumulative spirals by Myrdal's process of circular causation, by Merton's self-fulfilling prophecy, and by some just noted aspects of cognitive dissonance theory, not to speak of more routine reinforcement and feedback processes. As a result, any change in the direction of a process—the turnaround or dialectical reversal or *Umschlagen*—takes us by surprise, except, perhaps, for the outbreak of revolution in its classic form.

It is ironic that Myrdal proposed his notion of circular causation in order to get away from the self-equilibrating models in economics and sociology and from their conservative, laissez faire implications. For, in a sense, he threw out the revolutionary baby with the conservative bathwater. According to his analysis, the cumulative processes of discrimination, deterioration, and underdevelopment, disastrous as they are, do not awaken by themselves any counterforces—the only exception is the intellectual who observes things from the outside and somberly predicts that they will get much worse unless some appropriate action is taken. The many insurgent and radical social scientists who have embraced this sort of model have thus fallen unwittingly into a profoundly undialectical and, what is worse, unperceptive and unimaginative way of thinking.

One important way of rekindling perception and imagination and of developing an alertness to dialectical, as opposed to purely cumulative, social processes is to pay attention to the unintended consequences of human actions. This is extraordinarily well illustrated by the Peruvian story. Here both the training in citizenship the military received (though not in the actual form it took at CAEM) and the suppression of the guerrillas in the Sierra were activities purposefully designed to ensure the maintenance of the status quo; but in combination they had unintended side effects which led to irreversible social change.

The concept of unintended consequences of human actions has of course a distinguished ancestry. Intimated by Vico and propounded as a paradox by Mandeville, it was developed systematically by Adam Smith and his contemporaries. But the concept was always cast in one particular mold: a set of rather unprepossessing activities, such as the pursuit by everyone of his own material gain, was shown to have edifying consequences because through their unintended side effects these activities would guarantee the overall functioning, stability, and rationality of the existing social system.

Perhaps it is because many of the later critics of this way of thinking were social reformers that its rich potential for understanding and expecting social change, rather than equilibrium, rationality and optimality, has not been actively exploited. The idea that change, particularly major social change, is something to be wrought by the undeviatingly purposeful actions of some change agents is certainly far more widespread than the view that change can also occur because of originally unintended side effects of human actions which might even have been expressly directed toward system maintenance.

The possibilist will not contend that the predominant view of change is wrong; but he will challenge its predominance by collecting evidence supporting the alternative point of view. The Peruvian story was one case in point, but since it is a personal interpretation of still unfolding events, I shall invoke some more authoritative examples.

In the first place, I can refer to two anthropologists who attempted, a few years ago, to give a comprehensive account of the "human revolution" and proposed as their principal theoretical construct the following principle which they called "Romer's rule," "after the paleontologist A. S. Romer who has applied it so effectively . . . in his own work":

> *The initial survival value of a favorable innovation is conservative, in that it renders possible the maintenance of a traditional way of life in the face of changed circumstances.*

The authors continue:

> Later on, of course, the innovation may allow the exploration of some ecological niche not available to the species before the change; but this is a consequence, not a cause.
>
> One of Romer's examples concerns the evolution of Devonian lungfishes into the earliest amphibians. The invasion of the land was feasible only with strong fins (which in due time became legs). But strong fins were not developed "in order to" invade the land. The climate of the epoch was tempestuous; the water level of the pools in which the lungfishes lived was subject to sudden recessions. There was thus selection for those strains of lungfishes which, when stranded by such a recession, had strong enough fins to get back to the water. Only much later did some of their descendants come to stay ashore most of the time.[32]

32. Charles F. Hockett and Robert Ascher, "The Human Revolution," *Current Anthropology* 5 (June 1964): 137.

In other words, the lungfishes' attempt at system maintenance (the desire to get back to the water and thus to remain amphibians) leads here to system change. A similar view of change and innovation is put forward by an economist in a book on agrarian development under population pressure.[33] Initially, so the author shows, population growth in primitive agricultural communities leads merely to reduction of fallowing and consequently to lower output per man hour. But, at the same time, the intensification of agriculture may cause work habits to become more regular and more efficient, and larger numbers may lead to new forms of the division of labor. These secondary effects can then "set off a genuine process of economic growth."[34]

It should not be inferred from these two examples that change via unintended side effects is in any way restricted to "lower forms of life" such as animals or "primitive people." Efforts to maintain or restore a social organization or a way of life or a standard of living that is threatened or weakened have yielded unintended innovational change in modern societies just as among the lungfish. At the threshold of the modern age, the discovery of America originated in an effort at "system maintenance," in the search, that is, to keep *up* or restore maritime contact with India. Many technical inventions which then led to further important transformations of technology, occurred as a result of sudden interruptions of normal trade flows due to war or blockade and the consequent need to maintain prior output levels through the production of substitutes. Industrialization in many countries, particularly among the twentieth-century latecomers, was similarly brought underway not so much by the will to industrialize as by the need to keep up the supply of consumer goods whose importation became suddenly impossible during the world wars and the Great Depression.

In short, history could be viewed as the process of men in general, and the ruling classes in particular, continually outsmarting themselves in their efforts to reproduce and maintain the existing order.

33. Esther Boserup, *The Conditions of Agricultural Growth* (Chicago: Aldine, 1965).
34. Ibid., p. 118.

Change that occurs in such manner as a result of unintended side effects can be compared from several points of view to the kind of voluntaristic change that is brought about consciously by some change agent, be he a revolutionary or an agricultural extension officer. In the first place, the unintended change is often likely to be more revolutionary than change brought about by the most revolutionary of change agents, for the simple reason that the imagination of the change agent is severely limited by his immediate experience and historical precedent. More important, unintended change is of course far more difficult to detect and to block by the forces opposed to change; for that matter, these forces often participate unwittingly yet actively in bringing it about. On the other hand, unintended change may be less satisfying to those profiting from it than voluntaristic change, since it "falls into one's lap" without either advance planning or sustained struggle.

Actually these two types of change are little more than analytically useful distinctions; most of the time they will be found to be closely intertwined in the real world. For example, voluntaristic change will often take over after unintended change has done the spadework and created conditions in which the outline of previously hidden possibilities of change can begin to be perceived by an activist change agent. In other situations, such voluntarist activists may be futilely trying to make "the last revolution," as Régis Debray put it, but since they draw all the fire and monopolize the attention of the pro-status-quo forces, they make it even easier for the unintentional processes of change to come to fruition. Elements of both these combined situations are present in the Peruvian story.

Such, then, are some of the devices which the possibilist can use to sharpen the perception of available avenues toward change. There are probably quite a few others. For these devices cannot be expected to trace out by themselves new, hitherto undiscerned avenues; they are only meant to help defend the right to a non-projected future as one of the truly inalienable rights of every person and nation; and to set the stage for conceptions of change to which the inventiveness of history and a "passion for the possible" are admitted as vital actors.

PART I

Elaborating *The Strategy of Economic Development*

1. Economics and Investment Planning: Reflections Based on Experience in Colombia

It is to be welcomed that economists have decided to explore systematically the question of investment criteria for economic development which is the subject matter of this conference. With so much development planning taking place in the world today and with economists frequently occupying key positions in the planning apparatuses, it does not seem fair either to the public in the underdeveloped countries or to the economists themselves to leave undefined the nature of the contribution which our profession can aspire to make. To entertain and encourage exaggerated notions of our abilities will sooner or later invite reactions of the type: "But the Emperor has nothing on!" To refuse to take a stand on a country's vital development problems, on the other hand, would be an avowal of bankruptcy on the part of the social science whose principal subject of inquiry has long been defined to be the allocation of scarce resources between competing ends.

Perhaps the time has come to state clearly what is the type of question about planning which has to be resolved by the engineer or the politician rather than by the economist and what is, on the contrary, the area where the latter is supreme or can at least provide useful guidance. To make such distinctions is rendered difficult not only because the economist naturally partakes in the universal desire for power and finds it difficult to admit that there are limits to his prowess, but also because he is usually endowed with more literary ability than the engineer. Moreover, the politician prefers to have the planning decisions presented in scientific

This essay was written for a conference in 1954, after I had spent two years in Bogotá as economic adviser. It is the first paper I wrote on general problems of economic development; a number (but by no means all) of its points were later worked out more systematically in *The Strategy of Economic Development*. Reprinted by permission from *Investment Criteria and Economic Growth*, MIT Center for International Studies (New York: Asia Publishing House, 1961), pp. 33–53.

terms as long as his requirements are satisfied. Thus the lot of writing up development plans usually falls to the economist and this fact produces the optical illusion that economics as a science can yield detailed blueprints for the development of underdeveloped countries.

What, in all honesty, can it yield? To begin, what is it yielding at present for this purpose?

The Value of Aggregative Analysis

A highly interesting effort is currently being made by individual economists and by such agencies as the United Nations Economic Commission for Latin America to relate various macroquantities of the economic system in such a way as to obtain some guidance for the basic economic policies of underdeveloped countries. By constructing models involving the national income, the population increase, the average and marginal capital-output ratios, and the propensity to save, and by using the results of intensive statistical investigations concerning the range of these parameters, it is possible, for example, to gauge how much foreign capital is required to achieve a desired rate of growth of national income per head. By combining the income-elasticity of demand for a country's exports with the probable increase in income of its customers, its own propensity to import, and again the desired rate of increase in per capita income, it is possible to arrive at broad conclusions concerning the necessary speed of industrialization. The needed growth in agricultural output and investment can be similarly derived on the basis of certain reasonable food consumption trends, assumed transfers of population from agriculture to industry, etc. The guidance which an individual country can derive from this type of work is important: it might in due time influence attitudes toward taxation, foreign capital, and toward a balanced development of industry and agriculture.

Thus far, however, generalizations involving large aggregates of the economic system have somehow seemed to be lacking in ready applicability to the specific problems that confront the practical planner. He knows he should be on the lookout for low capital-output ratios, but is also made to realize that the calculations relating output to investment are either not possible or, if possible, are far from conclusive in the type of social overhead investment (transportation, power and water supply, irrigation, etc.) he is most likely to deal with. He knows that he is supposed to pay close attention to the balance of payments effect of new investment, but again he is most frequently concerned with projects that are expected to have a pervasive effect on the productivity of the economy rather than with specific export-raising or import-saving proposals. Finally, he realizes that agriculture and industry should be developed in step, but the improvement in agricultural methods is a discouragingly slow and decentralized process, so that our economist is generally content to leave this matter to the specialist unless he can promote a large-scale irrigation scheme or discover some kind of patent formula for the relief of a country's agricultural ills such as, in Colombia, the switching of agriculture from the eroding slopes to the plains and of livestock raising in the opposite direction. But, in this latter case, the actual investment of funds in transportation, power, and industry is rather poorly balanced by the outpouring of mere good advice with respect to agriculture.

It appears, then, that the economist is still on firmest ground when dealing with the largest aggregates of the economy such as consumption, savings and investment, and imports and exports. In advising on the securing of a balance between these aggregates at the highest possible level for savings and investment, he has at his disposal a whole arsenal of proven monetary, banking, fiscal, and foreign exchange techniques and, with some ingenuity, can always obtain the satisfaction of producing a variant of his own. But this task is generally that of the financial adviser and does not satisfy the planner-economist interested in the composition rather than the size of a developing country's investment.

Is it true then that, aside from the very general guidance received from aggregative analysis, all the economists can do is, in the words of a U. N. report, "to soak themselves thoroughly in the facts of each particular case and then use their best judgment as to what will be the most desirable directions of movement"?[1] As a critic of the report puts it, the underdeveloped countries are thus cast in the role of "inanimate materials" which are to be given shape by "the intuitions of the artist-planner."[2]

The main thesis of the present paper is that this absurd conception of the role of the economist engaged in development planning has been due to overemphasis on the confection of "overall, integrated development programs" and to a neglect of the search for a body of principles and meaningful generalizations which would permit the economist to be concretely helpful in the location and elaboration of promising, specific investment projects. In line with this position, I shall try to do some debunking in the first part of the paper while attempting to be constructive in its second part.

THE MYTH OF INTEGRATED DEVELOPMENT PLANNING

There are two principal reasons for which the economist should make far less of the "integrated, overall development planning" than has been the fashion: first, this planning involves in reality very little creative effort; and secondly, if such effort were required, economics would have very little to contribute.

The first point is dealt with below at greater length; suffice it here to say that, in broad outline, the principal areas of needed development are usually fairly obvious and the economist does not invent an investment pattern, but merely extrapolates the existing one while making room within it for some of these obvious priority areas. The second point is more central to my critique: if national development and investment programs are to have any validity from the point of view of economics, they must mean, for example, that the last million pesos of scheduled expenditures on education will have approximately the same impact on the growth of the national product over the years to come as the last million pesos

1. *Measures for the Economic Development of Underdeveloped Countries,* Report by a Group of Experts appointed by the Secretary General of the United Nations (New York, 1951), paragraph 151.

2. S. H. Frankel, *Economic Impact on Underdeveloped Societies* (Cambridge, Mass.: Harvard University Press, 1953), p. 94.

to be spent on transportation. I believe, however, that such a claim cannot validly be made by economists for their development programs.

In the first place, economics cannot really go beyond the statement that transportation and education are both important; within extremely wide limits set by common sense rather than economics, the determination of the proper share of these two sectors in a development program will be made intuitively and arbitrarily. If there is at all a reasoned decision as to the apportionment of investment funds between these two sectors, it will have to be based on a fundamental conviction as to whether the change of environment intended to change the people should take precedence over attempts to change the people directly—a question to which economics can supply no answer.

But there is another, more immediately practical reason for which it is ordinarily impossible to claim that the marginal contributions to future output of the various sectors of a development program are in fine balance, namely, the heterogeneous character of the figures included in the investment budget. There is indeed usually such a wide variation between what might be called the reality content of these figures that a comparison between their probable impact on the economy is quite out of the question. Some of the figures will be pure guesses or extrapolations from the past, some very general targets ("so many hospital beds"), and only a few will stand for specific projects whose nature is precisely known and whose financing assured, such as the construction of a steel mill or the building of a hydroelectric power station at a certain site. Obviously it is impossible to compare the social marginal utilities of an expenditure which is known in all its details to another whose nature only is given, but whose precise characteristics have not been defined so that it may turn out to be a good, bad, or indifferent investment provided it takes place at all. I submit, therefore, that the principal task of the economist, before committing himself to any one investment pattern, is to give all his figures for sector investment the same reality content.

THE MEANING OF "POOR," AND OF "GOOD" PLANNING

We are touching here on an important area of semantic confusion. The term "poor planning," so often heard in Colombia, is never used in reference to the apportionment of total investment funds among the principal sectors of the economy; it rather designates a highway that has been built where there is no traffic, an irrigation scheme in an area with adequate rainfall, etc., etc.[3] "Good planning" means simply to have studied and prepared thoroughly a given project, that is, to have ascertained whether it corresponds to a real need, whether proper engineering and market studies have been made, whether full financing has been assured so that it will not remain half completed for years, and whether alternative ways of filling the same need have been explored and rejected for good reasons. "Good planning" does not and, I believe, should not mean that all possible alternative uses for the funds which are to be spent on the project have been explored and rejected. This is a matter which countries such as Colombia, and possibly all countries, can leave, with Burke, to a "wise and salutary neglect."

Thus development planning can proceed from the basic diagnosis of the root causes of a country's poverty and backwardness directly to the elaboration of concrete, rationally laid out sector projects. The elaboration of "overall, integrated development programs" is not essential, and in fact might be harmful. The economist-planner should not forget that his own skill is one of the

3. A minister of finance graphically describes this type of poor planning in his annual report: "One of the most picturesque and at the same time disturbing chapters is the way public buildings are constructed in our country. In Colombia we have an irresistible addiction for the monumental. A school for a municipality which can supply 120 pupils, will be built with a capacity for 500. A building where 15 or 20 offices are to be located—the post-office, the telegraph, the municipal court—must have at least 8 floors to achieve any dignity, even though in that locality there is no electric power for an elevator. The electric power plant whose construction is requested with the utmost urgency, must have a capacity of 3000 kW even though the potential consumption of the town does not exceed 200" (Antonio Alvarez Restrepo, *Memoria de Hacienda 1951* [Bogotá: Imprenta Nacional, 1952], pp. 188–89).

very scarce resources in underdeveloped countries. If he devotes it primarily to the elaboration of comprehensive investment programs projecting everything ten or more years ahead, he runs the risk of bringing about, in the economic sphere, a counterpart to a state of affairs which André Siegfried found characteristic, some twenty years ago, of political life in many Latin American countries: the contrast between fine theory and wretched practice.[4] Similarly, the pretense of total, integrated economic planning could and often does coexist quite amicably with, and may serve to cover up, unregenerated total improvisation in the actual undertaking and carrying out of investment projects.

The need for comprehensive planning is sometimes explained by referring to the water, power, or transportation shortages which have occurred in a city, region, or country and, so it is argued, might have been avoided had there only been in existence a properly integrated development program. This seems to me equivalent to saying that a person has run out of gas because he incorrectly planned, or failed to plan, his gasoline purchases in relation to his purchases of other commodities. While this statement is formally correct, it might be more helpful to tell that person to watch his gasoline gauge the next time. Similarly, an electric power shortage may be attributed to the fact that no overall economic plan was drawn up or that investment in power has not received the proper priority within such a plan; but it seems more useful to point out that it can ordinarily be traced to faulty sector planning and, even more frequently, to the great difficulties in properly carrying out well-designed sector plans in fields such as electric power, where the time lag between plan and execution is particularly long and which therefore require a steadiness of purpose, a stability in administration and similar qualities often in short supply in underdeveloped countries. The dispersal of efforts to please every province, the maintenance of rates that do not

4. That is, between constitutions with their assurance of free elections, their rights of the individual, their checks and balances, etc., and the realities of arbitrary exercise of dictatorial power. See André Siegfried, *Amérique Latine* (Paris: A. Colin, 1934), p. 100.

permit the setting aside of reserves, the frequent changes in plans and personnel—these are usually the principal factors making for inadequate investment in power and hence for insufficient power supplies and the ones that have to be dealt with if there is to be any improvement. "Assigning a higher priority to power in the overall investment program" would be of little avail.

It may be objected that recent economic history of developing countries contains several cases of calculations of demand for power, water, etc. that have gone wrong because a region or a city has suddenly developed at a much faster pace than previously. But how could "overall planning" be of help in these cases? Because of the time lag between plans and realization, a power shortage is almost bound to develop in such instances, as it would be too hazardous in a capital-poor country to plan the expansion of so capital-intensive an industry as electric power on the basis of mere hopes for a sudden acceleration in economic growth. Thus when an acceleration actually occurs, a power shortage will make itself felt until such time as new projections taking into account the quickened pace of development bear fruit in the form of newly installed capacity. Anyone who has lived in a country caught in the drive for development knows of many towns and regions whose inhabitants are convinced that they stand on the threshold of a tremendous era of prosperity. Sudden rapid advances actually do occur here and there, but it is surely better to let some temporary shortages in public utilities develop in these instances than to waste the country's capital resources by preparing for explosions of economic progress everywhere.

My conclusion is that the appearance of certain shortages and bottlenecks in the process of economic development is most frequently due to inadequate planning and administration within the sector in which the shortage occurs; and that, when they occur in spite of perfect planning and administration within this sector, they are unavoidable concomitants of a process of accelerated economic development.

OVERALL VS. SECTOR PLANNING

The practical consequence of the foregoing considerations is that the economist-planner should bring his talents primarily to bear on the elaboration of well-planned sector projects. In actual fact, the examination that is generally given to a single project by the most exacting critics does hardly ever go beyond the criterion that there be an obvious need for the goods or services to be supplied by it and that it be well planned per se. In spite of all the insistence on "overall" planning, I have yet to see a project that is thus well conceived rejected by national or international agencies disposing of investment funds on the ground that the investment required is too high considering the need for monetary stability and for "balanced" development. In Colombia, the only case to my knowledge into which this kind of consideration has thus far entered at all was that of the Paz de Rio steel mill. Nevertheless, the report of the International Bank Mission, which objected to the project, carried only one extremely vague sentence about the fact that the money involved in Paz de Rio might be put to better use elsewhere in the economy,[5] while several pages were devoted to specific technical strictures against the project.[6] Thus, even in a case where there was undoubtedly a strong feeling that a given investment project was too big for the economy regardless of its desirability *per se* and technical merit, it was sensed that an effective attack against it could only be made in terms of the imperfections of the project itself rather than in terms of some undefined alternative uses of resources.

The accent here is on the word undefined. Let us assume that the economist is convinced that our particular project, although well planned itself, does not have the highest priority in terms of the economic development of the country; unless he can say in detail what the alternatives are, unless he can produce projects in a state of readiness-to-be-undertaken similar to the one he attacks, he will not and *should not* be listened to. The reason for this position is that there exist not only conceivably better uses for the

5. "The tremendous amount of capital involved, particularly U.S. dollars, would return much greater yields to Colombia invested in other sectors of the economy" (*The Basis of a Development Program for Colombia* [Washington, 1950], p. 426).

6. Ibid., pp. 419–28.

funds, but many worse ones as well, and that these are the ones that are surely going to be undertaken if no ready alternative is provided by our objecting economist. Of still less force would be the economist's position if he were to argue that a given project endangers the country's monetary stability; if the project is useful and well planned, why not make room for it by compressing through general fiscal and monetary measures some types of consumption and all nondescript investment activities which are probably of a low-priority nature? Again, it is only when these activities have become "descript," that is, have themselves been incorporated in rationally planned projects and programs, that it will be possible to advise against such a policy of general squeeze in favor of the few projects that have really been well laid out.

In summary, underdeveloped countries are characterized not only by a low rate of investment, but also by the low efficiency of much of the investment that is actually undertaken. This is due in part to the many false starts that will necessarily be made before a country's economy is really launched on a secure course, and in part to the lack of qualified engineers, agronomists, economists, etc., who can produce really useful and well thought through, specific investment projects. Such projects are naturally at a premium, are most likely to and should go through, irrespective of any stricture against them on alternative-use-of-resources or danger-to-monetary-stability grounds. In fact, they are all that is usually left behind from the "integrated development programs" elaborated and announced with much fanfare. Thus, in the investment field, the only important achievement of the International Bank Mission to Colombia was the highway and railroad program, which was also the only one to have been spelled out in fairly concrete terms.[7]

BIASES IN THE DETERMINATION OF HIGH-PRIORITY AREAS

Thus the most important task for the economist is to make a contribution to the elaboration of sensible sector programs and spe-

7. The report of the mission has, of course, had a considerable educational value, besides exerting an important and continuing influence on monetary, fiscal, and foreign exchange policy.

cific investment projects. But before this task can be undertaken he has to satisfy himself as to the areas of highest priority in which he feels that he should make this contribution. This determination may represent a formidable problem in a country whose economy is underdeveloped and stagnant. But in a country like Colombia, which, though still insufficiently developed, has been making rapid strides, the very growth that has taken place usually creates stresses and shortages which point conclusively to principal areas that have lagged behind or whose natural growth must be accelerated if further all-round progress is to be assured. Thus the most superficial observer of the Colombian economy will realize that transportation and electric power are key factors conditioning further growth. Improvements in agricultural methods, changes in land utilization and education of the farmers are other obvious objectives to correct the lagging behind exhibited by agriculture. The growth of cities generally makes imperative an improvement and expansion of public utilities such as waterworks and sewers. It appears, then, that the selection of priority areas does not represent much of a problem, at least in the type of country I have been concerned with.

One word of caution is nevertheless called for. The economist should be aware of existing biases in this field so as to be able to direct his attention to sectors which may have been neglected. We may list a few such biases. Democratic governments depending on popular elections will tend toward an undue dispersion of the public investment effort so as to mend fences in all regions of the country. "Strong" governments, on the other hand, are apt to concentrate too much on a few spectacular showplaces. All governments are likely to show a preference for projects that can be inaugurated, and therefore will often neglect maintenance of existing capital and investment in human capital, such as education and health (outside of the building of schools and hospitals which can be inaugurated, but which represent only a very small part of the effort necessary to improve health and education). This neglect is also due to a frequently encountered attitude of discouragement on the part of the rulers of underdeveloped countries toward their own people (and of the people toward themselves): advancement can only be visualized as a result of their transformation by the machine and a modern environment; the idea that through improved education and health man might meet the machine at least half way is not often encountered.[8]

It is interesting to notice that the biases of the foreign economist-planner may work in the same direction as those of the local government. His stay in the country is limited and he wants to make a visible imprint on the country's economy. He, too, is therefore going to try to change the face of the country rather than its people and, confronted with pervasive poverty and inefficiency, is likely to concentrate on a few big projects whose execution can be guaranteed as a result of foreign technical, engineering, and financial assistance, rather than on programs that require laborious improvements in organization and methods or the application of native skills and efforts at many points of the economic system. Finally, it is probably correct to say that this bias is not entirely absent from the decisions of the large international lending agencies. They also are looking for short cuts to economic development and are ready to let themselves be persuaded that they have found them in the form of a hydroelectric project, a few arterial roads or an irrigation scheme. And it is hardly necessary to point out that such projects always have the backing of politically powerful contractors and other business interests.

The foregoing is not meant as an argument against the big "steel-and-concrete" projects. Provided they are well laid out, they not only may provide, as already pointed out, a better use of investment funds than the scattered efforts which would probably be undertaken in their absence, but they might also fire the imagina-

8. "With respect to health and education, our country, just as most of Latin America, still finds itself in a state of deplorable backwardness. Unfortunately our mentality is such that there is no drive to push for a solution of these problems. Our people take a passionate interest in the realization of public works, gather in throngs in our small towns to clamor for a road, a building, or a bridge. Such matters agitate our crowds, disturb our press, and eventually bring about joint action by the authorities and the people to overcome difficulties and obstacles. Nothing similar happens with respect to the problems which concern the health of the body and the spirit" (Alvarez Restrepo, *Memoria,* p. 155).

tion of a hitherto stagnant society and awaken many previously dormant energies. Nevertheless, it seems important for the economist to realize that there is, in addition to the strong arguments in favor of these projects, a natural strong bias toward them on the part of governments, economic advisers, international lending agencies, and business interests alike. Maybe we should force our economic adviser to spend at least half of his time helping in the elaboration of projects in the unglamorous, but nonetheless essential, fields of education, small industry, improvement of agricultural methods, etc.!

THE CONTRIBUTION OF THE ECONOMIST TO SPECIFIC INVESTMENT PLANNING

So much for the choice of the areas in which the economist is to make his contribution. We now come to the nature of this contribution itself. It is in this field that, I feel, the economist has not been ambitious enough while overreaching himself in the area of "overall planning." Once a sector of the economy, say electric power, has been designated as a priority area for investment, the next step is usually to call in a group of consulting engineers who will be in charge of drawing up a specific plan for the expansion of power generating facilities.[9]

The economist, to be sure, will review the plan in the end and will make some perfunctory analysis of the proposed investment relating it to total investment and to national income, with the likely result that he will pronounce the plan as sound and bankable. But should he not have a more important role than this one of acting as usher and high-level messenger boy for the people who make the real decisions? In other words, does the economist not have a contribution to make when such vital matters as road *vs.* railroad, hydroelectric *vs.* thermoelectric power are being decided, or even when alternative techniques for road construction are being discussed?

Clearly economics can produce a number of significant consid-

9. At this writing, a joint French-American mission, formed exclusively by engineers from Electricité de France and Gibbs and Hill, Inc., is in Colombia for this purpose.

erations which the planning engineer should take into account when making his cost calculations.[10] In the first place, the economist, with his knowledge of general economic conditions and problems, will call attention to the indirect and qualitative implications of alternative techniques to reach a given end. Thus he will point out that while as a connecting link between two points a railroad may be more effective and economical than a road, the latter has the advantage of being a powerful vehicle of colonization for the territory that lies between the two points. In the choice between coal and water as a source of power, he might point out that in computing the cost to the economy of thermal power, one should take no or only partial account of the wages paid to the coal miners; this unorthodox cost calculation could be justified by the fact that the opportunity cost of the mined coal is far lower than its actual cost in a situation in which the labor will be drawn from the overpopulated countryside where its marginal productivity is extremely low.

THE CRITERION OF CAPITAL EXTENSIVENESS

For the economist to be taken seriously in specific investment planning, it is perhaps not enough that he can produce from time to time stimulating remarks and observations of this kind. What is required of him is a body of generalizations which can be referred to by those who are in charge of elaborating specific projects. The only generalization which one meets again and again in economic literature is the one concerning the need to economize the principal scarce resource of capital-poor countries, that is, capital.[11]

This precept is of only limited usefulness as guidance when one attempts to select priority areas for investment in general. Frequently, as we have seen already, investment in public utilities, transportation, etc., is the one that may often be expected to have

10. I do not mention here the study of markets. The projection of demand may be considered a branch of economics, but has in reality become an integral part of engineering surveys and reports.

11. This criterion and a number of others are developed in detail in W. Arthur Lewis, "The Industrialization of the British West Indies" *Caribbean Economic Review* 2, no. 1 (May 1950): 1–61.

an igniting effect on development throughout the economy and that must therefore be undertaken in spite of its capital-intensive character.[12]

Can we save the rule for a more limited field, that is, the technique to be used in undertaking a given investment and in designing the technology of a given plant? A discussion of this point was contained in a document of the United Nations Economic Commission for Latin America[13] which called attention to the fact that underdeveloped countries have a far greater interest in the output-raising than in the labor-saving features of modern technology. The report recognized that these two characteristics are inextricably intertwined in industrial processes, but ended with a plea for the creation of an institute of technological research whose task it would be to develop productive processes particularly suited to economic conditions in capital-poor countries. The idea was debated again in the Conference on Iron and Steel Industries in Latin America which was held in Bogotá two years ago. The consensus was that, even though some theoretically known processes for the production of iron and steel might be more suited to Latin American conditions because of their more labor-intensive character and their smaller scale than the processes in current usage in the industrial centers, Latin American countries could not possibly afford to invest large sums in processes which had never been tried out anywhere on a commercial scale.[14]

12. One author suggests that the criterion might still be valid if we "arrange all our projects along a scale . . . and measure their merit in terms of capital extensiveness at the point where their end products reach the consumer" (Konrad Bekker, "The Point IV Program of the United States," in *The Progress of Underdeveloped Areas,* ed. Bert F. Hoselitz [Chicago: University of Chicago Press, 1952], p. 242). Since, however, undertakings to which an electric power plant, a steel mill, or a road will give rise are hardly ever a matter of detailed planning, this type of calculation cannot ordinarily be made. Therefore, the criterion, as modified by Bekker, has little practical guidance value though it may serve to relieve the economist who advises in favor of a steel mill of undue anxiety and guilt feelings.

13. *Problemas teóricos y prácticos del crecimiento económico* (Mexico: Naciones Unidas, 1952), pp. 5, 18–21, 42.

14. United Nations, Economic Commission for Latin America, "Estudio de la Industria Siderúrgica e Informe sobre la Reunión de Expertos celebrada en Bogotá," mimeographed (February 1953), vol. 1, pp. 124–25.

This is probably a decisive argument against the idea of devising an entirely new technology for use in underdeveloped countries. What remains possible is to transplant to these countries processes which have been successfully employed in the industrial centers at an earlier stage of their development. In a certain number of traditional industries where technical progress has been mainly identified with further mechanization rather than with product improvement, this is certainly an avenue worth exploring systematically and jointly by economists and engineers. But even with this severe restriction of the field of applicability of the only universally accepted criterion as to investment planning, a further note of skepticism must be sounded. There are very few historical examples of nascent industries in developing countries that have failed to take advantage of a "late start" by appropriating the last word in production techniques.[15] Even in those cases where this policy is unjustified from the point of view of resource use, the psychological realities of the situation make adoption of antiquated technology highly unlikely. The entrepreneur of an underdeveloped country wants to create something that really contrasts with the backward surroundings, he wants to "épater" visitors from the United States; in short, he just will not be content with anything but the most modern equipment if the cost of its installation can

15. This is part of what might be termed the "investment demonstration effect" to complement the consumption demonstration effect whose threat to capital formation Ragnar Nurkse stresses in *Problems of Capital Formation in Underdeveloped Countries* (New York: Oxford University Press, 1953), pp. 57 ff. It seems to me that Nurkse's theory overlooks two crucial points: (1) The fact that the attraction of higher standards of living and of consumers' goods to be found in the advanced countries provides the people of the less developed countries with an incentive to increase their effort and productivity; after all, one of the principal obstacles to development has always been known to be the *limitation of wants* in primitive societies. (2) The fact that the demonstration effect applies to investment just as much as to consumption. This is particularly evident in the great effort made by the national and local authorities in Colombia to provide the citizens with what are today considered the essentials of modern living, from street lighting to supermarkets and divided highways. A considerable volume of additional investment is naturally required by the provision of these facilities and would probably not take place were it not for their demonstration by countries such as the United States.

at all be justified. And a justification is readily supplied by the ambitious and unstable social legislation of today's underdeveloped countries which convinces the entrepreneur that the most labor-saving machinery is barely trouble-saving enough for him.

On the whole, then, the main principle which economics has proposed as guidance for detailed investment planning is likely to have a rather narrow field of practical application. Nevertheless, it is important that in examining investment projects the economist ask whether capital is being expended in a particularly lavish and unnecessary way and whether it is exposed to special risks. It is on the latter ground that an underdeveloped country should stay away not only from technical processes that have not been tried out elsewhere, but also from industries which are in a phase of rapid technological progress and transformation, since a capital-poor country cannot afford the sudden and premature obsolescence of capital equipment that is characteristic of such industries.[16]

INVESTMENT CRITERIA DERIVED FROM SOME CHARACTERISTICS OF UNDERDEVELOPED ECONOMIES

Defective Maintenance

The first generalization about investment planning in underdeveloped countries was an immediate derivation from the fact that these countries are poor in capital. There are other propositions that can be made about these countries which, while not quite as incontrovertible (nor as tautological!), still have a great deal of general validity and serve to develop further criteria. To stay on the subject of capital, the observer is invariably struck not so much with the lack of capital formation (it is difficult to *see* a lack) as with the poor use of existing capital. I am not now referring to the large amount of poorly planned investment on which I commented earlier, but rather to the lack of maintenance of existing capital that is well worth maintaining. Let us accept this as a rather common failing without delving, at this point, into its anthropological reasons. It would appear then that on the basis of this observation the following criterion for investment planning could be devel-

16. For a very different view of this matter, see chap. 3, pp. 92–94.

oped: priority should be given to investments, industries, and technical processes which either hardly require maintenance or *must* have maintenance because its absence carries with it a very high penalty, that is, leads to accidents or immediate breakdown rather than to slow deterioration in the quantity and quality of output. The fact that the performance of the airlines in Colombia is excellent, that of the railroads mediocre, and that of the roads outright poor can be explained in terms of this criterion: nonmaintenance would lead to certain disaster in the case of airplanes, but roads can be left to deteriorate for a long time before they finally disappear, and railroads occupy a somewhat intermediate position from this viewpoint.

The foregoing observations naturally do not mean that underdeveloped countries should concentrate exclusively on airlines and forget about road construction. But they do lead to the conclusion that these countries may well make more of a success of industries with a complicated technology which must be maintained in top working order and efficiency than of industries which only require simple machinery and a few simple operations.

The criterion can also be useful for the selection of technical processes for a given industry; an interesting example is provided by road construction in Colombia, as explained by the consulting engineer who until recently was in charge of supervising the International-Bank-financed road construction and reconstruction program:

> We made one major concession in our planning to the recognized maintenance organization problem, and it sounds odd, at first thought. We encouraged the construction of low-type bituminous surfaces on relatively low-traveled routes, where this use would not ordinarily be justified in this country. We assumed that, with the increasing truck and bus industry in the country, local pressure would be applied to the Ministry to repair the deep holes which will develop in cheap bituminous pavements if maintenance and retreatment is delayed, and that such pressure would be greater than if a gravel and stone road is allowed to deteriorate. Gravel and

stone surfaces disappear at the rate of 20 to 40 tons per kilometer per year, and its loss may not be detected until the base is damaged. In other words, neglect of a bituminous surface is more obvious than neglect of a gravel or stone surface.[17]

It is possible that the absence of adequate maintenance is only one particularly important and striking aspect of the comparative proficiency of underdeveloped countries in the technical, as opposed to the administrative, fields of industry.[18] I believe that quite frequently the technical operation of industry is fairly competent, but that much is left to be desired in accounting, full use of cost—and quality—control methods, training and organization of the labor force, and utilization of raw materials and by-products. Naturally, a direct effort should be made to correct deficiencies in these increasingly important fields. But if our judgment is that, even in the best of circumstances, there is going to be a continuing lag in these respects, this should be taken account of in investment planning, by selecting projects and techniques where these matters are of relatively minor importance, or, as in maintenance, where a high penalty attaches to their neglect.

The Impact of Secondary on Primary Production

A further criterion for investment planning can be derived from an observation of the working of economic progress in underdeveloped countries. In spite of the apparently common sense advice to the effect that these countries should start by developing industries based on their own primary production, they have often industrialized heavily on the basis of imported materials. Three principal industries in Colombia, for instance, textiles, beer, and tires, relied initially entirely on imported cotton, barley, and rubber. In due course, the Colombian economy has made an effort to supply these raw materials and at present self-sufficiency is being

17. From a letter to the author from Forrest Green, Professor of Highway Engineering at Purdue University.

18. See, for a detailed discussion of this subject in relation to one industry, United Nations, *Labor Productivity of the Cotton Textile Industry in Five Latin American Countries* (New York, 1951), passim.

achieved in barley and cotton and the beginning of rubber production on a plantation basis is also being made.

This type of seemingly inverted development, from secondary to primary production—which finds a counterpart in the often noted movement of capital accumulated in trade toward industry and from there to agriculture—is in reality quite natural: all manufacturing in underdeveloped countries starts out as an isolated daring venture in what is held to be a hostile environment. The entrepreneur, no matter whether he is a national of the country or a foreigner, is fully aware of this situation and wishes the least possible contact and integration with, and dependence on, the local economy—excepting, of course, the local consumers of his products. Because of the inadequacy or outright absence of "social overhead capital," he has to supply his own water and electric power, he has to train his workers, must install his own machine and repair shops, retail outlets, etc., etc.

Thus for a long time there prevails a general climate in which nobody can, or feels he can, rely on anybody else. This often results in difficulties for the growth of enterprises since the director is loath to delegate authority to subordinates. But it makes even more powerfully for large-scale integrated operations since obviously one can rely least of all on outsiders. For this reason, industrial operations based on local materials are generally undertaken only—at least in the first stages of development—where the production or extraction of these materials and their transformation are combined under the same management, as is usually the case in refining of ores and of sugarcane, in the production of cement and bricks, etc. An equivalent solution of this raw material problem exists when a safe, dependable foreign source of supply is available.

The difficulty about starting an industry whose raw material can only be supplied by many local, independent primary producers is that usually the primary product lacks the quality and uniformity necessary for industrial operations, and that its supply is unreliable and ordinarily insufficient. But this situation can be remedied once an industry is established, for then the local producer will make a determined effort to take advantage of the availability of an assured market by satisfying the industry's requirements. When the manufacturer on his part finds that the domestic product is as good as the imported one, he is likely to lose his original "domophobia," and if he does not, a few governmental measures (import duties, compulsory admixture of locally grown materials) are likely to help. The end result of this process—which could never have taken place the other, "normal" way round, that is, by starting with the primary production—is considerable productive progress throughout the economy of the developing country.

Here we have then another criterion useful in the planning of investment projects and processes: to achieve balanced progress in agriculture and industry it may often be best to promote first industries and particularly those industries which, while relying initially on imported materials, are potential mass buyers of potential domestic crops. Special precautions are necessary, on the other hand, in planning industries that have to rely entirely on independently produced domestic materials without disposing of the safety valve represented by imports. It is probably because of the difficulty of adapting and expanding domestic primary production for industrial operations simultaneously with the setting up of the industry, that there has thus far been in Colombia so little development of food processing industries, for example, canning of vegetables and tropical fruits, which at first sight would seem ideally suited to the country.

The primary objective of the preceding pages was to demonstrate that by deduction from elementary observation of the economic and sociological reality of underdeveloped societies, the economist can elaborate criteria which may enable him to make a highly useful contribution to the process of detailed investment planning.

To the only factors that usually enter investment decisions, that is, cost of production, availability of labor force and of raw materials, access to and size of markets, he will be able to add a series of criteria that will provide further orientation and elements of judgment as to the advisability of different investments. Thus prospective ventures should be examined not only from the above, traditional points of view, but the following questions should also be asked:

1. What is the capital extensiveness of the process intended to be used compared to alternative available processes?
2. Is the investment planned to take place in an industry that is in a stage of rapid technological transformation?
3. What kind of penalty attaches to failure to maintain equipment?
4. What role is played by administrative as opposed to purely technical proficiency?
5. What is the potential impact of various industrial projects on primary production?

Considerable research with the object of classifying various industries and industrial processes according to these criteria could be done by economists working jointly with engineers. More criteria could certainly be developed by economists working jointly with anthropologists. By bringing to bear on investment decisions a number of important considerations which are almost totally neglected today, the end result of such research would be a considerable improvement in the formulation of development programs and projects. Besides, progress along these lines would make it possible for the economist to make a far more useful, interesting, and operational contribution than the continued pursuit of mirages, be they even attractively labeled "integrated development programs."

2. Economic Development, Research and Development, and Policy Making: Some Converging Views

With Charles E. Lindblom

When, in their pursuit of quite different subject matters, a group of social scientists independently of each other appear to converge in a somewhat unorthodox view of certain social phenomena, investigation is in order. The convergence to be examined in this paper is that of the views of Hirschman on economic development, Burton Klein and Wiliam Meckling on technological research and development, and Lindblom on policy making in general. These three independent lines of work appear to challenge in remarkably similar ways some widely accepted generalizations about what is variously described in the literature as the process of problem solving and decision making. Before discussing the interrelations of these views, we will give a brief description of each.[1]

HIRSCHMAN ON ECONOMIC DEVELOPMENT

A major argument of Hirschman's *Strategy of Economic Development* is his attack on "balanced growth" as either a sine qua non of development or as a meaningful proximate objective of

Reprinted by permission from *Behavioral Science* 7 (April 1962): 211–22.

1. Another line of related work is represented in Andrew Gunder Frank's "conflicting standards" organization theory. It is sufficiently different to fall outside the scope of the present article, but sufficiently similar to be of interest to anyone who wishes to explore further the areas of unorthodoxy described here. See A. G. Frank, "Goal Ambiguity and Conflicting Standards: An Approach to the Study of Organization," *Human Organization* 17 (1959): 8–13; and A. G. Frank and R. Cohen, "Conflicting Standards and Selective Enforcement in Social Organization and Social Change: A Cross-Cultural Test" (paper delivered at the American Anthropological Association Meeting, Mexico City, December, 1959).

development policy. His basic defense of unbalanced growth is that, at any one point of time, an economy's resources are not to be considered as rigidly fixed in amount, and that more resources or factors of production will actually come into play if development is marked by sectoral imbalances that galvanize private entrepreneurs or public authorities into action. Even if we know exactly what the economy of a country would look like at a higher plateau, he argues, we can reach this plateau more expeditiously through the path of unbalanced growth because of the additional thrusts received by the economy as it gets into positions of imbalance.[2]

Take an economy with two sectors that are interdependent in the sense that each sector provides some inputs to the other and that the income receivers of each sector consume part of the other sector's final output. With *given* rates of capital formation and increase in the labor supply, it is possible to specify at any one time a certain pair of growth rates for both sectors that is optimally efficient from the points of view of resource utilization and consumer satisfaction. This is balanced growth in its widest sense. Unbalanced growth will manifest its comparative initial inefficiency through a variety of symptoms: losses here, excess profits there, and concomitant relative price movements; or, in the absence of the latter, through shortages, bottlenecks, spoilage, and waste. In an open economy, a possible direct repercussion is a balance of payment deficit. In other words, sectoral imbalances will induce a variety of sensations—presence of pain or expectation of pleasure—in the economic operators and policy makers, whose reactions should all converge toward increasing output in the lagging sector.

To the extent that the imbalance is thus self-correcting through a variety of market and nonmarket mechanisms, the economy may be propelled forward jerkily, but also more quickly than under conditions of balanced expansion. Admittedly, the process is likely to be more costly in terms of resource utilization, but the imbalances at the same time *call forth* more resources and invest-

2. Albert O. Hirschman, *The Strategy of Economic Development* (New Haven: Yale University Press, 1958).

ment than would otherwise become available. The crucial, but plausible, assumption here is that there is some "slack" in the economy; and that additional investment, hours of work, productivity, and decision making can be squeezed out of it by the pressure mechanisms set up by imbalances. On the assumption of a given volume of resources and investment, it may be highly irrational not to attempt to come as close as possible to balanced growth; but without these assumptions there is likely to exist such a thing as an "optimal degree of imbalance." In other words, within a certain range, the increased economy in the use of given resources that might come with balanced growth is more than offset by *increased resource mobilization* afforded by unbalanced growth.

A simplified geometrical representation of balanced vs. unbalanced growth is as follows: let there be two sectors of the economy, such as agriculture and industry, whose outputs are measured along the horizontal and vertical axes, respectively. Let point U be the point at which the underdeveloped economy finds itself and D or D' the goal at which it aims. At this stage, assume

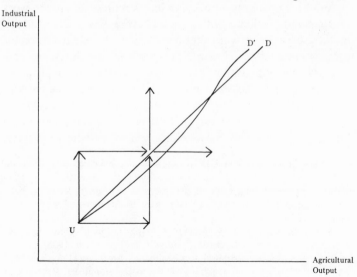

Figure 2.1. Balanced vs. Unbalanced Growth

certainty and unanimous agreement about this goal. Balanced growth then aspires to a movement along such a line as *UD* or *UD'*. At the end of each investment period the economy would find itself producing outputs corresponding to successive points on such lines[3] (see Figure 2.1). Unbalanced growth means to strike out first in one direction (see arrows) and then, impelled by resulting shortages, balance of payments pressures, and other assorted troubles, in the other. Hirschman argues that by traveling along this circuitous route, which is likely to be more costly because of the accompanying shortages and excess capacities, the economy may get faster to its goal. Note that there are several varieties of unbalanced growth with varying degrees of pressure. For instance, to start by developing industry is likely to introduce more compelling pressures (because of the resulting food shortages, or, if food is imported, because of the balance of payments difficulties) than if the sequence is started by an expansion in agricultural output.

KLEIN AND MECKLING ON RESEARCH AND DEVELOPMENT

Another apparently converging line is represented in the work of Klein and Meckling, who have for several years been studying military experience with alternative research and development policies for weapons systems.[4] They allege that development is both less costly and more speedy when marked by duplication, "confusion," and lack of communication among people working along parallel lines. Perhaps more fundamentally, they argue against too strenuous attempts at integrating various subsystems into a well-articulated, harmonious, general system; they rather

3. We introduced line UD' to suggest that balanced growth is not necessarily linear. "Balance" implies that one knows what the appropriate proportions are at each stage of development, but not necessarily that a constant proportion between two or more absolute rates of growth must be preserved.

4. See B. Klein and W. Meckling, "Application of Operations Research to Development Decisions," *Operations Research* 6 (1958): 532–63; B. Klein, "A Radical Proposal for R and D," *Fortune* (May 1958): 112; and idem, "The Decision-Making Problem in Development," RAND Corporation Paper no. P-1916 (Santa Monica, Calif., 19 February 1960).

advocate the full exploitation of fruitful ideas regardless of their "fit" to some preconceived pattern of specifications.

Suppose a new airplane engine is to be developed and we know that it ought to have certain minimal performance characteristics with respect to, say, range and speed. A curve such as *SS* in Figure 2.2 may represent this requirement. Is anything to be said here in favor of approaching the goal through an unbalanced path, rather than through shooting straight at the target?

The first and perhaps most important point made here by Klein and Meckling is that there is no single point to shoot at, but a great number of acceptable combinations of the two performance characteristics (shown in Figure 2.2 by the set of all points lying to the northeast of the curve *SS*). It is perfectly arbitrary for anyone to pick out a point such as *S′* as *the* target to shoot at even though this point may be in some sense the expected value of the desired technological advances. The argument then proceeds to show that because of this wide range of acceptable outcomes, and because of the uncertainty as to what is achievable, *any* advance in the northeasterly direction (such as *PP′*) should be pushed and

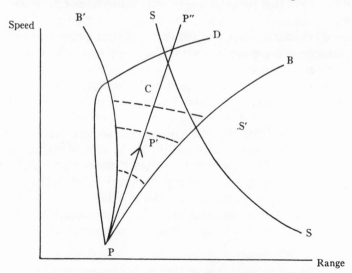

Figure 2.2. Alternative Paths of Development of
Two Performance Characteristics

capitalized on, rather than bent at great effort in the direction of any arbitrarily predetermined target.

The assumption here is that inventions and technical progress follow a "path of their own" to which we should defer: in other words, instead of getting upset at an early stage of development with the "lack of balance" between the two performance specifications (the engine that is being developed is all speed and very little range), we should go on developing it as best we can without reference to point S'. The simplest reason for this is that we may land anyway with a combination of the two characteristics that is acceptable for the purpose at hand: at P'' we have much more speed than we originally bargained for and enough range.

But then there may be other, more interesting reasons why "a wise and salutary neglect" of the balance between the two performance requirements may be desirable in the earlier stages of research and development. A second possibility is that, as an invention or technological advance matures and is fully articulated, possibilities of adjustment may appear that are not present earlier. In Figure 2.2 we represent this phenomenon by two boundaries PB and PB' that limit the range within which trade-offs between the two characteristics (along the dotted curves) are possible. If these boundaries diverge as shown in our figure, then we should postpone our attempt at trade-offs until we reach the range of greater flexibility (point C).

Third, sometimes the new product that is being developed and which at one stage seemed to be so top-heavy with one of our two requirements will veer around along the path PD and, in the course of its "natural" development, will acquire the required amount of the second characteristic. To be sure, to assume that this will inevitably happen would require that one places his faith in some basic harmonies, similar to the Greek belief that the truly beautiful will possess moral excellence as well.[5]

Most of what has been said for products with several characteristics applies also to systems with several complementary compo-

5. To assume the existence of such basic harmonies may be foolish, but it certainly helps us in making crucial decisions such as choosing a wife or a profession.

nents. But some of the problems in which we are interested come into sharper focus when we deal with systems where individual components can be independently worked at and perfected. Here also Klein and Meckling advocate full articulation of the components, even though this may mean uneven advances in their development and disregard for their overall integration into the system at an early stage.

Once again, a principal reason is uncertainty. The final configuration of the system is unknown, and knowledge increases as some of the subsystems become articulated. In the first place, knowledge about the nature of one subsystem increases the number of clues about the desirable features of another, just as it is easier to fit in a piece of a jigsaw puzzle when some of the surrounding pieces are already in place. Second, if two pieces (subsystems) have been worked at independently, it is usually possible to join them together by small adjustments: what is important is to develop the pieces, even though they may not be perfectly adjusted to each other to start with.

Obviously if the subsystems are being perfected fairly independently from one another it is likely that one of them will be fully developed ahead of the others, a situation quite similar to that where one sector of the economy races ahead of another. Also it is likely that even if they reach the point of serviceability together, some of them will be "out of phase" with the others, as in the case of a hi-fi system with an amplifier that is far too good for the loudspeaker.[6]

6. Klein gives a straightforward exposition of the logical and empirical differences between development decisions and decisions to maximize the use of existing resources. He again advocates looseness in goal-setting and gradual, oblique, or multiple approaches to the goal. In doing so, Klein now emphasizes the contrast between the decision maker in established production processes who accepts the relatively small uncertainties he faces as a datum, and the development decision maker whose chief purpose is to reduce the huge variance of the initial estimates so that successive investment and production decisions can be made with increasing degrees of confidence. In addition, he argues that it is of rather secondary interest to the developer to achieve an efficient combination of inputs. His main interest is achieving a breakthrough to a new product or to radically improved performance characteristics. See Klein, "The Decision-Making Problem in Development."

LINDBLOM ON POLICY MAKING

A third converging line is represented in Lindblom's papers on policy-making processes.[7] These papers aspire to fairly large-scale generalizations or to what, in some usages, would be called theory construction; while the points of departure of Hirschman and Klein and Meckling are two widely different, but still fairly specific, problem-solving contexts. The differences among the studies in this respect make the convergences all the more noteworthy.

Lindblom's point of departure is a denial of the general validity of two assumptions implicit in most of the literature on policy making. The first is that public policy problems can best be solved by attempting to understand them; the second is that there exists sufficient agreement to provide adequate criteria for choosing among possible alternative policies. Although the first is widely accepted—in many circles almost treated as a self-evident truth— it is often false. The second is more often questioned in contemporary social science; yet many of the most common prescriptions for rational problem solving follow only if it is true.

Conventional descriptions of rational decision making identify the following aspects: (1) clarification of objectives or values, (2) survey of alternative means of reaching objectives, (3) identification of consequences, including side effects or by-products, of each alternative means, and (4) evaluation of each set of consequences in light of the objectives. However, Lindblom notes, for a number of reasons such a synoptic or comprehensive attempt at problem solving is not possible to the degree that clarification of objectives founders on social conflict, that required information is either not available or available only at prohibitive cost, or that

7. C. E. Lindblom, "Policy Analysis," *American Economic Review* 48 (1958):298–312; "Tinbergen on Policy Making," *Journal of Political Economy* 66 (1958): 531–38; "The Handling of Norms in Policy Analysis," in M. Abramovitz, ed., *Allocation of Economic Resources* (Stanford: Stanford University Press, 1958), pp. 160–79; "The Science of 'Muddling Through,'" *Public Administration Review* 19 (1959): 79–88; "Decision Making in Taxation and Expenditure," in Universities National Bureau of Economic Research, *Public Finances; Needs, Sources, and Utilization* (Princeton: Princeton University Press, 1961).

the problem is simply too complex for man's finite intellectual capacities. Its complexity may stem from an impossibly large number of alternative policies and their possible repercussions from imponderables in the delineation of objectives even in the absence of social disagreement on them, from a supply of information too large to process in the mind, or from still other causes.

It does not logically follow, Lindblom argues, that when synoptic decision making is extremely difficult it should nevertheless be pursued as far as possible. And he consequently suggests that in many circumstances substantial departures from comprehensive understanding are both inevitable and on specific grounds desirable. For the most part, these departures are familiar; and his exposition of them serves therefore to formalize our perceptions of certain useful problem-solving strategies often mistakenly dismissed as aberrations in rational problem solving.

These strategies, which we shall call "disjointed incrementalism," are the following:

A. Attempt at understanding is limited to policies that differ only incrementally from existing policy.

B. Instead of simply adjusting means to ends, ends are chosen that are appropriate to available or nearly available means.

C. A relatively small number of means (alternative possible policies) is considered, as follows from A.

D. Instead of comparing alternative means or policies in the light of postulated ends or objectives, alternative ends or objectives are also compared in the light of postulated means or policies and their consequences.

E. Ends and means are chosen simultaneously; the choice of means does not follow the choice of ends.

F. Ends are indefinitely explored, reconsidered, discovered, rather than relatively fixed.

G. At any given analytical point ("point" refers to any one individual, group, agency, or institution), analysis and policy making are serial or successive; that is, problems are not "solved" but are repeatedly attacked.

H. Analysis and policy making are remedial; they move away from ills rather than toward known objectives.

I. At any one analytical point, the analysis of consequences is quite incomplete.

J. Analysis and policy making are socially fragmented; they go on at a very large number of separate points simultaneously.

The most striking characteristic of disjointed incrementalism is (as indicated in I) that no attempt at comprehensiveness is made; on the contrary, unquestionably important consequences of alternative policies are simply ignored at any given analytical or policy-making point. But Lindblom goes on to argue that through various specific types of partisan mutual adjustment among the large number of individuals and groups among which analysis and policy making is fragmented (see J), what is ignored at one point in policy making becomes central at another point. Hence, it will often be possible to find a tolerable level of rationality in decision making when the process is viewed as a whole in its social or political context, even if at each individual policy-making point or center analysis remains incomplete. Similarly, errors that would attend overly ambitious attempts at comprehensive understanding are often avoided by the remedial and incremental character of problem solving. And those not avoided can be mopped up or attended to as they appear, because analysis and policy making are serial or successive (as in G).

While we cannot here review the entire argument, Lindblom tries to show how the specific characteristics of disjointed incrementalism, taken in conjunction with mechanisms for partisan mutual adjustment, meet each of the characteristic difficulties that beset synoptic policy making: value conflicts, information inadequacies, and general complexity beyond man's intellectual capacities. His line of argument shows the influence of pluralist thinkers on political theory, but he departs from their interest in the control of power and rather focuses on the level of rationality required or appropriate for decision making.

POINTS OF CONVERGENCE

If they are not already obvious, specific parallels in the works reviewed are easy to illustrate. Compare, for example, an economy that is in a state of imbalance as the result of a sharp but isolated advance of one sector and a weapons system that is out of balance because a subsystem is "too good" in relation to the capacity of another system. Just as for a sector of the economy, it is possible that a completed subsystem is "too advanced" only in comparison with some preconceived notion, and that actually its unexpectedly high performance level is quite welcome, either because it improves upon overall system performance or because it happily compensates for the lag of some other component behind the norms originally set. On the other hand, a component can be "too advanced" in a real sense, as in a hi-fi set, where the performance of a component depends not only on its capacity but also on inputs from other components. This situation corresponds exactly to that of an economy in structural imbalance. The laggard components turn into bottlenecks for the full utilization of the avant garde component's capacity. Yet even though such a system or economy represents in itself an inefficient utilization of inputs, it may nevertheless be a highly useful configuration if it is conceived as a stage in the development process. For it may be expected that attempts will be made to improve the weaker subsystems or sectors so that the capability of the stronger ones may be fully utilized. In the process, the weaker systems or sectors may be so improved that they become the stronger ones, and the stage thus set for a series of seesaw advances which may carry the overall "goodness" of our system or economy beyond what might have been achieved by maintaining balance.

For both economy and weapons system we are talking in terms of probabilities. There can be no certainty that with one avant garde subsystem readied the others will dutifully be put in place or improved. The existence of the Maginot line along the French-German border failed to call forth a corresponding effort along the Belgian frontier to guard against the possibility of a German strategy aimed at circumventing the line.

This example illustrates an important point: a "system" or economy is never quite finished. Today's system or economy-in-balance is likely to turn into tomorrow's subsystem or economy-out-of-balance, because of unforeseeable repercussions, newly emerging difficulties, unanticipated counterstrategies, changing tastes or techniques, or whatever other forces with which the system or economy has to deal. But these repercussions, difficulties, and counterstrategies could not possibly be fully visualized in advance. The transportation system consisting of highways, gasoline and repair stations, and automotive vehicles is found incomplete, first because of inadequate accident prevention, and later also because of smog. The new system of defense against infections through antibiotics is suddenly "out of balance" because of the development of new varieties of drug-resistant microorganisms. In these cases, it would have been impossible to foresee the imbalance and incompleteness that emerged clearly only after the new system had been in operation for some time.

Once it is understood that a system is never complete or will never stay complete, the case against spending considerable effort on early integration and simultaneous development of subsystems is further strengthened. For if we do achieve early integration and simultaneity, we are much more likely to succumb to the illusion that our system is actually complete in itself and needs no further complements and watchfulness than if we had built it up as a result of seesaw advances and adjustments which do not provide for a natural resting place.[8]

As another specific illustration of convergence, consider the sequence of moves in problem solving as described, on the one

8. The examples of the Maginot line, of automobile traffic, and of antibiotics bring up an additional problem. In the latter two cases, the incompleteness of the system is forcefully brought to our attention through accidents and eye irritation, and through new types of infection. The trouble with some other systems that turn into subsystems is that the mutation may not be so easily detected, or that it may be detected only when it is too late, as was precisely the case with the Maginot line.

There is a real difficulty about the meaning of "too late." The imperfections of automobile traffic and antibiotics were discovered too late for the victims of accidents and new-type infections, but not too late, we hope, for the rest of us. The defects of the Maginot line were discovered too late to save France in 1940, although not too late to win the war against Hitler. This suggests that there may be cases where we cannot afford to do our learning about the imperfections and imbalances of a system through the hand, in developmental terms by Hirschman, Klein and Meckling and, on the other hand, in political terms by Lindblom. Recall the picture of desired progress where we wished to move from one fixed point (the present) to another fixed point in a two-dimensional diagram. From existing levels of output in industry and agriculture (or range and speed in aircraft) we wished to move to higher levels for both. Imagine a situation in which two parties with different preferences want to go off in two different directions. Lindblom argues that in this situation the best way to make progress is through "mutual adjustment," i.e. by a series of moves and countermoves in the course of which a higher plateau can be reached even without prior agreement about the eventual goal. "Individuals often agree on policies when they cannot agree on ends. Moreover, attempts to agree on ends or values often get in the way of agreements on specific policies."[9] Furthermore, it is possible, and even likely, that the value systems of the two parties will move more closely together once an advance that is tolerable to both has been achieved. "The decision-maker expects to learn about his values from his experiences and he is inclined to think that in the long run policy choices have as great an influence on objectives as objectives have on policy choices."[10]

---

failures, irritations, and discomforts that are the natural concomitants and signals of the imbalance. Such situations present us with a well-nigh insoluble task, similar to the one which would face a child who had to learn to walk without being permitted to fall. Here the temptation is particularly strong to prepare in advance a perfect theoretical solution. Yet we know from all that has been said that reliance on such a solution would be most likely to bring about the failure one is seeking to avoid. One way of dealing with situations in which we feel we cannot afford to learn "the hard way" is to develop institutions whose special mission it is to be alert to and to detect existing and developing system imbalances: in a democracy, some institutions of this kind are a free press and an opposition party. For national defense a certain amount of interservice rivalry may serve the same purpose, as each service has a vested interest in pointing out the "holes" in the other services' systems.

9. Lindblom, "Tinbergen on Policy Making," p. 534.
10. Lindblom, "Decision Making in Taxation and Expenditure," p. 309.

Lindblom's reasoning reinforces the others. It parallels Klein and Meckling's emphasis on the inevitability of moving forward through move and countermove, in what appears an arbitrary, somewhat aimless fashion, rather than Hirschman's stress on the efficiency of such a sequence in squeezing out additional resources. Nevertheless, the idea that unbalanced or seesaw advances of this kind are efficient in some sense is also present. Instead of focusing on the limited supply of decision makers and on the desirability of placing some extra pressures behind investment decisions, Lindblom emphasizes the limited supply of knowledge and the limited area of agreement that exists among the various power-holders, and visualizes a series of sequential adjustments as a way to maximize positive action in a society where ignorance, uncertainty, and conflict preclude not only the identification, but even the existence, of any "best" move.

But we can do better than illustrate parallels. We can explicitly identify the principal points of convergence.

1. The most obvious similarity is that all insist on the rationality and usefulness of certain processes and modes of behavior which are ordinarily considered to be irrational, wasteful, and generally abominable.

2. The three approaches thus have in common an attack on such well-established values as orderliness (cf. Hirschman's "model of optimum disorderliness"[11]), balance, and detailed programming; they all agree with Burke that some matters ought to be left to a "wise and salutary neglect."[12]

3. They agree that one step ought often to be left to lead to another, and that it is unwise to specify objectives in much detail when the means of attaining them are virtually unknown.

4. All agree further that in rational problem solving, goals will change not only in detail but in a more fundamental sense through experience with a succession of means-ends and ends-means adjustments.

11. Hirschman, *Strategy*, p. 80.
12. An even higher authority might be invoked, namely the Sermon on the Mount: "Take therefore no thought for the morrow, for the morrow will take care of the things of itself."

5. All agree that in an important sense a rational problem solver wants what he can get and does not try to get what he wants except after identifying what he wants by examining what he can get.

6. There is also agreement that the exploration of alternative uses of resources can be overdone, and that attempts at introducing explicitly certain maximizing techniques (trade-offs among inputs or among outputs, cost-benefit calculations) and coordinating techniques will be ineffective and quite possibly harmful in some situations. In a sense more fundamental than is implied by theories stressing the cost of information, the pursuit of certain activities that are usually held to be the very essence of "economizing" can at times be decidedly uneconomical.

7. One reason for this is the following: for successful problem solving, all agree it is most important that arrangements exist through which decision makers are sensitized and react promptly to newly emerging problems, imbalances, and difficulties; this essential ability to react and to improvise readily and imaginatively can be stultified by an undue preoccupation with, and consequent pretense at, advance elimination of these problems and difficulties through "integrated planning."

8. Similarly, attempts at foresight can be misplaced; they will often result in complicating the problem through mistaken diagnoses and ideologies. Since man has quite limited capacities to solve problems and particularly to foresee the shape of future problems, the much maligned "hard way" of learning by experiencing the problems at close range may often be the most expeditious and least expensive way to a solution.

9. Thus we have here theories of successive decision making; denying the possibility of determining the sequence *ex ante,* relying on the clues that appear in the course of the sequence, and concentrating on identification of these clues.

10. All count on the usefulness for problem solving of subtle social processes not necessarily consciously directed at an identified social problem. Processes of mutual adjustment of participants are capable of achieving a kind of coordination not neces-

sarily centrally envisaged prior to its achievement, or centrally managed.

11. At least Hirschman and Lindblom see in political adjustment and strife analogues to self-interested yet socially useful adjustment in the market.

12. All question such values as "foresight," "central direction," "integrated overview," but not in order to advocate laissez faire or to inveigh against expanded activities of the state in economic or other fields. They are in fact typically concerned with decision-making and problem-solving activities carried on by the state. In their positive aspects they describe how these activities are "really" taking place as compared to commonly held images; and insofar as they are normative they advocate a modification of these images, in the belief that a clearer appreciation and perception of institutions and attitudes helpful to problem-solving activities will result.

Although many of these propositions are familiar, they are often denied in explicit accounts of rational decision making; and at least some of them challenge familiar contrary beliefs. Either the convergences are an unfortunate accident, or decision-making theory has underplayed the degree to which "common sense" rational problem-solving procedures have to be modified or abandoned. Account must be taken of man's inertia, limited capacities, costs of decision making, and other obstacles to problem solving, including uncertainty, which is the only one of the complicating elements that has been given sustained attention. And most investigations of uncertainty have been within the narrow competence of statistical theory.

POINTS OF DIFFERENCE

These similarities in approach, with their widely different origins, structures, and fields of application, are even better understood if their remaining points of difference are identified.

The basic justification for rejecting traditional precepts of rationality, planning, and balance is somewhat different for the three approaches here examined. For Lindblom it is complexity, i.e. man's inability to comprehend the present interrelatedness and future repercussions of certain social processes and decisions, as well as imperfect knowledge and value conflicts. For Klein and Meckling it is almost entirely future uncertainty, i.e. man's inability to foresee the shape of technological breakthroughs, or the desirability of letting oneself be guided by these breakthroughs if and when they occur, instead of following a predetermined sequence. For Hirschman it is the difficulty of mobilizing potentially available resources and decision-making activity itself; the inadequacy of incentives to problem solving, or, conversely, the need for inducements to decision making.

Although Klein's and Meckling's concern with future uncertainty could formally be viewed as a special case of Lindblom's problem of inadequate information, their treatment of the research and development problem is different enough from Lindblom's treatment of information inadequacies to argue against its being so viewed. Hirschman's concern with inducements to problem-solving activity is quite different from either Lindblom's or Klein's and Meckling's concern with limits on cognitive faculties. He argues not that men lack knowledge and capacity to solve problems in an absolute sense, but that there is always some unutilized problem-solving capacity that can be called forth through a variety of inducement mechanisms and pacing devices. These different reasons for supporting the same conclusions make the conclusions more rather than less persuasive, for the reasons supplement rather than invalidate each other.

That they are complementary reasons is, of course, indicated by the overlap of the Lindblom and the Klein–Meckling approaches on the problem of imperfect information, and by some Hirschmanlike concern for research and development incentives in the Klein–Meckling study. It is also true that Hirschman develops as a secondary theme the difficulties of ignorance and uncertainty in economic development. For instance, his partiality toward "development via social overhead capital shortage" is based in part on the position that shortages and bottlenecks remove uncertainty about the direction of needed overhead investments. Similarly, he emphasizes the importance of unforeseen or loose complementarity repercussions, such as "entrained wants" that arise in the course of development, and asserts that imports are helpful in inducing domestic production because they remove previous doubts about the existence of a market.

From the differences in the main thrust of the respective arguments, certain other major differences emerge, differences which do not deny the convergences, but which, on the other hand, ought not to be submerged by them. For example, Hirschman's argument that a very heavy reliance on central planning will often be inappropriate for underdeveloped countries looks superficially parallel to Lindblom's argument that partisan mutual adjustment can sometimes achieve efficiencies that could not be achieved through overambitious attempts at central omniscience and control. Yet on closer scrutiny, Hirschman's cautions about centralism only secondarily refer to the general difficulties of managing complex affairs that strain man's incentives and intellectual capacities. Instead he argues that a conventional, centrally planned attempt to define and achieve a balance among many varied lines of development will be less helpful than a similarly central attempt to estimate and manage the critical linkages through which economic growth is forced or induced.[13]

Hirschman's explicitly declared view of decision making for economic development is almost entirely one of central planning, or at least problem solving by persons—such as planning board managers or officials of international agencies—who assume some general responsibility toward the economy as a whole, and whose point of view is therefore that of a central planner. Hirschman's policy maker or operator is, with only a few exceptions, such a person or official; and Hirschman's prescriptions are always addressed to such a person. By contrast, Lindblom's policy maker is typically a partisan, often acknowledging no responsibility to his society as a whole, frankly pursuing his own segmental interests; and this is a kind of policy maker for whom Hirschman, despite his between-the-lines endorsement of him, makes no explicit place in his formulation of the development process.

13. This argument against the attempt at balanced growth is quite different from Hirschman's other argument that balance in growth is not desirable even if achieved.

A further important point of difference between Hirschman and Lindblom appears to lie in Hirschman's emphasis on discovering and utilizing the side effects and repercussions of development decisions, as compared to Lindblom's readiness to recommend at any given "point" neglect of such repercussions. It is indeed a major thesis of Hirschman that analysis of a prospective investment project should above all try to evaluate its effect on further development decisions instead of conventionally concentrating on its own prospective output and productivity. Specifically, every decision should be analyzed to discover its possible "linkages" with other decisions that might follow it. For example, a prospective decision to encourage the importation of some consumer goods, such as radios, should consider not simply the economy's need for these goods but the probability that their importation will in time lead to a decision by domestic investors to assemble them locally, as well as the "linkage effects" of such assembly operations on further domestic production decisions.

Hirschman's *Strategy* is both an attempt to uncover such linkages and a prescription issued to developers to uncover them in every possible case. Lindblom suggests that this kind of by-product, the indirect consequences of a decision that flow from the decision's effect on still other decision makers will often escape the analyst in any case; hence he should not try to always anticipate and understand it, but instead should deal with it through subsequent steps in policy making, if and when it emerges as a problem. Since, as Lindblom sees it, policy making is not only remedial and serial but also fragmented, both intentionally and accidentally neglected consequences of chosen policies will often be attended to either as a remedial next step of the original policy makers or by some other policy-making group whose interests are affected. Hence policy as a complex social or political process rises to a higher level of comprehensiveness and rationality than is achieved by any one policy maker at any one move in the process.

The contrast between Hirschman and Lindblom on this point can be overdrawn, however. For one thing, Hirschman feels that calculations which purport to give greater rationality to investment planning may often interfere with development, because they

81

typically do not and cannot take the "linkages" into account; whereas more rough-and-ready methods may be at least based on hunches about such linkages. Second, Hirschman's practical advice to policy makers is similar to Lindblom's when he tells them to go ahead with unintegrated and unbalanced projects on the ground that, in an interdependent economy, progress in some sectors will serve to unmask the others as laggards and will thereby bring new pressures toward improvement. In his general prescription, more implicit than explicit, that development planners try to move the economy wherever it can be moved, that is, seize on readiness to act wherever it can be found, Hirschman is endorsing Lindblom's suggestion that many consequences can best be dealt with only as they actually show themselves.

As a further point of difference, it is implicit in what has been said in the preceding paragraphs that Hirschman's thinking about secondary effects is preoccupied with possible bonuses to be exploited, Lindblom's with possible losses to be minimized. Again, the difference is easy to overstate: Hirschman too is at times concerned with possible losses, even if Lindblom has not explored at all the possibility of bonuses. Hirschman, however, relies on correct diagnosis of linkages for protection from damaging side effects; and his position is therefore parallel to his position on exploiting bonus effects. Only secondarily[14] does he count on Lindblom's remedial, serial, and fragmented kind of process for minimizing losses.

As Hirschman would now give uncertainty, complexity, and value conflict a more central place in justifying his conclusions on economic development policy,[15] so also Lindblom's and Klein's and Meckling's analyses could be strengthened by taking into account the fact that the policies they defend could also be justified because they permit mobilization of resources and energies that could not be activated otherwise. Perhaps these latter analyses could go beyond the statement that the processes of research

14. Hirschman, *Strategy,* pp. 208 ff.

15. This was done later in my *Development Projects Observed* (Washington: Brookings Institution, 1967), chap. 2, particularly pp. 75–85.

and development and of policy making are of necessity piecemeal, successive, fragmented, and disjointed; they could try to define typical sequences and their characteristics, similar to Hirschman's "permissive" and "compulsive" sequences. Once the intellectual taboo and wholesale condemnation are lifted from some of the policies Klein, Meckling, and Lindblom defend, it becomes desirable to have a closer look at the heretofore incriminated processes and to rank them from various points of view. It is useful to ask questions such as the following: as long as we know that a system is going to be out of balance anyway when the subsystems develop, what type of imbalance is most likely to be self-correcting? An answer to this question could affect the desirable distribution and emphasis of the research and development effort.

One problem deserves to be mentioned again. The processes of economic development, research and development, and policy making must all rely on successive decision making because they all break new, uncertain ground. Therefore these processes must let themselves be guided by the clues that appear en route. Snags, difficulties, and tensions cannot be avoided, but must on the contrary be utilized to propel the process further. The trouble is that the difficulties are not only "little helpers," but may also start processes of disintegration and demoralization. An intersectoral imbalance sets up a race between the catching-up, forward movement of the lagging sector and the retrogression of the advanced one. The greater the pressure toward remedial positive action, the greater is the risk if this action does not take place. There is a corresponding situation in systems development. The more a system is out of balance, the greater will presumably be the pressure to do something about it, but also the more useless is the system should no action be forthcoming.

All three approaches therefore have one further characteristic in common: they can be overdone. There are limits to "imbalance" in economic development, to "lack of integration" in research and development, to "fragmentation" in policy making which would be dangerous to pass. And it is clearly impossible to specify in advance the optimal doses of these various policies under different circumstances. The art of promoting economic development, research and development, and constructive policy making in general consists, then, in acquiring a feeling for these doses.

This art, it is submitted by the theories here reviewed, will be mastered far better once the false ideals of "balance," "coordination," and "comprehensive overview" have lost our total and unquestioning intellectual allegiance.

3. The Political Economy of Import-Substituting Industrialization in Latin America*

There is now a new school of thought on Latin America which casts the whole matter into a biblical mold and amounts to transposing the doctrine of original sin onto the social terrain. Here is a summary of this thesis: Latin America, with its evil destiny, was forced into the world capitalist system by the European powers right after Columbus and the Conquest. A great many calamities derive from this historical fact, yet they are small if compared to what happens during the next stage when the Continent is fully inserted into the international order organized by the "truly" capitalist nations, with Great Britain at the helm. That stage is reached in the nineteenth century after Independence. Subsequently, with export-led growth really taking hold, the evils become even greater and more numerous. But this is not the end of Latin America's "purgatory in life." Another phase of expiation and, in a way, of even greater degradation was yet to come. It duly arrived with "inward-looking" development and "dependent" industrialization whose adverse repercussions and insuperable limitations have been described ad infinitum.

Such reasoning makes one wonder whether the first and foremost trouble with Latin America was not perhaps the departure of Columbus from the port of Palos. . . . its basic weakness [consists in] the complete failure to understand the contradictory character of every social process.

—Aníbal Pinto Santa Cruz

*Reprinted by permission from *The Quarterly Journal of Economics* 82 (February 1968): 2–32. The opening quotation comes from "Diagnosticos, Estructuras y esquemas de desarrollo en América Latina," mimeographed (Santiago: Escuela latinoamericana de sociologia, November 1969), pp. 3–5.

DISENCHANTMENT WITH INDUSTRIALIZATION IN LATIN AMERICA

Not long ago, industrialization ranked high among the policy prescriptions which were expected to lead Latin America and other underdeveloped areas out of their state of economic, social, and political backwardness. In the last few years, however, considerable disenchantment with this particular solution of the development problem has set in. The present paper will survey some characteristics of "import-substituting industrialization" (ISI) in an attempt to appraise its evolution and the principal difficulties it has encountered. Some purely economic aspects of the problem will be discussed, but particular attention has been directed to interrelations with social and political life. The ease with which such interrelations could be suggested—mostly in the form of tentative and untested hypotheses—indicates serious neglect by social scientists of a fertile terrain.

To set the stage for our inquiry it is useful to illustrate, through quotes from Latin America's most prominent economists, the change in attitude toward industrialization as a cure of the area's ills. In his well-known "manifesto" of 1949 Raúl Prebisch said:

> Formerly, before the great depression, development in the Latin-American countries was stimulated from abroad by the constant increase of exports. There is no reason to suppose, at least at present, that this will again occur to the same extent, except under very exceptional circumstances. These countries no longer have an alternative between vigorous growth along those lines and internal expansion through industrialization. Industrialization has become the most important means of expansion.[1]

Thirteen years later, Prebisch wrote another basic paper on Latin America, in a sense his farewell message to his Latin American friends upon assuming his new post as Secretary-General of

1. *The Economic Development of Latin America and Its Principal Problems* (New York: United Nations, 1950), p. 6. See chap. 13 for a more detailed account of the Prebisch and ECLA doctrines.

the United Nations Conference on Trade and Development. Here industrialization is presented in a rather different light:

> An industrial structure virtually isolated from the outside world thus grew up in our countries. . . . The criterion by which the choice was determined was based not on considerations of economic expediency, but on immediate feasibility, whatever the cost of production . . . tariffs have been carried to such a pitch that they are undoubtedly—on an average—the highest in the world. It is not uncommon to find tariff duties of over 500 per cent.
>
> As is well known, the proliferation of industries of every kind in a closed market has deprived the Latin American countries of the advantages of specialization and economies of scale, and owing to the protection afforded by excessive tariff duties and restrictions, a healthy form of internal competition has failed to develop, to the detriment of efficient production.[2]

If we take a look at the writings of Celso Furtado, the shift in the climate of opinion stands out even more starkly. In 1960, after a decade or more of rapid industrial advance, Furtado celebrated the resulting "transfer of decision centers" from abroad to Brazil in almost lyrical terms:

> By now the Brazilian economy could count on its own dynamic element: industrial investments supported by the internal market. Growth quickly became two-dimensional. Each new impulse forward would mean an increasing structural diversification, higher productivity levels, a larger mass of resources for investment, a quicker expansion of the internal market, and the possibility of such impulses being permanently surpassed.[3]

2. *Towards a Dynamic Development Policy for Latin America* (New York: United Nations, 1963) p. 71.

3. Celso Furtado, "The Brazilian Economy in the Middle of the Twentieth Century," mimeographed (Israel: Industrial Conference on Science in the Advancement of New States, 1960), p. 5. See also chap. 13, p. 303.

Only six years later, after Brazil had suffered a series of political and economic setbacks, a disillusioned Furtado wrote:

> In Latin America . . . there is a general consciousness of living through a period of decline. . . . The phase of "easy" development, through increasing exports of primary products *or through import substitution* has everywhere been exhausted.[4]

Considering these two pairs of quotes one could easily conclude that we have here an instance of the acceleration of history. The phase of export-propelled growth (*crecimiento hacia afuera*) in Latin America lasted roughly from the middle of the nineteenth century until the Great Depression; and it took another twenty years, from 1929 to the Prebisch manifesto of 1949, before the end of export-propelled growth became official Latin American doctrine. Then came the next phase of Latin American growth, *crecimiento hacia adentro* or growth via the domestic market. It gathered strength during the Depression and World War II, flourished briefly in both theory and practice during the fifties and was pronounced either dead or a dud in the sixties. It looks, therefore, as though the acceleration of technical progress in the developed countries were matched in the underdeveloped ones by an increasingly rapid accumulation of failures in growth experiences!

As will be seen, there may be considerable exaggeration in the announced failure of import-substituting industrialization just as, in spite of the supposed demise of export-propelled growth, Venezuela, Ecuador, Peru, and Central America achieved notable economic gains in the two postwar decades through rapidly growing exports of petroleum, bananas, fishmeal, and cotton, respectively. While *fracasomania,* or the insistence on having experienced yet

4. "U.S. Hegemony and the Future of Latin America," *The World Today* 22 (September 1966): 375. My italics. Detailed critiques of the ISI process in Latin America can be found in two influential articles: Maria de Conceicão Tavares, "The Growth and Decline of Import Substitution in Brazil," and Santiago Macario, "Protectionism and Industrialization in Latin America," both in *Economic Bulletin for Latin America* 9 (March 1964): 1–61 and 62–102.

another failure, certainly has its share in the severity of the recent judgments on industrialization, the widespread criticism of ISI—in Pakistan and India very similar problems are being discussed—indicates that there is real substance to the concern that is being expressed. But the rapidity of the reversal in the climate of opinion makes one rather suspect that ISI had, from its very onset, both positive and negative aspects, with the latter simply coming into view a few years after the former. Our inquiry will therefore start out with a brief survey of the principal characteristics which set off ISI from other types of industrialization.

FOUR IMPULSES OF IMPORT-SUBSTITUTING INDUSTRIALIZATION (ISI)

Wars and depressions have historically no doubt been most important in bringing industries to countries of the "periphery" which up to then had firmly remained in the nonindustrial category. The crucial role of the two world wars and of the Great Depression in undermining acceptance of traditional ideas about the international division of labor between advanced and backward countries is well known.[5] But industrialization has not only been the response to sudden deprivation of imports; it has taken place in many erstwhile nonindustrial countries as a result of the gradual expansion of an economy that grows along the export-propelled path. As incomes and markets expand in such a country and some thresholds at which domestic production becomes profitable are crossed, industries come into being without the need of external shocks or governmental intervention—a process I have described

5. Apparently even earlier crises had positive effects on industrial growth in Latin America. The following quote is instructive: "There is no ill wind that does not blow some good . . . the crisis the country is going through is tremendous—and yet this is a perfect wind for national industry. Many of our industries have had a more or less vigorous protection through customs duties. But all of this would not have been enough had it not been for the crisis of 1875 which gave the impulse to industry and for that of 1890 which strengthened and diffused it." Quoted from *El Nacional* in Adolfo Dorfman, *Desarrollo industrial en la Argentina* (Rosario, 1941), p. 11. My translation.

as "import-swallowing"[6] and which has been perhaps more aptly termed industrialization through "final demand linkage," as distinct from the continuation of the process via backward and forward linkage effects.[7] Gradual import substitution in response to the growth of domestic markets accounts for the widespread establishment of industries which have substantial locational advantages because of the weightiness of the product (cement, beer) and of those, such as textiles, whose market is large even at low per capita incomes.

Over the past two decades import-substituting industrialization has, of course, no longer been exclusively a matter of natural market forces reacting to either gradual growth of income or to cataclysmic events, such as wars and depressions. It has been undertaken in many countries as a matter of deliberate development policy, carried out no longer just by means of protective duties, but through a wide array of credit and fiscal policy devices, through pressures on foreign importing firms to set up manufacturing operations as well as through direct action: the establishment of state-owned industries or, increasingly, of development corporations or banks which are then entrusted with the promotion of specific ventures.

It is useful to keep in mind these distinct origins of ISI—wars, balance of payments difficulties, growth of the domestic market (as a result of export growth) and official development policy— in focusing on the distinctive characteristics of the process.

Clearly, there is not just one ISI process. An industrialization that takes place in the midst and as a result of export growth has a wholly different *Gestalt* from one that feeds on foreign exchange deprivation. For example, in the latter situation it seems much more likely that inflationary developments will accompany the in-

6. Albert O. Hirschman, *The Strategy of Economic Development* (New Haven: Yale University Press, 1958), chap. 7.

7. See Melville H. Watkins, "A Staple Theory of Economic Growth," *Canadian Journal of Economics and Political Science* 29 (May 1963): 141–58; and Richard E. Caves, "Vent-for-Surplus Models of Trade and Growth" in *Trade, Growth and the Balance of Payments,* Essays in honor of Gottfried Haberler (Chicago: Rand-McNally, 1965), pp. 95–115.

dustrialization process than in the former. Or, to proceed to one of the alleged—and often criticized—characteristics of the industrialization process itself, namely its tendency to concentrate on nonessential, luxury-type goods. This tendency to give importance to what is unimportant will be present only when the primary impulse to industrialization arises out of unexpected balance of payments difficulties which are fought routinely by the imposition of quantitative import controls. The controls will aim at permitting continued supply of the more essential good traditionally imported at the cost of shutting out nonessentials and will thus cause domestic production of the latter to become especially profitable.

It is easy, however, to make too much of this situation. Of the four motive forces behind ISI—balance of payments difficulties, wars, gradual growth of income, and deliberate development policy—only the first leads to a bias in favor of nonessential industries. The last, deliberate development policy, is likely to produce exactly the opposite bias; and the remaining two causes are neutral with respect to the luxury character of the industry. Wars cause interruption of, or hazards for, all international commodity flows, essential or nonessential, and therefore provide a general unbiased stimulus to domestic production of previously imported goods. The same is true for the stimulus emanating from the gradual growth of markets. It seems likely, therefore, that the role of nonessential goods within the total ISI process has been exaggerated by the "new" critics who, in stressing this role, sound almost like the old-line Latin American laissez faire advocates who were forever inveighing against the introduction of "exotic" industries into their countries.

CHARACTERISTICS OF THE INITIAL PHASE OF ISI

Industrialization by Tightly Separated Stages

No matter what its original impulse, ISI starts predominantly with the manufacture of finished consumer goods that were previously imported and then moves on, more or less rapidly and successfully, to the "higher stages" of manufacture, that is, to intermediate goods and machinery, through backward linkage effects. The process can and does start here and there with capital or even intermediate goods insofar as such goods are imported prior to any industrialization because they are needed in connection with agricultural or transportation activities. Machetes, coffee hulling machines, trucks and fertilizers are examples. In the textile industry, the crushing superiority of machine spinning over hand spinning, combined with a lesser advantage of machinery in weaving, has made sometimes for the installation of spinning mills ahead of weaving mills, especially in countries where a strong handweaving tradition had not been previously destroyed by textile imports from the industrial leaders.

But the bulk of new industries are in the consumer goods sector and as they are undertaken in accordance with known processes, on the basis of imported inputs and machines, industrialization via import substitution becomes a *highly sequential,* or *tightly staged,* affair. Herein lies perhaps its principal difference from industrialization in the advanced countries. This aspect is so familiar and seemingly inevitable that it has not received quite the attention it deserves. It is the basic reason for which the ISI process is far smoother, less disruptive, but also far less learning-intensive than had been the case for industrialization in Europe, North America, and Japan.

This is not the place for renewing the discussion over the advantages or drawbacks of an early or late start in industrialization. Suffice it to point out, however, that those who have stressed the advantages of a late start have often had in mind the ability of newcomers to jump with both feet into a newly emerging dynamic industrial sector (as Germany did with chemicals) instead of remaining bogged down in sectors that had long passed their prime (as England in textiles and railways construction). But the "late latecomers" with whom we are concerned here are not apt to jump in this fashion. Industrialization is here at first wholly a matter of imitation and importation of tried and tested processes. Consider by way of contrast the following description of the establishment of new industries in advanced countries:

> Young industries are often strangers to the established economic system. They require new kinds or qualities of

materials and hence make their own; they must overcome technical problems in the use of their products and cannot wait for potential users to overcome them; they must persuade customers to abandon other commodities and find specialized merchants to undertake the task. These young industries must design their specialized equipment and often manufacture it.[8]

Not much of this travail occurs when a new industry is introduced into the "late late" starting countries. It is in this connection that one must be on guard against studies purporting to show that the history of industrialization is substantially the same in all countries, working its way from light consumer goods industries, to heavy and capital goods industries, and eventually to consumer durables. The apparently similar pattern of the earlier and "late late" industrializers in this respect conceals an essential qualitative difference. Even when the earlier industrializers were predominantly in the light consumer goods stage (from the point of view of labor force or value added), they were already producing their own capital goods, if only by artisan methods. As Marx wrote: "There were mules and steam-engines before there were any laborers whose exclusive occupation it was to make mules and steam-engines; just as men wore clothes before there were tailors."[9] But the "late late" industrializers will import, rather than make, their clothes until such time as they are able to set up a tailor in business all by himself. This situation forecloses, of course, for a considerable time any fundamental adaptation of technology to the characteristics of the importing countries, such as the relative abundance of labor in relation to capital. Whether and to what extent such an adaptation is desirable is an idle question under these circumstances; given the sequential pattern of industrialization, there is remarkably little choice. ISI thus brings in complex tech-

8. George Stigler, "The Division of Labor is Limited by the Extent of Market," *Journal of Political Economy* 59 (June 1951): 190.

9. *Kapital,* 1 (Vienna-Berlin, 1932), p. 399. This passage and the previous one by Stigler were brought to my attention by Nathan Rosenberg's article "Capital Goods, Technology, and Economic Growth," *Oxford Economic Papers,* 15 (November 1963): 223–24.

nology, but without the sustained technological experimentation and concomitant training in innovation which are characteristic of the pioneer industrial countries.

"Late" vs. "Late Late" Industrialization

The "late late" industrialization sketched so far may be contrasted not only with that of the presently advanced industrial countries in general, but particularly with that of the so-called latecomers among them. The "late" industrialization of countries like Germany, Italy and Russia has been depicted by Gerschenkron through the following propositions:

1. The more backward a country's economy, the more likely was its industrialization to start discontinuously as a sudden great spurt proceeding at a relatively high rate of growth of manufacturing output.

2. The more backward a country's economy, the more pronounced was the stress in its industrialization on bigness of both plant and enterprise.

3. The more backward a country's economy, the greater was the stress upon producers' goods as against consumers' goods.

4. The more backward a country's economy, the heavier was the pressure upon the levels of consumption of the population.

5. The more backward a country's economy, the greater was the part played by special institutional factors designed to increase the supply of capital to the nascent industries and, in addition, to provide them with less decentralized and better informed entrepreneurial guidance; the more backward the country, the more pronounced was the coerciveness and comprehensiveness of those factors.

6. The more backward a country, the less likely was its agriculture to play any active role by offering to the growing industries the advantages of an expanding industrial market

based in turn on the rising productivity of agricultural labor.[10]

Of these six characteristics only the last one applies unconditionally to the late late industrializers. Special institutions designed to supply capital and entrepreneurial guidance (point 5), became important in most of Latin America after the ISI process had already been underway as a result of private, decentralized initiative for a considerable time. As to the remaining four points, almost the opposite could be said to hold for our late latecomers. Their industrialization started with relatively small plants administering "last touches" to a host of imported inputs, concentrated on consumer rather than producer goods, and often was specifically designed to improve the levels of consumption of populations who were suddenly cut off, as a result of war or balance of payments crises, from imported consumer goods to which they had become accustomed. Even though the rates at which new plants were built and at which their output expanded were often respectable, the process thus lacked some of the essential characteristics of Gerschenkron's "great spurt."

As a result, late late industrialization shows little of the inspiring, if convulsive élan that was characteristic of the late industrializers such as Germany, Russia and Japan. This is perhaps the basic reason for the feelings of disappointment experienced by Latin American observers who had looked to industrialization for a thorough transformation and modernization of their societies.

Naturally, the difference between the two types of industrialization must not be overdrawn. At least one experience in Latin America, that of Brazil during the fifties, came fairly close to the picture drawn by Gerschenkron: sustained and rapid progress of steel, chemical and capital goods industries during this decade was here combined with a "special institutional factor designed to increase supply of capital," namely inflation, and even with the flowering of a "developmentalist" (*desenvolvimentista*) ideol-

10. Alexander Gerschenkron, *Economic Backwardness in Historical Perspective* (Cambridge, Mass.: Harvard University Press, 1962), pp. 343–44.

ogy.[11] But what looked like the hopeful beginning of a "Brazilian economic miracle" was thrown into disarray by the political crises and related economic and social setbacks of the sixties. The gloom that pervades the Latin American mood at present stems precisely from the convergence of frustrations over the unexciting character of late late industrialization in most Latin American countries with the despair felt over the stumblings of the one country whose advance had assumed the more inspiring characteristics of the "great spurt."

The Sources of Entrepreneurship

A number of important characteristics of late late industrialization remain to be surveyed. What has been said so far permits, first of all, some discussion of the sources of entrepreneurship. As industry is started primarily to substitute imports, those engaged in the foreign trade sector are likely to play a substantial role in the process. This is the reason for the industrial prominence of (a) the former importers of Lebanese, Jewish, Italian, German, etc., origin, and (b) of the large foreign firms intent on maintaining their market and therefore turning from exporters into manufacturers. Once again, however, it is useful to distinguish between an industrialization which is brought underway under conditions of expanding income from exports and one that is ignited by deprivation of previously available imports (due to war or balance of payments troubles). Only in the latter situation are local importers and foreign exporting firms likely to be the main promoters of industrial enterprise. When foreign exchange income is expanding, one may rather expect industrial opportunities to be exploited by indigenous entrepreneurship. Under such conditions, the importing interests are apt to be well satisfied with their lot and activity;

11. While not included in the six points cited above, support by a vigorous movement of ideas has been stressed elsewhere by Gerschenkron as a characteristic of late industrialization. See, for example, his *Economic Backwardness*, pp. 22–26. For a survey of developmentalist-nationalist ideas in Brazil during the fifties, see Frank Bonilla, "A National Ideology for Development: Brazil" in K. H. Silvert, ed., *Expectant Peoples: Nationalism and Development* (New York: Random House, 1963), pp. 232–64.

industrial development will run clearly counter to their short-run interests, especially when it requires the imposition of even a moderate level of protection. Some evidence in support of our distinction may be cited: in both Brazil and Colombia, coffee booms in the late nineteenth and early twentieth centuries gave rise to periods of industrial expansion led by domestic entrepreneurs who were in no way tied to the importing interests.[12] The latter, on the other hand, were prominent in these and other Latin American countries during the high pressure drives toward import substitution which marked the world wars and the Great Depression.

The importance of foreigners, of minorities or, generally speaking, of non-elite-status groups in the total industrialization process has on occasion been held responsible for the fact that industrial interests do not wield in Latin America the political influence and social prestige which have been theirs in the older industrial countries. Insofar as the phenomenon is real, it can also be explained by the kind of industries most characteristic of the first phases of import-substituting industrialization: opinions of the owners of soft drink bottling plants or of cosmetic or pharmaceutical industries are unlikely to command as much attention as those of steel and machinery manufacturers. In addition, the industrialists of the leading industrial countries always gained considerable influence by virtue of being exporters; as such they achieved prestige abroad, acquired contacts and gathered information—all accomplishments that were highly prized by their governments.[13] This source of influence is quite unavailable to the import-substituting

12. Warren Dean, "The Planter as Entrepreneur: The Case of São Paulo," *The Hispanic American Historical Review* 46 (May 1966): 138–52; Luis Ospina Vásquez, *Industria y protección en Colombia (1810–1930)* (Medellín: E. S. F., 1955), chap. 8.

13. In Germany, for example, social prestige was granted to industrial entrepreneurs only to the extent that they were active in "fields which made a direct contribution to Germany's economic strength [such as] coal, steel, chemicals, industrial engineering" or that they exploited "the all-important export markets" (William N. Parker, "Entrepreneurial Opportunities and Response in the German Economy," *Explorations in Entrepreneurial History* 7 [October 1954]: p. 32).

industrialists who are usually aiming only at supplying the domestic market.[14]

The Exuberant Phase of ISI and Its Political Consequences

A final characteristic of the early phases of import-substituting industrialization is the growth pattern of the newly established industries. It has been suggested that

> output curves in newly established import-substituting industries have tended to be kinked, rising rapidly when exports are being replaced, but flattening out when further growth of demand has been grounded in the growth of domestic income. Profits have also followed this kinked pattern. Thus industries have moved rapidly from high profit and growth to precocious maturity, at which point they fall back to monopolistic quiescence with lower profit rates, a reduced level of investment, and aging plant and equipment.[15]

The extent to which the kinked pattern of output growth is really a fact rather than an inference from the nature of import substitution remains to be established. After all, newly established industries have to overcome initial production and organization problems, they encounter some sales resistance due to preference for the imported product so that the early portion of their sales data may still approximate the logistic curve which has given a good fit for the time shape of the expansion of many industries in

14. The proposition that the comparative *lack* of political power of the industrialists can be explained by the *lack* of industrial exports becomes perhaps more convincing when one states its positive counterpart: namely that the continuing political influence of the land-owning interests throughout the period of industrialization in Latin America is explained by the continuing almost total dependence of the capacity to import on exports of primary products. This point is made for Brazil in Francisco C. Weffort, "Estado y masas en el Brasil," *Revista Latinoamericana de Sociologia* 1 (March 1965): 53–71.

15. David Felix, "Monetarists, Structuralists and Import-Substituting Industrialization," in W. Baer and I. Kerstenetzky, eds., *Inflation and Growth in Latin America* (Homewood, Illinois: Irwin, 1964), p. 384.

the advanced countries.[16] Nevertheless, it is probably legitimate to speak of a particularly "easy" phase of import substitution when the manufacturing process is entirely based on imported materials and machinery while importation of the article is firmly and effectively shut out by controls. Under such conditions, the early experience of the new manufacturers is likely to be most gratifying. It is this phase of import substitution that gives rise to the often noted exuberance and boom atmosphere during which demand is easily overestimated. In any event, low duties or preferential exchange rates for machinery imports make for lavish orders. As a result, the new industry is likely to find itself saddled with excess capacity as soon as it reaches the kink.[17]

It is tempting to speculate about the psychological-political consequences of this pattern of industrialization. Progressive Latin Americans had long hoped that industry would introduce new, much-needed disciplines into the behavior of their governments. The very nature of industrial operations—their precision, the need for exact timing, punctuality, reliability, predictability and all-around rationality—was expected to infuse these same qualities into policy making and perhaps even into the political process it-

16. Simon S. Kuznets, *Secular Movements in Production and Prices* (Boston: Houghton Mifflin, 1930). Arthur F. Burns, *Production Trends in the United States since 1870* (New York: National Bureau of Economic Research, 1934).

17. Even if expansion plans of competing firms are known all around and there is no excessive optimism, demand tends to be overestimated for two special reasons: with protection the price of the domestically produced product is going to be higher than that of the imported one; and market studies based on import statistics often overestimate the domestic market for the new domestic industry also because the statistics usually include a fair volume of specialty products which the domestic industry is unable to supply. In the case of intermediate products, however, demand may be *under*estimated for an important reason: by looking primarily at the volume of imports of such products as an indication of the room for substitution, the analyst would overlook opportunities that arise as import substitution is undertaken with respect to products which use the intermediate good as an input. See Samuel A. Morley and Gordon W. Smith, "On the Measurement of Import Substitution," *American Economic Review* 60 (September 1970): 728–35.

self. This sort of inference was based on the nature—or supposed nature—of industrial operations at the plant level. It disregarded, however, the larger financial and economic aspects of the process which had, of course, a much more direct and determining impact on politics. Thus the ease with which new industries were installed in spite of dire warnings and often in the midst of war and depression, the rapid growth they experienced and the handsome profits they realized during the first phases made import-substituting industry appear as a new incarnation of some primary product that would suddenly erupt with an old-fashioned world market boom. Little wonder, then, that the hoped for achievement of rationality in economic policy making and in the political process in general failed to occur. On the contrary, the "exuberant" phase of import substitution was accompanied by flamboyant public policies which badly overestimated the tolerance of the economy for a variety of ventures, be they income redistribution by fiat, the building of a new capital, or other extravaganzas. Here we can do no more than touch upon these matters; but it may be conjectured that in their very different ways, Perón, Kubitschek, Rojas Pinilla, and Pérez Jiménez could all be considered victims of the delusions of economic invulnerability fostered by the surprising early successes and rapid penetration of industry into a supposedly hostile environment.

THE ALLEGED EXHAUSTION OF IMPORT SUBSTITUTION

Then, suddenly, the honeymoon was over and the recriminations began. Import-substituting industrialization was officially added, as we have seen, to the long list of certified *fracasos* in Latin American policy making. We shall now attempt to sort out and evaluate some of the elements in this reversal of opinion.

Four principal accusations have been leveled against the industrialization process as it has appeared in Latin America:

1. Import-substituting industrialization is apt to get "stuck" after its first successes, due to the "exhaustion of easy import substitution opportunities"; it leaves the economy with a few relatively high-cost industrial establishments, and with a far more vulnerable balance of payments since imports consist now of semi-

finished materials, spare parts and machinery indispensably required for maintaining and increasing production and employment.

2. Import-substituting industry is affected by seemingly congenital inability to move into export markets.

3. The new industries are making an inadequate contribution to the solution of the unemployment problem.

4. The new industries often tend to be established as branch plants and subsidiaries of foreign firms and thereby foster a new type of "dependency" for Latin America.

In the following we shall concentrate on the first two critiques; the other two cannot be adequately discussed within the limits of the present essay.[18]

A Naive and a Seminaive Exhaustion Model

The argument on ISI getting stuck is put forward in several forms. Most frequently and crudely, the assertion is made that the process faces "exhaustion" after a certain period during which the "easy" import substitution opportunities are taken up. Exhaustion evokes the image of a natural resource available in strictly limited quantities which is being depleted; and we must ask now to what extent the image is sensible. One model which could underly the exhaustion concept is an exceedingly simple one: at any one point of time, a country imports commodities A, B, C . . . ; the annual import volumes of these commodities are M_A, M_B, M_C . . . Next, one assumes the existence of economies of scale such that the minimum economic sizes of plants which are to produce these various goods can be unequivocally defined. If the annual capacities of such plants are designated by P_A, P_B, P_C, . . . then import substitution opportunities are limited to those products (say, A, C, E, . . .) for which imports (the M's) exceed the minimum economic sizes (the P's).

This would be a truly naive model rationalizing the exhaustion concept, and it is perhaps too much of a caricature of what the critics of import substitution have in mind. The more sophisticated

18. See chap. 11 for some observations on the fourth critique.

among them, at least, do realize that the first steps of ISI open up new opportunities for the establishment of domestic manufactures through both income and backward linkage effects. In the first place, the domestic production of A, C, and E creates new incomes which may enlarge the market for a number of additional final demand goods to the point where their domestic production becomes, in turn, feasible. Secondly, domestic production of A, C, and E, which is *ex hypothesi* set up on the basis of imported inputs, opens up new opportunities for the establishment of domestic manufacturing facilities turning out these inputs.

The income effect is likely to result in a convergent series of new investment opportunities. Thus it postpones exhaustion in relation to the naive model, but does not overcome it. When backward linkage effects are taken into account, however, the exhaustion concept tends to evaporate unless it is bolstered by some additional assumptions.

Again a rather naive, let us call it "seminaive," exhaustion model could be built up as follows. Industry A requires imported inputs $a_1, a_2, a_3, \ldots a_i \ldots$; industry C inputs $c_1, c_2, c_3, \ldots c_i \ldots$ and so on. It seems plausible that imports of any individual input, such as $M_{a1}, M_{a2}, M_{a3}, \ldots M_{ai} \ldots$ should be smaller than M_A had been before domestic production of A started. On the other hand, it could be surmised (and frequently is unquestioningly assumed) that minimum economic plant size increases as one ascends to "higher" stages of production. If this is so, then we have $P_{ai} > P_A$ while $M_{ai} < M_A$. Under these circumstances the chances that imports will exceed the minimum economic sizes for any large number of imported inputs for A, C, and E decrease rapidly as one ascends via backward linkage toward the higher stages of production.

Criticism of the Seminaive Model: The Importance of Policy

I believe that something like this seminaive model is indeed in the minds of those who speak of exhaustion. For this reason it is useful to spell it out, for as soon as that is done, it is easy to perceive where such an exhaustion model goes wrong and what are, therefore, the requirements of an industrialization process that would "beat" exhaustion.[19]

Two modifications of the model serve to make it look both more realistic and less exhaustion-prone. In the first place, some of the inputs needed for the initial import-substitution industries are likely to be identically the same (steel, paper, glass are needed as intermediate inputs in a wide variety of final demand products). As a result of this product convergence of industrial processes the a_i's are not always distinct from the c_i's and e_i's, so that imports of a number of intermediate goods may well be larger than the previous imports of final demand goods.[20]

Secondly, it is of course not necessarily true that minimum economic plant size increases regularly as one ascends toward the higher stages of production. I am not aware of any systematic study relating to this point. But it is well known, for example, that automobile assembly plants deal with a number of suppliers and subcontractors for many needed components, just as a single steel plant will draw for its supply of coal on several mines. Large capacity plants do characterize the technology of a few important intermediate and basic products; but at every stage—particularly in the machinery and equipment industries which, in a sense, rep-

19. One way of staving off the exhaustion predicted by the naive or seminaive model would be to enlarge total market size, either for *all* products through the amalgamation of several national markets, or for *some* products particularly important for industrial progress, through appropriate income redistribution within a given national market. Accordingly the formation of common markets and a redistribution of income which would result in larger domestic markets for mass-produced articles have held an important place in the discussions that arose after the "exuberant" phase of ISI was over. There can be no doubt that the creation of a larger market through either or both of these moves would contribute much to dynamic industrial growth. But we wish to argue here that they are not the only available instruments or, in other words, that market size is not as rigid and definite a barrier as the exhaustion thesis claims.

20. Moreover, because of this product convergence the opportunities for import substitution are much greater, in the case of intermediate goods, than appears from a look at the import statistics. See n. 17 above.

resent the "highest" stage of production—small and medium-sized establishments are also to be found.[21]

If we put these two considerations together, one particularly favorable possibility appears: minimum economic size could providentially be, and in fact often is, large in those industries for whose products (steel, glass, paper) the convergence phenomenon is important. But even apart from such a happy coincidence, the preceding considerations make the exhaustion concept lose the physical and predictable definiteness it had assumed with the previous models. It appears instead that the difficulties that may well dog the backward linkage process are to a considerable extent a matter of economic environments and policies, instead of being determined exclusively by objective quantities such as market and minimum economic plant sizes.

We have a few more words to say on the latter topics before we turn to the economic and sociopolitical reasons for which the backward linkage process may or may not get stuck. It must be recognized that one implication of the above considerations is to stress even more the importance of market size. In the seminaive exhaustion model, market size sets definite limits to the number of industries which a given country can set up. With increasing market size, an additional number of industries, all of larger size than could be accommodated previously, become possible. But if one gives up the idea that minimum economic size and stage of production are closely correlated, the advantages of market size can become larger rather than smaller, for a larger market permits the installation not only of an industry requiring that market, but, in its wake, of a host of other plants supplying that industry; the required market size of these plants may be much smaller, but they could not be established without the prior establishment of the

21. For striking evidence on the smallness of the typical machine tool firm in the United States and on low concentration ratios in the industry, see Murray Brown and Nathan Rosenberg, "Prologue to a Study of Patent and Other Factors in the Machine Tool Industry," *The Patent, Trademark and Copyright Journal of Research and Education* 4 (Spring 1960): 42–46. One reason for this situation is that capital/labor ratios are typically low in the machinery industry.

industry requiring the larger market and which might therefore be called the "bottleneck industry."

These considerations make us understand better the tremendous importance of market size (so well illustrated by the exceptional achievements in Latin America of Mexico and Brazil) if the backward linkage process is to be vigorous. But they also lead to some interesting policy conclusions: with the seminaive model, the industrialization process is bound to stop at a given point. It can be likened to the ascent of a mountain which gets steeper all the time; the country is the mountain climber and the larger it (or rather its market) is, the higher up the mountain it gets. If this were really so, there would not be much point in pushing it up a bit higher through special incentives or promotion of public enterprise, and any infant industry protection should be uniform. But if we abandon the seminaive model, the mountain alters its shape; at one point its slope does become forbiddingly steep, but then it flattens to turn up again only much later. Under those conditions it becomes exceedingly important to climb the forbidding portion (the bottleneck industry) of the mountain as then the traveling can be continued with ease for some time. In other words, the existence of the bottleneck industries is a powerful argument for special protection, or direct promotion, and even better, for efforts to export the portion of the industry's output that cannot be accommodated by the domestic market. In any event, public policy is very much back in the saddle with this view of the industrialization process.

A further remark along similar lines. The phenomenon of product convergence can also be utilized to help a country negotiate the steeper slopes of its bottleneck industries. When an intermediate product industry faces inadequate domestic demand and cannot therefore be established on an economic scale, it is possible to canvas possibilities for setting up industries which might generate additional demands for the bottleneck industry's output. While this may be difficult in practice, the argument leads to a counsel of caution in policies directed against so-called "nonessential" industries: the demands for intermediate products emanating from these industries can be very precious in permitting *essential* intermediate product industries to be established.

ECONOMIC, POLITICAL AND TECHNOLOGICAL DETERMINANTS
OF BACKWARD LINKAGE

While the preceding considerations ended up by stressing the
importance of policy, they were still focused on the *mechanism* of
industrialization through backward linkages. We must now ad-
dress ourselves directly to the political economy of the process.

The importance of market size and of an adequate supply of
foreign exchange in setting some limits to the process is undoubted; nevertheless, the industrialization processes of countries
which are not too dissimilar with respect to these constraints still
display considerable variation so that curiosity is aroused about
the role of other factors, such as the behavior of private industrialists and of public authorities.

As is well known by now, the setting up of an industry based
on imported inputs has two contradictory effects: it becomes possible, and in some to be defined ways attractive, to set up industries
producing inputs for the initial industry; but at the same time, the
very establishment of that industry sets up resistances against
backward linkage investments. Several reasons for such resistances had already been noted in my *Strategy of Economic Development:*

> The industrialist who has worked hitherto with imported
> materials will often be hostile to the establishment of do-
> mestic industries producing these materials. First, he fears,
> often with good reason, that the domestic product will not
> be of as good and uniform quality as the imported one. Sec-
> ondly, he feels that he might become dependent on a single
> domestic supplier when he could previously shop around the
> world. Third, he is concerned about domestic competition
> becoming more active once the basic ingredients are pro-
> duced within the country. Finally, his location may be wrong
> once the source of supply of the materials he uses is
> thoroughly altered. For all these reasons, the interests of the
> converting, finishing, and mixing industries are often op-

posed to the establishment of domestic sources of supply for the products that they convert, finish, or mix.[22]

Another powerful factor making for resistance has since received much attention: high tariff protection for the initial industry combined with low or zero tariffs or preferential exchange rate treatment for the industry's inputs.[23] The greater the difference between the level of protection accorded to the import-substituting industry and that applying to its imported inputs, the more will the profit margin of the industry depend on preventing domestic production of the inputs. For it is a fair assumption that the backward linkage industries would, once established, be eligible for a level of protection similar to that benefiting the initial import-substituting industry, and it is at least doubtful whether the initial industry can obtain a compensatory tariff increase for its own output or, in general, whether the resulting increase in costs can be passed on to the consumers without loss in sales volume.

For those various reasons, the newly established industries may not act at all as the entering wedge of a broad industrialization drive. The high customs duties on their outputs, combined with low (or negative) duties on their inputs, could almost be seen as a plot on the part of the existing powerholders to corrupt or buy off the new industrialists, to reduce them to a sinecured, inefficient, and unenterprising group that can in no way threaten the existing social structure. Indeed, like the workers' aristocracy in Lenin's theory of imperialism, these pampered industrialists might go

22. Hirschman, *Strategy*, p. 118. I am quoting myself here because the critics of ISI have sometimes taken me to task for having overrated the power and automaticity of the backward linkage process.

23. See, for example, Santiago Macario, "Protection and Industrialization," and R. Soligo and J. J. Stern, "Tariff Protection, Import Substitution and Investment Efficiency," *Pakistan Development Review* 5 (Summer 1965): 249–70. A general critique of import substitution on the grounds that the concentration on, and strong protection of, consumers goods it usually implies make for misallocation of resources, for obstacles to further industrial growth, and for a bias in favor of consumption is in John H. Power, "Import Substitution as an Industrialization Strategy," *Philippine Economic Journal* 5 (Second Semester 1966): 167–204.

over to the enemy—that is, make common cause with agrarian and trading interests which had long been opposed to the introduction of "exotic" industries.

The possibility that the industrialists who first appear in nonindustrial countries may not be all that much in favor of dynamic industrial development leads to an interesting sociopolitical puzzle. Sociologists and political scientists have frequently deplored the weakness of the middle class and particularly of the industrialists in Latin America, its lack of self-assertion and its failure to influence public affairs. Earlier we have tried to account for this phenomenon by some characteristics of late late industrialization. But at this point, one begins to wonder whether it would really be a good thing if the new industrialists were much more self-assertive and powerful than they are—perhaps they would then really be able to choke off further industrialization, something which generally they have not been able to do! Considering what we called the tightly staged character of late late industrialization it may in fact be preferable for the governments of the late late industrializing countries to be run by *técnicos,* by groups of planner-technicians, rather than by the new industrialists themselves. It has been in fact due to the regulations issued by the *técnicos* of the Kubitschek administration that backward linkage was enforced rapidly in the Brazilian automotive industry in the late fifties. In Mexico, on the other hand, assembly plants had existed for decades without any progress being made toward the local manufacture of motors and parts until measures similar to those in Brazil were adopted in the sixties. Thus the resistance of the initial industrialists to backward linkage combine with other already noted characteristics of late late industrialization to enhance the potential contribution of public policy to the process.[24]

But we dare not rely on such policies emerging simply because they are needed and because we issue a call for them. Could

24. That a policy of forcing backward linkage investments has problems and pitfalls of its own is shown in Leland L. Johnson, "Problems of Import Substitution: The Chilean Automobile Industry," *Economic Development and Cultural Change* 15 (January 1967): 202–16.

the resistance to backward linkage be overcome otherwise than by state action? While the resistances of the new industrialists are perfectly rational, one cannot but feel that they are based on a myopic, excessively short-run view of the development process. In this manner, we can supply a concrete justification for the view of a Brazilian sociologist according to which the traditional Western, Puritan-ethic-imbued, rational, profit-maximizing businessman is not really the type that is most needed in the situation of Latin America; what is required, he feels, are entrepreneurs who can identify themselves with the general developmental aspirations of their society, be it even at the expense of some rationality in their everyday business operations.[25]

But, once again, one cannot rest content with issuing a call for the *desenvolvimentista* entrepreneur; it would be more useful to be able to explain his appearance or nonappearance by a series of economic and social factors. This will be our next task. While it is true that backward linkage meets with certain resistances and obstacles, we have yet to inquire about the existence of other forces working in the opposite direction, that is, in the direction of making backward linkage work. This appraisal of the comparative strength of forces and counterforces is probably the key to understanding why industrialization has been more vigorous and continuous in some developing countries than in others—long before they ran up against any barriers of market size.

As is the case for the start of late late industrialization, so will the continuation of the process through backward linkage be strongly influenced by the industrializing country's balance of payments. The opposition of the initial industrialists to backward linkage investments is likely to be considerably reduced if they occasionally experience curtailments, due to foreign exchange shortages, in the flow of imported inputs; on the other hand, the backward linkage investments require availability of foreign exchange for the importation of machinery. Consequently it is likely that some alternation of foreign exchange stringency and abun-

25. Fernando H. Cardoso, "The Industrial Elite" in S. M. Lipset and A. Solari, eds., *Elites in Latin America* (New York: Oxford University Press, 1967), pp. 96–99.

dance would be optimal from the point of view of generating both the motivation and the resources required for the process. I have previously made this point[26] and considerable attention has been paid to the foreign exchange constraint.[27] Hence, it will be more useful to focus here on other forces affecting the process. There surely exist many situations in which some backward linkage investments are neither impossible in the light of foreign exchange availabilities, nor wholly compelled because of previous searing experience with foreign exchange shortages. We are interested here in the conditions that make for vigorous continuation of industrialization in these situations.

In line with our previous arguments, we posit a certain level of resistance of the new industrialists to the manufacturing of currently imported inputs. The resistance, while rational on the part of the initial industrialists, is undesirable from the point of view of the economy in the sense that profitable production of some inputs is assumed to be possible provided some average or normal level of protection is extended to them. In other words, there is room for, but resistance against, further industrialization along reasonably efficient lines of comparative advantage.[28] We now inquire what

26. *Strategy,* pp. 173–76.

27. See, for example, Carlos F. Díaz-Alejandro, "On the Import Intensity of Import Substitution," *Kyklos* 18 (1965): 495–511.

28. In somewhat more rigorous terms: the established, protected industries are earning excess profits which they would lose if industries supplying inputs to them were to be established with a "normal" level of tariff protection. The excess profits of the first ISI industrialists thus have an interesting contradictory character: they set up resistances against further industrialization, but at the same time they represent an obvious and attractive source of possible finance for that very process. Protection of the backward linkage industries achieves quite simply the needed transfer: as is now familiar, this protection lowers the level of effective protection of the industries catering to final demand. The numerous studies which have lately been devoted to the topic of effective protection have paid little attention to this important mechanism, presumably because they were rooted in the desire to denounce the evils and inefficiencies of ISI. That some of these evils are possibly self-liquidating as ISI proceeds, that an industry protected by infant industry tariffs can "grow up" not only because those tariffs are reduced, but because supplier industries with their own tariff protection

conditions other than balance of payments developments could make this resistance weaken or disappear.

The principal point to be made here is very simple: the resistance is almost wholly premised on the supposition that manufacturing in the higher stages of production is going to be undertaken by entrepreneurs other than the already established initial industrialists (or other than members of his immediate family). For if he himself undertakes it, most of the listed objections to the expansion of manufacturing via backward linkage fall to the ground. Thus, the fear of unreliability and poor quality of the domestic article should abate and the fear of domination by a monopoly supplier will disappear entirely. True, domestically produced inputs may have to be purchased at a higher price than was paid for the previously imported product which was perhaps obtained duty free or bought at some preferential exchange rate. But even if the increase in input costs that comes with domestic manufacture cannot be passed on, vertical integration would take the sting out of it; for the decrease of profits in one operation of an integrated industrial concern does not seriously matter if that decrease is compensated by the emergence of profits in another, newly established operation. To realize such profits the industrialist who contemplates the manufacture of hitherto imported inputs will usually have to obtain for those inputs some "normal" level of protection. It must be assumed, therefore, that he does not consider existing customs duties and exchange rate preferences as unchanging parameters immune to his will and influence; the opposite assumption is sometimes made in the literature on import substitution (with pessimistic consequences for the prospects of ISI), but it is manifestly unrealistic for most investment decisions.

If the disposition of the initial industrialists themselves to move farther back into the industrial structure is an important

---

spring up, was specifically suggested by W. M. Corden in his fundamental article, "The Structure of a Tariff System and the Effective Protective Rate," *Journal of Political Economy* 74 (June 1966): 229. But this implication of the theory of effective protection seems to have been forgotten by the many researchers who have followed in Corden's footsteps.

element in overcoming obstacles to the backward linkage process, a brief inquiry into the factors making for a disposition of this sort is in order.

The economist can contribute a general reason for which backward linkage investments are likely to be carried on by the new industrialists themselves: the mere fact that they have been earning profits and are therefore presumably looking for new investment opportunities. Once the new industries have reached the point at which imports have been wholly substituted so that horizontal expansion is no longer profitable, vertical expansion into the "higher stages" of production may well offer the best available and, in any event, the most obvious outlet for investment funds that have accumulated as a result of the profitable operation of the existing industries. The availability of profits from the first phase of import substitution thus provides a generalized incentive for the successful import-substituting industrialist to plunge once again, naturally after appropriate modification of the tariff and exchange rate policies affecting the products whose manufacture is to be undertaken. The likelihood that the new industrialist will look in this particular direction, is increased by two interrelated factors: one, by the special difficulty of moving into export markets, to be commented on in the next section; and secondly by what we called the sequential or "tightly staged" character of late late industrialization. The industrialist manufacturing a final demand good during earlier cycles of industrialization was likely to call into life domestic producers of inputs and of the required machinery; therefore, once he was no longer able to expand his domestic sales volume, he found the higher stages already occupied by others and was therefore impelled to look elsewhere, including to exports, for further expansion. The situation is very different when production is undertaken wholly on the basis of imported inputs.

The availability of profits and resulting search for new profitable investment opportunities act, as has been said, as a general counterweight to the hostility toward backward linkage investments on the part of new industrialists. Whether or not this counterweight will outweigh the hostility is difficult to say. Under the worst of circumstances the combination of the two forces may result in a dog-in-the-manger situation: the new industrialists are able to prevent others from entering the backward linkage arena, but are not sufficiently motivated to enter it themselves.

To carry the analysis a bit further and to account for the different degrees of strength which the backward linkage dynamic has displayed in different countries, it is tempting to make a brief foray into the realm of sociology. The eagerness of an industrialist to move into related fields of activity instead of being satisfied with his existing operation based on imported inputs, may, for example, be reinforced if he has the feeling that his sons are locked into his own class and career. If an industrialist's sons are able and eager to enter the professions or the government, there is no need for father to think about finding new industries for the sons to expand into and to manage (preferably one for each son so they won't fight). But if industrialists look down on government and the professions, or if the latter look down upon the former, or, as happens frequently, if dislike and disdain are mutual, or simply, if the social distance between the industrialists and other groups is considerable, then the advantage of providing jobs for the family may fully compensate for the inconveniences, headaches, and even for minor monetary sacrifices that may be entailed by backward linkage investments. It appears once again, although from a rather different angle, that it is perhaps not a bad thing for the initial entrepreneurs to belong to a group of immigrants or of some other outsiders, with no immediate prospects of joining the established upper class or of moving into politics or the professions.

Social distance is bred by geographical distance. For this reason, one might expect that an industrialization process which, at least in its beginnings, is strongly identified with one or several centers other than the national capital stands a better chance to spill over vigorously from one industry to another than one which has its base in the capital city itself. The importance of having a somewhat isolated, inbred and self-consciously proud industrial center during the early stages of industrialization is demonstrated by the roles played by São Paulo, Monterrey, and Medellín. No similar pioneering center outside the capital city arose in Chile and

Argentina, and it is perhaps not a coincidence that these two countries have provided the critics of the ISI process with far better examples of its alleged irrationality and propensity to exhaustion than Brazil, Mexico, and Colombia.

A final subject of speculation is the differential impact of technology on the comparative strength of the linkage process in different industries. When a backward linkage effect points to an industry which is technologically quite distinct from the one requiring the input, the input-utilizing industrialist is less likely to be attracted to the input-producing industry than if the latter is closely related to processes and techniques with which the industrialist is already familiar. For example, the backward (and forward) linkage dynamic may show more spontaneous vigor in the "inbred" metalworking and chemical industries than in, say, the textile industry whose inputs come in large part from technological strangers such as, precisely, the chemical industry. Thus the backward linkage dynamic may be held back at some point simply by "technological strangeness." This point is of particular importance for the machinery industry since machinery is usually a technological stranger to the industry in which it is utilized. An inquiry into the technological determinants of the differential propensity of different industries toward linkage investments could be of considerable value. To identify and then to remove this sort of bottleneck should be a principal task of public agencies concerned with industrial development.

The purpose of the preceding observations was to convince the reader that there is far more to the vigor or weakness which late late industrialization displays in various countries than minimum economic size of plants, market size and even foreign exchange availabilities. We have left the naive and seminaive exhaustion models far behind and have instead generated a highly complex "field" of forces and counterforces. If the reader feels a bit confused, we have achieved our purpose: for essentially we wished to show that the process is not nearly so straightforward and constrained as it has recently been made to look, and that it depends far more on public and private acts of volition than has sometimes been granted as well as on numerous economic, sociological and technological factors which remain to be investigated.

THE INABILITY TO EXPORT MANUFACTURES: "STRUCTURAL" CAUSES AND REMEDIES

It is hardly necessary to stress how desirable it would be for our late late industrializing countries to become exporters of the outputs of their new industries:

1. Through exports they would overcome whatever obstacles of market size limit their growth or prevent their establishment.

2. Through exports they would loosen the balance-of-payments constraint which may otherwise prevent capacity operation of existing industries as well as establishment of new industries.

3. Finally, by competing in world markets, industries would be forced to attain and maintain high standards of efficiency and product quality and would thereby acquire defenses against oligopolistic collusion and decay to which they often succumb in highly protected, small local markets.

Unfortunately, the intensity with which one would wish for exports of manufacturers from the late late industrializers is matched by the solidity of the arguments which appear to foreclose any real prospects of success in this direction.

Once again, the arguments are familiar: the new industries have been set up exclusively to substitute imports, without any export horizon on the part of either the industrialists themselves or the government; the foreign branch plants and subsidiaries, which have taken an important part of the process, often are under specific instructions not to compete abroad with the products of the parent company; even more decisive than these obstacles deriving from attitudes and institutions, is the fact that the new industries, set up behind tariff walls, usually suffer from high production costs in countries that are, moreover, permanently subject to strong inflationary pressures—hence there is no real possibility of these industries competing successfully in international markets even if they were disposed to do so.

These are weighty arguments and they seem to meet the test of a satisfactory explanation in that they put one's mind to rest. But do they? After all, there are many industries which started out producing for the home market and eventually spilled over into foreign markets. Prior, successful acceptance of a manufactured commodity in the home market has even been considered to be a prerequisite for successful exporting.[29] Secondly, foreign firms have been known to be quite adaptable in their manufacturing and export policies. Just as they have been coaxed by national policies to produce or procure domestically a larger proportion of their inputs, so they could be induced to engage on export drives. Finally, even the most impressive explanation of the inability to export—the cost disadvantage of new industries set up under tariff protection—loses some of its persuasiveness when one remembers that protection of industries in Germany and the United States has not prevented considerable success of those protected industries in world markets. Industrialization of the nineteenth century latecomers was in fact frequently accompanied by both tariff protection and a vigorous export drive which threatened the previous dominant position of the old established industrial countries in a number of important markets. Again, the behavior of the late late industrializers could not be more different and it now begins to appear that we may be in need of some further, perhaps more fundamental explanations of the inability to export that afflicts them. While such a "structuralist" strategy of problem solving may show the problem to be even more deeply rooted than had been thought it can also uncover new, hitherto unsuspected ways of attacking it.[30]

One additional explanation of the difficulty of exporting has already been given in the preceding section. It was asserted that in view of the sequential character of industrialization, late late industrialists looking for new profitable business opportunities will frequently have the option between investing in backward linkage industries and expanding into export markets, whereas late industrialists had primarily the latter course open to them since the

29. S. B. Linder, *An Essay on Trade and Transformation* (New York: Wiley, 1961), pp. 87 ff.

30. A general plea for "structuralist" analysis of Latin American economic problems along with a good bibliography is to be found in Osvaldo Sunkel, "El trasfondo estructural de los problemas del desarrollo latinoamericano," *Trimestre Economico* 34 (January–March 1967): 11–58. For an interpretation of structuralism as a strategy for problem solving, see my *Journeys Toward Progress* (New York: Twentieth Century Fund, 1963) pp. 210–16 and 231–35.

backward linkage industries were already in existence. Little wonder, then, that the late late industrialists decide to stay cozily at home much longer than the late industrialists who were under a far greater compulsion to make the plunge into foreign markets if they were going to expand. It would therefore be unrealistic to expect an industry to become an exporter before it has truly taken root in the country through a variety of the more obvious backward linkage investments. And the expeditious undertaking of these investments is therefore desirable not only per se, but also as a necessary way station to the opening of the export phase.

Another structural reason for the inability to export derives from the circumstances under which resources have been channeled into the industrial sector in many Latin American countries. Industrial investments became attractive not only because of customs protection, but additionally because of the combination of internal inflation, overvaluation of the currency, and exchange controls. In effect, maintaining an overvalued exchange rate meant that the exporters of traditional primary products would receive a smaller real income than with an equilibrium or undervalued exchange rate. At the same time, the overvalued exchange rate permitted the acquisition at favorable prices (in domestic currency) of those imports that were let in by the control authorities. And since machinery and essential industrial materials enjoyed preferential status, the overvalued exchange rate acted in effect as a mechanism to transfer income from the traditional export sector to the new industries.[31]

At the same time, however, the overvalued exchange rate acted as a bar to exports from these industries. This probably was not a serious drawback and certainly was not felt as such during the earlier stages of import-substituting industrialization when exports on the part of the nascent industries were not a real prospect. But as a vigorous industrial establishment grew up in various countries

31. Alexandre Kafka, "The Theoretical Interpretation of Latin American Economic Development," in H. S. Ellis, ed., *Economic Development in Latin America* (New York: St. Martin's Press, 1961), p. 21; and Celso Furtado, "Industrialization and Inflation," *International Economic Papers* 12 (1967): 101–19.

one may well ask the question why a different institutional arrangement was not chosen. For example, why not tax the export sector, subsidize the new industries and do away with the overvalued exchange rate so that industrial exports are encouraged? To ask this question is to answer it: in most Latin American countries such a course would have been politically impossible. The power of the groups tied to the primary export sector would hardly have permitted so direct an assault, as is attested by the strong, permanent and occasionally successful pressures that were exerted against the indirect squeeze of the sector which Latin American monetary authorities had more or less inadvertently stumbled on. The great advantage of the inflation-cum-overvaluation arrangement was in fact not only that it resulted in an indirect rather than direct squeeze of politically and socially powerful groups, but that this mechanism was an unintended and, for a long time, an unnoticed by-product of a course of action which had the perfectly respectable objective of "defending the national currency against depreciation."[32]

Viewed in this way, the inability to export manufactures appears as the price which had to be paid for building up an industrial sector under adverse sociopolitical conditions. Should we then perhaps be simply gratified that industrialization was contrived at all, and be happy to pay the price? Not necessarily. As industrialization proceeded, the desirability of the overvaluation device became increasingly questionable from the point of view of industry itself. For overvaluation not only impeded exports, but interfered, in ways already analyzed, with the vigorous exploitation of the backward linkage dynamic. Moreover, in several countries, industries became sufficiently vigorous and integrated so that the help stemming from the procurement of a few imported inputs at

32. The policy originated, ironically enough, in an attempt to *defend* the export interests, e.g., in the case of Brazil, to maintain the cruzeiro price of coffee in the face of falling world market prices during the Great Depression. This policy led to an increase in the money supply, and thereby caused domestic inflationary pressures which would eventually result in the inflation-cum-overvaluation arrangement. Cf. Furtado, *Industrialization and Inflation,* p. 103.

bargain prices (via the overvalued exchange rate) was bound to be more than offset, for an increasing number of firms, by the loss of potential profits that could have been realized through the exports at a nonovervalued rate of exchange. It could thus be suggested that, at a certain point, overvaluation of the currency turned from a stimulus to industrial progress into a drag on it.

It appears that the much advertised noncompetitiveness of Latin American industry may be rooted more in the failure to modify institutions than in any inability to bring down real costs. The question then arises why the industrial interests have not vigorously pressed for institutional arrangements—export subsidies, preferential exchange rates, or more radically, an exchange rate that is undervalued rather than overvalued—that would make exporting profitable. Are there some grounds on which industrialists could be basically *reluctant* to commit substantial resources to an export drive?

This question leads to a third structural reason for—or speculation about—the difficulties of exporting. It has to do, once again, with the distribution of power in Latin American societies. To stage an export drive, an industrialist must frequently make special investments in research, design and packaging; he must assemble a specialized sales force, delegate considerable authority, launch an entirely different advertising campaign; in short, he incurs special risks and new overhead costs which will be recoverable only over a comparatively long period of successful exporting. Therefore, an industrialist will consider exporting only when he can be sure either that the basic institutions and policies which vitally affect his foreign operations are highly stable or, as a minimum, that his interests will be given the most serious attention when these institutions and policies are altered.

In effect, we have just spelled out a "prerequisite" for a determined and successful export drive for manufactures: to undertake such a drive with all its risks and special costs, the industrialist class must feel reasonably sure that it can control certain crucial fiscal and monetary policies of its government. Differently put: only a cohesive, vocal, and highly influential national bourgeoisie is likely to carry industrialization beyond relatively safe import

119

substitution to the risky export-oriented stage. It will be noted that this assertion—the industrialists do not export because they are not influential—completes the second half of a vicious circle whose first half asserted that the ISI industrialists are lacking in influence because they are not "conquering foreign markets" (see p. 97 above). Obviously we should not take inordinate pride in having fashioned a new vicious circle or in having identified a new prerequisite to the economic progress of the developing countries. Rather, we shall consider in a moment ways of breaking out of the circle and of doing without the prerequisite or of finding, à la Gerschenkron, a substitute for it. But we must nevertheless pause at this point in our reasoning and take notice that conditions for a strong export drive by the private sector are highly unfavorable in Latin America: in no country of that continent do the industrialists feel securely in control of vital economic policies affecting them. Policy makers positively cultivate unpredictability and distance from interest groups; at the same time, they are highly manipulative. Changes in fiscal, monetary, and foreign exchange policies are therefore frequent while communication about these changes with the affected interest groups is infrequent. These are the sociopolitical traits that account, perhaps more fundamentally than the cost-price structure of the new industries, for their poor export performance.

Having uncovered ever more cogent reasons for the inability to export, have we encounterd by the same token a "fundamental" remedy? One way of staking such a claim would be to expect that, as a result of our analysis, Latin America will change the nature of its politics and that its powerholders will henceforth become less manipulative and more communicative. Unfortunately analysis is not likely to act as so powerful a solvent. But is it really necessary to wait until a trusting and intimate relationship between the industrialists and the policy makers emerges or is it conceivable that countries which find it difficult to establish such a relationship could travel an alternative road?

A radical reaction to the problem would be for the state itself to take over the foreign merchandising function. The spectacle of the state rendering difficult or impossible the performance of an important function by the private sector and then taking over that function because the private sector is ostensibly falling down on the job, is by no means uncommon. If this course of action has not been taken so far for the export of manufactures, one reason is that the importance of this function is only beginning to be appreciated. Also, state enterprise is hardly likely to be at its best in selling a wide variety of manufactures in foreign markets; for, by its nature, this task requires levels of initiative, flexibility, risk-taking and de-centralized decision making which it has been difficult for state enterprise to attain.

A less radical and more promising solution would be for the state simply to take an active role in promoting exports by private enterprise. As already mentioned in connection with exports from foreign-owned branch plants and subsidiaries, the state could very well tie the granting of tax and other incentives to the attain-ment of export targets in a manner analogous to that with which backward linkage has been enforced in the Brazilian automobile industry. From the point of view of the industrialists, such a policy would have the advantage that one sector of the bureaucracy would become committed to the export drive and could then be relied on to do battle with those sectors whose policies interfere with the success of the drive.

Quite a different solution consists in leaving alone, at first, the obstacles to exporting that derive from the actions of one's own government and in concentrating instead on those that are caused by other governments. This is in fact what is being attempted at present through the United Nations Conference on Trade and De-velopment and its campaign for preferences for the manufactures of developing countries in the markets of developed countries. Perhaps this request can be viewed more sympathetically than it has been if it is considered as a compensation to the exporters of the newly industrializing countries for some of the extra burdens they must bear because of the policies and frequent policy changes of their own governments. In this reasoning, one may also discern a hope that such preferences would be temporary: once exports in volume would have been achieved, the first half of the vicious circle we have identified—industrialists are not influential be-cause they do not export, and they do not export because they are not influential—would have been shattered. There would then be hope that government policies would become more finely attuned to the needs of the exporting industrialists who might therefore dispense in due course with the special privileges obtained from other governments.

The need for common markets among developing countries can also be better appreciated from this perspective. The common markets would not only provide preferential treatment for the industrialists of the participating countries; for these mutual arrangements to be durable, monetary and foreign exchange policies would have to become more uniform and stable than they have been; and such a development would be even more important than the customs preferences themselves in promoting exports from the common market countries, not only to each other, but also to third countries. It is, however, precisely the prospect of less freedom of movement in monetary and foreign exchange policies which makes national governments so skittish about entering effective common market commitments.

Finally our problem could be alleviated by developments in the structure of international trade in manufactures. According to some observers, countries of recent industrialization should be acquiring a comparative advantage in certain types of highly standardized industrial products.[33] To sell such goods abroad may not be possible, in a number of lines, without special international market and firm connections, but it does not require either expensive advertisement campaigns or any special adaptation to foreign tastes and conditions. As a result, the overhead cost of exporting would be cut and the risks deriving from the instability or unpredictability of official economic policies would be correspondingly reduced.

In the preceding pages an attempt has been made to describe the varieties and characteristic features of import-substituting industrialization, and to derive from them sociopolitical consequences which in turn affect the process. Among the characteris-

33. Raymond Vernon, "International Investment and International Trade in the Product Cycle," *Quarterly Journal of Economics* 80 (May 1966): 202–07.

tics of ISI the possibility of proceeding sequentially, in tightly separated stages, because of the availability of imported inputs and machinery, plays, as was shown, a particularly commanding and complex role, direct and indirect, positive and negative.

Thus, the sequential or staged character of the process is responsible not only for the ease with which it can be brought underway, but also for the lack of training in technological innovation and for the resistances to both backward linkage investments and to exporting that are being encountered. The most important consequence of sequentiality, however, is the fact that it has become possible for industrialization to penetrate into Latin America and elsewhere among the late latecomers without requiring the fundamental social and political changes which it wrought among the pioneer industrial countries and also among the earlier group of latecomers. The repercussions of this situation on the industrialization process itself are ambivalent: on the one hand, the lack of political power of the new industrialists means, as we have just seen, that exporting meets with political and institutional, rather than purely economic, obstacles; on the other hand, this very lack of power neutralizes in various ways some of the possible adverse effects of sequentiality, for example, the resistance of the new industrialists to backward linkage.

In addition, the fact that import-substituting industrialization can be accommodated relatively easily in the existing social and political environment is probably responsible for the widespread disappointment with the process.[34] Industrialization was expected to change the social order and all it did was to supply manufactures! Hence one is only too ready to read evidence of total failure into any trouble it encounters.

This paper has by no means denied the various difficulties which the ISI process is apt to experience; in fact, they have on occasion been shown to be more deepseated than had been thought. At the same time, our exploration of the characteristics of the process has made it possible to discern avenues toward continued industrial growth that remain open to the late latecomers.

34. See below, chap. 15, pp. 331–33, for an elaboration of this point.

4. Industrial Development in the Brazilian Northeast and the Tax Credit Scheme of Article 34/18

SUDENE, the federal development agency for the Brazilian Northeast, was created in December 1959 to coordinate the many state and federal agencies operating in that traditionally underdeveloped region of Brazil, and to produce an "integrated, comprehensive" regional development program.[1] While the agency has set about this task over the past seven and a half years with remarkable energy and persistence, it was perhaps to be expected that no matter how integrated its plans, some of its numerous programs should have turned out to be more successful than others. By far the most significant development to have taken place over the past few years in the Northeast, has been an industrial spurt set off by a powerful tax credit provision which made it attractive for private capital from the more developed areas of Brazil to seek out investment opportunities in the Northeast. Established by Article 34 of the law approving SUDENE's first Plano Diretor (Law no. 3995 of 14 December 1961), and modified by Article 18 of the law approving the agency's 1963–65 program (law no. 4239 of 27 June 1963), this provision is known in Brazil, and will here. be referred to, as the "fiscal incentives of Article 34/18" or simply as "Article 34/18."

In spite of its comparatively recent institution, the Article 34/18 mechanism has become a complex legal, administrative and institutional system. Our first task is to describe the system in its essentials. Thereafter we shall assess its quantitative and

Reprinted by permission from *The Journal of Development Studies* 5 (October 1968): 5–28.

1. The history of the Northeast as an underdeveloped region in Brazil and of the many attempts to grapple with this problem, including the establishment and first steps of SUDENE, is traced in my *Journeys Toward Progress* (New York: Twentieth Century Fund, 1963), chap. 1, pp. 1–92.

qualitative impact. The final section is an appraisal of the economics of this novel technique of industrial development.

THE TAX CREDIT SCHEME

Basic Features

The basic principle of Article 34/18 is the permission granted to all Brazilian corporate entities *(pessôas jurídicas)* to cut their income tax liability in half, provided they invest the saved half in Northeastern projects approved by SUDENE. The income tax rate stands at 30 per cent, so that the tax saving can be substantial. As a first step, the tax savings (34/18 funds) are deposited in a blocked account at the Bank of the Northeast of Brazil (BNB); these deposits revert to the Federal Treasury if they are not committed to specific, approved projects within the three calendar years following the date of the deposit.

The projects in which the tax savings are invested must not only be approved by SUDENE as being of interest to the development of the Northeast; they must also be combined with fresh funds *(recursos próprios)*. Originally the minimum percentage of fresh funds in a project's equity was set at a flat 50 per cent. Since mid 1966 (decree no. 58.666–A of 16 June 1966), the minimum percentage of fresh funds can be set at 25 per cent, 50 per cent, or 75 per cent, depending on the merit of the project as determined by SUDENE according to an elaborate point system (Article 8 of the same decree).

An extremely important feature of the mechanism is the fact that this matching of tax savings with fresh funds must only occur at the level of the project, not at the level of the individual taxpayer. In other words, the individual taxpayer or rather, deposit holder, does not need to contribute fresh funds; he may contribute his deposits to a venture that is organized by a corporate group willing to contribute the needed fresh funds and eager to minimize this contribution by bringing together as much 34/18 money as is permissible. Most ventures are organized by this technique of matching the promoter of the enterprise (and whatever deposits he may own), to the deposits of others. The latter make a purely financial investment, usually in the form of preferential nonvoting stock, so that the group providing entrepreneurial and managerial leadership as well as fresh funds can exercise full control.

In addition to the facilities available under Article 34/18, new (as well as existing) industries can be granted the usual battery of privileges such as income tax exemptions, tax deductions for a number of years, customs duty exemptions on imported equipment and the like. More important than these standard incentives is the availability of bank credit. The BNB stands ready to extend to industrial enterprises loans up to 50 per cent of the needed capital assets at a highly advantageous interest rate (12 per cent which compares with commercial bank interest rates, of 30 to 40 per cent). In this way, projects that are allowed to raise up to 50 per cent of their equity through 34/18 deposits, need to supply only 25 per cent of total capital assets required through fresh funds (25 per cent fresh funds, 25 per cent 34/18 deposits, 50 per cent BNB loan). In the case of high-merit projects which are eligible for the 75 per cent–25 per cent equity split, the fresh fund requirement drops from 25 per cent to 12.5 per cent of total assets, as a result of the facilities offered by the BNB. In practice, however, firms which fall into this category do not normally find it worth their while to apply for a BNB loan, in part because of the additional delay involved, in part because of the BNB requirement that *all* fixed assets of the borrower be mortgaged to it.

Some additional prefinancing and financing facilities are available from state banks and financial agencies (Bandepe in Pernambuco, CODEC in Ceará, etc.).

The Trend toward Liberalization

The principal feature of the system is the availability of otherwise blocked funds for Northeastern investment. As will be seen below, taxpayers have taken advantage of the deposit privilege in rapidly increasing numbers and amounts, and the need to utilize these deposits effectively has led to a series of legal administrative changes—all in the direction of liberalizing the rules under which investment can take place. The principal changes are as follows:

1. Originally only firms whose capital was 100 per cent Brazilian were eligible to invoke the 50 per cent tax credit; this provision, which was laid down in 1961 (by Article 34) was eliminated in 1963 (by Article 18).

2. Originally only industrial enterprises in the Northeast could receive financing under the system; later on, agricultural and telecommunications projects were included.

3. Originally, as already noted, 34/18 deposits could only be used up to 50 per cent of the project's total equity; this ceiling was raised in 1966 to 75 per cent.

4. Originally the 34/18 deposits had to be contributed in the form of equity. Even though subscriptions to the capital were permitted to take the form of preferential nonvoting stock (nonnegotiable for at least five years), the equity requirement still made it difficult to organize some ventures, particularly in the case of *expansion* of existing firms. The assets of these firms were usually greatly undervalued because of inflation; moreover, in the case of agricultural enterprises, undervaluation of assets is widely practiced because of the ensuing real estate tax savings. To finance the expansion of an existing industrial or agricultural firm through issuance of stock to 34/18 deposit holders, would mean that the established owner-managers of the firm would find themselves in a minority position intolerable to them. However, to make the application of 34/18 deposits possible, a decree of 1964 (paragraph *13* of Article *13* of decree no. 55334 of 31 December 1964—a provision frequently referred to as "13/13"), permitted 34/18 deposits to be applied in the form of loan capital, on condition that they be repayable after a minimum grace period of five years.[2] It is my understanding that some of these loans are being made available with monetary correction clauses.

---

2. The intent of the legislator was obviously to make these loans as long-term as possible. An error was made in the drafting of the decree, however, and the wording calls for repayment, after the five-year grace period, "in annual instalments not *inferior* to twenty per cent each" when what was meant must surely have been the opposite—20 per cent was intended as the maximum limit of yearly repayments of principal. But the letter of the decree has prevailed.

5. Further use of 34/18 deposits was permitted to service foreign loans (particularly under an IDB credit line to the BNB), contracted by Northeastern firms to the extent of one-half of principal and interest, as long as the loan had served to increase the fixed assets of the firm (SUDENE resolution no. 1162 of 5 February 1965).

6. Finally, since September 1966, 34/18 deposits may be used within certain limits for purposes of reinforcing the working capital of Northeastern firms (Article 1 of decree no. 59001 of 5 August 1966, and Article 1 of decree no. 60462–A of 13 March 1967).

All these measures tend in the direction of broadening and facilitating the absorption of 34/18 deposits which have accumulated in steadily increasing amounts at the BNB. A related phenomenon is the staking of claims to these funds by other government entities: in recent months the permission to use 34/18 funds has been extended to the Amazonas region whose development is now to be guided by a new agency, SUDAM, modeled on SUDENE, as well as to certain deserving country-wide programs, such as tourism and reforestation.

How the System Works

So much for an outline of the principles governing the scheme. Something must be said now about its actual working. Here two topics are of interest: the role played by SUDENE and the formation of what we shall call a "captive capital market" through which 34/18 deposits are channelled to the individual sponsors of projects.

1. *Administration of the system by SUDENE.* Any project proposing the use of 34/18 funds must be approved by SUDENE. On the average, the processing of an application is said to take three to four months. SUDENE's role does not terminate with the approval; it must also authorize the actual release or disbursement *(liberação)* of 34/18 funds from the blocked deposits at the BNB, in accordance with the progress of the project and the simultaneous application of the required fresh funds.

At the beginning, the system was intended as a highly administered one. The privileges of Article 34/18 were felt to be so considerable that SUDENE saw its role as screening out projects which did not meet high standards of priority or essentially. In line with the general trend already sketched, the criteria of admission became far more flexible as time went on and deposits mounted. The 1966 decree which institutes three categories of projects with the ability to enlist 34/18 deposits to the extent of 25 per cent, 50 per cent and 75 per cent of total funds needed may look like a step toward a more highly administered system. Actually it was the opposite: the decision concerning these three possibilities is made in accordance with an objective point system which takes account of various characteristics of the proposed venture, such as location, number of employees, type of industry, etc. In this manner every project is more or less automatically given a rating and all, or almost all, are approved, even though a few may only be able to call on 34/18 deposits in the amount of 25 per cent of needed funds.

At present, the control of SUDENE is said to be required not so much to influence the direction of industrialization, as to avoid two types of malpractice:

a) Firms may be tempted to overstate the actual cost of the project so as to be able to finance, through 34/18 funds, a larger share of the total investment than that permitted by law.

b) Firms may announce projects without a serious intention to go ahead, in order to prevent competing firms from coming in, while continuing to supply the Northeastern market from their existing production facilities in the Center–South.[3] To avoid this sort of maneuver SUDENE must be able to ascertain the seriousness of prospective applicants; it has also been given the authority to revoke approval already given to a project if the firm has not started on actual construction eight months after SUDENE has given it the go-ahead (resolution no. 2810 of 15 February 1967).

While the approval and release procedures are bound to make for some delay and red tape, it was my impression in Recife that

3. It is understood that the rejection of the Firestone project by SUDENE was based on this consideration.

the SUDENE staff in charge of these matters is dedicated, competent and honest. This impression was nicely confirmed by a prominent São Paulo industrialist who declared emphatically what a pleasant surprise it was for him to deal with the SUDENE *técnico* after having been exposed for years to the indolent, inefficient and frequently corrupt ways of the São Paulo and Rio bureaucracies. Ironically, the SUDENE *técnico,* widely feared at first because of his alleged revolutionary objectives, may thus be turning into a major asset for the development of the Northeast under the auspices of private capitalistic enterprise.

2. *A captive capital market.* Another notable institutional aspect of the system is the mechanism which has evolved to make Article 34/18 deposits available to the projects actually undertaken. As can be seen from Table 4.1, the number of depositors

TABLE 4.1   Firms *(Pessôas Jurídicas)* Paying Income Tax and
Article 34/18 Deposit Holders

	Income tax returns filed[a]	*Deposit holders[b]*	%
1962	334,258	1,909	0.6
1963	380,986	2,951	0.8
1964	407,448	4,625	1.1
1965	214,303	13,949	6.5
1966	243,272	19,832	8.2

a. Data from *Boletim Estatístico da Divisão do Imposto de Renda.*
b. Data from SUDENE/Rio.

(twenty thousand at the end of 1966) has grown rapidly over the past years as the advantages of the system have come to be better appreciated. While still less than 10 per cent of the total number of *pessôas jurídicas* filing income tax returns (many of them never pay any tax), this number includes many small and medium-size firms as well as almost all large firms.[4]

4. Among the latter the only exception consists of foreign (particularly U.S.) firms some of which apparently decided not to take advantage of the

If we look at the number of approved projects, on the other hand, we find that up to the end of May 1967 about 570 projects had been approved. The vast disparity between numbers of deposit holders and of projects, immediately raises the question: how does each project collect its 34/18 deposits? Occasionally there is no problem, as in the case of a firm, such as Willys Overland, which has a project as well as large deposits of its own and has no need to fill up the allowable portion of its equity with 34/18 funds belonging to outsiders. But in most cases, outside funds are required, and to collect them, financial intermediaries have sprung up in large numbers. These are located primarily in the main financial centers of São Paulo and Rio where the large and medium-size depositors are to be found. These brokers try to obtain an exclusive right to certain projects and then go "from door to door" selling shares to various deposit holders. Lists of deposit holders are available from SUDENE and BNB, so that the business is open and highly competitive. (So much so that some firms are said to have put up signs reading: "We are not interested in discussing investment opportunities for our 34/18 funds.") The deposit holders are charged a fee, which is reported to run from 5 to 8 per cent. Since the supply of funds has been larger than the demand for them, the brokers frequently have to share the commission with the entrepreneurial firm which put the project together, had it approved, and supplied the fresh funds. Some large firms, such as Volkswagen, are acquiring a highly diversified portfolio of Northeastern stocks. Many firms are facing the decision whether to put together a project of their own or to invest in someone else's project. The mechanism has an interesting by-product. Several large firms (for example Romi, the lathe manufacturer), which have remained closely held corporations in the South, have dozens of partners in the Northeastern subsidiaries. As a result, the corporate structure of firms in the backward area is more modern than that in the Center-South.

34/18 system because to do so would increase their income tax liabilities in their home country in an equivalent amount—with the further cost of having to pay that amount in U.S. dollars.

TABLE 4.2   Deposits under Article 34/18 during 1965 (By states)

State	Millions of new cruzeiros	%
São Paulo	95,7	55.4
Guanabara	39,3	22.7
Rio Grande do Sul	11,8	6.8
Minas Gerais	7,3	4.2
Paraná	4,2	2.4
Pernambuco	3,6	2.1
Bahia	2,7	1.6
Sta. Catarina	2,3	1.3
Ceará	2,1	1.2
All others	4,0	2.3
Total	173,0	100.0

Source: Bank of the Northeast of Brazil.

TABLE 4.3   Deposits under Article 34/18 during 1965
(By size classes)

New cruzeiros		Deposit holders		Amount of deposits
		Actual numbers	% of Total	% of Total
0–	500	4,081	30.5	0.5
500–	1,000	1,898	14.2	0.8
1,000–	2,000	1,590	11.9	1.4
2,000–	4,000	1,908	14.3	3.2
4,000–	6,000	862	6.5	2.6
6,000–	8,000	556	4.2	2.5
8,000–	10,000	386	2.9	2.6
10,000–	15,000	573	4.3	4.2
15,000–	20,000	345	2.6	3.6
20,000–	50,000	663	5.0	12.1
50,000–	100,000	228	1.7	9.2
100,000–	250,000	169	1.3	15.0
250,000–	500,000	67	0.5	13.7
500,000–1,000,000		26	0.2	11.0
1,000,000–5,000,000		14	0.1	18.0
Total		13,366	100.0	100.0[a]

a. Total amount deposited in 1965 was 172 million new cruzeiros.
Source: Bank of the Northeast of Brazil.

In any event, there is now lively interest in investment opportunities in the Northeast among a large and important group of Brazilian investors. This does not mean that the deposit holder will invest in any project that is offered to him, even though his deposit faces extinction after three to four years. While deposit holders are naturally anxious to invest, they are nevertheless reported to be fairly "choosey" and the brokers must make a real sales effort.

Table 4.2 gives a breakdown of the deposits by states from which the preeminence of São Paulo and Rio is readily apparent. Table 4.3 shows a breakdown by size classes and reveals another aspect of the concentration of deposit holders—the 107 largest holders account for 41 per cent of the total amount deposited. In view of this concentration it appears likely that most small deposit holders experience difficulties in investing their funds, in spite of the many brokers who naturally tend to concentrate their activity among the larger and medium-size holders. This is recognized by the BNB and ways of pooling the smaller deposits in investment funds or trusts are now under consideration.

The Lag of Disbursements behind Deposit Accumulations and the Alleged Drain of Working Capital

It is one of the basic characteristics of the 34/18 system that investible funds become available as a result of taxpayers using the option to deposit half of their income tax liability in a blocked BNB account, prior to the actual use of those funds in a specific investment project. A lag between availability of funds and disbursement is therefore not only inevitable, given the complex tasks of preparing new industrial projects, getting them approved by SUDENE and then built, but to some extent it is the driving force of the system since the availability of funds (as well as the threat of their reversion to the treasury if they are left unutilized), makes for an active search for investment opportunities on the part of both independent promoters and deposit holders. The extent of the lag appears from Table 4.4. This table reveals also a substantial acceleration of project preparation and disbursement during 1966–67 in part because of the various new steps toward

TABLE 4.4   Lag between Deposits and Their Utilization
(Millions of new cruzeiros)

	34/18 deposits	Share of 34/18 funds in approved projects	Disbursements of 34/18 funds for approved projects
1962	6	—	—
1963	7	7	0.1
1964	36	26	3
1965	172	35	8
1966	252	152	37
1967 (first 4 mos.)	N.A.	105	43

Source: BNB and SUDENE

more liberal use of the funds. Actual disbursements are just now beginning to make a dent in the available deposits. Actually, a lag of two to three years between the setting up of the system and the large-scale disbursement of funds for the construction of industrial projects is hardly excessive. Nevertheless this lag has been an easy target of criticism. In particular, it is being said that the 34/18 system is draining the rest of the country of funds for the purpose of building up "uneconomic" industry in the Northeast at a time when a shortage of working capital was being felt by many existing, efficient firms in the Center–South. It is already clear from the previous table that what has taken place is a shift in the availability of *short-term bank credit* from the Center–South to the Northeast, since most of the 34/18 funds were not disbursed for plant construction purposes, but were accumulating in deposits at the BNB. This shift was in itself highly significant for the economic development of the Northeast: it permitted the BNB to extend its commercial banking operations and thereby spared economic activity in the Northeast the contractions imposed on the rest of the economy by official anti-inflationary policies in the recent past. In other words, if the rate of growth of the Northeast during the past three years has been higher than that of Brazil as a whole,[5] the credit for this perform-

5. This experience contrasts sharply with earlier recessions or stabilization crises which ordinarily hit the Northeast harder than the "dynamic" Center–South. See my *Journeys,* p. 36.

ance must be given, not to actual new industrial investments (which have been unimportant until quite recently), but rather to the *lag* of investment behind deposit accumulations which permitted comparatively easy credit conditions to prevail throughout the region.

In an attempt to defend itself against the accusation that it does not know how to utilize the funds flowing to the Northeast, SUDENE has prepared some statistics purporting to show that the prospective need for 34/18 funds—based on projects already approved and on project applications currently being processed —already exceeds the funds presently available. As a result, SUDENE explains, almost with pride, its budget of industrial projects is actually suffering from a deficit. While such an argument may be useful as a debating point, it must of course be understood that no deficit exists in any meaningful sense. Only if the 34/18 legislation were wholly abolished tomorrow, would this sort of comparison of future commitments against presently available resources make sense. As the flow of 34/18 deposits can be expected to continue for some time, deposit resources are ample and are well able to accommodate the demand arising from current industrial projects. Of course, should the spurt in project applications continue, the point may well be reached at which future disbursements would be likely to exceed the anticipated availability of deposit funds from past accumulations and current inflow. But for the time being one hardly needs to worry about this danger.

Just as Brazilian industrial entrepreneurs and SUDENE have been far from investing all the 34/18 funds which were accumulating at the Bank of the Northeast, the latter has in turn been incapable of utilizing in its short-term lending all of the resulting temporary accumulation. To the extent that "absorptive capacity" was lacking even in this respect *no drain at all* was caused to the rest of the country: for the BNB simply left the deposits it was not able to use in its commercial lending business at the Bank of Brazil which in turn makes these funds available through its nationwide banking services.[6] Table 4.5 shows that

6. There are some indications that, in addition, the Bank of Brazil reduced its lending activity in the Northeast as the BNB expanded its

during the last two years of rapid accumulation of 34/18 deposits (1965 and 1966), the BNB was able to utilize only about one-half of its new resources while maintaining the other half in deposits at the Bank of Brazil. Interestingly, this situation changed fundamentally during the first five months of 1967 when the BNB lent out all of the new deposits it received, perhaps because it followed a more aggressive lending policy than before.

The Alleged Fiscal Drain

Another criticism of the system has of course been that it constitutes a drain, not on bank and business liquidity, but on the treasury. In the short run, one cruzeiro deposited under Article 34/18 is obviously a tax cruzeiro lost—even though it has been argued that if the scheme fulfills its purposes, it will pay for itself even from the point of view of the treasury, as new taxable capacity is created in the Northeast.[7] For such reasoning to carry weight, however, it must be shown that taxable capacity is more easily created in the Northeast through private sector investments than through other conceivable applications of the funds, such as more public spending. The argument would thus merge into a general justification of the scheme (see section 3).

How big is the drain on the treasury? Table 4.6 shows in its first three columns that corporate taxpayers have been using their tax credit privilege in increasing amounts, but also that use is by no means universal. If every *pessôa jurídica* were to use the privilege, 34/18 deposits would be equal to income tax collections; in 1966 they were just one-half of collections.

The statistic which gives cause for concern in the table is the comparison between the deposits and the cash deficit—it looks as though half of the deficit could be wiped out by an elimination

---

own. Such a development would reinforce the point that there has been far less of a "drain" of funds from the rest of the country to the Northeast than would appear from the gross figures of the 34/18 deposit accumulations.

7. This point is made by Rubens Costa, president of the BNB, in an article "O que o Nordeste espera de São Paulo" in *Fôlhas de São Paulo* (13 August 1967).

TABLE 4.5 34/18 Deposits at the Bank of the Northeast (BNB), and BNB Deposits at the Bank of Brazil (B.B.)
(Millions of new cruzeiros)

	34/18 deposits at BNB at end of year	BNB deposits at B.B. at end of year	Increase in 34/18 deposits during year	Increase in 34/18 deposits at B.B. during year
	(1)	(2)	(3)	(4)
1962	6	4	—	—
1963	13	4	7	—
1964	46	14	33	10
1965	186	77	140	63
1966	369	168	183	91
1967 (through May)	422	168	53	0

Sources: BNB Relatórios and Revista Bancária.

TABLE 4.6 34/18 Deposits Compared to Corporate Income Tax Collections, Budget Deficit, and Total Treasury Cash Receipts
(Millions of new cruzeiros)

	34/18 deposits	Corporate income tax	34/18 deposits as % of income tax	Cash deficit	34/18 deposits as % of cash deficit	Cash receipts	34/18 deposits as % of cash receipts
	(a)	(b)		(c)		(c)	
1962	5.9	62	9.5	280.9	2.1	497.8	1.2
1963	7.2	138	5.2	504.2	1.4	930.8	0.8
1964	36	219	16.4	700.0	5.1	2,000.0	1.8
1965	172	406	42.4	587.9	29.3	3,237.5	5.3
1966	252	501	50.3	586.6	43.0	5,350.0	4.7

Source: a. SUDENE/Rio.
b. Boletim Estatistico da Divisão do Imposto de Renda.
c. Proposta Orcamentária para 1967.

of the 34/18 tax credit privilege. Two comments are in order here: first, the percentage is as high as it is only because the deficit is low and therefore relatively innocuous; were it to go up substantially—it has shown some such propensity lately—the percentage of 34/18 funds would diminish correspondingly. Secondly, the matter is placed in a more correct perspective by comparing the 34/18 deposits to total cash receipts of the treasury (columns 6 and 7); it appears that these deposits account at present for just about 5 per cent of these receipts. To single out the 34/18 deposits as "responsible" for half of the deficit is perfectly arbitrary: clearly there must be many other ways in which receipts can be increased or expenditures cut by 5 per cent.

SIZE AND STRUCTURE OF THE NEW INDUSTRIAL ESTABLISHMENT

To appraise the quantity and quality of the industrial development stimulated in the Northeast by the tax credit mechanism, one has to compare investment now under way as a result of the scheme with the preexisting industrial base. Such a comparison requires a number of heroic statistical assumptions and manipulations, but since it is the only way of gauging the real importance of the new industrial development, the attempt is worthwhile.[8]

Size of the Investment in Relation to the pre-34/18 Base

By the end of May 1967 total investment represented by industrial projects taking advantage of the Article 34/18 mechanism amounted to NCr$1,811 million (in 1967 cruzeiros—see Table 4.7).[9] When this figure is compared to an estimate of the indus-

8. This section of the essay owes much to the collaboration of Judith Tendler.

9. This figure includes both approved projects and projects still being processed by SUDENE (em análise). As pointed out in sec. 1, the approval process in SUDENE has changed from one of weeding out and rejection of projects, to their classification according to the percentage of 34/18 funds which they are qualified to receive. Most projects that get to be "in analysis," therefore, are subsequently approved. Leaving these projects out of the figure would underplay the results being achieved, because of the current acceleration in the program: the "in analysis" projects as of 31 May 1967, amount to more than the total investment of 34/18 projects approved during the year 1966.

TABLE 4.7 34/18 Project Approvals and BNB Releases
(Millions of new cruzeiros)

	Approved 34/18 projects		BNB releases for 34/18 projects	
	Current prices	1967 prices[a]	Current prices	1967 prices
1963	36.4	170.9	0.09	0.4
1964	133.4	327.0	3.3	8.1
1965	138.9	225.5	8.0	13.0
1966	335.4	400.2	37.4	44.6
1967[b]	697.8[c]	687.8[d]	91.8	91.8
TOTAL		1,811.4		157.9

a. An average of the FGV wholesale price index for the first five months of 1967.
b. Up to 31 May 1967.
c. NCr$271.8 million of approved projects, and NCr$426.0 million of projects in analysis on 31 May 1967. Since almost all projects in the "analysis" stage are subsequently approved, and since the approval procedure averages about four months, the "analysis" projects are included here with the approved projects for 1967.
d. The 1967 price is different from the "current price" because it is assumed that the projects in analysis already contain some monetary correction for future inflation. To roughly account for this, the projects-in-analysis investment figure is assumed to represent May 1967 prices, which are deflated to the January–May 1967 price level.

trial capital stock existing in the Northeast just before the Article 34/18 mechanism became effective, it is found that *34/18-induced investment will double the industrial capital stock in the Northeast*. This statement is based on an estimated value of NCr$1,801 million (also in 1967 cruzeiros) for the industrial capital stock of the Northeast in 1964.[10]

It may be questioned whether it is legitimate to attribute all of the new investment to Article 34/18. Certainly some industrial investment which is taking advantage of the tax credit privilege would have taken place in any event. But considering the large quantitative jump and the substantial qualitative change characteristic of the new investment (see next section), there is little doubt that the Article 34/18 mechanism deserves credit for the bulk of the new ventures.

Of the total investment (including uncompleted starts), it appears from the figures on BNB releases that about 25 per cent has already been put into place.[11] This means that Article 34/18 has already contributed to a 25 per cent increase in the capital stock of the Northeast during the first three and a half years of its existence. It can be seen from the year-by-year breakdown of investment in projects approved and of BNB releases (in 1967 cruzeiros), that the 34/18 mechanism has only now started to get under way. The total investment represented by approved proj-

10. This estimate is obtained by applying a capital-output ratio of 2.5 to the income generated by the industrial sector of the Northeast as available from the regional breakdown of gross national product statistics elaborated by the Getulio Vargas Foundation. Actually the last year for which such a regional breakdown is available is 1960, but it was possible to update it to 1964 on the basis of an industrial product index supplied by BNB. The 2.5 capital-output ratio seems reasonable for a region like the Northeast where light industry has so far predominated. While it is of course subject to a wide margin of error the calculation aims only at conveying the order of magnitude involved in the industrial development now taking place in the Northeast.

11. BNB releases for 34/18 projects amounted to NCr$157.9 million (1967 cruzeiros) up to 31 May 1967. Up to this time, the average contribution of 34/18 deposits in total investment has been about 35 per cent. Multiplying these BNB releases by the reciprocal of 0.35 gives an estimate of the total resources invested in 34/18 projects: NCr$448.6 million.

ects has grown from NCr$170 million in 1963 to NCr$687 million in 1967—a fourfold increase. BNB releases gained momentum even more recently—over one half of the releases to date were made in the first five months of 1967.

Industrial Structure

Another important aspect of 34/18 investment is its relationship to the existing industrial structure in the Northeast. The region's industry is weighted toward agricultural product processing and light consumer industries, with sugar refining, oilseed processing and cotton textiles in particularly prominent roles. The share of capital, intermediate and durable consumer goods in the Northeast's industrial product (about 30 per cent), is considerably smaller, as can be seen in Table 4.8, than it is for Brazil as a whole (about 60 per cent). Taking a measure for existing industry that is more comparable to the fixed investment data available for new projects, such as installed horsepower in industry (column 3 of Table 4.8), one finds the same overwhelming share of traditional industries. The distribution of investment represented by 34/18 projects, on the other hand, shows the opposite relationship between "modern" and "traditional" goods—it approximates the distribution that exists for Brazil as a whole.[12] The projects subsidized by the 34/18 mechanism, in short, are bringing a more diversified and sophisticated industrial structure to the Northeast, with sharply increased representation of industries that are both dynamic and rich in linkage effects.

Location

The distribution of 34/18 projects among the Northeast states (Table 4.9) does not break the existing pattern of industrial location in the region. The greatest amount of 34/18 investments will go into Bahia,[13] with Pernambuco following close behind. The

12. The proposed steel complex for Bahia—USIBA—has been excluded from the calculation of percentage shares of various industries in 34/18 investment. The USIBA undertaking is quite large—NCr$94 million—and there is some doubt as to whether and when it will be undertaken.

13. The NCr$304 million to be realized in Bahia includes NCr$94 million for USIBA, which is still at the talking stage. Without USIBA, Bahia is in third place in total amount of 34/18 investment.

TABLE 4.8 Structure of Industrial Product in the Northeast

	Value added—% of total (1962)		Installed horsepower capacity in industry northeast % of total (1959)	Investment represented by approved 34/18 projects
	Brazil	Northeast		
Capital, Intermediate, and Durable Consumer Goods	58.8	29.2	30.2	67.4
Nonferrous metals	5.0	6.3	10.0	9.4
Metallurgy	12.4	2.7	2.3	8.7
Comm. and electrical materials	5.6	0.1	0.02	3.3
Transport material	10.2	0.4	0.3	6.7
Mechanical industry	3.2	0.2	0.2	2.3
Lumber	2.5	1.0	2.4	1.6
Paper and cardboard	2.9	0.9	2.8	0.5
Rubber	2.0	0.9	0.2	0.5
Leather and furs, etc.	1.0	1.2	1.5	0.1
Chemical and pharmaceutical	14.0	15.5	10.5	34.3
Traditional Consumer Goods	41.2	70.8	69.3	32.7
Furniture	2.0	1.5	0.9	0.4
Textile	13.8	26.7	26.8	18.2
Clothing, shoes, handcraft	3.4	1.7	0.2	1.4
Food products	13.2	30.4	38.8	7.9
Drinks	2.6	3.9	1.5	3.9
Tobacco	1.9	4.3	0.3	—
Printing	2.5	1.9	0.7	0.4
Miscellaneous	1.8	0.4	0.1	0.5
TOTAL	100.0	100.0	100.0	100.0

Sources: SUDENE and BNB/ETENE

TABLE 4.9   Industrial Projects Approved, by State, up to April, 1967
(*Millions of new cruzeiros*)

States	Total investment projected	%	No. of projects	%
Bahia	304.0	36.2	47	18.5
Pernambuco	288.6	34.4	88	34.6
Alagôas	121.5	14.5	15	6.0
Ceará	39.6	4.7	43	17.0
Paraíba	23.6	2.8	28	11.0
Rio Grande do Norte	22.2	2.7	9	3.5
Sergipe	17.4	2.1	7	2.6
Minas Gerais	13.3	1.6	3	1.2
Piauí	5.0	0.6	8	3.1
Maranhão	4.4	0.5	6	2.4
TOTAL	839.6	100.0	254	100.0

Source: SUDENE

third place of Alagoas is misleading—as can be seen by its low ranking in the number of projects—because 90 per cent of the funds to be invested represent one project for a caustic soda plant. Ceará is in third place in number of projects and amount invested (not including Alagoas). The 34/18 projects, then, flow to the already established centers of economic activity in the Northeast —Salvador, Recife, and, to a lesser extent, Fortaleza. Many of the Bahian investments are based on the petroleum in the Recôncavo region.

Of the three Northeast centers, Bahia has the locational advantage in terms of supplying the national market. Pernambuco seems to be the center of an import-substitution development (in relation to southern Brazil), carried out by the very producers of the former imports—Southern industrial firms such as NORLAR (refrigerators), Fiat-Lux (matches), Willys Overland (jeep assembly), Brahma and Antarctica (beer and soft drinks), Romi (lathes), Microlite (electric batteries), Tintas Coral (paints). Ceará's 34/18 projects are more in line with the traditional structure of Northeastern industry: they are on a smaller scale than those of Pernambuco and Bahia (which explains Ceará's high rank in number of 34/18 projects and low rank in total investment) and concentrate on processing of cotton and foods, clothing, furniture, etc.

Employment

The 34/18 projects approved up to June 1967 will give rise to 67,800 new jobs. This figure compares to a total industrial work force of 176,800 in 1959. A new job will be created for every NCr$20,580 invested,[14] just about US$7,600 at the current rate of exchange. This certainly is not an encouraging labor-capital ratio for a region with problems of unemployment but it is the inevitable counterpart of the already noted change in industrial structure toward capital and intermediate goods. The ratio, which is characteristic of industrial investment in Brazil in general, does

14. In 1967 cruzeiros, total investment projected for 34/18 projects up to May, 1967, amounts to NCr$1,395.4 million. Dividing by the amount of new jobs created gives NCr$20,580 per job.

not take into account the activities which will spring up to service these 34/18 industries. It is precisely in these service industries that the labor-capital ratio is much higher than in the more basic industries that comprise the 34/18-induced industrialization.

ECONOMIC APPRAISAL

The preceding sections have shown that the incentive system of Article 34/18 has been turned into a highly effective and flexible policy instrument and that it is about to achieve a substantial expansion and diversification of the Northeastern industrial establishment. We must now examine (1) whether the same objective could be more efficiently achieved by different policy instruments and (2) whether the system could be *too effective* in the sense of causing an excessive and uneconomic allocation of industrial capacity to the Northeast. These questions call first of all for a comparative economic appraisal of various policy instruments for regional industrial development.

Regional Industrial Development: Available vs. Suitable Policy Instruments

At the outset of this inquiry, one crucial observation is in order: some of the principal policy instruments available for industrial development at the *national* level are simply unavailable when it comes to a *region* within a country. Herein resides the peculiar difficulty of stimulating industrial development within a region: protective tariffs have probably been the most widely used policy instrument in stimulating industrialization, but when it comes to fostering "infant industries" in region A in competition with an already established industrial center in region B within the same country, this cannot ordinarily be done by means of protective tariffs—unless region A secedes to form a separate nation.

Similarly an underdeveloped region has no monetary and exchange rate autonomy and is therefore unable to use (against the developed region) the peculiar combination of inflation, overvaluation of the currency and import controls which, in the not very distant past, served Brazil and other countries so well in assuring new industries both high prices for their outputs and low import prices for their inputs and needed equipment.

Fortunately there exists one important policy instrument that is available to an underdeveloped region: the allocation of *public* funds through the national budget. But this mechanism serves normally to finance public works and various infrastructural investments for the region and therefore has at best indirect effects on industrial development. Actually the policy of inducing industrialization through infrastructural investments is particularly unsuitable to an underdeveloped region within a developing country.[15]

As an alternative, public funds could be made available to some specially designed financial institution which would provide loan and perhaps equity capital to Northeastern industrial ventures. The Bank of the Northeast had in fact been established in 1952 to operate at least in part along just such lines, but its performance testifies that this approach meets also with considerable difficulties.[16] With the successful tax credit experience as counterpoint, the reason becomes clear. The approach via a regional development bank lacks one of the most important assets of the present scheme: the urgent personal involvement of dozens of experienced corporate managers from the Center–South who have some savings to invest—savings which, because of the three-year limit, are highly perishable—and who also have some managerial and entrepreneurial skills to spare. The mobilization for the underdeveloped region of managerial and entrepreneurial ability and energy that is available in the advanced region of a developing country is perhaps one of the principal arguments in favor of our scheme.[17]

In sum, the dilemma of industrial development through private

15. See my *Strategy of Economic Development* (New Haven: Yale University Press, 1958), p. 94.

16. See my *Journeys,* pp. 58–66.

17. Such mobilization is particularly desirable and effective when managers and entrepreneurs are "underemployed" because of stagnation or slackened growth in the advanced region—a situation characteristic of Brazil since 1963. From this point of view, the timing of the scheme was remarkably fortunate.

enterprise in an underdeveloped region is that on the one hand, the most powerful policy instruments, such as customs protection, are unavailable to the *region;* on the other hand, the policy instruments that are readily available to the region are not particularly suitable to the promotion of industrial development through private enterprise. Through the Article 34/18 mechanism Brazil has found a way out of this dilemma—it has converted the *available* into a *suitable* policy instrument.

Comparison with Tax Exemptions for New Industries

The mechanism of Article 34/18 is a far more powerful instrument than the income tax exemptions which have been a standard feature in many programs to promote industrialization. The Puerto Rican experience is one particularly well known and advertised example. Income tax exemptions for new industries make a profitable venture more profitable; but they do nothing to reduce the loss of an enterprise in case it turns out *not* to be profitable. Therefore, to the extent that investment is held back by uncertainty, i.e. by the fact that the subjective probability of losing a given amount of money exceeds some tolerable level, income tax exemption is ineffective as a stimulus to investment. The mechanism of Article 34/18, on the other hand, is not handicapped in this way: by reducing the amount of equity the entrepreneur has to supply for a given venture, it automatically reduces the size of the loss he will suffer in case there is a loss.[18]

Here lies the principal incentive effect of the tax credit mechan-

18. In technical terms: the entire probability distribution of expected outcomes is shifted to the right, rather than only its positive portion. In fact, if the 34/18 deposit holders come in as ordinary shareholders, then the effect of the mechanism on the prospective outcomes for the entrepreneurial group is to reduce their loss in case there is a loss *and also* their profits in case there is a profit. In other words the effect is the exact opposite of the tax exemption device which fails to reduce the prospective loss, but increases the expected profit. Since 34/18 deposit holders are usually preferential shareholders, the effect is somewhat more complicated. There will be an increase in the prospective profit (along with a decrease in the prospective loss) provided the profit rate is larger than the dividend rate payable out of profits on the preferential shares.

ism: not so much that the cost of capital to the entrepreneur is zero—we shall see presently that this is not really so; but the amount of the equity which the entrepreneurial group has to supply is drastically cut and the resulting financial gap is normally filled not by creditors, but by partners who are made to share, through the 34/18 mechanism, in the risks of the venture.

It has often been said that uncertainty about prospective costs and markets rather than the outright absence of profitable investment opportunities is the principal obstacle to industrial investment in a populous, but underdeveloped region such as the Northeast;[19] if this is correct, then the mechanism which has been evolved is ideally designed to overcome the obstacle.

Is the Cost of Capital Zero?

From the point of view of the Northeastern industrial sector, the 34/18 money is indeed costless since the only alternative for the region as a whole is loss of the money to the treasury; but, fortunately for the efficient use of 34/18 funds, this situation is not the one facing the individuals who make the investment decisions.

In the first place, we may consider the most usual case where the entrepreneurial group does not own any 34/18 deposits or at least not nearly enough to fill the allowable 34/18 quota of the equity. Here the 34/18 mechanism means, as just noted, that a capital market in which a portion of the firm's capital can be readily raised is made available to the entrepreneurial group. But this capital is not "costless" any more than it is in any other capital market.

Take next a firm which has established a substantial blocked 34/18 deposit at the BNB with which it may establish a Northeastern venture all by itself. It is true that the alternative to making this deposit is to pay the same amount in income taxes to the treasury—thus there is no cost, from the point of view of

19. In technical terms, once again: what holds back entrepreneurial activity in an underdeveloped region is not the expected value of all possible outcomes which may well yield a satisfactory profit rate, but the wide dispersion of the outcomes around the expected value, with a large portion of the probability distribution lying in the loss area.

the firm, to establishing the deposit. Thereafter, however, the firm has the option of either starting a project of its own (in which case it must contribute some fresh funds), or of contributing its deposits to someone else's project. There exists therefore a real opportunity cost of using the funds *in one's own project:* it means to forgo a financial investment in another project. Firms are therefore going to engage in a search for the most profitable investment opportunities available in the region.

Effects of the System on Efficiency—Comparison with Customs Duties

In general, it is my opinion that the mechanism activates the investment decision, but does not impair essential disciplines making for efficient firm behavior. For example, the assets corresponding to the 34/18 funds are entered into the books of the new firms at their actual market value and are then duly depreciated so that, once again, what is a subsidy for the region as a whole is not sensed as such by the individual firm which will consider its operation as profitable only if its sales proceeds exceed outlays *including* depreciation allowances on *all* assets.

In this, as well as in several other respects, the tax credit mechanism compares favorably to customs duties. It is well known that customs duties, once established, are considered by the protected industry as a birthright which will never again be taken away. Hence, if the protected firms are price makers and if the protection exceeds (as it frequently does) the level required for an efficient firm to make "normal" profits, the excess level of protection afforded is likely to result in lower levels of efficiency than are achievable. There is nothing in the 34/18 mechanism to impair efficiency in this manner.

Another important superiority of the tax credit incentive over customs duties resides in the comparative uniformity of the former as compared to the usual wide dispersion of the latter. Orthodox economists who recognize the force of the infant industry argument for protection, have on occasion withdrawn from an out-and-out advocacy of free trade to the proposal of a *uniform* tariff rate such as 20 or 30 per cent. Such a tariff system would permit the establishment of some industries which could not survive without such protection, but at least it would select the most economic among these industries. Now it appears that the tax credit mechanism is largely equivalent to such an orthodox policy of protection. In the Northeast, the advantages it confers used to be entirely uniform among different firms and even with the differentiation of firms into three categories eligible for different equity proportions (25, 50 and 75 per cent) of 34/18 funds, uniformity remains far greater than in the case of customs tariffs. Thus the danger that highly inefficient industries might become established under the system is far smaller than in the case of industries growing up behind a customs wall, some segments of which always tend to be unreasonably high.

Furthermore, the 34/18 system complies with another long-standing injunction of the economist: it brings the costs of industrial promotion to the community, and to the national treasury, out in the open and thereby ensures a periodic reexamination of the continued need for paying these costs. Already there has been some public discussion over the merits of continuing the 34/18 system. Two attempts to pare down its benefits have been made under the Castello Branco administration and have been only narrowly fought off by strong protests from the Northeast. Further reexamination will no doubt take place from time to time. In this connection it must be noted that the 34/18 system can be phased out or discontinued without any adverse effects on the profitability of *existing* firms even though they have become established as a result of the system. In this respect also, the 34/18 system is a more flexible instrument of industrial promotion than customs duties. For the reduction of the latter can imperil the very life of firms which have grown up under their protection and such a reduction is therefore a far more delicate operation, both economically and politically.

The Question of Capital Intensity

Is it then impossible to find any fault whatever with the tax credit system? Not quite. The obvious objection to it is that it cheapens the cost of capital or, at the least, that it increases the availability of capital to entrepreneurs so that the industries which are being established in the Northeast are likely to be more capital-intensive and less labor-intensive than they might be under a "neutral" incentive system. The trouble is that the best known "neutral" system, i.e. protective customs duties, is, as already noted, not available to an underdeveloped *region* within a developing country. Besides, when a method is sought that will activate *investment* decisions it is simply more efficient to subsidize capital rather than labor: for spending on capital predates spending on labor and a subsidy of any given size is therefore far more efficient in stimulating the investment decision if it is applied wholly to capital than if it were spread in some fashion over both investment (capital) and operating (labor) expenditures.

It is my impression that the capital bias of the 34/18 system has not led to serious distortions in the technologies of firms that chose to become established in the Northeast. With or without Article 34/18, firms tend to use the latest technology without too much adaptation in the labor-intensive direction, except for internal transportation and, occasionally, multiple-shift operation. The effect of Article 34/18 on this tendency is marginal.

In this connection, one undesirable practice of SUDENE should nevertheless be mentioned: the reluctance to let the fresh funds be supplied in the form of secondhand machinery brought from São Paulo or abroad to the Northeast. This reluctance is due primarily to the difficulty of setting a price on such machinery and hence to the possibility of evasion of the "fresh funds" requirements. There is also a general feeling that "we don't want any more junk in the Northeast" (the unsatisfactory experience of COPERBO—a synthetic rubber plant near Recife based on alcohol from sugar cane—with partially secondhand machinery from the United States is often cited as a case in point). Nevertheless it seems a pity to forgo the valuable opportunities for using comparatively labor-intensive technologies which might be opened up for the Northeast by a more hospitable, if selective, attitude to secondhand machinery, a large supply of which is becoming steadily available in the Center–South.[20]

On the Appropriate Level of the Tax Credit Privilege

For the reasons given in the foregoing sections, the tax credit system deserves a high rating as a policy instrument for industrial promotion in an underdeveloped region. It solves a difficult institutional problem—the search for an equivalent for tariff protection and similar measures available to a nation but not to a region—and does so, moreover, in a way that avoids some of the efficiency-impairing effects and other drawbacks of the more usual policy instruments such as custom tariffs. Two questions remain to be examined. First, are there any ways of appraising the appropriate level of the tax credit privilege? Second, how long should the privilege be retained?

Some general remarks may start the discussion of the first question. The successful development of a region which has for long remained far behind the economic achievements of the country as a whole is a matter of changing ingrained attitudes, both of self-deprecation within the region and of prejudices against it, its people and resources in the rest of the country. The need is therefore for strong *incentives* which will lead to investment in the region in spite of these frequently irrational, but none the less real obstacles. The hope is that the ensuing favorable experience will in due course lead to a change in traditional attitudes.

The fact that regional underdevelopment is so hard a nut to crack has at least one positive counterpart. In the fight against inflation, for example, it is always very important to watch out lest the goal of stability be overshot and the economy land in the opposite evil, deflation. But such a worry need not burden the policy maker in the fight against regional underdevelopment. The danger that the opposite type of regional imbalance will be

20. The reasons for which use of secondhand machinery is desirable in a capital-poor and labor-rich economy are (1) that the labor-output ratio is increased because more labor is employed in using and maintaining the machinery and (2) that the capital-labor ratio is reduced because of the low purchase of secondhand as compared to new machinery.

created as a result of the efforts to remedy the existing imbalance is very remote.

Nevertheless, there must be concern about the danger of misallocation of resources. While the decision to correct a serious regional imbalance will usually imply some sacrifice of overall economic growth for the purpose of narrowing interregional income differentials, such a sacrifice can obviously become counterproductive. For example, it would be unfortunate if the 34/18 funds were to lead to the establishment of wholly uneconomic activities, such as the hauling of raw materials over long distances to the Northeast and then the return of the finished product to the South, merely for the purpose of taking advantage of the available 34/18 funds.

What has already been said about the way in which individual firms view these funds makes it unlikely that many uneconomic decisions of this kind will be taken. It is nevertheless of interest to evaluate the degree of protection afforded to a firm by the tax credit privilege, to work out, so to speak, the "customs duty equivalent" for the 34/18 mechanism, for in the case of customs duties we do have an approximate idea of what is a "normal" level of infant industry protection as opposed to one that is likely to induce a host of uneconomic investment decisions.

Suppose an industrial firm with fixed assets worth 300 that have an average life of ten years, and with a capital-gross output ratio of 3:1. Annual output will then be valued at 100, including 30 for depreciation allowances. Suppose now that the *whole capital* is given to the firm free of charge. In this case the firm receives in effect a subsidy of 30 in comparison to other firms that are not in this fortunate position. In order to receive an equivalent subsidy via tariffs, the firm ought to be able to sell its output at 130 instead of at 100, thanks to a tariff of 30 per cent. The somewhat surprising conclusion from this example is that the payment of even a 100 per cent subsidy for the cost of a firm's fixed assets is equivalent to a far from prohibitive rate of tariff protection provided the firm is not too capital-intensive. The tax credit privilege in the Northeast has resulted on average in a contribution, out of 34/18 funds, of 35 per cent to the capital assets of new firms.

Hence, in our example, the customs duty equivalent of the arrangement is 35 per cent of 30 or a moderate 10.5 per cent, even on the assumption (which has been seriously questioned above) that the 34/18 funds are sensed as "free" by the firms making the investment.

The tariff protection equivalent for a substantial capital subsidy is so low for the simple reason that no matter how highly subsidized their fixed assets, firms must still meet current labor and materials expenditures which in most manufacturing operations are liable to exceed depreciation allowances by a substantial margin.

Our conclusion is that there is no great danger of serious misallocation of resources resulting from the 34/18 mechanism, except in the case of highly capital-intensive industries. Here the customs duty equivalent of the 34/18 device may be fairly high and a good case can therefore be made for special vigilance on the part of SUDENE over industrial proposals in this category.

On the Phasing Out of the Tax Credit Privilege

Obviously the tax credit privilege should not remain in force forever. Once it has done its job of administering a decisive push to industrial investment activity in the Northeast it can be safely phased out. But given the degree of industrial backwardness of the Northeast—with 31 per cent of Brazil's population it produced only 8 per cent of the country's industrial output in 1960—there is much to be said for retaining the device until self-propelled industrial growth in the region is well under way. It may be useful to set a quantitative target for the beginning of the phasing-out process: for example, it could be provided that the system would remain substantially unchanged until the Northeastern share of the national industrial product has increased from its present level to at least *one-half* of the share of the Northeastern population in the total population—which is not a very ambitious target. While perfectly arbitrary, the setting of such a target would introduce a somewhat higher rationality into the matter than if it were left to depend on day-to-day decision making and on recurrent fights between a revenue-conscious minister of finance and Northeastern pressure groups. The North-east and SUDENE can only gain from making it quite clear that they expect to relinquish their present privileges at some unde-termined time in the future when "justice will have been done."

CONCLUSION FOR BRAZIL

The current industrialization drive, brought under way by the Article 34/18 mechanism, is by far the most significant economic advance to take place in Brazil's Northeast for many decades; it is probably also the most encouraging growth story to come out of Brazil since the *desenvolvimentista* fifties. It must be stressed once again that this story is now just barely unfolding: only in the last year or so has spending for industrial construction reached respectable levels and the resulting increase in industrial output will not be clearly visible for at least another year or two. But the institutions to administer the industrial expansion are now in place and are functioning well; a considerable interest in oppor-tunities opening up in the Northeast has been created among the entire Brazilian community; and attitudes about the region's in-dustrial capabilities and prospects are changing rapidly.

The current transitional stage has permitted two types of mis-understandings: on the one hand, the 34/18 program has been criticized for being ineffective, for merely leading to a drain of badly needed liquid funds from the "dynamic center" and the treasury without really achieving anything in the Northeast which is said to lack in "absorptive capacity." On the other hand, some voices begin to be heard to the effect that the Northeast has *had* its industrial boom and that the time has come, in the interests of "balanced development," to direct the resources of the 34/18 system toward agriculture in the Northeast or toward other regions. It is hardly necessary to point out that both these views are equally wrong: the Northeast is now developing a substantial absorptive capacity for the funds made available through the tax credit system; on the other hand, the fact that a few dozen fac-tories are now being built does not mean that the Northeast or any one particular Northeastern city is as yet in the throes of an industrial boom that needs to be throttled in the interests of sectoral or geographical balance.

There is little doubt that problems of inadequate agricultural productivity and of defective patterns of land tenure remain as acute as ever in the Northeast. But it is unlikely that the 34/18 system can make as fundamental a contribution to agricultural progress as it is making to the expansion of industry. Progress in agriculture depends in part on patient research and extension work, in part on political decisions regarding land tenure, as well as on public investment in irrigation, transportation, and education. Actually, the increase in industrial activity and employment can itself make an important indirect contribution to agriculture, by enlarging the market for agricultural products and by consequently bringing increasing pressure on the *zona da mata* to substitute food crops and livestock for the traditional, but increasingly uneconomic, sugarcane.

A strong argument can thus be made for not "rocking the boat" at the present time and for permitting the Northeastern industrialization drive to reach maturity.

CONCLUSION FOR OTHER UNDERDEVELOPED REGIONS

The demonstrated effectiveness of the tax credit mechanism in stimulating industrial development in Northeastern Brazil and the general advantages of the device as analyzed here should make this particular policy instrument attractive to "developers" in other lands. To forestall indiscriminate imitation we should note, however, that the success of the scheme has depended on a number of distinctive features of the Brazilian scene.

First, Brazil was already endowed with a highly advanced region which could mobilize not only considerable tax savings for the underdeveloped Northeast, but also entrepreneurial and managerial skills which were perhaps no longer fully employed in the Center–South.

Secondly, the Northeast had recently acquired a strong regional development agency which proved able to supply the flexible administrative controls required by the scheme.

Thirdly, Brazil has enough unity as a country and a civilization that it is not threatened by disruptive conflict in consequence of one inevitable effect of the scheme: the ownership of a large part of the new Northeastern industries by "outsiders" from the Center–South.

It is easy to think of countries with underdeveloped regions or sectors which are not nearly as favorably situated with respect to these three factors as Brazil and where, therefore, the scheme may not be applicable or successful.

I prefer to end, however, on a visionary rather than on a cautionary note by mentioning a proposal which was suggested by one particularly enterprising as well as competent management consultant of São Paulo: that thought be given to an application of the tax credit device on the *international* scale. Perhaps we have here a means of rekindling interest in international development aid and of placing it more on a people-to-people basis than hitherto? I have elsewhere made an attempt to elaborate such a proposal;[21] suffice it to say here that international aid is badly in need of institutional imagination and that the tax credit scheme has a strong claim to our attention since it has already proved itself in the context of interregional development.

21. See chap. 10, below.

PART II

Addressing the Rich Countries: Critiques
and Appeals

5. Primary Products and Substitutes: Should Technological Progress Be Policed?

The economic profession comes very close to having its own two party system: one party extols, the other criticizes the price system. In almost all the great theory and policy issues the lines are neatly drawn and the parties solidly arrayed against one another. The problem before us is notable in that it provides an exception to the rule. Both parties, e.g. Hayek and Keynes twenty years ago, or Bauer and Myrdal today, appear to be in basic agreement that the fluctuations of commodity prices are in

This paper was part of a symposium on commodity price stabilization and development in primary producing countries organized by *Kyklos* and published in two issues of that journal in 1958 and 1959. It is reprinted here by permission from *Kyklos* 7 (1959): 354–61.

The discussion was occasioned by a paper of Ragnar Nurkse which criticized various price stabilization schemes on the ground that they interfere with incentives to shift resources. Instead, he argued, primary countries should adopt general measures of countercyclical fiscal policy to counteract some of the undesirable consequences of fluctuations in the world price of their principal export commodities. Unless otherwise noted, the references to authors in the paper are to their contributions to the symposium.

The policy proposal of this paper—that technical "progress" may under some circumstances have to be "managed" because of deleterious side effects—met at the time the "contemptuous dismissal" referred to in the introductory essay (p. 29). In the meantime, of course, the intellectual climate has changed to such an extent that the idea is almost commonplace. It is noteworthy, nevertheless, that attention to the noxious side effects of technology is still confined almost wholly to local and domestic repercussions such as air and river pollution. For example, in the otherwise excellent report of the National Academy of Sciences, *Technology: Processes of Assessment and Choice* (U.S. Government Printing Office, July 1969) no mention is made of the damage that might be inflicted by technical progress in one country on the economies of other countries, or of possible institutional safeguards the international community might wish to erect in the face of such contingencies.

some sense excessive. The lively comment which was evoked by Ragnar Nurkse's suggestive proposal was caused fundamentally by the fact that his paper could be interpreted as a dissent from this bipartisan agreement. He appeared to consider as valuable adjustment mechanisms the much decried "gyrations" of commodity prices provided means were found to maintain general stability of prices and business activity in the primary producing countries. In his concluding note, however, Nurkse agreed that "relative movements [of commodity prices] may have been far too erratic" and even suggested in a footnote a possible mechanism for avoiding excessive fluctuations.[1]

In spite of this unanimity, fluctuating commodity prices are very much with us; in fact, they appear to be at this writing the one international economic problem which the Western world has not even begun to solve. Much remains to be done for international cooperation in economic development, monetary management and business cycle control; but one cannot help thinking that in all of these areas important forward steps have been and are constantly being taken. With respect to our problem, on the other hand, no such optimism is yet justified.

Indeed, for the time being the problem is becoming rather more serious as the exporters of primary products are industrializing. In the course of this process raw and semifinished materials tend to replace finished consumer manufactures as a principal import category. Sudden sharp declines in export proceeds become of greater concern under such conditions since they mean drastic curtailment of economic activity and employment rather than, as before, postponement of final purchases for consumption or investment. Thus, at least until these developing countries emerge as exporters of manufactures in their own right, the task of avoiding excessive fluctuations of primary product prices clearly takes on new importance and urgency.

How are we to explain our failure to act or to inspire action? Is it due to the very unanimity of the economic profession, i.e. are we less energetic and effective in realizing our ideas when by so

1. 1958 *Kyklos* Symposium, pp. 263–64.

doing we cannot claim victory over an antagonist? Or have we presented policy makers with so large a variety of equally attractive schemes that, bewildered, they have been unable to choose?

The most plausible explanation is perhaps that for a long time we had placed our trust in remote rather than direct control. We thought, with some justification, that once the advanced industrial countries achieved a reasonable degree of stability as well as continuous long-term growth, the problem of fluctuating commodity prices would disappear. But the business cycle, although far from dead, seems to have outgrown its youthful excesses, the industrial countries have, on the whole, achieved considerable economic expansion and, nevertheless, the commodity problem is still very much with us. Varying a well-worn saying that is no longer applicable in its original version, we may assert that when the industrial countries sneeze, commodity prices contract pneumonia; and, worse from the point of view of indirect therapy, some commodities seem to experience violent ups and downs rather independently of the business cycle.

WHEN ARE PRICE FLUCTUATIONS EXCESSIVE?

The conviction is growing that we must after all proceed to a direct attack on our problem. Now the question that the *Kyklos* discussion has raised in my mind is: What is the nature of the "excessive" fluctuations which we wish to eliminate? The usual answer "fluctuations around the trend" is most unsatisfactory since the trend itself is unknown and is likely to be modified by any action taken to moderate the fluctuations.

As Nurkse, Bauer-Paish and others have stressed, we do not want to lose the equilibrating adjustments in supply and demand that stem from relative price changes. Fluctuations will then be called excessive if, usually as a result of short-term supply or demand rigidities, they are larger than is indispensably required to do the job of restoring balance between long-run demand and long-run supply. Limiting ourselves to the supply side, we may distinguish between three possibilities of this kind.

1. In the first place, it is conceivable that, given a large price rise (fall), supply will simply not increase (decrease) beyond

what might have been equally well achieved with a smaller price rise (decline). This is the case where output, even over the long term, can expand or contract only by a certain amount. Ordinarily, we would here want to hold price movements down to the minimum required to achieve our output goals. Any fluctuations beyond this minimum would still permit us to reach these goals, but they would also involve unnecessarily large unsettling effects on the general price level and on socioeconomic conditions and policies in general. Being rather unrealistic this case primarily serves to set off the other two possibilities.

2. Next, price fluctuations can be said to be excessive when, far from being pointless, they are too effective in calling forth or in choking off supply and demand. Here we enter the realm of the cobweb, with high prices and the consequent supply reactions of producers in one period leading to overproduction and disastrous price drops in the next. The case for damping fluctuations has always largely rested on this type of situation which is indeed characteristic of many primary commodities—of tree crops with their long delayed yields and of minerals because of the long time that must elapse until new projects begin to yield an output stream.

The desirability of moderating price fluctuations cannot be questioned if the underlying supply position is as described in either (1) or (2), and the fact that the task is difficult and can be and has often been bungled is hardly a valid argument against trying again.

3. But fluctuations can be excessive in an even more serious sense: in addition to supply overreactions on the part of the primary producers themselves, they may lead to irreversible responses on the part of other economic operators.

In the first place, large increases in the price of a country's principal commodity may mean that the country loses its comparative advantage in some of its secondary exports. Sharp fluctuations in the prices of the primary producing countries' principal export products are therefore perhaps responsible for the failure of the many attempts at diversification.[2] To come to this con-

2. Cf. United Nations, *Commodity Survey, 1957,* chap. 3.

clusion we must assume that the behavior of the producers of "other" exports is asymmetrical; namely, that once discouraged from producing and exporting they are not easily coaxed back into these activities. This seems a realistic assumption, at least with respect to traditional secondary exports.

On the other hand, sudden and large price increases may encourage the equally irreversible start of substitute production in the importing industrial countries, as Singer has pointed out. It is plausible that, for any given price rise, the supply reaction of substitute producers would depend on the speed with which the rise occurs; if it comes about through a violent spurt the eventual increase in supply may be much larger than if the same price movement is administered in small doses over a period of time. Similarly, of course, a sudden increase in price may send indignant consumers to search for more or less close substitutes when they might offer less resistance to a gradual rise even though ultimately it would reach the same proportions. In effect, therefore, sharp fluctuations in price are likely to lead to downward shifts in supply (and perhaps also demand) schedules; they act as a powerful stimulus to the encroachment of the chemical and other new-product industries of the developed countries on the markets of the primary producers.

COULD STABLE PRICES STIMULATE SUBSTITUTE PRODUCTION?

When fluctuations are deemed to be excessive in this third meaning stabilization clearly serves not only the purpose of smoothing oscillations around some not-to-be-disturbed trend; in fact, one of its principal objectives would be to alter the trend which, in the circumstances described, would be increasingly adverse to the primary producers if fluctuations were permitted to continue. Stabilization is sought less for its own sake than as a means of slowing down technological progress in one of its more unwelcome aspects.

In other words we are back in the realm of "indirect control," but instead of aiming at the indirect control of commodity price fluctuations through general stabilizing policies, we now hope to

165

encourage diversification and to hold back the onrush of "creative destruction" by keeping a tighter rein on commodity prices.

But here a doubt arises. True, many important inventions of substitute products and processes can be traced back to wars and to periods of high prices and uncertain supply. In the meantime, however, technological advances in chemistry, metallurgy, etc., have become institutionalized and stand in only limited need of the stimulus provided by temporarily high prices and shortages in natural materials. Moreover, stabilization may provide such a stimulus in a different, but perhaps equally powerful fashion inasmuch as it would provide the research laboratories of the industrial countries with a "sitting duck" target. Certainly this is the way in which success in stabilization has affected competition among primary producers; new low-cost producers have always come upon the scene when agreements among existing producers resulted in a prolonged period of stable prices.

Examining the influence of effective stabilization on supply, Henry Wallich has suggested that commodities may be divided into those whose output is likely to be stimulated by stabilization and those whose supply would on the contrary be expanded by fluctuations.[3] Actually, if the preceding considerations are correct, one and the same commodity (so defined as to include its immediate substitutes) could react positively to *both* stabilization and violent fluctuation. Conceivably there might be some intermediate degree of fluctuation which is optimal for the purpose of preventing the development of substitute production: it would be too mild to put much extra pressure behind the search for substitutes and too strong to provide would-be substitute producers with the "economies of certainty." But it is clearly out of the question for economic policy to aim at such a highly theoretical optimum. Once again, therefore, we may have to abandon our hopes for indirect control, and the problem of the displacement of natural by manufactured materials may have to be met head on.

3. Henry C. Wallich, "Stabilization of Proceeds from Raw Material Exports," in Howard S. Ellis, ed., *Economic Development in Latin America* (New York: St. Martin's Press, 1961), pp. 350–53.

IS THERE A CASE FOR INTERFERING WITH TECHNICAL PROGRESS?

This is an even more distasteful prospect for economists than that of controlling prices through some sort of direct control. Interfere with technical progress! The otherwise rather enterprising United Nations experts who wrote the report on *Commodity Trade and Economic Development* (1953) solemnly abjured any such intentions: "We are strongly opposed to retarding technological progress for the sake of avoiding the pains of adjustment which inevitably attend progress." And they went on to advocate a father-knows-best attitude in case the industrial countries were to encourage the production of substitutes through subsidies: "Industrial countries are not in the habit of following such a course unless there are weighty reasons."[4]

Is it really necessary to be so horror-struck at the mere thought of policing in some fashion the process of technological innovation in spite of the fact that its repercussions can be truly calamitous? If today a way were found to produce chemically a product with a satisfactory coffee flavor at competitive prices, should we just let events take their ruinous course among the Latin American and African economies whose prospects for development rest so largely on maintaining foreign markets for the coffee bean? I know of no economic theorem which tells us that intervention in such cases is necessarily and always bad or even that it should be limited exclusively to aid in relocation, retraining and reemployment.

The basic conditions under which technological progress will result in economic gains for society as a whole are labor mobility and full employment. A cost-reducing innovation is bound to increase total output only if the displaced high-cost producers can find alternative employments. Within the Western industrial nations, and during the last 150 years, mobility has ordinarily proven sufficiently high so that interference with innovation has seemed unwarranted except in special situations. When hardships developed for certain groups or regions, the role of the

4. New York: United Nations, 1953, p. 79.

167

state was usually limited to relief and was later extended to aid in relocation, retraining and reemployment. The obligation to give such assistance was recognized only gradually by the Western societies as they became more "integrated," to use Myrdal's phrase. The combination of mobility with assistance which exists today within these countries creates an ideal setting for the unleashing of technological progress: the economic operators can be exposed to the full force of innovational and competitive pressures (a) because they are generally mobile and (b) because if some operators come to be seriously hurt—because of insufficient mobility—in the course of the rough economic game that is being played, the nation as a whole will come to their assistance. Actually assistance had to be given only rarely because mobility of resources was generally sufficient to take care of the adjustment problems created by innovation. If mobility had been less, a heavier load would have been thrown on readjustment assistance. Some questions might then have been raised about the correctness of a policy that is only allowed to repair the damage wrought by technological innovation, but never to prevent it. The possibility of such questioning is clearly shown by the protective measures that have been taken in various countries to shelter existing, relatively immobile operators in the cases of truck vs. railroad transportation,[5] margarine vs. butter, and recently in India, handloom vs. machine weaving.

In international relations, the possibly deleterious repercussions of technological innovation in one country on the economies of other countries have been even more ignored than the corresponding disturbances within national territories. The reason

5. In this respect it is interesting to note that transportation economists are not at all agreed with the United Nations experts that substitution of an old product by a new one is always technical progress and should never be guarded against. Serious consideration is for instance given in Europe to the question of compensating the railroad industry for the fact that it must carry on certain nonremunerative passenger lines as a public service and for other factors that mean higher money costs for railroad transportation in comparison to truck services, without a corresponding disparity in social costs. Cf. A. M. Milne, *The Economics of Inland Transport* (London: I. Pitman, 1955), pp. 139 ff.

for this neglect is clearly not that mobility is higher between than within countries, but rather that "integration" has been so much lower. In other words, whatever happened to other countries as a result of inventive and innovational activities in our country was "none of our business." As long as our country gained that was all we needed to know and to consider. This attitude, however, is becoming obsolete; and the interesting feature, from the point of view of the topic here discussed, is that on the international level, "integration" is decisively outpacing resource and labor mobility: we feel and increasingly assume a measure of responsibility for the effects of our actions on the economic destinies of others, but we are not opening our doors to them.[6] This situation may therefore make it necessary to reappraise a policy that was elaborated for handling our problem within national boundaries under exactly opposite conditions, with "integration" coming in as a supplement and almost as an afterthought and with the main adjustment task being shouldered by mobility.

Since "integration" is so far ahead of mobility on the international level, a policy that is confined to repairing the damage can imply huge costs; as an alternative, a policy of screening and steering innovations from the point of view of their international economic repercussions may have to be given serious consideration.

Of course technical progress should not nor could it be "locked up"; but neither should it be allowed to run amok. This is not the place to discuss in detail the arrangements through which we might hope to escape from a dilemma that has become so familiar to all of us as a result of the advances in nuclear physics and space technology. I merely wish to suggest that economists have good reasons of their own to make a contribution to this momentous topic.

6. Moreover, the ability of primary producers to shift without serious economic loss out of their existing lines of specialization through *internal* mobility may be severely limited if their participation in world trade is best interpreted in terms of the "vent-for-surplus" theory of international trade. For an illuminating rehabilitation of this theory, see H. Myint, "The 'Classical Theory' of International Trade and the Underdeveloped Countries" *Economic Journal* 68 (June 1958): pp. 317–37.

6. *Abrazo* versus Coexistence

Let me comment on the provocative proposal to "deemphasize the inter-American tie" and to concentrate on the building up of Latin American, rather than inter-American, institutions. The proposal is made, nota bene, as a means to improve relations between Latin America and the United States; the argument is that we will get along better if we frankly recognize and assert our separateness from one another instead of straining to live under the same roof and to make a great show of friendliness and harmony.

To support this position, the point is sometimes made that Latin America is only one of several areas of the world in which the United States takes a preeminent interest; under these circumstances, we cannot expect Latin Americans to maintain an exclusive or preferential tie with us. It can be argued, indeed, that the United States would gain much, not only from a deemphasis of the inter-American relationship, from a damper on the hollow phraseology of hemispheric solidarity, but that we should welcome a decrease in our involvement in the Latin American scene. The fact is that our position of power in the area is not at all commensurate with the high degree of involvement in its economic life. As a result, we are clearly getting the worst of both worlds: the degree of control and influence we exercise is in fact quite limited, yet we get blamed for whatever goes wrong. Thus there may be much to be said, from a purely selfish point of view, for

This short paper is part of a discussion on the basic orientation of United States economic and political policies toward Latin America between "Ypsilon," Lincoln Gordon, and myself which took place in 1960 and which was published in the volume noted below. The proposal to "deemphasize the inter-American tie" on which the paper comments at the outset, was put forward by Ypsilon.

Reprinted by permission from *Latin American Issues—Essays and Comments,* ed. A. O. Hirschman (New York: Twentieth Century Fund, 1961), pp. 59–63.

encouraging greater contacts of the Latin American countries with each other, and with third countries.

But the case for separateness goes deeper. As all developing nations, but perhaps more so because of their geographical position and the claims of the "Spirit of Pan-Americanism," the Latin American countries find themselves faced with a dilemma: on the one hand, they wish to industrialize and modernize, hence, they have to and wish to become more like us in many respects; but this means precisely that they must strive at the same time for some countervailing differentiation from us if they are to maintain or acquire a sense of their own individuality. Accordingly, the more successful are their efforts at development and modernization, the stronger their desire for self-assertion, at least outside of the realm of technology, is likely to become.

It follows that if we want Latin American development, we must learn to live with this correlative drive toward self-assertion. Yet, to respect and value "otherness" seems to be one of the basic difficulties in our relations with "others." We practically have to be told to our faces that we are good only to be buried before we recognize otherness and give up the "conviction that once we become acquainted with people throughout the world, we will discover that they are basically the same as we: reasonable people, that is, who, when we have explained our basic concepts and value systems to them will warmly embrace our way of life." This "sentimental one-worldism [which] has made basic understanding and cooperation so elusive"[1] has, strangely enough, become even more entrenched as a result of the presence of the Soviet bloc: here we have a group of countries with which we accept to have *nothing* in common; therefore, so we conclude all too easily, in the "free world" there ought to be *total* accord on ideals and objectives. Just because we have resigned ourselves to mere coexistence with the Soviet bloc, we expect to live with everyone else in the intimacy of shared goals and agreed values.

Actually, of course, coexistence may be an excellent term for the relations at which we should realistically aim with many coun-

1. F. B. Pike, ed., *Freedom and Reform in Latin America* (Notre Dame, Ind.: University of Notre Dame Press, 1959), p. 14.

tries *outside* the Soviet bloc. The difficult stage of development through which they are passing may require that their position toward us be distant and reserved and that the solutions to their problems be emphatically different from ours. It is a measure of our naïveté that Nixon's proposal upon his return from Latin America—let us "have an 'abrazo' for democratic leaders but a formal handshake for dictators"[2]—was hailed as a tremendous advance in our thinking about United States–Latin American relations. It did not occur to anyone, it seems, that the "democratic leaders" might not particularly care for our *abrazo,* that, in the particular atmosphere of nationalistic exaltation in which these leaders frequently come to power, they might even fear it as a kiss of death, since their political appeal may in part rest on their *not* being embraced by us.

It may be mentioned in passing that our striving for consensus and full-blown understanding results naturally enough in the opposite emotion after it has been repeatedly rebuffed. Accordingly we have today in the United States a not negligible group of scholars and Latin American specialists who have become disgruntled and hostile to their very area of specialization—always a sad spectacle.

A further unpleasant result of our insistence to achieve a full consensus with others who are just as insistent on not agreeing with us is that we drive them toward more and more extreme and hostile positions. Our very reasonableness and eagerness to understand may drive others to unreasonableness and eagerness to offend. We must at least consider the hypothesis that others disagree with us not because either their or our thought processes have been imperfect, but because they attach a positive value to disagreement with us. Wherever this is so a successful attempt on our part to eradicate the disagreement (with respect to one issue) can only lead to it popping up somewhere else, probably in more virulent form. In general, aggressive and offensive behavior may at times be resorted to in order to fend off an unwelcome embrace

2. This proposal was later reaffirmed in Milton Eisenhower's "Report to the President" of 27 December 1958, (Washington, D.C.: Department of State Publication 6769), p. 15.

and would not be indulged in if we were not such determined suitors.

A corollary of my position is that it may be ill-advised to advertise Puerto Rico as the model Latin Americans ought to study, meditate and imitate. Puerto Rico's advances are impressive indeed, but are likely to be discounted because it can never be conclusively proved that its economic progress has not been bought at a price in national independence which other Latin Americans are unwilling to pay. Let us note that they would thus reject the lessons of Puerto Rican development for reasons very similar to those for which we ourselves urge them not to pay any attention to the undoubted economic gains of countries in the Soviet orbit.

But the most important reason for which I would strongly support a lessening of the emphasis on inter-American solidarity is that in this fashion we would actually increase the range of practical cooperation in problem-solving activities between the United States and Latin America. Our present image of hemispheric relations is that we share quite a few basic values and that we can gradually achieve agreement on others provided we are all reasonable and progressive; and our programs of technical and financial assistance are presumed to be based on this kind of consensus. But this image is largely a fiction: the United States and the Latin American countries are not undertaking a series of joint actions because they pursue well-defined and fully shared goals; rather, ties may be established and strengthened as we jointly engage in common programs in the course of which we may be pursuing quite different goals, at least initially.

A frank recognition of this situation may help to enlarge considerably the area of cooperation and the number of problems we can tackle through joint efforts: there is no need to have a consensus on the value of the price system as a mechanism for allocating resources in order to take certain common and common sense steps to deal with clearly excessive fluctuations of commodity prices. There is no need to agree on comprehensive development plans in order to support a wide variety of obviously useful and productive projects. The United States need not and should not withdraw its support from a common market in Latin

America because it feels that some Latin American supporters of the common market have objectives that are anathema to us. In these and many other fields, instead of requiring consensus and harmony at the outset, we may hope for a rapprochement of initially divergent views as a possible byproduct of common and successful action.

It is indeed on this basis that we solve many of our domestic problems. Strangely enough, in our international relations we frequently act as though we believed that political science must stop at the water's edge, a proposition that is even more untrue than the one it paraphrases.

7. Second Thoughts on the Alliance for Progress

When President Kennedy proposed his *alianza para el progreso* to the assembled Latin American ambassadors on March 13, he was making a new bid for cooperation in economic and social development. The Bay of Pigs debacle has made it harder for this program to succeed. But it may well run into some difficulties of its own. For it is just possible that the failure of the CIA to gauge correctly the Cuban situation is only one manifestation of a more general misreading of the mood of Latin America and of the realities of inter-American relations.

The new program, however, represents significant progress. It promises to be a vast improvement over past doctrines which held that Latin America's economic development could safely be left to private capital, occasionally supported by credits from the International and Export-Import Banks. True, in the last two years or so of the Eisenhower administration, this policy underwent considerable modification under the impact first of the Nixon trip and then of the Cuban revolution. Now it has been repudiated: Latin America is to receive a fair and perhaps a preferential share of U.S. foreign aid.

Further, certain traditional negative or hostile attitudes are being revised. The United States is "ready to cooperate in serious, case-by-case examinations of commodity market problems." The Export-Import Bank has announced that it will grant credits for the export of equipment and machinery even to government-controlled enterprises, thereby ending its doctrinaire and ineffectual but still highly irritating refusal to cooperate with petroleum monopolies such as Mexico's Pemex and Brazil's Petrobras. Finally, the United Nations Economic Commission for Latin America, long abhorred in Washington for its "wild" theories but

Reprinted by permission from *The Reporter* (25 May 1961): 20–23. © 1961 by The Reporter Magazine Company. This article had actually been completed before the Bay of Pigs invasion of April 1961, but since publication took place shortly after that event, some references to it were inserted.

highly influential in many Latin American finance ministries and planning boards, is to be given an important place in the effort to accelerate Latin America's economic growth.

The principal new feature in the Kennedy administration's program is the emphasis on social change and reform. The ten-year plans that the Latin American nations are invited to formulate as a basis for our aid are not only to "establish targets and priorities" or to "insure monetary stability," along lines familiar from past foreign aid; they are also to "establish the machinery for vital social change." Congress was immediately requested to appropriate $500 million for "social development" projects in the fields of land use, housing, water supply, health, and education. Here again, allocation and disbursement of the funds are to be conditioned on "the willingness of each recipient nation to improve its own institutions, make necessary modifications in its social patterns, and mobilize its own domestic resources in a program of development."

Thus both the immediate and the longer-term programs are built on a new criterion for foreign aid: the willingness on the part of the recipient nations to undertake fundamental reforms of social structure.

It is gratifying to see the policy of our government array itself frankly and openly alongside the forces making for social progress in Latin America. But if we care for the attainment of what we are after, we ought to recognize that with this new policy we are entering uncharted territory. Unlike the Russians, we do not have much experience in promoting social change abroad.

A NEW BASIS FOR AID?

Long before foreign aid became a matter for governments to handle, private capitalists sought assurances that their funds would not be wasted. One approach, which held sway for many decades and even centuries, was to scrutinize the direct uses to which the money was put, to evaluate whether the proposed project was sound in itself, i.e., promised to be profitable or useful. It does not require a high degree of sophistication, however, to realize that even the soundest project can go wrong if the borrower's own resources are poorly used. As a result, the demand has long been made that the borrower should have not only sound projects but also a general economic policy favorable to development.

This demand has shown itself in several ways. The one currently most popular is to request that the borrower formulate a "consistent, integrated" program for development, and to grant aid on the basis of such programs. The Eisenhower administration followed a less demanding line: everything would work out well—at least in Latin America—provided only that a country achieved monetary stability and established a "favorable investment climate." The frequent admonition to "put your house in order" had this meaning: stop inflation and welcome foreign capital.

In Latin America these requirements are frequently alleged to have included not only the nondiscriminatory treatment of foreign capital and a minimum of stability in the relevant legislation, but also the readmission of private capital, domestic and foreign, to areas of economic activity, such as the production of petroleum, that had been taken over by the state. Whether or not official pressures in this direction were exerted in such countries as Argentina (successfully) or Brazil (unsuccessfully) will have to be investigated by some future historian.

Castro's rise to power made the United States favor a more intensive use of public funds as a principal instrument of foreign policy. At the same time, it compelled a reexamination of what we wanted to achieve through an increase in U.S. aid. The Cuban revolution could not have occurred had there not been basic faults in the organization of Cuban society and legitimate, highly exploitable popular grievances. Thus, it was argued, if a new Cuba was to be prevented in Latin America, every effort should be made to correct similar faults and prevent similar grievances. "Put your house in order" suddenly acquired a different content. Even in the last months of the Eisenhower administration, it came more and more to mean, "Improve your land tenure system, distribute your tax burden more equitably, erase slums and illiteracy." This emphasis on social reform has now been vigorously affirmed by the new administration.

FINANCING SOCIAL JUSTICE

The new formula will inevitably present problems of great difficulty. How shall we judge whether a country is taking sufficiently bold steps in the direction of social justice to be entitled to aid? How are we to gauge whether a given program is likely to achieve adequate progress in eliminating ingrained patterns of exploitation? Progressive legislation has frequently been meaningless or blissfully unenforced in Latin America. Moreover, certain types of social justice may have been overdone. There is much evidence, for example, that Cuba's very ambitious social security legislation of the pre-Castro era had created rigidities that seriously retarded the industrial development of that island.

A given set of measures may be considered likely to result in a more equitable distribution of income, but the decisive question, however elusive may be the answer, remains: will these measures be adequate to lessen the *feeling* of social injustice?

Obviously we have neither the intellectual tools nor the time to make such evaluations; we will have to be content with the more modest goal of enhancing the attention that the governments of Latin America are giving to the main social causes of discontent in their countries. Perhaps the knowledge that financing is to be available for projects in the "social" areas will indeed stimulate their interest. But here the utmost alertness will be required, since a government that does not of itself have the impulse to undertake real reforms will find it only too easy to invent a variety of projects (e.g., ambitious colonization schemes in faraway jungle lands) that lend themselves to the massive expenditure of aid but are designed to evade rather than to attack the country's real social evils.

Thus we may be in a dilemma: if a country has the will to improve the condition of its lower classes, the proffered funds may not be needed, while if such a determination is lacking, the offer of funds will not in itself create it. In all our foreign aid ventures, we bank on the existence of an intermediate type of situation: a government is presumed to be teetering on the edge of taking a step in the right direction, but can overcome the resistances and ensuing difficulties only if it obtains control of additional funds. The chances of foreign aid making a difference in this fashion varies. For example, foreign aid is likely to increase the total amount of investment, although usually not on a dollar-for-dollar basis. Under present procedures, it is also likely that foreign grants and loans will lead to a somewhat more careful technical and economic analysis of projects than would otherwise take place. But the likelihood that foreign aid will play the decisive role in important areas of public policy such as tax and land reform is much smaller, especially since the prospect of receiving foreign aid has traditionally been one reason for which countries have been able to avoid and postpone harsh decisions of fiscal discipline.

Our new policy raises even more bothersome questions. Let us assume that it is successful; would there not then be something distasteful to the Latin Americans about our having financed social justice for them? Receiving gifts always makes for emotional strains. But it is far less hurtful to pride and dignity to accept food and machines from the "richest nation in the world" than to risk being beholden to it for such intangible and invaluable achievements as independence, or social progress, or cultural advance. Some of those Latin Americans who have long been struggling to make their countries better places to live in will receive our new policy with mixed feelings at best.

For various reasons, then, our intervention may well produce a substantial realignment of forces and groups in the countries concerned. The fight for social reforms is always hard, but it used to have the compensating attraction of being a real fight. It therefore called forth a certain type of supporters, some of whom may well lose interest once the fight has the blessing of all the authorities. Nationalist elements will certainly find fault with any reform the United States espouses and will shift either to defending the status quo or to advocating more radical measures. Thus, compromise solutions that might otherwise have been found may not materialize, and independent opinion could become more deeply divided as a result of our intervention—with the desired social reforms farther away than ever. Have we already forgotten the great and bitter lesson of the European Defense Community, which went down to its defeat in the French parliament largely because we supported it so openly and insistently? This episode should have taught us that the engineering of social and political change abroad requires more than a proclamation that we favor it. Our persistent illusions in this respect can perhaps be explained by the fact that it costs us great efforts to arrive at the decision of supporting European unification or Latin American land reform. By the time we have laboriously convinced ourselves of the worthiness of these causes, we think that "implementation" will be simple.

Of course, it is just at this point that the difficulties begin. Frequently we "discover" problems that have a long history of sometimes effective, sometimes abortive attempts at solution. Recently, for example, we have "discovered" the urgency of doing something about Brazil's northeast, largely because the peasant leagues that have sprung up in that area and have taken over a few half-abandoned sugar estates are obvious points of penetration for "Fidelismo." But the northeast, with its periodic droughts and its failure to participate in the general progress of the country, has been troubling Brazil for almost a century: the first big drought took place in 1877–1880. One government bureau established to combat the recurrent droughts has just celebrated its fiftieth anniversary; a whole literature has sprung up about the problem. Similarly in Colombia, land reform has been "around" as an issue and object of policy making for decades. Advances in some directions have been achieved, and delicately balanced alliances are constantly forming and breaking up. In this kind of situation, uninformed pressure from us to "get going," far from playing a decisive part, may well cast us in the role of bull in the china shop.

How to Change an Image

Clearly, the new administration seeks to change the image of the United States that has long prevailed in Latin America. According to this image our concern with the area is inspired by strategic and selfish economic considerations. Furthermore, we are supposed to be allied everywhere with big business and big landowners. A change of this image is indeed desirable, but there is some question whether we can realistically aim at becoming, by a few ringing proclamations and the disbursement of some funds, the patron saint of the Latin American social revolution.

To attain the good relations we aim at, it might be more dignified and more effective if we tried first of all to destroy the old image by such practicable measures as turning the Panama Canal over to a hemisphere-wide organization; working out a mutually satisfactory status for our private investments, including gradual withdrawal where desired; and reducing obstacles to the imports of Latin American products.

The giving of aid would then take its proper place as part of a policy designed to rebuild confidence and to overcome the prejudices and animosities that burden our relationship at present. Viewing aid in this perspective, we would emphasize our willingness to engage in numerous obviously useful cooperative tasks on the technical, local, regional, and national levels. In the course of the widespread cooperation that would ensue, we would have many opportunities to identify ourselves with land reform, low-cost housing, or other social development projects. Such projects have been and are continuously being elaborated in many Latin American countries. Thus far, we have not been able to help in their financing—and therefore have been without influence in shaping them—partly because our lending criteria called for loans that were "directly productive" or because we vetoed the use of dollar loans for expenditures in local currency.

We should make it quite clear that these restrictions are a thing of the past and that we are prepared and indeed eager to make some contribution in the "social development" areas. But this is a far cry from the pretense of taking command of the fight for social justice in Latin America.

These misgivings about our new Latin American policies may go back to one basic worry: the whole idea of a new alliance, be it even an "alliance for progress," may not strike the right tone, given the prevailing mood of many influential intellectuals and policy makers of Latin America. They, like their Asian or African counterparts, are not interested in alliances with either us or the Russians. They want to chart an independent and somewhat unpredictable course between the two principal power blocs. They know, after all, that their bargaining power derives largely from not allying themselves definitively with either bloc. Moreover, they desperately want to find their own way to modernity and development.

Actually, there are perhaps more reasons for the new Latin American leaders to seek an arm's length relationship with us than for the Asians or Africans. In this hemisphere we have long been the dominant power, and if the Latin Americans wish to have their share of the "winds of change," as they surely do, they will want to loosen the ties that bind them to us and look for new connections, not only with Western Europe and Japan but also with India and the new African states. If we seek to keep them too close to us, there is the danger that they may bounce much further away.

The illusion that after years of frustration and alienation an alliance can be manufactured overnight by well-meaning phrases may have something in common with the illusion that the hold of an authoritarian régime that has effected a social revolution can be shaken loose by the landing of a few hundred volunteers. The tragedy is that the Bay of Pigs disaster may make us more inclined toward demanding that Latin Americans declare themselves for us or against us. We could make no greater mistake. We must learn how to cooperate with the increasingly influential groups of new nationalists who wish to experiment with new forms of social and economic organization and recoil from any outspoken commitment to us. In other words, we may well have to choose between *alianza* and *progreso*.

8. Critical Comments on Foreign Aid Strategies

The most articulate reflection of a new mood of disillusion with foreign aid and past reliance on capital plus technical assistance is the recent article in *Foreign Affairs* by Ambassador John Kenneth Galbraith.[1] Readers are told that the development process can hardly be expected to be brought under way and that an infusion of financial aid and experts will be useless unless there be present in the to-be-aided society (1) "a substantial degree of literacy" and an "educated elite of substantial size"; (2) "a substantial measure of social justice"; (3) "a reliable apparatus of government and public administration"; and (4) "a clear and purposeful view of what development involves."

This is a counsel of perfection. In no advanced industrial country were these four conditions realized prior to industrialization. Moreover, if these four conditions were found to be present in any country today, that country could easily dispense with foreign financial and technical assistance; in fact, it should probably be an exporter of such assistance, with the United States as a recipient!

The Galbraithian conditions should supply, therefore, a final *reductio ad absurdum* of one approach to foreign aid that has dominated American thinking during the whole postwar period: the "will to believe"—rooted perhaps in the need to so persuade the Congress—that foreign aid is the "missing component," the "catalyst" whose addition will surely bring the alchemy of the development process to its climactic reaction: self support, "take-off," or bliss in general. The search for the components that have to be in place so that foreign capital and technical assistance from abroad can play this sure-fire role has focused successively on monetary stability, on a "favorable investment climate," on "in-

Reprinted by permission from *Development in the Emerging Countries,* by Robert E. Asher et al. © 1962 by the Brookings Institution.

1. "A Positive Approach to Foreign Aid," *Foreign Affairs* 39 (April 1961): 445–46.

tegrated development programs," and lately on land and tax reforms. The diagnosis of "the experts" has thus fluctuated wildly, in line with the ideological preferences of the moment and with the lessons of the latest disaster.

If only as much attention had been devoted to the successes as to the failures, we should have noticed that whenever development occurs, it does so invariably in the absence of one or several of these "required" components or preconditions. In nineteenth century Germany, it occurred without much primitive accumulation of capital and in Italy without the Protestant ethic, to mention some of the earlier theories on prerequisites; and during the postwar period, Brazil experienced development in the absence of monetary stability, and Colombia even in the absence of public order, not to speak of land reform.

These experiences cast great doubt on the whole notion of preconditions or prerequisites. In fact, I believe with Gerschenkron that the only generalization one can make about the development of latecomers is that they will not follow the sequence of their predecessors, but will insist on changing it around or on skipping entirely some stages as well as some "preconditions." Therefore, I continue to advocate that in their research, the experts pay special attention to the emergence and possible rationality of new or inverted sequences. When they discover an "obstacle," such as poor public administration or uneconomic land use, their job does not consist in merely advising its removal; they ought to explore also how, by moving the economy forward elsewhere, additional pressure (economic and political) could be brought on the obstacle to give way.

I am at present engaged in the detailed analysis of sequences in economic policy making around particular problems such as land reform or inflation or regional imbalance in three Latin American countries.[2] In each case I am seeking answers to the questions: At what particular point, under what combination of pressures, after what kind of learning process, are new insights about the nature of the problem acquired? When and why does

2. This study resulted in my *Journeys Toward Progress* (New York: Twentieth Century Fund, 1963).

it suddenly become possible to take effective action after decades of ineffective legislation and tinkering?

But let me return to my theme. The rich countries might as well reconcile themselves to the fact that they will never be called on to give aid to a country unless it is afflicted with many, more or less loosely interrelated, facets of backwardness or obstacles to development. In this view, aid is a way of getting involved in the recipient country's battle against these obstacles. At first, the best the United States can do when joining the battle is often to follow Napoleon's maxim *"on s'engage; puis on voit."* Little by little, after getting committed and "seeing," that is, learning about the country's problems, some hypotheses should emerge about the sequence in which a country is likely to attack successfully the multifarious obstacles. In the search for the best hypothesis, those who administer aid programs should use what Dr. Carl Rogers, the psychotherapist, calls "client-centered therapy." The well-known similarity in characteristics exhibited by underdeveloped countries at any one stage of development is matched only by the far less noticed variety of sequences and processes through which they move from one stage to the next. For example, the wide range of means by which one particular obstacle can be overcome was strikingly if somewhat inadvertently illustrated by Frank Tannenbaum when he wrote recently that Mexico acquired a feeling of pride in its own identity and achievements through its protracted revolution, whereas Brazil achieved similar confidence in its own destiny through the publication of a book, namely, Freyre's classic *Masters and Slaves*.

But there remains a serious question that is really the basic one to which Ambassador Galbraith was addressing himself. What if we have acquired the conviction that no further progress is possible unless a corrupt government gets ousted or a thorough-going land reform is instituted? Far be it from me to say that such situations are inconceivable. But perhaps Americans today are a little too ready to jump to this kind of conclusion. In reaction to the Cuban events they wish to rid themselves in a hurry of what Robert Heilbroner has called "American ostrichism," by which he means the earlier lack of attention to the social struggles and tensions that have so important a bearing on the course of development. At last, Americans have become painfully aware that it may be impossible to effect significant economic progress as long as aid actually strengthens those who are opposed to the social changes without which economic advance is impossible or meaningless.

Naturally, if the situation is the one depicted in the Communist textbook where the government is entirely the expression of one homogeneously reactionary and parasitic ruling clique while the country's popular energies and developmental resources wait to be unshackled through revolution, little can be said in favor of making aid available until the revolution has taken over. If this is the situation, the best thing for the United States Operations Mission to do is to join the rioting students or the backbush guerillas. But ordinarily reality is not that simple: the government in question may be unwilling to decree (or its parliament may be unwilling to vote) certain reforms that the United States Mission thinks are desirable; at the same time it may be anxious to undertake a variety of unexceptionable tasks of economic development. If the reforms are as central to further progress as the American experts think they are, these other tasks will either be impossible to carry out in the absence of the reforms, or they will make the need for the reforms even more compelling than before. Both eventualities bring the reforms closer, for they either force the hand of the government or hasten its downfall.

In this perspective, financial or technical help is justified, provided we realize the kind of difficult game in which we are involved and are not caught unaware by the outbreak of crisis. By helping in peripheral tasks of economic development or by proving that such ventures are bound to fail within the existing socioeconomic framework, one is waging a kind of guerilla warfare against the holdouts of reaction and backwardness at the center. From this point of view even the failure of a technical assistance mission can have its uses: nothing demonstrates as clearly the need to undertake thorough-going land reform as the failure of an attempt to establish an equitable land tax system.

Foreign aid does not necessarily always work to the benefit of the group that happens to be in power. It is desired by governments to enhance their prestige, but may turn out to undermine it. Frequently, foreign aid is requested to stave off reforms, but it may be made to accelerate them. The exploration and utilization of such disruptive and subversive potentialities of aid is perhaps particularly important for the United States as long as it is neither much given to guerilla warfare proper nor apparently very good at it. In order to be able to use aid in this fashion and not to be unduly surprised by the explosive consequences, one should devise ways of giving aid in a fashion that does not imply a wholesale endorsement of the programs, objectives, and values of the recipient government. Aid givers should learn to cooperate with other governments in a variety of tasks, fully aware that the governments giving and receiving aid are pursuing objectives that overlap initially only to a very small extent. This way of using financial and technical assistance implies techniques quite different from those toward which the United States's aid program is now gravitating. To underwrite a development program—which appears to be the new formula, to be applied the world over— may be the appropriate technique when there is a rather complete meeting of minds. But not to underwrite a development program may be just as important at times; and it need not mean the absence of an overall design, or resignation to having just a collection of random projects. It may be a deliberate choice to remain aloof from full cooperation while giving support to certain aspirations. It may be useful to identify different types of aid policies appropriate to different constellations so that we will stop looking for the one best policy applicable to all possible circumstances.

9. The Stability of Neutralism

Suppose two powerful, industrialized countries, called Usonia and Russonia, compete by means of capital exports and other forms of "aid" for influence in various underdeveloped countries, typified by Thirdonia. We are interested in exploring whether anything can be said about the resulting relations between total aid, the proportions of the total supplied by each of the powers, the political position of Thirdonia, and particularly about the stability of that position. Usonia and Russonia, even though antagonistic over a wide range of issues, may come to perceive a community of interest in such stability, or at least in the avoidance of utter instability, for sudden large-scale changes in alignment on the part of Thirdonia could increase the risk of war between the two powers to a point not desired by either.

Aid from each of the two powers is likely to be influenced by the political alignment of Thirdonia as expressed, for example, by the proportion of votes it casts in the United Nations General Assembly in line with Usonia's or Russonia's wishes. Aid received from Usonia may be assumed to be the larger, the more closely aligned Thirdonia is with Usonia, with a similar aid-giving behavior holding for Russonia. For the time being, we shall suppose that complete alignment with Usonia yields the same flow of aid as does complete alignment with Russonia.

Figure 9.1 (a, b, and c) portrays some of the principal resulting possibilities when political alignment is shown on the horizontal axis and the amount of aid received on the vertical axis. In Figure 9.1a aid from Usonia declines linearly and aid from Russonia increases in the same fashion, as Thirdonia takes up political positions farther removed from Usonia and closer to Russonia; in Figure 9.1b aid from both decreases little as Thirdonia moves toward neutralist middle ground; while in Figure 9.1c aid is cut to the bone as soon as Thirdonia ceases to be a faithful

Reprinted by permission from *The American Economic Review* 54 (March 1964): 94–100.

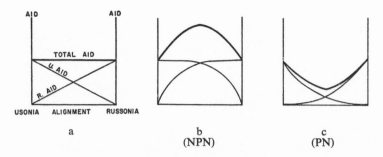

Figure 9.1. Types of Symmetrical Aid-Giving Behavior
by Usonia and Russonia

camp follower. The total aid flow available to Thirdonia results
from adding up the two individual aid flows from Usonia and
Russonia and is shown as the heavy line or curve in the figures: it
is invariant with respect to political alignment in *a,* and exhibits
either a maximum or a minimum for the neutralist position depending on whether the aid-giving behavior of the powers corresponds to the one portrayed in *b* or in *c.*

We have just derived the transformation curve or opportunity-
set available to Thirdonia if aid-from-Usonia and aid-from-Russo-
nia are considered as two commodities which can be "produced"
in differing combinations, depending on the country's position between the two powers. The three possibilities just discussed are
shown along traditional lines in Figure 9.2 where one of the two
commodities is measured along the horizontal and the other along
the vertical axis. Aid-giving behavior of Figure 9.1*b* which does
Not Penalize Neutralism *(NPN)* is now seen to result in the traditionally shaped transformation curve, while Figure 9.1*c*-type insistence on substantial identification on the part of the aid givers
results in the opposite shape (labeled *PN* for Penalization of
Neutralism).

Consider next the preference functions of Thirdonia for aid
from Usonia and Russonia. Again we may distinguish between
three principal possibilities shown in Figure 9.3. First, Thirdonia
may be exclusively interested in maximizing aid: in this case its
indifference map will consist of straight lines such as *MM* (for

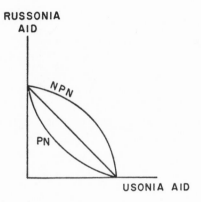

Figure 9.2. Thirdonia's Opportunity-Sets

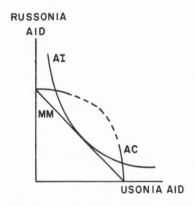

Figure 9.3. Thirdonia's Indifference Functions

Mercenary Maximization of aid) forming a 45° angle with the axes along which the two aid flows are measured. The next possibility is that a country puts a high value on independence as well as on aid and feels that, for any given total, its independence is the greater, the more the ratio of Usonia aid to Russonia aid approaches unity. Such a preference would result in the traditionally shaped indifference curve, labeled *AI* (for Aid plus Independence.)

A third conceivable preference pattern exists. Thirdonia could prefer complete alignment with one of the two superpowers to a middle position, either because it has a liking for a strong, ideological stance or because it does not wish to be suspected of playing Usonia off against Russonia for the sake of material advantage or for some other reason. Given any fixed amount of aid, the country prefers getting it all from one source rather than through any combination of the two aid givers. The resulting shape of the preference pattern is shown in the curve labeled *AC* (for Aid plus Commitment); the middle portion of this curve is dotted to indicate that, at any point of time, a country exhibiting this preference pattern is likely to find itself on one or the other end of the curve and is likely to visualize only immediately adjacent positions.

We can now join our "transformation" and "indifference" curves (Figures 9.2 and 9.3), and one important result follows immediately. The traditional point of stable equilibrium is achieved by joining the *NPN* curve of Figure 9.2 with the *AI* curve of Figure 9.3. In other words, if Thirdonia's preference pattern is such that it values both aid and independence, a stable point is best achieved through aid-giving behavior on the part of Usonia and Russonia that does not penalize neutralism. Should aid be reduced strongly as soon as Thirdonia ceases to be wholly aligned with one or the other aid-giving powers (curve *PN* of Figure 9.2), then a potentially unstable situation results from the *AI*-type of preference. The highest *AI* curve could touch the *PN* curve at two widely distant points, between which the aid-receiving country would be indifferent. Even if there is only one point of tangency, small real or imagined shifts in the position of the two similarly shaped curves could produce a drastic shift of the optimal point, i.e., a sudden switch in Thirdonia's position in relation to the two superpowers. Hence, if an underdeveloped country is known to have the Aid-plus-Independence type of preference and if both Usonia and Russonia, in the interest of reducing the risk of war, are intent on preventing sudden shifts in the world power balance through shifts of positions on the part of less developed countries, then they ought to adopt the aid-giving behavior of Figure 9.1*b,* which does not penalize neutralism.

Looking at some of the other conceivable combinations of the transformation curves of Figure 9.2 and of the indifference curves of Figure 9.3, we find that Mercenary Maximization *(MM)* of aid is compatible with stability only if neutralism is not penalized *(NPN* curve of Figure 9.2*b)*. Small real or imagined shifts in the supply curve of aid of a linear or *PN* type could produce a complete flip-flop on the part of a country that is only interested in squeezing the maximum aid out of the two competing powers.

What happens if a country puts a positive value on ideological commitment to one of the aid-giving powers and hence has a preference function of the *AC* type? In this case, the more stable situation appears to result from the transformation curve following the *PN* rather than the *NPN* type. In other words, if Thirdonia likes commitment, the most stable situation is created through the aid-giving countries responding to and reinforcing this attitude by penalizing decisively any straying from the commitment path. It is possible to speak of stability in this situation only if Thirdonia, which is by definition aligned with one of the aid-giving powers at the outset, does not visualize a switch all the way to the other camp (its preference curve is defined at any one time only for one or the other end of the *AC* curve of Figure 9.3).

At this point in our reasoning we perceive that, in contrast to the usual assumption of economic theory, the shapes of the transformation and indifference curves in our model are *not* independent: clearly, the *NPN* and *AI* curves, on the one hand, and the *PN* and *AC* curves, on the other, "belong" together and generate each other. A Thirdonia with the *AI*-type preference will see its behavior rewarded and its correctness confirmed by finding that its opportunity-set is in fact *NPN;* and the realization on the part of Usonia and Russonia that Thirdonia is *not* "playing off one against the other," but is genuinely interested in keeping at an equal distance from both, may induce them to adopt the kind of aid-giving behavior that does not penalize neutralism. On the other hand, the *AC*-type of preference on the part of Thirdonia will generate expectations of unbending loyalty on the part of the country to which it professes to be committed; should these expectations be disappointed ever so little, aid is likely to be reduced drastically, in accordance with the *PN* pattern.

Unstable situations exist nevertheless and can now be viewed as a result of transitional departures from the two basic stable situations, *NPN-AI* and *PN-AC*. Suppose we start out with preference system *AC* and opportunity-set *PN*. An unstable situation can then arise because Thirdonia shifts its preference pattern to *AI* while Usonia and Russonia hold fast to *PN* instead of switching to *NPN*. A potentially unstable situation results, in other words, if a previously committed country shifts to a neutralist or independent position and its previous mentor cannot reconcile itself to the loss of its dominant influence and attempts to coerce the country back to the fold. The possible, and indeed likely, result is that the country will move even farther away.

Another case of instability would occur in the following situation: Suppose Thirdonia has the neutralist *AI*-type of preference, but the aid-giving countries have adopted the *NPN* aid-giving behavior simply as a means of cajoling Thirdonia into becoming a satellite; after a while they may then tire of waiting for this hoped-for event and try a more coercive policy of the *PN* type —Thirdonia's choice would be unpredictable.

The model could no doubt be complicated considerably in various ways, for example, by introducing time more explicitly into the analysis. Suppose that the longer Thirdonia continues as Usonia's or Russonia's satellite, the more it will tend to be taken for granted with a consequent decline in aid received—such aid-giving behavior could easily be shown to give rise to instability.

Another realistic complication of the model may be briefly discussed. Suppose that the maximum aid flow that can be obtained by Thirdonia I from Usonia is larger than that which Russonia can be expected to provide, while the opposite holds for Thirdonia II. This means that the opportunity-set facing these two countries is no longer symmetrical with respect to the coordinates. Figure 9.4 assumes that the relevant opportunity-sets are of the *NPN* type and that both Thirdonias have the same neutralist *AI*-type preference pattern. It is clear then that the two countries will select different foreign policy positions and would receive their aid in different proportions from the two superpowers even though they have basically the same neutralist attitude. For this reason, it is impossible to detect (to "read off") the extent or sincerity

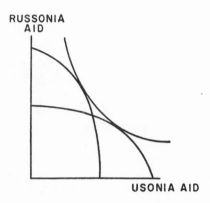

RUSSONIA
AID

USONIA AID

Figure 9.4. Two Equally Neutralist Thirdonias with
Different Opportunity-Sets

of their neutralism merely from the proportion of total aid received from one of the two contenders for influence (or from the proportion of votes cast in the United Nations General Assembly in line with the wishes of either Usonia or Russonia).

Thus far we have assumed (see Figure 9.1) that the aid-giving behavior of Usonia and Russonia is symmetrical. Naturally this need not be—indeed is not likely to be—the case. An interesting combination results if Usonia exhibits the *NPN* behavior of Figure 9.1*b* and Russonia the *PN* behavior of Figure 9.1*c*. The outcome could well be, as shown in Figure 9.5, that total aid will once again be invariant with respect to Thirdonia's political alignment. If Thirdonia is neutralist and therefore has the *AI*-type preference function, it will now select the political position that will equalize aid from both camps and will therefore tend to take up the political position *P* on Figure 9.5, rather close to Russonia. This situation will be exasperating to Usonia whose contribution to Thirdonia's development equals that of Russonia. As a result, Usonia will now be tempted to imitate Russonia and withdraw to the *PN*-type of aid-giving behavior. This sequence would lead to the unstable *AI-PN* combination we have already discussed. Suppose, however, that instead of Usonia adopting Russonia's be-

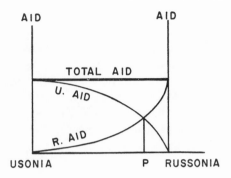

Figure 9.5. Asymmetrical Aid-Giving Behavior

havior, Russonia for some reason goes over to Usonia's *NPN*-type behavior; we would now be back to the stable *NPN-AI* combination, and Thirdonia would assume a truly neutralist position, equidistant from both blocs. The irony would be, in this case, that Russonia's more generous aid-giving policy would have led Thirdonia to move politically away from Russonia.

Another step toward the real world is taken if we allow for multilateral aid agencies or for aid-giving countries other than Usonia and Russonia. Taking the most worrisome unstable case where a neutralist country faces aid-giving behavior that penalizes neutralism (the *AI-PN* combination), it appears that the function of multilateral aid or of aid from countries other than the two superpowers may well be to restore stability by stepping up aid from these sources as Thirdonia moves to neutralist ground. In this way the total aid available to Thirdonia from all three sources of aid could approximate the *NPN* rather than the *PN* shape and stability would be restored. It is conceivable that Usonia and Russonia, realizing the domestic policy constraints under which they operate, find it difficult in their bilateral relations with Thirdonia to adopt anything but the *PN*-type of aid-giving behavior; it would then make good sense for them to foster deliberately multilateral aid or aid from other industrial countries in such a way as to compensate for their inability to make their own bi-

195

lateral aid-giving behavior conform to the requirements of stability.

Finally, it might be tempting to analyze how the behavior of each of our three principal actors is shaped by expectations about that of the other two. But before the resulting complications are explored, it was perhaps worth while to show that a simple static model can account satisfactorily for a variety of real-life situations and can even yield some suggestions for policy.

10. Foreign Aid: A Critique and a Proposal

With Richard M. Bird

Foreign aid is as Janus-faced an institution as can be found. It redistributes income from the rich to the poor and can thus serve to speed the latter's development. At the same time, in a world of sovereign nations foreign aid is an instrument of national policy which can be used by the rich to acquire influence and to increase their power.

While foreign aid might never have come into this world without its appeal to both national and transnational interests, it has also suffered from the resulting ambiguity about its "real" function. Unlike pure power instruments such as national military establishments, on the one hand, or overt redistribution mechanisms like the progressive income tax, on the other, foreign aid has never been firmly institutionalized. It has led a precarious existence, bolstered from time to time by cold war conflicts and then flagging again as immediate dangers passed, or the lack of a "domestic constituency" in the aid-giving countries made itself more strongly felt, or certain unpleasant side effects of aid giving became apparent. Lately signals of a new crisis in aid giving have multiplied in the United States; there is disaffection and disenchantment as well in Western Europe and perhaps in the Soviet Union, and foreign aid is none too popular even in the recipient countries.

The first part of this essay attempts a partial explanation of this state of affairs through a critique of basic concepts underlying present aid programs of the United States as well as some multilateral ones. The second part of the paper discusses an alternative mechanism of transferring aid, which would avoid some of the more conspicuous difficulties that have been encountered. The two parts of the paper are not tightly integrated, however: it is

Reprinted by permission from *Princeton Essays in International Finance*, no. 69, July 1968.

quite possible for a reader to agree with our critique while disagreeing with the proposal, and vice versa.

A CRITIQUE OF PROGRAM AID

Current practice in foreign aid dates from the new principles introduced by the Kennedy administration in the early sixties. Essentially, this country's doctrine moved at that time to embrace what has since become known as the "program approach" to foreign aid.

From Project to Program Aid

The "project approach" had predominated through the fifties. The World Bank had been enjoined by its very statutes to extend loans only on the basis of specific projects (in transportation, power, agriculture, and so forth). The first activity of the United States in the field of aid to underdeveloped countries was technical (Point Four) assistance, which had necessarily a project content and which evolved naturally into capital assistance with a similar content. Important departures from this practice occurred in countries on the periphery of the Soviet bloc. To a number of these countries the United States extended massive military as well as economic assistance, with the latter being usually justified in terms of short-term import or budgetary requirements.

By 1960 criticism of the project approach was widespread. It was easy to show how development depended not on a few specific projects, but on an adequate overall investment effort, with respect to both aggregate size and composition, and how ill-designed fiscal, monetary, and foreign exchange policies could undercut the positive contribution of any individual project to economic growth. Economists further pointed out that the donor country was not really financing the project for which it was ostensibly granting funds, but rather the "marginal" project which the aid recipient would have just given up had he not been handed the additional resources for a project which he probably would have undertaken in any event.[1] For these reasons, so it was

1. For a critique of this view, see Richard M. Bird, "The Influence of Foreign Aid on Local Expenditures," *Social and Economic Studies* 16 (June 1967): 206–10.

argued, a look at the total spending pattern of the recipient country is essential if one wishes to have some assurance that the aid funds are put to productive use. Finally, it was pointed out that project aid necessarily implies a series of biases and perverse incentives: it encourages the aid recipient to prepare large capital projects, to exaggerate the foreign-exchange portion of the total cost of these projects, and to favor public infrastructure projects, which are most easily financed through loans or grants extended from one government to another for project purposes.

While these criticisms of the project approach all contributed to a change in the climate of expert opinion, another important reason for going from project to program aid was the desire to increase the level of aid to some key countries and to provide a solid institutional basis for aid giving at this higher level. Program aid was conceived as aid given "in bulk" on the basis of a general understanding between donor and recipient about the latter's development program and principal economic policies. (Other terms frequently used in connection with program aid are, in ascending order of euphemization, "leverage," "incentive programming," "making sure of self-help.")

As a result of what was then thought to be the model case of India, the accent was at first primarily on achieving agreement on the recipient's development plan, its size, priorities, and the resulting "resources gap" to be filled by aid in its various forms. But, in most developing countries development plans are primarily statements of intention. Further, in the rare country with a highly operational development plan, the fulfillment of the plan's objectives would depend crucially, among other things, on "appropriate" fiscal, monetary, and other economic policies. In Latin America, moreover, program aid under the Alliance for Progress was to be forthcoming not only in connection with a broad agreement on economic development objectives, but was to be premised also on advances in social development that depended on the enactment and implementation of reforms in land tenure, income taxation, educational opportunity, and the like.

The Two Aid Bargains Compared

The general idea of moving from the project to the program

approach consisted, therefore, in laying the groundwork for a substantial and steady flow of aid through a meeting of minds between donor and recipient on central economic programs and policies of the recipient country.

When the matter is put in this way, the formidable difficulties of the program approach begin to appear. No doubt, by moving the discussion between donor and recipient from where to build what kind of power station to fiscal, monetary, or agrarian reform policies, one is turning from peripheral to central issues of the recipient's decisions. But is that a good thing? We shall now argue that this move raises at least as many problems as it solves.

To facilitate the discussion, it is useful to attempt at this point a conceptual distinction between "pure" project and "pure" program aid. In the real world this distinction will of course be blurred, as these two archetypes of aid hardly ever appear in their pure forms. Hence it should be understood that our subsequent discussion does not cover every conceivable case of project or program aid, but tries to catch the essential difference between two diverse forms of aid giving. Moreover, we do not aim at extolling project aid, with whose problems and drawbacks we are familiar, but rather at bringing out, with project aid as a backdrop, the heretofore largely neglected political implications and side effects of program aid.

As a starting point for the discussion, we may imagine that aid is given in the form of a check drawn by the donor to the order of the recipient, without conditions or strings of any kind. This unconditional aid can then turn into conditional aid along two principal routes.

First, the donor can insist that the money be spent for certain specific purposes: the result is pure project aid as here defined. Secondly, the donor may require that the recipient country change some of its ways and policies as a condition for receiving the funds: this is our definition of pure program aid.

From the point of view of the recipient, there is a fundamental difference between the two bargains which may conceivably accompany the transfer of aid funds. Pure project aid forces the recipient country to substitute to some extent the donor's investment preferences for its own insofar as the use of the aid funds is concerned. As a result, the recipient country lands in a situation it senses as inferior to the one in which the same amount of aid would be available unconditionally. Nevertheless, the aid permits the country to achieve a position in which it is unequivocally better off than without aid, in the sense that more funds are forthcoming for some purposes while, generally speaking, investments that the country would have made in the absence of aid will not be curtailed. Thus, the conditions attached to pure project aid are not likely to arouse strong hostility in the recipient country and do not require the policy makers to sacrifice any important objective which they would have been able to pursue in the absence of aid.

The situation changes significantly in the case of the bargain characteristic of pure program aid. The commitment a country undertakes in connection with this type of aid is typically of the following kind: to increase investment and decrease consumption, to increase the share of the private sector and decrease that of the public sector, to devalue the currency and thereby alter relative price relationships within the country, to throttle inflation and therefore strike a blow at the particular interest group whose turn it is to benefit from the next inflationary appropriation, credit expansion, or rise in prices or wages; and so on, and so forth. In all these instances, compliance with the conditions attending program aid makes one group within the recipient country worse and another better off than before. The bargain preceding the granting of program aid also implies that the aid-receiving government will alter its previous policy-mix in such a way as to sacrifice in some measure objective A (say, a larger public sector) to objective B (say, growth).

Economists who have discussed the concept of community welfare have long been divided into two groups: those who deny, and those who affirm, that meaningful statements can be made about increases or decreases in collective welfare when, as a result of economic change, one group gains at the expense of another. There is no need for us to enter into this discussion, except to note that its protracted and stubborn nature testifies to the fundamental difference between the two situations that we have just described. With pure project aid, the recipient government can achieve all of its preaid objectives (plus some additional aid-financed ones) and no group in the country need be any worse off. With the type of conditional program aid discussed here, the objectives of public policies will be reshuffled and some domestic group is likely to be hurt. Even though the total resources available to the country are increased through the aid, the hurt group cannot be directly compensated, at least in the short run, for its loss, by the very terms of the aid agreement.

We should mention here one particularly important way in which project aid shades off in the real world into program aid. When the project donor spends its funds on, say, a certain kind of power station, it will often have views, and will attempt to have them prevail, on such matters as accounting practices, power rates, administrative autonomy, and perhaps even public versus private ownership of the utility. Project aid may then also involve policy changes that would hurt some groups or individuals. Even in this case, however, an important difference between project and program aid remains. Program aid is usually given in connection with changes in central economic policies of the recipient, whereas the policy changes the donor is liable to insist on in connection with project aid are germane to the construction and operation of the project and are therefore likely to be concerned with matters that are at some remove from the central policy concerns around which the more important group conflicts rage.

The Program Aid Bargain Further Considered

It will, of course, be argued that whatever sacrifice is entailed by the policy changes required by the program aid bargain is more than fully compensated by the other side, namely the aid package itself. The fact that aid is accepted on these terms could be considered as evidence that there is nothing to worry about. After all, the recipient government could have refused aid (as Burma did in general, and Brazil and Colombia at one time or another, in connection with assistance from the International

Monetary Fund) if it felt that the conditions were too harsh. But this application of the notion of revealed preference misses several points. In the first place, we were intent on showing the difference between two forms of conditional aid giving and on pointing out that the cost of obtaining aid is of a different nature in the two cases. Secondly, it is a gross oversimplification to treat a government entering the program-type bargain on foreign aid like a consumer buying himself a bag of apples. Since aid, in this case, has as its counterpart a shift in national objectives and in the short-term fortunes of different social groups, the bargain will be considered a bad one by the circles that value highly the objective that has been sacrificed and by those groups whose interests have been hurt. Hence, the very bargain that gives rise to program aid can and will be attacked directly by these circles and groups as being damaging to the national interest as they define it. Pure project aid is ordinarily immune to this kind of destabilizing side effect. Precisely for that reason, those who attack it will often resort to alleging that it is impure and carries some unavowed and excessive cost in terms of general economic or political policy commitments. In other words, to be effective, an attack on project aid will attempt to prove that it is really program-type aid.

The difference between a country or a country's government adopting certain changes in its central economic policies as a quid pro quo for aid and a consumer disbursing cash for a pound of apples goes deeper still. The program aid bargain is effective only if the government is genuinely convinced of the positive value of the policies it has adopted in conjunction with the aid— if there has been, that is, a genuine meeting of minds between donor and recipient about the economic policy measures conducive to development. It is as if the consumer were not only made to hand over the cash, but were asked to positively enjoy this act instead of sensing it as a cost. Moreover, the commitment of the recipient government is ordinarily not just to a single policy action, but to a policy that requires implementation through a practically infinite series of actions. A more correct comparison of the program aid bargain would therefore be to the decision of a person who joins the monastic orders: he does not usually consider his vows of poverty and chastity as a payment for the promise of eternal afterlife, but as something to be valued and perhaps enjoyed directly and independently of that promise.

One matter is already becoming clear: for the commitments entered into in the course of program aid negotiations to be faithfully adhered to, the recipient government ought to be so convinced of the correctness of the policies to which it commits itself that it would have followed these policies even without aid. Paradoxically, therefore, program aid is fully effective only when it does not achieve anything—when, that is, no quid pro quo (in the sense of a policy that would not have been undertaken in the absence of aid) is exacted as the price of aid. (It is ironical that, at least when it is effective, program aid is vulnerable to the very charge that has long been levelled—wrongly, we think—against project aid: namely, that one can never be sure that the project thus financed would not have been undertaken even in the absence of aid.)

In these situations, the donor would set himself the task of rewarding virtue (or rather, what he considers as such) where virtue appears of its own accord.

This is indeed a modest and manageable task, but it is also one that does not usually satisfy the donors. Precisely because the institutional basis and public opinion support of aid are so precarious in the donor country, the proponents and dispensers of aid have quite naturally felt compelled to make extraordinary claims for what aid can accomplish. The most persistent of these claims has been that aid acts as a "catalyst." This term is meant to convey that aid makes the difference between stagnation (or perhaps deterioration) and vigorous economic growth of the recipient country, or between the recipient being hostile and being friendly to the donor country. To these traditional and exaggerated claims for aid, a new variant has been added by the program approach: namely, that aid, properly conditioned, makes the difference between the recipient following the "wrong" and adopting the "right" economic policies.

In this fashion, then, aid is not seen in the role of rewarding virtue, but in the role, infinitely more difficult, of bringing virtue into the world. Now the fact that aid is known to be available *if* certain policies are followed will sometimes serve to strengthen a domestic group genuinely and independently convinced of the correctness of these policies and it is therefore not inconceivable that aid will on occasion help this group to come to power. This is the ideal case in which program aid acts first as a catalyst and then achieves so complete a meeting of minds and so full a sharing of values and objectives between donor and recipient that from then on they will march hand in hand toward a better future.

We have on purpose drawn a caricature, for it is our conviction that this picture of program aid as a catalyst for virtuous policies belongs to the realm of rhapsodic phantasy. At best, situations in which aid helps virtue to triumph in this fashion are the exception rather than the rule. The normal case is far more prosaic: the knowledge that aid is available if certain policies are adopted serves to make these policies more attractive and less costly than they would otherwise be. These policies will therefore often be adopted by aid-hungry governments in spite of continuing doubts of the policy makers themselves, resistance from some quarters within the government, onslaught against the "deal" from the opposition, and general distaste for the whole procedure.

Naturally, doubts and reservations are not voiced at the moment of the aid compact; hence the delusion on the part of the donor that there has been a full meeting of minds. But soon after virtue has been "bought" through aid under these conditions, the reservations and resistances will find some expression—for example, through half-hearted implementation or sabotage of the agreed-to policies—and relations between donor and recipient will promptly deteriorate as a result.

Problems Encountered in Buying Virtue through Aid

It may be argued that once a government has unequivocally committed itself to certain acts as a condition of receiving aid, there is a good chance that it will convince itself that these acts are truly in the national interest even though previously it may not have thought so. Psychologists have developed the theory of "cognitive dissonance" to analyze individual behavior in similar situations. The theory teaches that if a person engages in "discrepant behavior"—in acts, that is, which cannot be reconciled with what he considers to be his beliefs and values—he will attempt to reduce the resulting dissonance by changing his values in such a way that harmony is restored.

However, the theory also stresses another point that is crucial here: if the discrepant behavior is induced by either carrot or stick, there will be far less consequential value change than if the discrepant behavior occurs in some accidental, absentminded, or experimental fashion. If the behavior is rewarded (as it is, in our case, by the granting of aid), dissonance hardly arises, because, in accounting for his behavior to himself, the actor has a ready explanation and excuse for the fact that he did something contrary to his principles, opinions, or preferences. (For the same reason, declarations of support for a cause against which one has previously fought are unlikely to change a subject's prior beliefs when such declarations are exacted under torture.) Therefore, the very act of rewarding policy changes through aid undermines the determination with which these changes will be carried out and makes backsliding and sabotage more likely.

These considerations explain why certain types of policy commitments on the part of aid-receiving countries are more workable—and therefore have turned out to be more popular with the donors than others. The more workable and more popular commitments are precisely those that are highly visible, verifiable, measurable and, at their best, irreversible. One thinks of a revision of the customs tariff, of the imposition of credit restrictions in order to curb inflation, or, most typically perhaps, of a devaluation. In the latter case, there would seem to be little possibility of backsliding or of second thoughts. Yet, while devaluation cannot be retracted, its intended effects can usually be frustrated by subsequent monetary, fiscal, and wage-price policies. Hence, even in the case of devaluation, a government which harbors a feeling that it has been pushed into an unwise policy can often administer an "I-told-you-so" lesson to the donor just by omitting to carry out certain complementary policies after the devaluation.

In the case of other economic or social policies that sometimes have stood in the center of aid negotiations, the continued psychological resistance of the aid recipients to such policies after a formal compact has been sealed can manifest itself more directly and easily. Whether the aid negotiations were concerned with enlarging the private sector of the economy or with establishing the basis for a land reform, the commitments a government has undertaken in these areas can be rendered inoperative through bureaucratic harassment or through lack of administrative energy, respectively. The old Spanish colonial adage *"se acata pero no se cumple"* (one obeys but one does not comply) will thus be widely practiced once again, and properly so. A country which permits its key economic policies to be determined by this type of international negotiation finds itself in fact in a semicolonial situation and is likely to adopt all the time-honored methods of stealthy and indirect resistance appropriate to that situation.

The fact that certain commitments have less latitude in implementation and are therefore less prone to sabotage than others has naturally led to a preference of aid negotiators for these types of commitments. In this way we can explain the increasing tendency to make program aid depend on the taking of specific monetary and exchange rate measures and on the "appropriate" behavior of certain fiscal and monetary indicators, while less and less attention is paid to economic growth and social justice, supposedly the principal objectives of aid.

The Hidden Costs of Program Aid

The resistance of the recipient country to some of the policy commitments it has underwritten in the course of the aid negotiations is not the whole story. The general unhappiness about having had its arm twisted can find other outlets than backsliding on these same commitments.

In a simple model of international relations we may assume that, for the sake of independence, self-respect, and defense against accusations of being a satellite, the government of B, a poor country, is determined to maintain a certain average distance from country A, a great power and a potential donor. Country B measures this distance along two dimensions, the extent to which it adopts economic policies suggested by A and the extent to which it takes A's position on the leading issues of international politics. Under these conditions, a success on the part of the great power in having B "do the right thing" in economic policy will result in a strong urge on the part of B to compensate for this move in the direction of A by a move in the opposite direction in international politics. Only in this fashion can the desired average distance be maintained. That this model of international behavior is not completely unrealistic, in spite of its simplicity, can be shown by recalling a few episodes of the recent past: the attempt of the Quadros government in Brazil to move in the direction of a strongly neutralist posture in international relations after having adopted economic policies long advocated by the United States and the International Monetary Fund; to some extent, Pakistan's rapprochement with China; and, lately, a number of "surprising" foreign policy positions taken by the present Indian government just after it had finally been so "reasonable" in its decisions on domestic economic policy.

In this manner, a "successful" program aid negotiation in the course of which the recipient agrees to a variety of economic policies suggested by the donor may well have hidden, though considerable, costs: first, a direct cost to the donor in terms of the loss of certain diplomatic and foreign policy supports he thought doubly secure because of the aid extended; secondly, a serious loss of public support for the aid program in the donor country, as a result of what will be felt as ingratitude, hostility, and "irresponsible antics" on the part of the recipient. In this indirect fashion, the attempt at maximizing the productivity of aid by exercising "leverage" involves the risk of drying up the flow of aid at its very source.

Other Frictions Created by the Program Approach

Our case can be further bolstered by important differences between project and program aid related to the diplomacy of the aid process. Consider first the donor's claim to have his advice taken seriously on the ground that he contributes substantial resources. This claim is strong in the case of projects, where the donor's contribution often amounts to one-half or more of the total cost of the project. It is much weaker in the case of program aid, for here the donor's contribution is measured against the recipient country's national product or, at best, its total investment or imports. In such comparisons, the aid effort is almost always likely to look disproportionately small in relation to the important changes in national economic policies that are being sought.

Next, we may examine the donor country's implied claim that its own judgment is superior to that of the recipient. In the case of projects financed by the donor, the justification and credibility of the claim is usually quite strong. The donor country is likely to know more about the construction of highways and power stations than the recipient, simply because it is economically more advanced and has specialized knowledge in the areas in which it stands ready to finance projects. When it comes to appropriate economic policies to foster growth along with price stability and an acceptable distribution of income, the claim of the donor country to superiority is far more questionable. Frequently the donor country itself is far from having fully solved these very problems. Even if it has done better at them than the aid recipient, the applicability of its experience to the wholly different economic, social, historical, and political circumstances of another country must be much in doubt. The claim to superior knowledge is therefore fairly credible and innocuous in the case of project aid. It is not credible in the case of program aid—indeed, it is profoundly irritating.

The diplomacy of aid is even more directly involved in our final point. It is in the nature of the aid relationship that comparatively low-level officials of the donor country are paired off in aid negotiations with high-level officials of the recipient countries. This irksome difference in levels is far less pronounced in the case of project aid than program aid. In discussing the layout and specifications of a highway, an engineer of an aid mission or of the World Bank may perhaps exchange arguments at one point with the director of the highway agency of the aid-receiving country. But the matters discussed in conjunction with program aid relate, as we have seen, to central economic policies and issues. Given the centralization of decision making and the thinness of the elite in the typical aid-receiving country, these matters can ordinarily be decided only at the very top of the political structure, by the president and his minister of finance. And who are their counterparts around the negotiating table? At best, the director of the local aid mission and, usually, various mission staff members. In this way, program aid recreates a typical colonial situation in which the rulers of the recipient country have to deal as equals with, and often feel that they have to take orders from, persons who, within their own country, are miles away from the seat of power. There is no need to expand on the resentment created by this situation.

Recapitulation and Some Recommendations

These, then, are some of the disadvantages of the program approach to foreign aid. To recapitulate: the program approach will accentuate old and create new discord within the recipient country and it will erode the government's support; it will lead to attempts at backsliding and reneging on the commitments that have been entered into; it will have a hidden cost for the donor and will diminish public support for aid programs in the donor countries as it impels the recipient to assert his independence by moving away from the donor in areas not covered by the aid agreement; and the negotiations leading to program aid will prove highly irritating to the recipient, both because he will not recognize the claim of the donor to superior knowledge of the questions that are typically the subject of program aid negotiations and because the gap in the respective levels or ranks of those who do the actual negotiating between donor and recipient is painfully wide.

After this indictment of program aid, is there anything good to be said about it? Certainly there is. The main virtue of program aid has been to permit, in the early sixties, a considerable increase in the volume of aid extended to a number of countries. Two questions therefore arise. First, is it possible to change the practice of program aid in such a way as to avoid some of its more unpleasant side effects? Secondly, and more ambitiously, is it possible to go beyond both the limitations of project aid and the liabilities of program aid, and devise a wholly new approach? This question will be taken up in the next section.

The answer to the first question is not particularly difficult. The very analysis of the program approach that we have given yields a partial remedy; for, if the policy makers were fully aware of the political side effects of aid giving under the program approach, they would become more circumspect in its use.

Some specific recommendations also emerge from the preceding pages. Since, in our opinion, the program approach overreaches itself when it attempts grandiosely to bring virtue into the world, the explicit or implicit conditioning of aid on changes in policies of the recipient countries should be avoided. This does not mean that the donor cannot make his opinions and preferences known; but it does imply that elaborate arrangements should be made to divorce the exchange of opinions about suitable economic policies from the actual aid-giving process. The educational virtues of such discussions will be strengthened rather than weakened as a result. Finally, the donor should resist the temptation to measure "performance" of the recipient at frequent intervals by narrow quantitative indicators, when by its very nature such performance can be assessed properly only over a relatively long period of time by a combination of quantitative information and qualitative judgment.

AN ALTERNATIVE MECHANISM FOR FOREIGN AID

In spite of these possible avenues of improvement of current practices, the present aid-giving processes are sufficiently defective to warrant a search for new techniques—however utopian they may appear at first sight. To our minds, the basic requirements of a satisfactory aid technique are three in number: (1) it should permit the transfer of a substantial volume of funds to the poor countries, (2) it should not be tied systematically to the achievement of a meeting of minds on central economic policy decisions

211

of the recipient countries, and (3) it should still exert pressure toward the efficient use of the resources that are provided.

We shall now discuss a scheme that gives promise of satisfying these conditions and would have two important additional merits. First, it would place international development more on a people-to-people basis and thereby rekindle public interest in it. Secondly, it would institutionalize more openly and firmly than heretofore the redistribution of world income from the rich to the poor countries.

Like any new scheme, the one to be described here is replete with uncertainties and difficulties. Fortunately it lends itself to being introduced gradually and it could therefore initially supplement rather than replace existing resource flows. Once perfected in one country as a result of experience, the proposed alternative mechanism for transferring aid might largely supersede current bilateral programs and might also spread to other donor countries.

The essence of the plan is to involve the individual taxpayer of the donor countries in the foreign aid program. Instead of paying taxes for a package of government expenditures that includes foreign aid together with all domestic programs, taxpayers could elect to use a limited portion of their income tax obligation for contributions to one or several World Development Funds. These funds would not be administered by any government and would channel financial assistance to various investors, public and private, in developing countries.

For their "contribution to foreign aid" the taxpayers would receive a full tax credit from the Internal Revenue Service. Such a tax credit would require legislation, but not on an annual basis. In the last resort, the government would of course still be the donor to developing countries, in that its tax revenue would be reduced by the amounts that individual taxpayers were earmarking for foreign aid, but the resulting funds would not belong to the government and their allocation and uses—and, to some extent, their amount—would no longer be determined by it.

Before turning to the details of the scheme, a brief justification for handling national expenditures for foreign aid so differently from expenditures for all other purposes is in order. A national decision to extend financial assistance to developing countries

must necessarily be made by the established constitutional processes of each donor country and its implementation requires
action by existing national fiscal authorities. At the same time,
the foreign aid decision must be interpreted as the assumption, on
the part of the donor country and its citizens, of an obligation to
contribute to world development. But this intent of the foreign aid
decision stands in great danger of being jeopardized and per-
verted if the resulting funds are administered by donor-country
governments. Our discussion of program aid is suggestive in this
respect. Foreign aid that is supposed to transfer income from the
rich to the poor countries becomes all too easily, when it is administered by national governments, an instrument through which
the rich impose their will on the poor! The possibility and even
likelihood of this unfortunate mutation is a risk peculiar to foreign
aid expenditures, and strong institutional safeguards against it
are required. Here lies the basic justification for the break with
traditional canons of fiscal policy that is implicit in our tax
credit proposal. (The establishment of multilateral agencies such
as the World Bank has been one response to the need for moving
away from the extension of development aid by national governments, but the response has not fully met the need, both because
of the limited funds these institutions command and because they
depend entirely and directly on governmental contributions.)

The following discussion first outlines the basic mechanism of
tax credits and then treats the difficult problem of efficiently allocating the funds thus obtained.[2] Finally, some possible objections
to the scheme are considered, and it is contrasted to earlier tax
incentive proposals. At this stage, the proposal is necessarily quite
tentative. We have tried, nevertheless, to be concrete and specific,
primarily to explore the feasibility of the idea and to invite further
discussion.

The Tax Credit

In more detail, the tax credit mechanism might work somewhat as follows. Individual taxpayers could claim a full tax credit

2. The tax credit mechanism and a number of the other points made
here were suggested by the remarkable effectiveness of a somewhat similar
Brazilian scheme for regional development. See chap. 4 above.

for their foreign aid contributions, up to 5 per cent of their federal income tax or $10,000, whichever is smaller. A hypothetical average taxpayer with an adjusted gross income of $16,000 and a tax liability of $2,030 could, for example, obtain a tax credit of $102 under this scheme. The claim for credit would have to be substantiated by a receipt from the depository bank or other satisfactory documentation. The limits of 5 per cent and $10,000, while arbitrary, are designed to eliminate the possibility of undue influence by wealthy individuals on the operations of the development funds proposed below, and to hold the potential cost of the scheme to the treasury to reasonable dimensions. Corporations would not be eligible for this credit for similar reasons, the danger or suspicion of "private imperialism" being particularly acute in their case.

From *Statistics of Income* data it may be crudely estimated that the maximum amount that could have been made available for development in this way in 1965 was about $2.3 billion, compared with actual public economic assistance from the United States in the fiscal year 1966 of about $2.5 billion. Since incomes are now higher and aid lower, the potential of the tax credit scheme would at present be in excess of current aid levels. The important question of the probable actual yield of this incentive will be taken up later.

Return to the Investor

Apart from the psychic satisfaction of helping the poor of the world become less poor, the benefits which an individual might get from taking part in this scheme should be narrowly limited. For every $100 (or other round figure) deposited, the taxpayer would receive a "Share in Development." To avoid complications, this document should not be a marketable asset. The possibility may be held out, however, for such shares to earn a small return, on the order of $2\frac{1}{2}$ per cent a year for 40 years, until the face value of the "loan" is fully repaid. Whether or not this return is actually received would depend on the nature of the use made of the funds on average, as discussed below. Any such return would presumably be taxable as normal income to the taxpayer.

214

Another possibility might be to introduce a lottery feature with some such prize as a tourist trip to the less developed country or countries of the winner's choice.

Uncertain and small as these incentives would be, they should serve to make the tax credit option a preferred alternative to simply paying taxes. Their primary purpose is to maintain the interest and involvement of taxpayers in the progress of the less developed world without imposing serious service and transfer problems on the recipient countries.

How to Channel the Funds

One can envisage various ways in which the funds provided by the tax credit mechanism might flow to less developed countries from the United States or from any other developed countries that might adopt this idea. At one extreme, all the tax credit funds might be remitted by the depository banks to a single World Development Fund, which would then allocate them to different activities in different countries. This alternative does not attract us at all, since such a single fund would surely be tempted once again to influence the central economic policies of recipient countries and to engage in the leverage practices which have been criticized above.

At another extreme, every individual investor might search out some qualifying activity in some less developed country into which he would like to put his money. While the option of doing this might well be kept open (given the limits on the tax credit, the possibilities of abuse are negligible), it would clearly be impossible for most of those potentially affected by the tax credit to behave in this way. Nor would it necessarily be desirable, even if they could do so, for those activities in which individuals would prefer to put their money as investors are often very different from those which they would wish to finance to promote world development. Some compromise is needed to avoid monolithic bureaucracy, on the one hand, and self-centered individualism, on the other.

One possibility is for the funds to be channeled in some proportions (which could be reconsidered at periodic intervals) to special sections of the existing multilateral organizations, such as the World Bank and its affiliates, the Inter-American Development Bank, and the other regional banks now in the process of formation. This solution would have the advantage of avoiding the setting up of a new bureaucracy, but there is some question about channeling all available funds to these far from infallible international agencies.

Partly for this reason and partly to explore the possibilities of still more decentralized aid giving, we shall discuss here an alternative: to set up a number (say ten) of independent private organizations called "Development Funds" as agents for disbursing the funds collected through the tax credit. Each Fund would be managed by a small professional and administrative staff. Recruitment would be on an international basis from the considerable body of those in both private and public sectors, in both poor and rich countries, who now have relevant experience in the problems of investment and development.

The principal aim of these Funds would simply be to transfer available funds as quickly and as efficiently as possible to less developed countries. (In the event that the Funds could not invest the amounts provided by the tax credit within, say, three years, the money could revert to the treasury. This three-year rule applies in the Brazilian scheme for the development of the Northeast.) The rules outlined below would offer some guidance in this task, but the main test of success would, in the nature of the operation, have to be something as vague and general as the approval of the board of directors of the Fund. Each Fund might have a separate board of six to eight members, or there might be one general advisory board of sixteen to twenty members for all the Funds. In either case, at least half the membership of the board (or boards) should consist of citizens of less developed countries. No one country should have a majority on any board. The board members would serve in their private capacity and not as representatives of any country or organization. These stipulations are designed to emphasize the international and nongovernmental character of the Funds and to permit drawing as widely as possible on world competence in guiding their operations. How these boards and the Fund managements might be initially constituted and perpetuated is a matter for further study.

Some Operating Rules

The main restriction imposed on the investment policy of the Funds is that any project in which they invest should be partially financed by someone else. The required complementary investor (or investors) might be a local private entrepreneur, a local development bank, the government or a public enterprise, and perhaps also some other international lending agency, or any combination of these.

The requirement that someone else be willing to put up some of his own money for the project in question (probably a specified percentage of the total cost) is crucial to ensure efficient use of funds and to prevent the recipient country's considering the cost of capital to be zero. The percentage of the matching requirement might vary with the country: it might well be set at a lower level for the poorer countries. (In setting such general, though flexible, rules some of the economic criteria derived from the experience of present aid giving agencies might prove very useful.)

It deserves emphasis that the Funds would be institutionally neutral. The degree of their involvement in a country's economic life should not be affected by the way in which that country chooses to draw the borderline between the public and private sectors. The only generally unacceptable partners would be private foreign enterprises and bilateral lending agencies, although there could be exceptions even to this rule, particularly when it is clear that principal ownership and control rest in local hands.

Should the Funds be restricted to the financing of a limited list of certain "productive" or "essential" activities? For a number of reasons, we do not think so. It is up to the recipient countries to determine whether they want to be permissive or restrictive in this respect. Every sovereign country will evidently be able to restrict the access of its nationals to the Development Funds in any way it sees fit and the Funds should be left to use their best judgment, within those limits, without further direction.

The financing provided by the Funds should be flexible—equity, medium-term, or long-term loans, or a combination of these. For non-revenue-producing projects in the public sector the terms might be very soft—for example, a fifty-year loan, with a

217

ten-year grace period and a 2 per cent interest rate. For normally revenue-producing projects, public or private, the terms should be correspondingly harder both to encourage them to produce revenue in actual practice and to provide financing for other activities in the future.

Return Flow

Depending on the nature of the investment, payment of interest, principal, and dividends could be stipulated either in convertible or in local currencies. As most developing countries are at present either too debt-ridden or too poor to shoulder large additional amounts of international indebtedness, the net return flow stemming from the Funds' investments should be strictly limited. Some small inflow of foreign exchange from successful projects would be desirable to cover the administrative expenses of the Funds, and, as noted above, to enable them to pay out a small return of capital to the original individual "investors." Any such repayment to investors would depend on the average return to the Funds, since one taxpayer's money would not be distinguishable from another's. The backflow of dollars from past investments should not normally exceed that needed for these purposes, but if it did so occasionally it would provide a useful reserve and supplement to the ordinary resources of the Funds.

Since the Funds are conceived primarily as channels and should not end up controlling or owning enterprises in the less developed countries, even the payment of dividends, interest, and amortization in local currency requires careful consideration. One suggestion with merit is that the original individual investor might be allowed to designate his favorite charity or other nonprofit organization in the developing country as the recipient of such funds. This would, however, require too much cumbersome tagging of funds with individual names. An alternative proposal along similar lines is that each recipient country would designate or set up one or several nonprofit organizations which, on approval of the Development Fund concerned, would receive any repayments, stock sale proceeds, or profits and disburse such monies to worthy activities. This feature would offset to some extent the bias toward investment in revenue-producing activities in the private sector that might perhaps be considered inherent in the scheme, no matter how much the Development Funds might be directed to maximize economic development, rather than financial returns alone.

Fund investments in equity require special consideration. Again to avoid permanent entanglement of the Funds in the recipient countries' affairs, all such investment could be in nonvoting stock (as is the present practice of the International Finance Corporation) and one could require the Funds to turn over any such equity after a period of, say, ten years to the nonprofit organizations just referred to.

Competition and Coordination

The purpose of creating ten or twelve Funds instead of one is to encourage diversity and competition. It would therefore be best not to assign certain countries or groups of countries or certain types of investments to one Fund rather than another. In time, of course, one might expect the different Funds to acquire their particular areas of competence both regionally and functionally, but there seems no reason to specify in advance what these areas should be. Nevertheless, a few general rules in this regard might be useful to avoid undue concentration or neglect. For example, it might be specified that no Fund could have more than 50 per cent of its total investment in any country or type of activity. In general, more than one Fund could invest in the same country or the same activity. Such overlapping would in our view be something to be desired, both to increase the bargaining power of the poor countries, and to stimulate multiple approaches to the solution of the development problem.

Initially the monies collected under the tax credit scheme could be divided equally among the various Development Funds, but one could gradually relax this automatic distribution as the Funds began operating and building a distinctive record and personality on the basis of which each would appeal to the taxpayers. In view of the limited monetary return, the ensuing competition for the taxpayers' contributions would take place on the basis of the overall development performance of the Funds. Such competition would act as a spur to efficiency and would encourage a continuing search for better development strategies. Because the taxpayers would have to decide which Fund or Funds to favor, the competition would also serve to enhance and keep up the taxpayers' interest in the development process.

It may be hoped that, as a result of competition among the less developed countries, each will secure a "fair" share of the total funds available. This competition among recipients is another element of efficiency built into the scheme. Whatever the ensuing distribution of aid funds, it is quite unlikely to be as irrational, from the point of view of economic development, as it has been in actual practice over the past twenty years, when we have had central coordination over the distribution of bilateral aid granted by the United States and when Korea, Taiwan, Jordan, and Greece have been our overwhelming favorites, on a per capita basis. Nevertheless, some corrective mechanism ought to be available in case a country or group of countries, say, India and Pakistan, should be unduly neglected. In such case, it might be desirable for a central advisory board to suggest or direct that the taxpayer-investor should favor those Funds that specialize in South Asia or, alternatively, that each Fund should increase its outflow to India and Pakistan. (It is because of this eventuality that the initial choice of taxpayers about the Fund to which their money should go, while a useful device for encouraging participation and recognizing successful operation, cannot be binding.)

Another problem on which some central guidance may be needed relates to the point in time at which a heretofore aid-receiving country will have done so well that it should no longer have access to the special financial resources dispensed by the Funds. The managers of the individual Funds, interested in displaying a good performance, may want to keep such countries indefinitely among their clients. There may thus be some limited functions which should be handled by a central advisory board.

Parallels and Problems

Our scheme can be better understood by comparing it with other types of international capital movements and other types of tax credit arrangements. It is clear that we have created a hybrid between public and private capital movements. To some extent, the proposal could be considered an attempt to revive private portfolio investment—with the important difference that the source of the investment funds is public tax monies rather than private savings. Do we then have here a throwback to the "private profit at public expense" arrangement that characterized the guaranteed Indian railway bonds of the nineteenth century? Not really, since we have narrowly circumscribed the potential return to the private investors from their tax savings. In this fashion, we avoid in general the principal economic drawbacks of portfolio investment: the insistence of the investors on a high, fixed rate of return and the resulting periodic inability of the borrowing countries to service their debts. In our scheme, the investor will be grateful for even a minimal return since the opportunity cost of his investment is zero.

The activities of the Development Funds will have something in common with those of the World Bank, the International Finance Corporation, and the Inter-American Development Bank, but might perhaps be modeled more closely along the lines of such private organizations as ADELA (Atlantic Community Development Group for Latin America) and Edge Act financing corporations like the Chase International Investment Corporation. We are suggesting a great expansion in this kind of activity, funded by the tax credit option and oriented toward both the private and public sectors of the developing countries. An important difference from all these institutions is not only the source of the funds, but our plan to have the Development Funds function purely as one-time channels. There would be no return flow from interest, dividends, repayments, or stock sale proceeds beyond the sums needed for administration and for the limited (and uncertain) return to investors. In this fashion, all investments made by the Funds would eventually come to be locally owned and controlled.

The scheme could be criticized on the ground that, unlike direct investment, it does not provide for the transfer of managerial and technical skills along with the investment funds. The fact is, however, that such skills are already widely available through international technical assistance, management contracts, copro-duction schemes, and similar institutional arrangements. Recourse to such arrangements would be further stimulated and the skills of private enterprise and management would be amply drawn upon, if the scheme were adopted.

The proposed tax credit goes far beyond any tax incentives to investment in less developed countries presently available in the United States. A number of provisions in the present tax law have been advertised as such incentives. Present tax provisions do in fact place direct investment by American firms in less developed countries on a slightly more favorable basis than direct invest-ment by such firms in more developed countries. As a rule, how-ever, investment in the United States is even more favored because of the 7 per cent investment credit. (The major exceptions to this statement are those investors who can take advantage of the low tax rate applicable to Western Hemisphere trade corporations or of the privilege of tax deferral through tax haven subsidiaries.) Proposals to extend the investment credit to investment in devel-oping countries would simply put such investment on an equal footing with domestic investment in the United States. This is hardly a positive incentive policy, especially when, as is now ap-parently the preferred approach, the credit is to be extended country-by-country on a tax treaty basis rather than by statute, as with domestic investment.

The most generous tax incentive that has been seriously, though fruitlessly, discussed, a 30 per cent investment credit, would ad-mittedly constitute real favoritism at last. But favoritism to what? To *direct* investment by *American* firms—or to precisely the kind of foreign investment that carries with it all too often a set of problems and opportunities for friction at least as formidable as those accompanying program aid. Our proposal avoids these diffi-culties, as well as the need for recipients of the tax benefit them-selves to hunt down favorable investment opportunities. For these reasons, the proposad tax credit to individuals is totally different from anything that is now in the tax law or that has been con-templated.

Like all tax incentives, our proposal constitutes, of course, a special favoritism to certain activities, but we submit that it is an unneutrality as worthy as fostering private charities, probably more so than many tax-exempt foundations, and certainly more so than percentage depletion in the oil industry. The increased rigidity of budgetary policy implicit in any fiscal measure of this kind could be reduced, if desired, by making the percentage credit in any year variable between appropriate upper and lower limits, say, 3 and 8 per cent. A more basic justification for the special fiscal treatment of foreign aid implicit in our scheme has already been given at the beginning of this section.

Another traditional objection to tax incentives, and a harder one to answer, is that they are usually ineffective. We have no secure basis for estimating the probable flow of funds resulting from this proposal, or the cost to the treasury. For reasons suggested above, it would probably be greater than that under the other tax incentive proposals mentioned, which simply means it would be more effective in achieving the supposed aim. Most of those who bothered to take this option would probably be relatively well-to-do people, but this is hardly an objection, since it means the funding of the program would be more progressive in its incidence than that of the usual aid program. If we assume that the limits suggested above (5 per cent of the income tax, or $10,000) were adopted and that all of those with adjusted gross incomes of over $10,000 took advantage of the tax credit, the potential funding from this source in 1965 would have been on the order of $1.5 billion, but this is only the crudest of guesses. One might expect the initial amount available to be relatively small and to grow with time and success.

Despite all the points requiring further thought, it perhaps deserves reiteration that the proposed scheme avoids the problems of grappling with the "central issues" of economic policy and the consequent detailed interference in domestic economic policies of recipient countries that so mars the present public programs of foreign aid. It also avoids most of the traditional objections to increased reliance on foreign investment, primarily because there is no question of increased foreign "control" either by American corporations or by the U.S. government, nor even by the proposed Development Funds themselves. The scheme may seem overgenerous to the developing countries. For the reasons given in the first part of this paper, however, we are convinced that such generosity is in the best interests of the aid-giving countries themselves.

One most desirable side effect might be felt immediately as a result of a trial adoption. Considering the small and uncertain return the taxpayer might expect, we would have, for the first time, a concrete indication of how many people in the United States care enough about foreign aid to be willing explicitly to divert some of their tax dollars to it. Our initial assumption is that more aid is a good thing. This proposal would, if nothing else, enable us to know how many poeple agree with us.

11. How to Divest in Latin America, and Why

The President, in 1940, [recounted] that when he had visited Rio de Janeiro in 1936, President Getulio Vargas had told him that the bus lines in the capital were owned in Montreal and Toronto, and had asked: "What would the people of New York City do if the subways were all owned in Canada?" Roosevelt's reply had been: "Why, there would be a revolution." The President went on to say that he thought that, when foreign capital went into a Latin American country, the country should gain control of the utility or other business after the investment had been paid off in a period that might be set at twenty-five or thirty years. Thus, the country could look forward to gaining ultimate control of utilities and perhaps other foreign-financed corporations through having what Roosevelt called "an option on the equity."

—Bryce Wood

The dispute between Peru and the United States over the expropriation of the International Petroleum Company is only one of a monotonously long list of incidents and conflicts which call into serious question the wisdom of present institutional arrangements concerning private international investment. This paper will discuss the principal weaknesses of these arrangements, with particular emphasis on political economy rather than on economics proper, and will then survey a number of ways in which current institutions and practices could be restructured. It is written against the backdrop of rising nationalism and militancy in the developing countries, particularly in Latin America, and of an astounding complacency, inertia, and lack of institutional imagination on the part of the rich countries.

The basic position adopted here with respect to foreign private

Reprinted by permission from *Princeton Essays in International Finance*, no. 76, November 1969. The opening quotation comes from *The Making of the Good Neighbor Policy* (New York: Columbia University Press, 1961), pp. 358–59.

investment is that it shares to a very high degree the ambiguity of most human inventions and institutions: it has considerable potential for both good and evil. On the one hand, there are the celebrated and undoubted contributions of private international investment to development: the bringing in of capital, entrepreneurship, technology, management and other skills, and of international market connections, all of which are either wholly lacking in the poor countries, or are in inadequate supply given the opportunities and programs for economic development. On the other hand, foreign investment brings not only the dangers of economic plunder and political domination which are the stock-in-trade of the various theories of imperialism, but a number of other, more subtle, yet serious effects and side effects which can handicap the development efforts of countries placing prolonged and substantial reliance on private investment from abroad. The picture that has sometimes been painted of the career of foreign investment is that at one time, long ago, the negative aspects predominated: there was sheer exploitation of human and natural resources as well as crude power play in the early free-wheeling days, when capital followed the flag or was, on the contrary, the "cat's paw of empire"; but this unfortunate phase has been outgrown, so it is widely thought, with decolonization, with the worldwide assertion of national sovereign states and their taxing powers, and with the desire, on the part of modern foreign investors, to perform as "good corporate citizens" of the host country and as "partners in progress." Unfortunately, this edifying story of human progress is incomplete and one-sided. It can, in fact, be argued that certain negative aspects of foreign investment do not only continue to coexist with the positive ones, but typically tend to predominate over them as development proceeds, at least up to some point. These are the just-mentioned "more subtle" effects and side effects that will now be briefly explained.

PRIVATE FOREIGN INVESTMENT—AN INCREASINGLY MIXED BLESSING

The positive contribution of foreign investment to an economy can be of various kinds. In the first place, it can supply one of several missing factors of production (capital, entrepreneurship, management, and so forth), factors, that is, which are simply and indisputably not to be found in the country receiving the investment. This is the situation often prevailing in the earliest stages of development of a poor country. More generally, foreign investment can make it possible for output to increase sharply, because it provides the recipient economy with a larger quantity of comparatively scarce (if not entirely missing) inputs.

Another contribution of foreign investment, conspicuous in relations among advanced industrial countries and inviting often a two-way flow, is of a rather different nature: it can have a teaching function and serve to improve the quality of the local factors of production. By on-the-spot example and through competitive pressures, foreign investment can act as a spur to the general efficiency of local enterprise. This effect is likely to be particularly important in economic sectors which are sheltered from the competition of merchandise imports from abroad. Such sectors (services, industries with strong locational advantages) appear to expand rapidly at advanced stages of economic development. If foreign investment is successful in enhancing the quality of local enterprise, then its inflow will be providentially self-limiting: once the local business community achieves greater efficiency, there will be fewer openings for the demonstration of superior foreign techniques, management, and know-how. But what if local businessmen, faced with overwhelming advantages of their foreign competitors, do not respond with adequate vigor and, instead, deteriorate further or sell out? This is, of course, the nub of recent European fears of the "American challenge." I cannot deal here with this problem, but the fact that it exists has interesting implications for the topic at hand.

If foreign investment can fail to improve and may even harm the quality of local factors of production, then the question arises whether it may also, under certain circumstances, lead to a decrease in the quantity of local inputs available to an economy. In other words, could the inflow of foreign investment stunt what might otherwise be vigorous local development of the so-called missing or scarce factors of production?

This question has been little discussed.[1] The reason for the neglect lies in the intellectual tradition which treats international investment under the rubric "export of capital." As long as one thinks in terms of this single factor of production being exported to a capital-poor country, it is natural to view it as highly complementary to various local factors—such as natural resources and labor—that are available in abundance and are only waiting to be combined with the "missing factor" to yield large additional outputs. But, for a long time now, foreign investors have prided themselves on contributing "not just capital," but a whole bundle of other valuable inputs. In counterpart to these claims, however, the doubt might have arisen that some components of the bundle will no longer be purely complementary to local factors, but will be competitive with them and could cause them to wither or retard and even prevent their growth.

The possibility, and indeed likelihood, that international trade will lead to the shrinkage and possibly to the disappearance of certain lines of local production as a result of cheaper imports has been at the root of international trade theory since Adam Smith and Ricardo. This effect of trade has been celebrated by free traders through such terms as "international specialization" and "efficient reallocation of resources." The opponents of free trade have often pointed out that for a variety of reasons it is imprudent and harmful for a country to become specialized along certain product lines in accordance with the dictates of comparative advantage. Whatever the merit of these critical arguments, they would certainly acquire overwhelming weight if the question arose whether a country should allow itself to become specialized not just along certain commodity lines, but along factor-of-production lines. Very few countries would ever consciously wish to specialize in unskilled labor, while foreigners with a comparative advantage in entrepreneurship, management, skilled labor, and

1. Important exceptions are the articles by J. Knapp, "Capital Exports and Growth," *Economic Journal* 67 (September 1957): 432–44, and by Felipe Pazos, "The Role of International Movements of Private Capital in Promoting Development," in John H. Adler, ed., *Capital Movements and Economic Development* (New York: St. Martin's Press, 1967).

capital took over these functions, replacing inferior "local talent." But this is precisely the direction in which events can move when international investment, proudly bringing in its bundle of factors, has unimpeded access to developing countries. In the fine paradoxical formulation of Felipe Pazos: "The main weakness of direct investment as a development agent is a consequence of the complete character of its contribution."[2]

The displacement of local factors and stunting of local abilities which can occur in the wake of international investment is sometimes absolute, as when local banks or businesses are bought out by foreign capital; this has in fact been happening recently with increasing frequency in Latin America. But the more common and perhaps more dangerous, because less noticeable, stunting effect is relative to what might have happened in the absence of the investment.

As already mentioned, foreign investment can be at its creative best by bringing in "missing" factors of production, complementary to those available locally, in the early stages of development of a poor country. The possibility that it will play a stunting role arises later on, when the poor country has begun to generate, to a large extent no doubt because of the prior injection of foreign investment, its own entrepreneurs, technicians, and savers and could now do even more along these lines if it were not for the institutional inertia that makes for a continued importing of so-called scarce factors of production which have become potentially dispensable. It is, of course, exceedingly difficult to judge at what point in time foreign investment changes in this fashion from a stimulant of development into a retarding influence, particularly since during the latter stage its contribution is still ostensibly positive—for example, the foreign capital that comes in is visible

2. Pazos, "International Movements of Private Capital," p. 196. A. K. Cairncross expresses the same thought in discussing the contribution of foreign-owned branch plants and subsidiaries to economic development: "Their very power to break all the bottlenecks at once . . . can be, from the point of view of the host country, their most damning feature" (*Factors in Economic Development* [London: George Allen and Unwin, 1962], p. 181).

and measurable, in contrast to the domestic capital that might have been generated in its stead. One can never be certain, moreover, that restrictions against foreign investment will in fact call forth the local entrepreneurial, managerial, technological, and saving performances which are believed to be held back and waiting in the wings to take over from the foreign investors. Nevertheless, a considerable body of evidence, brought forth less by design than by accidents such as wars, depressions, nationalist expropriations, and international sanctions, suggests strongly that, after an initial period of development, the domestic supply of routinely imported factors of production is far more elastic than is ever suspected under business-as-usual conditions. If this is so, then the "climate for foreign investment" ought to turn from attractive at an early stage of development to much less inviting in some middle stretch—in which most of Latin America finds itself at the present time.

The preceding argument is the principal economic reason for anticipating increasing conflict between the goals of national development and the foreign investment community, even after the latter has thoroughly purged itself of the excesses that marred its early career. The argument is strengthened by related considerations pertaining to economic policy making, a "factor of production" not often taken into account by economists, but which nevertheless has an essential role to play. In the course of industrialization, resources for complementary investment in education and overhead capital must be generated through taxation, the opening up of new domestic and foreign markets must be made attractive, institutions hampering growth must be reformed, and powerful social groups that are antagonistic to development must be neutralized. The achievement of these tasks is considerably facilitated if the new industrialists are able to speak with a strong, influential, and even militant voice. But the emergence of such a voice is most unlikely if a large portion of the more dynamic new industries is in foreign hands. This is a somewhat novel reproach to foreign capital, which has normally been taken to task for being unduly interfering, wire-pulling, and domineering. Whatever the truth about these accusations in the past, the principal failing of the managers of today's foreign-held branch plants and subsidiaries may well be the opposite. Given their position as "guests" in a "host country," their behavior is far too restrained and inhibited. The trouble with the foreign investor may well be not that he is so meddlesome, but that he is so mousy! It is the foreign investor's mousiness which deprives the policy makers of the guidance, pressures, and support they badly need to push through critically required development decisions and policies amid a welter of conflicting and antagonistic interests.

The situation is in fact even worse. Not only does policy making fail to be invigorated by the influence normally emanating from a strong, confident, and assertive group of industrialists; more directly, the presence of a strong foreign element in the dynamically expanding sectors of the economy is likely to have a debilitating and corroding effect on the rationality of official economic policy making for development. For, when newly arising investment opportunities are largely or predominantly seized upon by foreign firms, the national policy makers face in effect a dilemma: more development means at the same time less autonomy. In a situation in which many key points of the economy are occupied by foreigners while economic policy is made by nationals it is only too likely that these nationals will not excel in "rational" policy making for economic development; for, a good portion of the fruits of such rationality would accrue to nonnationals and would strengthen their position.[3] On the other hand, the role and importance of national economic policy making for development increases steadily as the array of available policy instruments widens, and as more group demands are articulated. Hence the scope for "irrationality" actually expands as development gains momentum. That its incidence increases as well could probably be demonstrated by a historical survey of tax, exchange rate, utility rate and similar policies that were aimed directly or indirectly at "squeezing" or administering pin pricks to the foreigner, but managed, at the same time, to slow down economic growth.

The preceding pages have said next to nothing about the direct

3. For some interesting remarks along these lines, see Hans O. Schmitt, "Foreign Capital and Social Conflict in Indonesia," *Economic Development and Cultural Change* 10 (April 1962): 284–93.

cost to the capital-importing country of private international investment nor about the related question of the balance of payments drain such investment may occasion. While these matters have long been vigorously debated, with the critics charging exploitation and the defenders denying it, the outcome of the discussion seems to me highly inconclusive. Moreover, undue fascination with the dollar-and-cents aspects of international investment has led to the neglect of the topics here considered, which, I submit, raise issues of at least equal importance and suggest a simple conclusion: strictly from the point of view of development, private foreign investment is a mixed blessing, and the mixture is likely to become more noxious at the intermediate stage of development which characterizes much of present-day Latin America.

Hence, if the broadly conceived national interest of the United States is served by the development of Latin America, then this interest enters into conflict with a continuing expansion and even with the maintenance of the present position of private investors from the United States. Purely political arguments lend strong support to this proposition. Internal disputes over the appropriate treatment of the foreign investor have gravely weakened, or helped to topple, some of the more progressive and democratic governments which have held power in recent years in such countries as Brazil, Chile, and Peru. Frictions between private investors from the United States and host governments have an inevitable repercussion on United States-Latin American relations. In a number of cases such disputes have been responsible for a wholly disproportionate deterioration of bilateral relations. The continued presence and expansion of our private investment position and our insistence on a "favorable investment climate" decisively undermined, from the outset, the credibility of our Alliance for Progress proposals. Land reform and income redistribution through taxation are so obviously incompatible, in the short run, with the maintenance of a favorable investment climate for private capital that insistence on both could only be interpreted to signify that we did not really mean those fine phrases about achieving social justice through land and tax reform.

If these political arguments are added to those pertaining to economics and political economy, one thing becomes clear: a policy of selective liquidation and withdrawal of foreign private investment is in the best mutual interests of Latin America and the United States. Such a policy can be selective with respect to countries and to economic sectors and it ought to be combined with a policy of encouraging new capital outflows, also on a selective basis and with some safeguards.

THE "LOST ART" OF LIQUIDATING AND NATIONALIZING FOREIGN INVESTMENTS

Before the possible elements of such a policy are examined, it is worth noting that liquidation of foreign investment has frequently happened in the history of capital movements. But, as a result of convergent developments, such liquidation has strangely become a lost art. Worse, this art has not been properly recorded by economic historians. In part, this is so because economic historians, like both the advocates of foreign investment and its critics, have been far more interested in the tides of capital flow than in its occasional ebbs. Moreover, the tides have been more regular and easier to detect and measure.

Some of the "mechanisms" which in the past permitted partial liquidation of foreign investment have been the unintended side effects of such large-scale, sporadic, and wholly unedifying happenings as wars and depressions. The two world wars led to a substantial decline in both the absolute and the relative importance of foreign investment in the national economies of Latin America. In the first place, with most Latin American countries joining the Allies, German investments, a not unimportant portion of the total (think of all those prosperous breweries!), were expropriated. Secondly, the British were forced in both world wars to liquidate a good portion of their security holdings, in order to pay for vitally needed food, materials, and munitions. Some of these securities were acquired by the citizens of the countries for which they had originally been issued. Thirdly, Latin American countries acquired large holdings of gold and foreign currencies during the wars, as they continued to export their primary products, but were unable to obtain industrial goods from the belligerents.

These accumulated holdings made it possible for them to buy out some foreign investments in the immediate postwar period. The most conspicuous, but by no means the only, instance of this sort of operation was the purchase from their British shareholders of the Argentine railways by the Perón government in 1946. Finally, the wars led to a complete interruption of capital inflow. Since, at the same time, Latin America's industrial growth was strongly stimulated, the relative importance of activities controlled by foreign capital declined substantially.

The depressions which periodically afflicted the centers of capitalist development until the Second World War had similar results. Again, capital inflow would stop for a while during periods in which the Latin American economies frequently received growth impulses because, with foreign exchange receipts low, imports had to be throttled, giving domestic industrial production a fillip. Moreover, when overextended corporations based in the United States and Europe fell on hard times, a sound management reaction was frequently to retrench and consolidate. In the process, foreign branch plants and subsidiaries were sold off to local buyers, a process which has been well documented in the case of American investments in Canada during the depression of the thirties.[4] Sometimes, especially in the case of European firms, these transfers took the form of ownership and control passing into the hands of the parent company's local managers who, while of foreign origin, would eventually become integrated into the local economy. Finally, of course, there were cases of outright bankruptcy and forced liquidation.

The quantitative importance of these various factors remains to be established. But, in the aggregate, they must have had a substantial limiting effect on the foreign investment position in Latin America during the first half of the twentieth century.

Actually, a less cruel mechanism permitting the nationalization of foreign investment was also at work before the "good old days" of portfolio investment had been eclipsed by direct investment. While those days were of course by no means wholly good, port-

4. See H. Marshall, F. A. Southard Jr., and V. W. Taylor, *Canadian-American Industry* (New Haven: Yale University Press, 1936), pp. 252–62.

folio investment, which took primarily the form of fixed-interest bond issues, did have several advantages for the capital-importing country. Among these, the lower cost and the existence of a termination date have been mentioned most frequently. There is, however, one further property of portfolio investment which is of particular interest in the context of the present essay. This is the fact that nationalization of portfolio investment could take place at the option of the borrowing country and its citizens, who were free to purchase in the international capital markets securities that were originally issued and underwritten in London or Paris. I have collected (and hope eventually to publish) considerable evidence that these so-called "repurchases" of securities by nationals of the borrowing countries took place on a large scale in such countries as the United States, Italy, Spain, Sweden, and Japan in the late nineteenth and early twentieth centuries. They also occurred in much poorer countries, such as Brazil, and were in general so widespread that the phenomenon is referred to in one source as "the well-known *Heimweh* [homesickness] of oversea issued securities."[5] As a result of this *Heimweh,* then, an increasing portion of maturing bond issues often came to be owned by the nationals of the borrowing country, so that payment at maturity did not occasion any balance of payments problem.

This is not the place to speculate on the reasons for which the bonds issued abroad became so often a preferred medium of in-

5. J. F. Normano, *Brazil: A Study of Economic Types* (Chapel Hill: University of North Carolina Press, 1935), p. 157. Note also the following concluding passage of a standard treatise on pre–World War I capital flows: "One and all looked forward to the time when foreign capital with the restraints it imposed would no longer be needed. Each country wanted to buy back its public securities, to redeem its railways from foreign ownership, to withdraw from foreign lenders all share in the making of national policy. Some countries advanced toward this goal, the United States, the British Dominions, Japan, and Italy, for example; some slid further and further away from it, as did China and Turkey. In short, borrowers wanted to nationalize the capital which was active in their domains, to assure themselves that this capital was subordinate to the national powers. It became clear that debts are not the kind of bond which can unite the world" (Herbert Feis, *Europe: The World's Banker, 1870–1914* [New Haven: Yale University Press, 1930], pp. 466–67).

vestment for national capitalists; suffice it to say that patriotism or nationalism on the part of local investors probably had little if anything to do with it. Whatever the reason, it appears that international investment, as formerly practiced, permitted the gradual transfer, via anonymous market transactions, of foreign-held assets to nationals, entirely in accordance with the capabilities and wishes of the borrowing country's own savers.

Today's arrangements are totally different, of course. Transfer to local ownership and control of foreign-held subsidiaries requires either an initiative on the part of the parent company or a decision to expropriate on the part of the host government. A valuable mechanism of smooth, gradual, and peaceful transfer has become lost in the shuffle from portfolio to direct investment.

Up to this point, it has been established (1) that progressive liquidation and nationalization of foreign private investments is likely to become desirable in the course of economic development, and (2) that mechanisms to this end functioned, if unwittingly and irregularly, in the nineteenth and through the first half of the twentieth century, but have no longer been available over the past twenty-five years or so.

The purpose of recalling these mechanisms was to sharpen our institutional imagination and perception for substitute mechanisms which it may be desirable to put into place at the present time. An open and far-ranging discussion of various possible alternatives is obviously desirable. The following pages are meant as a contribution to such a discussion, rather than as a fixed set of proposals.

A SURVEY OF POSSIBLE DIVESTMENT MECHANISMS

An attempt will now be made to sketch possible answers to the following questions:

1. What arrangements should be made to permit the transfer to local ownership and control of existing foreign-held investments?

2. What arrangements should exist for this transfer in the case of new foreign investments?

3. To what extent should devices that are designed for the pur-

poses just indicated be modified in the light of other important objectives of the developing countries, such as the export of manufactures and the promotion of local centers of technological research and innovation?

These questions will be taken up in order, although there is considerable overlap between the answers to the first two questions.

An Inter-American Divestment Corporation

In the light of the above considerations, partial liquidation of existing foreign investments in Latin America is outstandingly important. The book value of direct investments by the United States in Latin America amounted to 11.9 billion dollars at the end of 1967, while the annual outflow of fresh capital from the United States (outside of reinvested profits) never reached 500 million dollars during the past five years, even on a gross basis. The steady increase in book values is, moreover, due more to the reinvestment of profits than to fresh funds newly invested. In other words, if the quantitative and qualitative role of foreign-controlled enterprise in Latin America is judged to be excessive, something must be done about the existing foreign firms operating in the area, rather than only about those that may conceivably establish operations there in the future.

Vital as it is, this subject has received much less attention than the desirable regime for new foreign investments. It is of course the politically most delicate part of the operation here contemplated. Also, from the economic point of view, the use of any capital and, worse, foreign exchange resources for the purchase of property rights over assets already located and functioning within the territories of the poor countries seems perverse to those who remain basically convinced that the pace of economic development is conditioned on little else than the availability of capital and foreign exchange. Those who are not so convinced and who take seriously the economic and political arguments developed earlier would see nothing fatally wrong in allocating a portion of the country's savings and foreign exchange resources to the purchase of foreign investments already in their midst. From the purely financial point of view, moreover, expenditure of foreign exchange for the purchase of existing foreign assets could in a number of cases be preferable to the indefinite servicing of these assets (depending on one's estimate of the applicable discount rate and of future earnings and remittance patterns). The trouble is that the recipient countries do not generally have the financial resources to seize these opportunities nor have they in fact been able to borrow or to use aid funds for this purpose. Moreover, even when local resources are available there may be difficulties in bringing seller and buyer together, because the foreign owners may be ready to sell at a time when the local investors are not quite ready to purchase or because the two parties have difficulty in agreeing on the value of the assets to be transferred, without a mutually-trusted third party.

A need exists, then, for a financial intermediary, an agency, that is, which has resources of its own enabling it to acquire foreign-owned assets and to hold them until such time as it can place them with local investors. Dr. Raúl Prebisch earlier this year proposed that such an agency should be established within the Inter-American Development Bank. This course may well be preferable, because of the special urgency of the Latin American situation, to a suggestion I made as early as 1961, but with total lack of success, to the International Finance Corporation (IFC) that it devote a portion of its resources to this task.

The proposed agency—I shall call it the Inter-American Divestment Corporation—would engage in several distinct types of operations. In some cases it could limit its role to that of arbitrator and guarantor. As just noted, it could help set the fair price of the assets to be transferred from the foreign to the domestic owners and, if payment is to be made over a period of years, it could guarantee the debtor's obligation and, to some extent perhaps, the convertibility of his currency into that of the creditor. One can imagine situations in which the purchaser would have to be granted longer terms than can or should be imposed on the seller, as is common in some agrarian reform operations. In this case, the corporation would need to supply funds of its own to bridge the gap between the two sets of credit terms. The most usual type of operation would presumably consist in the outright acquisition by the corporation of a controlling block of shares of the firm to be divested, without any fixed schedule of repurchase by local investors.

As in any foreign aid project, some contribution should be forthcoming from the local government as an earnest that it judges the particular divestment to be important enough for it to commit some resources of its own. As the Divestment Corporation acquires experience, it should be able to attract additional resources from the private investment banking community, much as is done by the IFC in connection with new ventures.

Which foreign-owned firms should be eligible for divestment assistance on the part of the corporation? In deciding this crucial matter, the corporation should probably take its principal cues from the governments of the host countries. Just as the doctor asks the patient where it hurts, so the corporation could periodically inquire among governments which are the firms where foreign ownership is felt to be irksome. In many cases there will be a history of conflict which will clearly point to the main trouble spots. One can also easily imagine situations in which governments are reluctant to point a finger at specific firms. For this and other reasons, it should be possible for private parties in the host country, for the foreign investors, and for the corporation itself to take the initiative in the divestment process which, in the end, will require the agreement of the host government as long as it is expected to contribute some of its own resources to each divestment operation.

An interesting question arises with respect to the eventual disposition of the equity which will be acquired by the corporation. One objection will surely be levied against the operation: Is it really desirable to transfer presently foreign-owned firms to local ownership when the new owners cannot but be drawn from the very small clique of already too powerfully entrenched local capitalists? History issues a warning here, for this very sort of thing happened in the second half of the nineteenth century when liberal parties came to power in a number of Latin American countries. The newly installed, anticlerical governments expropriated the sizeable lands owned by the Catholic church—and then proceeded to sell them at bargain prices to the landed elite. As a result, the concentration of landholdings became far more pronounced.

At the present time, the weight of concern over a similar development in case of nationalization of foreign investment varies no doubt from country to country, as well as from industry to industry within each country. Moreover, the corporation could make a deliberate attempt to broaden the basis of industrial ownership when it sells its portfolio. This should, in fact, be one of its principal functions. If foreign-owned assets were to be sold directly to local investors, it would be impossible not to sell to the few and the powerful. But, if an intermediary stands ready to hold the divested assets for some time, the outcome may be quite different. One attractive possibility is that the agency would sell, on the installment plan, a substantial portion, and perhaps a majority, of the equity of the erstwhile foreign firms to white- and blue-collar workers, with first choice being given to those who are employed in such firms. This would be a method of tapping entirely new sources of capital formation. Moreover, in this manner, the liquidation of foreign ownership would become the occasion for effectuating, by the same stroke, a more equitable distribution of income and wealth within the host country. As in the case of the Mexican *ejido,* special safeguards may then have to be established to protect the new asset holders against the temptation to sell out right away.

Those who have stressed the advantage of a late start have usually had in mind the technological windfalls accruing to the newcomers and their freedom from a declining industrial plant based on some previous but now passé phase of industrial expansion. For various reasons, these advantages have been more in evidence for Germany and Japan than for countries whose industrialization was much more tardy; but the latter could perhaps attempt some social leapfrogging, as, for example, in the manner just indicated.

It is quite conceivable, moreover, that the foreign investors themselves would take a more benign view of divestment if they knew that their assets were to be transferred to their workers and employees rather than to their local competitors or to some public agency.

The projected divestment operations via a financial intermediary could be made to serve another objective that is particularly important within the present Latin American setting. It could help create financial and, hence, managerial ties among firms located in several Latin American countries. In this form a foundation would be laid for truly Latin American multinational corporations.The absence of such corporations, combined with the ever alert presence throughout Latin America, of United States-controlled multinational corporations, accounts for much of the timidity with which Latin Americans have moved so far in the direction of a common market. Thus, the proposed divestment, combined with a measure of "Latinamericanization," rather than mere nationalization, of the divested enterprises could impart a much needed momentum to the integration movement.

By now, I hope to have convinced the reader that it is worthwhile to raise funds for the corporation. In part, such funds should simply be taken from the general pool of foreign aid monies. For the reasons indicated, the use of aid funds for this purpose could be eminently "productive," using this term in a wide and realistic meaning. The question what fraction of the total should be allowed to this purpose is no doubt difficult to resolve; but it is not more so than many other allocation decisions that are constantly made in practice without the guidance or availability of precise "cost-effectiveness" criteria.

Nevertheless, the nature of the proposed operation may point to special sources of finance that are not available for other purposes, so that the corporation would not have to compete for general-purpose aid funds. A first thought that comes to mind in this connection is that the opposition in the United States Congress to appropriations for foreign aid is now motivated, to an increasing extent, by apprehension over the way in which aid and its administration makes for uncontrollable and possibly escalating involvements by the United States in foreign countries. A program of financial assistance which would have disengagement as its principal objective might therefore gather more public support at this point than the conventional aid program. In fact, if such a program were presented separately from conventional aid, a new political coalition might get behind it so that in the political sense the funds accruing for our purpose could become truly additional. Appropriation for the corporation might also have other appeals. Aid for divestment is unexceptional from the points of view of both balance of payments and inflationary impacts. The dollars disbursed by the agency would immediately return in full to the divesting country, such as the United States, but they would not enter directly into that country's spending stream.

The program may be opposed on the ground that the taxpayer of the United States should not be asked to "bail out" its corporations that have engaged in foreign operations at their own risk. In reply it may be argued that a large part of the risk of recent foreign investments has already been taken over by the taxpayer, through the investment guaranty program. Moreover, the Divestment Corporation should be in a good position to minimize the "bail-out" aspect of its operations: one of its principal tasks would be to negotiate a fair price for the assets and to convince the foreign investors that are being bought out to accept deferred payment for a substantial portion of their claim.

In a search for special sources of finance, it is natural to eye those parties which stand to gain from the proposed operations. The beneficiaries, in a sense, are the foreign investors themselves. In the first place, they will receive a valuable new option—to sell out at a fair price—as a result of the contemplated arrangements. The proposed agency would in effect administer a program whose purpose is to prevent the confiscation of foreign-held assets by timely transfers of these assets. Obviously not all foreign-owned firms will be able to exercise the option. But the orderly liquidation of foreign ownership in the cases where it is particularly objectionable to the host country cannot help but be a boon to the remaining foreign-controlled firms. The presence in a country of foreign interests that are felt as irritants poses a danger for the prosperity and, indeed, the life of *all* foreign firms, no matter how constructive and popular they may be. Hence a contribution from all corporations with foreign assets can be justified. As long as firms are willing to pay a premium which insures them against the risks of actual confiscation, there is no reason why they should not contribute something toward a program which materially decreases these risks.

Another possible source of special finance for the divestment agency should be briefly mentioned. The agency may well be the ideal beneficiary of the much discussed "link" between the new monetary reserves created as a result of the Rio Agreement (the Special Drawing Rights) and the developing countries. The principal objection against any such link has been that the reserve creation should not become a mechanism for effecting permanent transfers of real resources from one set of countries to another. This objection would be largely met if the industrial countries used part of their allocation of Special Drawing Rights for the subscription of capital or bond issues of the Divestment Corporation. The partial use of the new reserves for the repatriation of foreign-held assets could not have an adverse effect on the intended increase in world liquidity, for the simple reason that this use, unlike others that have been proposed, would not entail any real tranfer of goods and services.

Built-in Divestment—a Garland of Schemes

Considering the mass of foreign investment, the Divestment Corporation will be able to operate only on a highly selective, ad hoc basis. The question arises, therefore, whether the institutional framework within which foreign investment is conducted should be modified with a view toward building into it a mechanism making for eventual divestment. This question is best discussed in considering desirable regimes for *new* investments. Whether any such regime could or should be extended to existing foreign-owned firms can be considered subsequently.

The topic has given rise to a considerable literature and to several proposals. For example, the desirability for foreign capital to become associated with local capital in joint ventures has been exhaustively canvassed. Whatever the merits of this device, its usefulness is now recognized to be limited. In many situations, particularly those involving the transfer of new and complex technology, complete foreign control and ownership is said to be required or desirable at the outset. For this reason, increased attention has been given—by such authors as Paul Rosenstein-Rodan, Paul Streeten, and Raymond Vernon—to the possibility of a gradual transfer of all or the majority of the new firm's capital to local ownership, in accordance with a fixed schedule.

This is a fruitful idea which should be spelled out in full institutional detail. Consideration should, for example, be given to the the granting of fiscal incentives to firms electing this option. In the capital-exporting countries, the parent company committing itself to gradual divestment of its foreign assets over a stated number of years could be given a credit against its income tax liability for some portion of its foreign capital outlays; alternatively or additionally, the firm could be exempted from all capital gains taxation on profits made in selling its foreign assets to local investors. The capital-importing country could facilitate divestment by allowing the foreign-owned company to pay income taxes in stock in lieu of cash. Such an arrangement would probably have to be restricted to economic sectors in which foreign enterprise is not competing with domestic enterprises. Where there is actual or potential competition, the arrangement would give an unfair cash-flow advantage to the foreign firm.

Gradual divestment over a given number of years normally means expenditure of scarce foreign exchange. It also requires the finding of local partners. The difficulties here are, first, that such partners are not always easy to come by. It would be necessary to designate some public agency of the host country, perhaps acting in cooperation with the Inter-American Divestment Corporation, as a residual buyer of the stock to be transferred from the original owners in accordance with a fixed schedule and a pre-arranged price formula. Another drawback of a direct sale of assets from the foreign owners to nationals has already been mentioned. The local buyers that would be found most readily may not be the most desirable, if advantage is to be taken of the unique opportunity afforded by divestment for diffusing ownership more widely than before. Finally, in most situations, there will be a need to agree on a "fair price" of the assets: the potential for conflict over this issue is almost as great as that over the actual presence of foreign investment.

These problems of a scheduled gradual sale of equity from foreigners to nationals point toward a simpler and more radical arrangement: namely, that a firm established with foreign capital be given a term of x years, at the end of which all or the major portion of foreign ownership would simply be vacated, without any compensation. Some of the ideas already discussed in connection with the Divestment Corporation can be utilized in deciding on the parties on which ownership should be bestowed at the end of the term. Up to a certain percentage, the foreign owners could distribute the stock directly to their employees and workers, or to their favorite local charity or foundation, and another portion would be handed over to the Inter-American Divestment Corporation for the purpose of fostering industrial integration. The new owners would be free to negotiate a management contract with the former owner-operators.

Arrangements which set a time limit on ownership have long existed in concession contracts. The major drawback of such arrangements has also long been known: they encourage early depletion and discourage keeping up with technical progress during the years immediately prior to expiration. In manufacturing, the former danger would be rather smaller than in mining, and the latter would be reduced if the divesting firm is scheduled to maintain a minority equity position and is interested in a continuing relationship with its erstwhile foreign branch through management contracts and other technical assistance services. Also, if the foreign owners know that they will be handing a substantial portion of the equity over to their workers and employees or to their favorite charity or foundation in the host country, they will presumably be more reluctant to squeeze their property dry in the last years than they might be if it were to be handed to the government. Nevertheless, the objection to a fixed termination date is serious enough to prompt consideration of yet another institutional design.

Limiting ownership of a firm to a certain time period, at the end of which that ownership lapses or "expires" automatically, is tantamount to setting a ceiling on the profits the firm can remit to its parent. Why not make explicit this implicit ceiling on profit remittances? Instead of specifying the number of years a firm may remain in foreign hands, it would, in other words, be conceivable to limit the total amount of profits a subsidiary could remit to its parent. This amount would be related to the capital originally committed to the project, as well as to any fresh funds brought in subsequently over and above reinvested profits. Such a regime for divestment would have incentive effects directly opposite to those of the traditional concession. Since the firm can make the pleasure of control and ownership last by remitting as little as possible, that is, by reinvesting all of its profits, the incentive to deplete and milk the subsidiary would be replaced by the incentive to reinvest (on the assumption that management, control, and growth are important motivating forces for the modern corporation).

It may be useful to pick a number for illustrative purposes. Suppose that the ceiling on remittances is 200 per cent of the originally invested capital. This could mean, for example, that a parent company would lose ownership of its subsidiary after it had received a 10 per cent dividend on invested capital for twenty years. The internal rate of return of such a financial result would be just short of 8 per cent. In other words, if a rate higher than 8 per cent were appropriate as a discount rate in the particular environment where the subsidiary operates, a financial situation in which 10 per cent would be earned for twenty years would be superior to one in which 8 per cent would be earned in perpetuity. Hence, the perishable nature of the investment need not impair decisively its rentability, particularly in the frequently encountered situations where the applicable discount rate is fairly high.

Consideration could be given to the question whether, in computing the aggregate "allowable" profit, some discount rate should apply to the dividend remittances themselves. If this were done, payments made at a later date would contribute less heavily to the eventual extinction of ownership than payments made in the first years of the new enterprise and the incentive to postpone and hold down profit remittances might be further strengthened. The arguments against any such complication are: first, that it is a complication; and, second, that the real burden of profit remittances for the host country does not depend so much on the country's national product, which can be expected to be larger in later years, as on its balance of payments, which could well be in a more critical position ten years after the initial investment than at the time at which the investment is made.

The last point highlights an important advantage of the scheme under discussion. One of the major complaints with respect to foreign investment has been that because of reinvestment of profits— which in turn are made possible in part through local borrowing— the book value of the foreign-owned firms is likely to grow apace during an initial period, so that eventual dividend remittances may be a multiple of the capital originally brought into the country. While the scheme here discussed encourages reinvestment of profits, it averts the threatening prospect of huge remittances which might be made once the firm's growth slowed down, when they could represent an unacceptable burden for the country's balance of payments.

In all fairness, it may well be asked, if cumulative profits are subject to a ceiling should they not be granted a floor in compensation? No doubt, such a floor could make the scheme much more attractive to the capital-exporting firms. The floor should obviously be at most 100 per cent of the initially invested capital and probably rather less, so as to preserve an adequate degree of risk. Suppose a payback of 50 per cent of the invested capital is to be guaranteed as a consideration for the 200 per cent ceiling that is imposed on profit remittances. The capital-exporting country could provide such a guarantee simply by permitting the parent company a tax credit against its income tax liability up to 50 per cent of the capital invested. As was pointed out before, such a tax credit may be desirable in any event in order to encourage firms that invest abroad to take advantage of the divestment options.

Once some of the divestment arrangements sketched out here

become available for new investments, it will be desirable for existing investments to be able to participate in them. Existing foreign firms should, of course, be eligible to operate under one of the several divestment options that will be offered to new firms. Once again, fiscal incentives granted by the capital-exporting or capital-importing country, or by both, could be used to make participation attractive. There is no particular difficulty in adapting to existing firms the options calling for gradual sale of equity or for outright divestment after a certain number of years. Problems are more likely to arise with respect to the option terminating foreign ownership after remittance of profits in some multiple of the originally invested capital. Applying this rule to the original capital of the existing firms may be too restrictive, yet taking the present book value as a yardstick may be too generous. Some middle ground between these two solutions may have to be found.

To what extent would the existence of the Inter-American Divestment Corporation keep existing firms from electing to convert to some of the automatic divestment procedures here advocated? If a firm could be sure that it would become an object of the tender mercies of the Divestment Corporation, it might well prefer that course to any automatic divestment arrangement (other than gradual sale of equity), since it would be paid for its assets instead of losing them outright after a certain lapse of time. Actually, this sort of "competition" from the Divestment Corporation is not a serious danger. In the first place, the Corporation will not have sufficiently large funds to make acquisition a likely prospect for the average foreign-owned firm. Secondly, given its limited resources, the Corporation will generally acquire the assets of existing firms under medium and long-term credit arrangements instead of paying cash. In these circumstances, foreign firms may often decide that they can do better under divestment schemes which allow them to manage their affairs and earn profits for a number of years ahead.

Combining Divestment with Other Objectives

The purpose of the preceding pages was to present, in bare outline, a variety of possible institutional arrangements for divest-ment. It is now necessary to consider how these arrangements could be modified if divestment conflicts with other important objectives of the developing countries.

For example, it has been pointed out by Raymond Vernon that foreign-owned firms have a special aptitude for contributing to the exports of manufactures from the developing countries. In many cases, of course, foreign branch plants have been criticized for exactly the opposite tendency, namely for the determination to confine themselves to the local market and to reserve all exporting to the parent company. Nevertheless, this is no necessary and permanent failing; the multinational corporation in particular is obviously able to establish an integrated network of manufac-turing facilities and commercial operations which could insert its individual producing units in different countries into a worldwide pattern of specialized production and internal exchange.

It looks, therefore, as though in some sectors some developing countries are likely to face a dilemma: continued foreign owner-ship or no exports. But in reality there is no need to make so difficult a choice. The dilemma can be transformed into a trade-off situation where both objectives are pursued simultaneously and one of them is only marginally given up for the sake of achieving a limited gain for the other. The schemes already put forward can easily be adapted to this end. Take the scheme under which a majority ownership ceases automatically at the end of x years. It would be relatively easy to introduce a variant such that a firm achieving exports of z per cent of its total output by the time the x years are up, would retain majority ownership for another y years. In this or some similar fashion, the built-in di-vestment provisions can actually serve to provide incentives for the achievement of other goals.

The same argument applies to such objectives as the pro-motion of regional integration and the establishment by foreign firms of centers of applied technological research. In these cases it is, of course, difficult to quantify performance. Nevertheless, an independent expert commission could be created with the task of appraising whether in any individual case the contribution of a foreign firm to, say, the implanting of technological research and innovation warrants a slowing down of the divestment schedule.

In the end, therefore, a developing country may spell out for foreign investors several distinct mixes of objectives, among which divestment would be only one; and each foreign investor could elect the particular mix that corresponds most closely to his taste and capabilities.

Rapid and incomplete as it is, the preceding survey of conceivable divestment arrangements will have given the reader a sense of the sizable alteration in the institutional environment for foreign private investment that is advocated here. Several questions are raised in consequence: (1) what would happen to the outflow of private investment funds if some of the arrangements spelled out were actually adopted as national policy by the developing countries of Latin America as well as by the capital exporters such as the United States? Would that outflow slow down to a trickle or come to a full stop? And (2) if the latter occurred would considerable damage be done to economic development in Latin America?

To answer the last question first, it is my belief that the larger countries of Latin America are today in a quite favorable bargaining position to insist on substantial institutional changes of the kind here indicated. The damage that would be inflicted on them if international capital took offense and stopped flowing to them is no longer what it might have been 100, 50, or even 25 years ago. Most literature and official reports about Latin America stress the continent's continuing poverty and problems. These laments have hidden from view the very real economic progress that has been accomplished over the last 25 years. With a per capita income of around 500 dollars and a population of 250 million people, the Latin American continent is now well supplied with both "light" and "basic" industries. Countries such as Brazil, Mexico, and Argentina produce a large and constantly increasing portion of the capital goods needed by their industrial establishment. A boycott of Latin America by international investment capital might reveal the strength and resilience and ability to *fare da sé* in a great number of areas which the Latin American industrial establishment has acquired, in much the same way in which the two world wars permitted its then fledgling industries to take vigorous steps forward. Perhaps Latin America really needs at this point a sort of "economic equivalent of war," a measure of insulation, that is, from the advanced economies that would permit it fully to deploy the potential for entrepreneurship, skills, and capital formation which it has accumulated over the past 25 years of continuing intimate contact. In other words, it is quite conceivable that a temporary suspension of the flow of private capital toward Latin America would be beneficial rather than calamitous for the area's growth. That Latin Americans can afford to make "demands"' from a position of strength was perhaps sensed when their official representatives started to speak in quite a new voice to the United States at the Viña del Mar conference of May 1969.

The question remains whether a boycott by private capital would necessarily result from a Latin American attempt to change the rules by which the game of international investment is being played. This is not at all certain. There are at least some signs that a number of private investors may be willing to operate in a substantially altered institutional environment. In the first place, they know how to bend with the wind—an example is the "Chilenization" of Kennecott and now also of Anaconda. Some farther-sighted corporations in mining and telecommunications are no longer waiting for pressures from the host countries to provide for "-ization" of substantial equity in their concession contracts. A few scattered experiments in divestment are also going forward under the auspices of IFC, ADELA, and of the AID guaranty program. Furthermore, where official ideology proscribes "private ownership of the means of production" altogether, private companies located in Western Europe and the United States have been able to do business via so-called "coproduction agreements" through which capital goods, technology, and skills are transferred, with repayment scheduled often in kind, on a medium or long-term basis. As a result, Western business firms find themselves in the ironical position of granting a better deal to their ideological foes than to their friends. Finally, a few small experiments in bringing manufacturing operations into an area and then turning them over to community ownership and control are now being tried out in the United States in some of the black ghettos; corporations such as Xerox and Aerojet have been pioneering in this field.

It may well turn out, then, that the corporation will once again justify its reputation for flexibility. The radical nature of the changes required should nevertheless be clearly visualized. If the corporation is celebrated as an institution, this is so to a large extent because it has permitted business to be carried on *sub specie aeternitatis,* by an organization, that is, whose life span has become as unlimited as that of older permanent institutions such as the nation-state and the church. It is here suggested that, in some of its foreign operations, the corporation ought to institutionalize its own demise. Having achieved deathlessness, it must rediscover how to die.

Putting it less brusquely, the corporation must learn how to plan for selective impermanence. Perhaps it would do so more cheerfully once it realizes that the same need exists increasingly for other institutions proud of their permanence, such as the nation-state. So, why not be a trail blazer?

PART III

Addressing the Developing Countries: A Bias for Hope

12. Economic Policy in Underdeveloped Countries

Little attention appears to have been given by economists and other social scientists to any analysis, systematic or casual, of the behavior of governments of underdeveloped countries as revealed by their economic policy decisions over a period of time. Nevertheless, in view of the considerable role played today by governments in the development process, it is clear that governmental behavior should be subjected to just as close scrutiny as is being given to the motivations and conduct of entrepreneurs.

In fact, in the absence of more knowledge about probable actions and reactions of governments, our best-intentioned technical assistance efforts are liable to fail. This conclusion is inescapable to anyone who has been watching the economists and other social science experts who are sent on foreign assignments. At the outset of their mission, they are likely to think that the principal problem they are going to be confronted with will be that of determining what ought to be done, e.g., in what sector the principal investment effort should be undertaken, and what monetary, fiscal, and foreign exchange policies should be adopted. But soon they realize that they have little trouble in deciding what to do or rather what to advise to do, while by far the largest portion of their time is devoted to energy-consuming and often frustrating efforts to put their ideas and proposals across.

Let me say that my remarks apply primarily to the important group of underdeveloped countries whose economies have already registered important advances. In such countries, a few obviously useful investment projects are always at hand; some monetary

This paper was written in 1956, upon my return from a four-year stay in Colombia as official economic adviser (1952–54) and private consultant (1954–56). It is reprinted here by permission from *Economic Development and Cultural Change* 5 (July 1957): 362–70. © 1957 by the University of Chicago.

and fiscal reforms usually cry out to be taken; certain changes in the institutional and administrative structure would no doubt further stimulate development. The story of a technical assistance mission is then the story of its successes and failures in having these projects, reforms, and changes firmly adopted. The huge difficulties of this task are not always properly appreciated, partly, I suspect, because, in order to do so, one must catch the experts themselves during their unguarded moments rather than rely on their reports to headquarters; and partly, because the whole tale here is in terms of personalities and of human passions, frailties, and frustrations which the experts, once they are "back home," are liable to forget as easily and completely as physical pain. And if they reminisce, it seems to them that they were facing fortuitous circumstances which do not lend themselves to any kind of generalized analysis.

Here they could be mistaken. After all, underdeveloped countries and their governments may find themselves typically in situations which make likely the adoption of seemingly irrational economic policies. It is also conceivable that the emergence of oscillations and even of inconsistencies in such policies could be predicted with a fair degree of accuracy from a knowledge of their economic structure and problems.

An analysis that would deal with these probabilities would permit the economic adviser to gain some understanding of the economic policies—good or bad—and of the resistance that he and his proposals are likely to encounter. Not only would it thereby contribute to his mental health—by saving him from unnecessary exasperation—but it might make him into a more effective operator. Indeed, the governments may also profit from knowing more about themselves. In the following I shall attempt to give some examples of this kind of analysis from selected areas of economic policy making.

ATTITUDES TOWARD NATIONAL DEVELOPMENT PROGRAMMING

There is no field of economic policy in underdeveloped countries that stands as much in the limelight as the programming of economic development. To have a five-year plan for economic development has become a matter of prestige, second only to the importance of having a first-class international airport near the capital. In this, as in many other respects, governments are more powerfully subject to the "demonstration effect" than individuals for the simple reason that communications between governments are far more developed than between citizens of different countries.

The reasons for which the adoption of development plans has proven so attractive, are well known: the plan or program is a concrete expression of the universal aspiration toward better living standards and the elaboration and adoption of such a program is a source of considerable popularity for any government; on various occasions, countries have found that the possession of a development program was an essential condition for being considered eligible for foreign assistance, or at least was helpful in connection with the application for such assistance; similarly, the existence of a program makes it easier for a government to secure additional domestic financing through taxation or other measures which by themselves would encounter considerable opposition; finally, a development program is a convenient device for the national government in dealing with the many requests for financial aid to which it is constantly subjected from its own agencies. It seems so much more convincing to tell the visiting mayor of a provincial town who comes to lobby for an aqueduct that no provision for this project is made in this year's portion of the five-year plan than simply to plead old-fashioned lack of funds, which in any event is an unsatisfactory explanation when aqueducts are being built at the same time for several other towns.

The development program is therefore a convenient restraint on the central government which permits it to push through high-priority projects without being sidetracked. This function of a development program is usually not the principal motive for adopting it in the first place, but the realization of its usefulness becomes often a major reason for continuing the experience. On the other hand, this very freedom-of-choice-limiting property of development programs can be felt as excessive, and then results in the frequently observed spectacle of a government acting in contradiction to the course of action which it had laid down for itself.

Sometimes such behavior reflects nothing but the inherent impatience of most governments of underdeveloped countries with any kind of limitation of their powers, whether such limitation is inflicted from the outside or is self-imposed, and whether or not it is rational. But often the violation by the country of its own development program is due to the unreasonable and excessive character of the constraints laid down in the program. Governments of underdeveloped countries appear to have a tendency to subject themselves to overly rigid rules of conduct which, later on, they find themselves inevitably unable to follow. From this viewpoint, one may discern a genuine, though unexpected similarity between the orthodox and rigid monetary and banking legislations adopted in many Latin American countries in the twenties and the "integrated," long-term development programs of today. These programs often pretend to commit governments firmly to an all-embracing investment pattern in spite of the avowed weakness of our knowledge about appropriate investment criteria and even though the character and reality content of the estimates which make up the program differ widely from one economic sector to another.[1] If, in some sectors, the proposed spending is based only on the vaguest kind of criteria and extrapolations, then there is a good chance that the program figures should be radically revised once detailed engineering and economic studies have been undertaken. If it were made perfectly clear upon the publication and acceptance of a development program, which are the sectors where proposed spending results from careful screening of individual projects that are ready to be undertaken, and which are the ones where no such detailed planning has as yet been possible, then governments could change their minds about parts of the program without feeling that they are toppling the whole laboriously erected structure.

It should be added that provision for possible changes in the program should be made even with respect to those parts which have

1. On this point, see chap. 1, pp. 44–45.

received careful attention and study, as even here it is unlikely that all the alternatives have been fully considered. The distinction which we have made between sectors where planning has been sufficiently thorough to warrant full commitment by the government to the program, and those where the planning is of so general a nature that the government should retain considerable freedom of action to modify the tentatively set goals as better knowledge becomes available, is clearly overdrawn. The plan will ordinarily consist of a series of sectoral programs and projects which can be ranked according to the quantity and quality of expert planning that has gone into them and which should then command correspondingly decreasing degrees of allegiance on the part of the national government.

After the many experiences with national economic planning which have not been wholly successful, it might be time to recognize that governments of underdeveloped countries exhibit, side by side with a "propensity to plan," a "propensity to experiment and to improvise." If this is so, is it really wise to identify the former propensity with everything that is sensible and virtuous and the latter with all that is unreasonable and sinful? Would it not be far better to proceed in accordance with the prescriptions of any elementary textbook in psychology and provide healthy and constructive outlets for both propensities? Admittedly, there is nothing more exasperating and demoralizing than the spectacle, frequently on display in underdeveloped countries, of half-finished structures in reinforced concrete which were intended to become government buildings, hospitals, stadiums, etc. While the lack of planning and the arbitrary reversal of previously taken investment decisions that are responsible for these unsightly "modern ruins" are deplorable, improvisation and experimentation must be recognized not only as irrepressible urges of governments, but also as a force which, properly directed, can be made to play a beneficial role in the development process.

For instance, even with the best of plans, governments of underdeveloped countries certainly cannot and should not give up the permanent search for new and better ways of using the country's natural resources. If the search is successful, the investment pattern laid down in any previously adopted program ought to be disturbed. In our planning for certain average rates of growth, we are apt to forget that these average rates were realized in the industrial countries only because some very much higher rates were achieved in some sectors, often as a result of experimentation and improvisation. In underdeveloped countries, many dynamic growth sectors remain to be discovered; many patterns of social organization conducive to economic progress remain to be identified; and much flexibility in programming economic development must be preserved to enable governments and investors to take advantage of changing trends in world markets and of the changing whims of international development capital. Here, then, is a wide area where governments can and should make the utmost use of their urge to be imaginative, unpredictable, and uncoercible.

UNDERSTANDING RECURRING INFLATION

Let us now try to understand why inflation is still so real a problem in many underdeveloped countries. Is it not widely agreed that economic development should take place as much as possible within the framework of monetary stability? Has it not been pointed out ad nauseam that inflation, while typically resulting from an attempt to accelerate the development process, is actually harmful to it because of the speculative and nonproductive investments in inventories, real estate, and foreign exchange hoards it brings in its wake?

The fact is that when inflation proceeds at a fast and rapidly accelerating rate, its disadvantages usually become so obvious that somehow a way—and the political courage—is found to stop it. But after a short period of stability, the pressures often start to build up again and prices resume their upward course. The most obvious explanation is that in a developing economy which disposes of an elastic monetary system, the effective demand for investment funds always tends to outrun the supply of savings. While this explanation is true, I do not believe that it is particularly helpful in tracing the inflationary process and in locating the best means to curb it.

In the first place, this standard explanation implicitly tends to consider savings and consumption as more or less given and investment as the quantity which must be adjusted. Recent experience in several developing countries has shown, however, that savings are definitely "institution-elastic", i.e., that with the appropriate instruments and institutions, considerable amounts of domestic savings can be mobilized. Instead of curbing investment, it may also be possible to restrain consumption, in particular consumption of imported luxuries or their equivalent, namely foreign travel by residents. This is really the economic rationale for the prohibition of luxury imports or the special high foreign exchange rates often applying to such imports and to foreign travel. While in advanced countries such measures may have little anti-inflationary effect as the great variety of domestic production permits considerable substitution of the prohibited imports by domestically available goods and services, the sharply limited range of quality articles produced in underdeveloped countries makes such substitution there impractical, so that import-curbing measures may effectively decrease consumption.

Finally, the investments-outrun-savings analysis of inflation concentrates attention unduly not only on investment as opposed to savings and consumption, but also on public investments within the investment total. Public investments are the only ones that are reasonably well known and over which economic policy makers and advisers have some measure of direct control. Private investments are usually assumed at some given level, their composition is not known, and the way in which they can be influenced—by monetary policy—is not subject to accurate evaluation. As a result, public investments have to bear the brunt of any adjustment following the realization that there exists an excess of intended investment spending over available savings, and it is somewhat ironic to note that the modern approach to monetary stability, which relies on investment planning, is likely to result in this bias against public investments.

Let us now try to understand a little more fully why inflation is so difficult to avoid in underdeveloped countries. One reason is that the conditions for monetary equilibrium are more stringent for them than for the advanced countries. In the latter, all we need

261

as a condition for price stability is an overall balance between investment and savings. In actual fact, balance has often been consciously achieved by having expected dissavings or inadequate savings by individuals and business offset by a surplus in the government accounts. In underdeveloped countries, on the other hand, it is likely that we will have to achieve monetary equilibrium by balancing separately the accounts of the government on the one hand, and of the nongovernment sector on the other—obviously a more difficult task. The reason is that the achievement of a budgetary surplus for any length of time is simply out of the question for the ministers of finance of a developing country.

Even in advanced countries where a considerable internal debt is outstanding and maturing every year, it is difficult to win public support for a fiscal policy aiming at a cash surplus. In underdeveloped countries, internal debts are either small or are held by the central bank, and there would be little understanding for a policy aimed at retiring this debt when so many essential projects need to be undertaken. As to the external debt, it is ordinarily increasing rather than decreasing in an active period of development. Thus, the best that can be hoped for from the public sector under these circumstances is a precarious balance which means that the private sector has to balance its accounts independently. In this respect, the business sector, beset by requests for high dividends and by strong expansion needs, can be relied upon to be a net spender. The only safety valve is represented by the traditional tendency of individuals to be net hoarders of cash. But this tendency is increasingly counteracted by the enlarged availability of mass consumption goods, by the gradual appearance of personal credit facilities, and by the conversion of cash hoards into bank deposits.

In spite of these complicating factors, monetary stability could still be achieved given a sufficiently strong will among the economic policy makers. I shall now argue that this will is none too likely to be encountered. In the first place, a shrewd finance minister of a developing economy may not be entirely unhappy to have to contend with *moderate* inflationary pressure as such pressures give him an opportunity and an excuse to reject the more extravagant among the projects that are constantly brought to him by the spending ministers, the local governments, and the autonomous development agencies. As long as monetary stability prevails, he is almost as vulnerable as though he had accumulated a large cash balance. He does not and cannot pretend to know precisely the limits of tolerance of the economy. Thus, for him to say, "This additional expenditure will start inflation again," is clearly much less convincing than, "With prices again on the rise, we cannot afford to add more fuel to the fire." Small inflation may therefore represent an effective line of defense against unplanned and unreasonable expenditures and, in fact, it may at times be needed to hold the line against big inflation.

It is not suggested that the minister of finance consciously manufactures inflation. But all he usually has to do to have some inflation is to relent just one day in his fight against it; and he may so relent because, consciously or unconsciously, he feels that he must be under some pressure to operate successfully in the particular environment of an underdeveloped, but developing economy.

A further reason for which a finance minister may not be putting up as stiff a fight as he might against some increase in the price level is that the more modern tax structure which has in recent years been introduced in many underdeveloped countries, makes their fiscal revenues less vulnerable to inflation than they used to be. Customs duties are now predominantly on an ad valorem basis with specific duties in a secondary or supplementary role. Lags in collection have been reduced. Most important, progressive income taxation now exists almost everywhere and this means that a rise in prices and incomes has actually the effect of continuously and irreversibly increasing the real incidence of the existing rate schedule without any need to make it steeper through legislative action.

It must be a slow rise, for if there is a galloping inflation the schedules will surely be revised; but if prices and incomes rise by say 5 to 10 per cent per year, the inflation may bring with it just about the desired degree of tax tightening. Incidentally, this effect which may be quite important over the years, ought to be taken into account when one analyzes the effect of inflation on income distribution.

CYCLES IN FOREIGN EXCHANGE AND FISCAL POLICY

Let us next consider briefly a closely allied area of economic policy, namely foreign exchange rates and controls. Here a characteristic cycle may often be observed: a country with an impossibly complex multiple rate and exchange control structure adopts one day an excellent reform which sweeps away all the complications and sets up a unitary exchange rate, possibly incorporating into revised customs duties the protection previously resulting from some features of the abolished multiple rates. As time goes on, however, differential exchange rates and controls infiltrate again here and there. This goes on for some time until the situation is once more so chaotic that the country is ripe for another thorough exchange rate reform.

A similar cycle can be observed with respect to fiscal policy. A common feature of the revenue structure of many underdeveloped countries is the excessive earmarking of taxes for specific expenditures, in other words the violation of the principle of budgetary unity. Every once in a while, the situation becomes so intricate and the general budget so anemic that a law is passed eliminating all earmarkings—but here also one may be sure that soon there will be backsliding into the old ways.

These gyrations in economic policy are precisely what seems so discouraging to observers or advising experts who do not realize that there is some method in this madness, but see only the flouting of their advice and the total inability on the part of the authorities to adhere to a once elected course of action. Since the kind of policy making we have described requires frequent disregard for principles that were just recently proclaimed as inviolate, it attracts persons who do not have any qualms about such disregard. In this way, the optical illusion is created that the frequent turnabouts in economic policy are due to the fact that a capricious minister is in power, when in actual fact the more pertinent causation may work the other way around. Unsavory jobs are usually handled by unsavory individuals. But if society wants these jobs to be done, it is surely wrong to focus on the individuals and to hold them uniquely responsible.

The tendencies that are disruptive of unitary exchange rate systems and of the unity principle in budgeting are directly related to the economic structure and problems of underdeveloped countries. For instance, special incentive export rates are bound to be tried from time to time in countries which feel that they rely too heavily on one or two commodities for their export earnings. Earlier in this essay, we have already presented one argument favoring special import prohibitions, or special exchange rates designed to deter certain imports. In case domestic inflationary pressures dictate a devaluation, it may also become necessary to grant temporary privileged status to some imports. Consider, for instance, equipment imports on the part of public utilities which are undertaking important expansion projects. Privileged exchange rate·treatment for such imports may become a desirable offset to the handicap resulting for public utilities from the usual lag of their rates behind rises in the general price level.

In public finance the special earmarking of tax revenues is usually associated with the expansion of the government's activities. As a new field for governmental responsibility, say low-cost housing, is recognized, a new source of revenue must be discovered. It is only natural that at first the expenditure and the revenue which finances it, are coupled together. In this way the new fiscal device becomes far more acceptable to public opinion which always suspects "waste" in the expenditure of general treasury funds.

The conclusion I draw from this is not that to understand everything is to forgive everything. But I do think that to understand some of these real problems under which policy makers of underdeveloped countries labor will help in making our technical assistance more constructive. For instance, the preceding reasoning would seem to indicate that we should avoid those "fundamental reforms" accompanied by solemn declarations of principle and resounding commitments "never to do it again." In any reform, it would seem far wiser to circumscribe and to regulate such practices as multiple exchange rates and earmarking of fiscal revenues than to prohibit them outright.

CYCLES IN THE ADMINISTRATION OF ECONOMIC DEVELOPMENT

Cycles in economic policy such as the ones we have just described with regard to exchange rates and fiscal policy are paralleled in the administration of economic development. They are particularly disturbing as, under the best of circumstances, public administration presents many deficiencies in underdeveloped countries. On the other hand, policy changes in this area are perhaps more easily condoned by the foreign observer, as all governments seem to experience considerable difficulties in creating a workable and durable administrative structure for the exercise of new functions in the economic field. For here lies the origin of the trouble: a government decides that it should undertake a new function or carry on an existing one much more effectively than heretofore. It finds that for this purpose administrative procedures prevailing within the government itself are too cumbersome and slow; that salaries are too low to attract the kind of talent one wants to secure; and, most important usually, that political pressure ought to be removed from the scene. As a result of all these cogent reasons, a new institute, corporation, bank, or agency, with semiautonomous status, is created and starts on its career accompanied by many high hopes on the part of its founders and the general public.

One trouble with this solution is that the government of a developing country is liable to encounter one economic function after the other that ought to be newly undertaken or that must be carried out more efficiently. Thus semiautonomous institutes soon begin to mushroom, until one day a new cabinet comes in and the economic ministers find that the existence of these institutes—to which many important taxes are assigned—makes budgetary and economic planning practically impossible, and that it sharply curtails their own power to the full exercise of which they were hopefully looking forward. The result is that a thorough reorganization is decided upon which places all the new agencies right back into the government and under the ministries.

The likelihood of such a development is enhanced by the fact that the presidents, directors, or managers of the institutes are usually high-powered individuals at the start, but are soon replaced by others of lower standing, whereas no such process of progressive downgrading applies to the holders of ministerial jobs. Moreover, the autonomous institutes do not fare so well if the governments take too seriously their autonomous status, for then they lack the political and financial support which they vitally need for their success. Finally, there exists a well-known and time-honored propensity in many underdeveloped countries to "solve" serious economic problems by means of legislation alone. This practice has often blocked real progress. Today many governments are apparently under the similar and similarly dangerous illusion that they actually solve a problem by setting up an institute to which they delegate the task of solving the problem.[2]

The preceding remarks are not meant to deny that the new tasks which governments need to undertake will often require institutional innovations. But they may be taken as a warning against advocating too freely the "autonomous institute free of political interference" as *the* solution. What is needed, besides a very few institutes of this kind, is primarily a reorganization of the economic ministries which would enable them to carry out some of the new functions efficiently through their own subdivisions, or through institutes closely integrated with them.

We have noted here some salient examples of the apparently inherent instability of economic policy in underdeveloped countries. While the specific causes of this kind of instability are different in each case, a few general remarks may be in order by way of conclusion.

In the first place, we must understand this instability as the re-

2. An elaboration of some of these points is in my *Development Projects Observed* (Washington, D.C.: Brookings, 1967), pp. 153–59.

flection of some very general characteristics of underdeveloped countries. After all, their political structures themselves are unstable and ill-defined, the legitimacy of their governments is often in doubt, and in general the powers of the state fail to be clearly bounded by custom or observed constitutional law.

Secondly, there is the desire to experiment and to manipulate. Anxious to use their newly won sovereignty to the full, confident that the basic potential of their economies leaves them some latitude for making mistakes, governments of underdeveloped countries are powerfully attracted by new gadgets in economic policy making. Just as they have made the transition from mule to airplane in one generation, so they pass easily from the complete absence of monetary controls to the imposition of complicated differential reserve requirements. In economic policy, however, the meaning of progress is not nearly as clear as in technology. There are many more possibilities of going too far and too fast and, unlike technical progress, policy is typically reversible. If it is reversed too often, demoralization results, not only among the foreign advisers, but—and this is far more serious— among the country's policy makers and the general public. An impression of unpredictability and of lack of purpose is created which may even be damaging to economic progress itself. A rift develops between the business community which acquires the feeling that it is the only real creator of wealth in the country and the government with its bungling and erratic policies.

Much is therefore to be said for trying to make governmental policies more stable. Our analysis has shown that this aim cannot be achieved by once-and-for-all reforms or programs. Underdeveloped countries will not tolerate any straitjackets. The money doctor who prescribes a uniform financial diet or the economic advisor who lays down a rigid investment pattern may be obeyed for a while, but soon he becomes a father image that must be destroyed. Account must be taken of the propensity to change and to experiment so that, when it is indulged in, it does not come as a revolt against intolerable restraints but as an action that is foreseen as well as regulated. Economic policy in underdeveloped countries will then continue to fluctuate, but the limits of these fluctuations should gradually become narrower and the oscillation between those limits slower, as experiences with diverse policies are assimilated.

For economic policy in underdeveloped countries to become more stable, two conditions must therefore be fulfilled: first the institutional framework must be elastic and must regulate change rather than proscribe it; and second, home-grown experience must be accumulated, and made to yield a body of home-tested principles. As economists we can contribute importantly to this process: we can help underdeveloped countries to understand themselves and their experiences.

13. Ideologies of Economic Development in Latin America

> Why is there so much wretchedness, so much poverty in
> this fabulous land . . . ? Ah, says one—it is the priests'
> fault; another blames it on the military; still others on the
> Indian; on the foreigner; on democracy; on dictatorship;
> on bookishness; on ignorance; or finally on divine punish-
> ment.
>
> —Daniel Cosío Villegas

This paper attempts to review the principal ideas on the character
of Latin America's development problems which have been and
are being put forward by Latin American writers and social scientists.[1] Such an undertaking, if at all successful, will be more than
a contribution to the history of ideas. We need not go all the way
with Keynes's dictum that "the world is ruled by little else" than
by the ideas, both the right and the wrong ones, of economists
and political philosophers to recognize the importance of these
ideas for the shaping of reality. Yet the subject is strangely
neglected. We are far better informed about changes in the balance of payments, terms of trade, capital formation, etc., of
foreign countries than about the climate of opinion, the alignment of contending economic theories on policy issues, or about
the emergence of new reform proposals. When we are called
upon to advise a Latin American country on economic policy it
is only natural that, hard pressed, we should first of all attempt

Reprinted by permission from *Latin American Issues—Essays and
Comments,* ed. A. O. Hirschman (New York: Twentieth Century Fund,
1961), pp. 3–42. The opening quotation comes from *Extremos de América*
(Mexico City: Tezontle, 1949), p. 105.

1. The term "ideology" (of economic development) is used here, without derogatory connotation, to designate any moderately consistent body
of beliefs, ideas or propositions, tested or untested, that aims at explaining
Latin America's economic backwardness and at indicating its cure.

to get at the "facts," a difficult enough undertaking. But frequently our advice will be futile unless we have also gained an understanding of the understanding Latin Americans have of their own reality.

What follows is a first, tentative and very incomplete inquiry into a subject with vast and virtually unexplored possibilities. It will be possible to consider only a few central ideas that have been proposed on the cause and cure of Latin America's economic backwardness. The author hopes that his effort will stimulate others—particularly Latin Americans—to give us more systematic studies in this field.[2]

FROM INDEPENDENCE TO THE FIRST WORLD WAR: THE AGE OF SELF-INCRIMINATION

Some of the best known ideologies of economic development have arisen or have become prominent and influential in countries whose economic progress was seriously lagging behind that of the industrial leaders. *Relative economic backwardness* is thus an important concept which Alexander Gerschenkron has used with powerful effect to explain the specific characteristics of the successive forward surges of France, Germany and Russia in the nineteenth century and to show how every one of these thrusts was accompanied by a specific set of ideas about the cause and cure of the lag that was to be overcome. With respect to these countries it appears that the greater the lag the more radical and exalted were the theories which fired the effort at catching up.

Unfortunately, this suggestive generalization does not seem to hold in Latin America (or, for that matter, in the other countries which are today considered to be underdeveloped). The lag of the Latin American countries behind the industrial and general economic progress of Europe in the nineteenth century did not then give rise to any indigenous theories, ideas or views about the nature of Latin America's development problem. The reason

2. For a survey of ideological themes encountered in "latecomers" outside of Latin America, see Mary Matossian, "Ideologies of Delayed Industrialization: Some Tensions and Ambiguities," *Economic Development and Cultural Change* 6 (April 1958): 217–28.

may be that for many decades after the wars of independence the problems of survival, organization and consolidation of the South American states in the midst of border disputes, internal revolts and civil wars stood in the center of public attention so that the "ideologues" concentrated first on the problem of political organization.

This is not the place to retrace the development of Latin American political thought. But it should perhaps be briefly recalled that the constitutions which were adopted by the new Latin American states were largely inspired, if not copied, from that of the United States while the "generous idea of the French Revolution" served as the ideological foundation for the new republics. With the constitutions being continually violated, suspended and rewritten by the numerous military dictators and with the actual political, social and economic conditions being extraordinarily far removed from Liberty, Equality and Fraternity, there developed in Latin America that characteristic divorce between ideology and reality which has been well characterized by Octavio Paz in his incisive essay on Mexico, *El laberinto de la soledad:*

> The liberal and democratic ideology, far from expressing our concrete historical situation, obscured it. The political lie installed itself almost constitutionally among our countries. The moral damage has been incalculable and reaches into deep layers of our character. Lies are something we move in with ease. During more than a hundred years we have suffered regimes of brute force, which were at the service of feudal oligarchies, but utilized the language of liberty.[3]

This permanent and painful "collision between theory and practice, between words and action, between content and form"[4] has been described by virtually all observers of the Latin American

3. Octavio Paz, *El laberinto de la soledad,* 2d ed. (Mexico: Fondo de Cultura Economica, 1959), pp. 110–11.

4. J. F. Normano, *The Struggle for South America* (Boston and New York, 1931), p. 206.

scene and we shall see that, far from dead, it has invaded new territories, such as economic and social policy making.

The inability of the political system to provide basic requisites of law and order, the spectacle of the strides made by Europe and the United States and the defeats and humiliations suffered (mainly by Mexico) at the hands of the Colossus of the North did lead, in the course of the nineteenth century, to considerable soul-searching on the part of Latin American intellectuals. They turned away from the revolutionary ideals and dreams which had served their countries poorly and became willing to settle for less than utopia. In the second half of the century, many came to preach "a practical sense of life," "an inquiring, experimental and practical mind," "rigorous scientific method" and "clearly defined, positive ends."[5] This state of mind found its most curious expression in the ideological support many of Mexico's outstanding educators and intellectuals gave to the long dictatorship (1884–1911) of Porfirio Díaz, the "honest tyrant" who was to bring order out of chaos and prosperity out of stagnation and misery. It is well to recall that Díaz was admired not only by Mexican intellectuals; Tolstoy among others hailed him as a "modern Cromwell" who used autocratic methods in guiding his country toward democracy.[6] Thus, under Porfirio Díaz, Mexico experimented with an idea that today has wide currency and application in the Middle East and Asia: namely, that one-man military rule can play a positive, tutelary role in a new country by ridding it of corruption, by giving it a vacation from disruptive political strife, and by guiding it firmly and efficiently toward modernity.

One reason why educators such as Justo Sierra threw their support to Díaz was their strong feeling that much time and patient work was needed to remedy Mexico's ills. Indeed, faced with the incapacity of Latin American societies to achieve stable,

5. Leopoldo Zea, "Positivism and Porfirism in Latin America," in F. S. C. Northrop, ed., *Ideological Differences and World Order* (New Haven: Yale University Press, 1949), p. 170.

6. Quoted in C. O. Bunge, *Nuestra América,* 6th ed. (Buenos Aires, 1918), pp. 309–10.

just and progressive government, they concluded that nothing less than a complete transformation of Latin American "character" and society was required and this was evidently a long-term task. The structure of society was to be improved through the formation of a middle class and patient education was needed thoroughly to reshape the Latin American character.

In this latter respect, feelings ran to an astonishingly high pitch. At the beginning of this century, some of the most widely read works by Latin Americans about themselves and their society consisted of little more than a seemingly endless and remarkably pitiless recitation of their vices and failures. Outstanding among these works were Bunge's *Nuestra América*[7] and Bomfim's *O parasitismo social e evolução: A América Latina* (Rio de Janeiro, 1903). Strongly influenced by the then fashionable determinism based on race and heredity, both books barely stop short of proclaiming the irreparable racial inferiority and progressive degeneration of all Latin America. Bunge's work, which is highly entertaining and which went through six editions, contains many valuable insights and in particular a masterful portrait of the *cacique,* but his whole analysis is built on the proposition that the three basic constituents of the Latin American character are laziness, sadness and arrogance![8]

Another highly interesting work in this category which deals specifically with economics is *Nuestra inferioridad económica: Sus causas, sus consecuencias* (Santiago, 1912) by the Chilean historian Francisco Encina. To him the principal reasons for the inadequate progress of Chile's economy are certain pervasive character traits such as lack of initiative, of perseverance and of morality, inability to cooperate, ostentatiousness, etc. These

7. The first edition was published in 1903.

8. Another and an extreme example of this literature is *Pueblo enfermo* by the Bolivian Alcides Arguedas, 2d ed. (Barcelona, 1910). In his famous epic *Os sertões* (1902), Euclides da Cunha celebrated the way of life of the rugged *sertanejo,* the man of the backlands of Northeastern Brazil; but even he repeated the consensus of contemporary opinion that mixing of the races means degeneracy. See the English translation of da Cunha's work under the title *Rebellion in the Backlands* (Chicago: University of Chicago Press, 1944), p. 84 f.

traits, in turn, are due to poor heredity and the wrong kind of education.[9]

Today, when we are more aware of the hypersensitive nationalism sometimes encountered in Latin America, it is worth while to recall this extraordinary orgy of self-denigration, self-laceration and pessimism which can be traced back to Simón Bolívar and to his famous statement that in Latin America "treaties are pieces of paper, constitutions are books, elections are fights, liberty is anarchy and life a torment."

How was this "sick continent" and this "ill people" to be cured? The Argentinians Sarmiento and Alberdi, writing in the middle and late nineteenth century, respectively, advised imitation of the U.S. model. Sarmiento wrote: "Let us achieve the stage of development of the United States. Let us be the United States."[10] Alberdi gave much the same advice several decades later: "In economics even more than in politics the best example for Americans to follow is America herself. In economics North America is the great model for South America."[11]

But the economic doctrines that were prevalent among the more prominent Latin American writers on social and economic affairs were even more strongly influenced by the British free trade and noninterventionist doctrines. Perhaps the successive governments were either too weak or too tyrannical for anyone

9. Encina has some surprisingly "modern" things to say. Thus he stresses the importance of entrepreneurship and employee morality as opposed to that of capital: "One frequently talks of business opportunities blocked by lack of capital; more numerous are those that fail to be utilized because of the lack of entrepreneurs and even more numerous those whose realization is impossible because of the incompetence and immorality of the employees" (p. 98).

Moreover, Encina probably ought to be recognized as the original discoverer of the "demonstration effect," which is dealt with at length. To quote just two sentences: "Observation shows that in a weak economy penetrated by a strong one, the capacity to consume increases more rapidly than the capacity to produce. . . . The desires to consume are communicated by imitation far more rapidly than the propensity to produce" (pp. 157–58).

10. Quoted in J. F. Normano, *Struggle, pp.* 208–29.

11. J. B. Alberdi, *Escritos póstumos,* vol. 1, *Estudios económicos,* (Buenos Aires, 1895), p. 522.

to think of advising that they take on additional functions. Also, as Celso Furtado suggests, Latin American nineteenth-century writers had their social roots among the large landholders and slaveowners and may therefore have shown little interest in building up a manufacturing establishment.[12] In this context it becomes significant that Alberdi failed to advocate industrialization for Latin America even though he hit on the idea that latecomers possess certain advantages—an idea which has been invoked elsewhere as a persuasive argument for industrialization.

> By preventing the rise of industry in her American colonies Spain benefited industrial Europe and handed to her a rich territory which now has to buy from the most advanced industrial nations. On the other hand the very backwardness of South America is an advantage. Instead of inheriting a bad industry, South America has at her disposal the most advanced European industry of the 19th century.[13]

It appears that in spite of his insight about the advantages of backwardness Alberdi is happy enough with the existing state of affairs which makes it possible for Latin America to acquire quality manufacturers in Europe.

THE INTERWAR PERIOD AND THE RISE OF ANTI-IMPERIALISM

Up to the first decade of the twentieth century this literature with its passionate self-criticism and its advocacy of laissez faire and a social and economic system similar to that of the advanced industrial nations was perhaps dominant. In the next phase we encounter a greater tendency to find fault with the outside world rather than with oneself. Correlatively, a search begins for specifically Latin American solutions to the area's economic problems. United States interventionism in Panama, the Caribbean and Mexico, the loss of face of Europe as a result of the First World War, and the Russian and Mexican revolutions all con-

---

12. Celso Furtado, *Formação econômica do Brasil* (Rio de Janeiro: Editôra Fundo de Cultura, 1959), p. 123.
13. Alberdi, *Escritos póstumos,* p. 591.

tributed to this change. Yet cohesive theories of social and economic reform were slow to emerge. The Mexican Revolution was remarkable in that it wholly belied the Napoleonic maxim that a revolution is an idea that has found bayonets—here it was rather the revolution which found its ideas as it proceeded with varying speed and over a large number of years along its pragmatic road.

Paradoxically, the most ambitious attempt at revolutionary theorizing about Latin American society arose in a country that up to this day at least has gone through a minimum of social change: I am speaking about Peru and the writings of Haya de la Torre and Mariátegui.

Haya de la Torre formulated his thinking in the early twenties, in an intellectual climate dominated by the October Revolution. He soon felt the need to differentiate himself from orthodox communism and set out to discover the peculiar character of Latin America's problems. Thus, he considered Lenin's definition of imperialism as the last stage of capitalism and noted that for the non-industrial countries, imperialism was rather their first experience with capitalism. For this reason, Haya de la Torre maintained that a revolution in Latin America could not be undertaken by the weak and submerged proletariat, but must also rely on the intellectuals and the middle classes, which, according to him, were endowed with far more fighting spirit in Latin America than in Europe.

Under these conditions, the struggle must be conducted under an anti-imperialist rather than an anti-capitalist banner. Action against imperialism was the first point of Haya's five-point program, the others being: political unity of Latin America, nationalization of land and industries, internationalization of the Panama Canal, and solidarity with the oppressed people and classes everywhere. But like some of these latter points (e.g., nationalization) Haya's anti-imperialism was subject to interesting qualifications. For Haya explicitly recognized Latin America's need for foreign capital, but, so he argued, if only Latin American countries stopped competing for foreign capital, and united in an anti-imperialist coalition, they could obtain it under far more favorable conditions since capitalist countries have a compelling need to export capital:

The naive thesis of our feudal rulers, vassals of imperialism, proclaims "every capital is good" while the antithesis of our passionate radicals says "we don't need foreign capital." The Aprista synthesis holds that as long as the present economic order lasts some capital flows are necessary and good and others unnecessary and dangerous; and that only the anti-imperialist state should control capital investment under strict conditions. The latter can be imposed in view of the compulsion to emigrate which is felt by the excess capital of the big industrial centers. *In our countries, the capitalist stage must therefore unfold under the leadership of the anti-imperialist State.*[14]

Stripped of rhetoric, this simply means that the state should exercise control over the direction of investment—a condition which is today frequently demanded by the foreign (e.g., World Bank) capital itself, rather than imposed upon it.

Haya's search for an "Indoamerican Way" rests upon closer inspection essentially on the desire for economic development without some of the disruptions and injustices that have marked the process elsewhere:

Why not build into our own reality "as it really is" the bases of a new economic and political organization which will accomplish the educational and constructive task of industrialism but will be free of its cruel aspects of human exploitation and national vassalage?[15]

Attribution of backwardness to imperialist exploitation, direction of economic development by the state, avoidance of the excesses that have marked the early stages of capitalist development in the West, and the community of interests of all of Latin America—these are basic ingredients of Haya's thought which as we shall see have left a deep mark on Latin American economic thinking.

14. Haya de la Torre, *El antiimperialismo y el APRA* (Santiago, 1936), p. 159. (Italics in the original.)
15. Ibid., p. 25.

A final element is the search for elements in the Indian or primitive past of Latin America that are not only worth preserving but that can be used in building a better social and economic order. Haya speaks eloquently about the dualism of the Peruvian economy and about the need to preserve and to build a new agrarian society on the collectivist tradition of the Indian economy. In the work of another influential Peruvian, the Socialist José Carlos Mariátegui (1895–1930), the preservation of the communal *ayllu* (corresponding to the Aztec-Mexican *calpulli-ejido)* and the call for its victory over the *latifundio* are principal themes.[16] Actually, U.S. anthropologists who have done field work in Peru have expressed serious doubts about the vigor of the communes and about the extent to which they still hold land in common, engage in reciprocal labor, etc.[17] Nevertheless, the continuing belief among intellectuals that it may be possible to build on the Indian past is in itself of interest. It is part of the attempt to find an "own" way to economic progress and social justice.

Whether or not the currents thus far reviewed qualify as economic theories, knowledge of this background is important to an understanding of contemporary thinking. For, essentially, the debate is still defined by two principal questions. One, where lies the responsibility for our lag? In ourselves or in the outside world which exploits us? Two, how can we make progress? By imitating others (the West or Russia) or by fashioning our own way?

THE PRESENT SCENE AND THE COMMANDING POSITION OF ECLA

The historical background which has been all too briefly sketched in the preceding pages serves to bring out the considerable change which has occurred in the discussion of Latin American economic problems during the last ten years: while economic ideas have previously had to be gleaned from political writings or

16. José Carlos Mariátegui, *Siete ensayos de interpretación de la realidad peruana* (Santiago: Editorial Universitaria, 1955), see the essay "El problema de la tierra," pp. 35–76.

17. Cf. Richard W. Patch, "How Communal Are the Communities?" American Universities Field Staff Report (New York, 1959).

279

from general essays on Latin American society, we now possess a voluminous literature dealing exclusively with Latin America's economic problems. By all odds, the central body of this literature is represented by the writings of the United Nations Economic Commission for Latin America (ECLA).

ECLA was organized in 1948 as a regional commission of the United Nations with its seat in Santiago, Chile. Its members are the twenty Latin American countries, the United States and the three European countries with possessions in the Western Hemisphere—Great Britain, France and the Netherlands. While its membership is thus wider than that of the Organization of American States with its twenty-one Western Hemisphere governments, it has, in reality, become much more a strictly Latin American affair than the OAS; unlike the latter, it has been able to avoid an undue dispersion of its activities and has largely achieved its objective of being considered as the recognized spokesman for Latin America's economic development.

The arresting feature of ECLA is that it possesses attributes not frequently encountered in large international organizations: a cohesive personality which evokes loyalty from the staff, and a set of distinctive beliefs, principles and attitudes, in brief an ideology, which is highly influential among Latin American intellectuals and policy makers. To a considerable degree, this achievement is due to ECLA's director, Dr. Raúl Prebisch, who, in 1949, while not yet heading the organization (he was appointed Executive Secretary in 1950), wrote that veritable ECLA manifesto, *The Economic Development of Latin America and Its Principal Problems*.

Before the principal thesis of this brochure is examined, it is useful to point out briefly that ECLA's twelve-year history can be divided into approximately three phases, in accordance with changes in the central locus of its interests and activities. During the first period—to about 1953—the ideology was forged, elaborated and tested with the help of such basic data on the Latin American economies as were being assembled; during the second period, intensive studies of individual Latin American countries were undertaken with the aim of "programming" their future economic development; and since about 1958, the principal interest of the organization has shifted to the intensive study and promotion of Latin American economic integration or cooperation, principally through the formation of a Latin American common market. It should be noted that the new interests of the organization have not superseded the old ones, but have rather resulted in an extension of its field of action.

The Elaboration of the ECLA Doctrine

In Latin America, reality is undermining the outdated schema of the international division of labor. . . . Under that schema, the specific task that fell to Latin America, as part of the periphery of the world economic system, was that of producing food and raw materials for the great industrial countries. There was no place within it for the industrialization of the new countries. It is, nevertheless, being forced upon them by events. Two world wars in a single generation and a great economic crisis between them have shown the Latin American countries their opportunities, clearly pointing the way to industrial activity.[18]

These opening sentences of Prebisch's brochure convey its militant flavor and mark their author as another great figure in the series of outstanding political economists who have preached protection, industrialization and "catching-up" to their respective countries.[19] In describing the plight of the "periphery" and the need for a policy of deliberate industrialization, Prebisch and ECLA created and adapted a series of arguments and tools of analysis.[20] It would be highly instructive to trace in detail the

18. Raúl Prebisch, *The Economic Development of Latin America and Its Principal Problems* (New York: United Nations, 1950).

19. See chap. 3 above for comments on "disenchantment with industrialization" as later voiced by Prebisch and ECLA.

20. In the following I am drawing also on ECLA's *Economic Survey of Latin America, 1949,* (New York: United Nations, 1950), part 1 of which (pp. 1–88) contains an elaboration of the Prebisch essay. A further development of the doctrine is in *Theoretical and Practical Problems of Economic Growth* (New York: United Nations, E/CN 12/221, 1951). A reformulation is in Prebisch, "Commercial Policy in the Underdeveloped Countries," *American Economic Review* 49 (May 1959): 251–73.

evolution of the ECLA doctrine and to relate it to Latin American political writings such as those of Haya and to Western economic theory. All that can be done here is to give a synopsis of the essential ingredients of the doctrine.

The basic emphasis is on the asymmetry in the relations between the "center" and the "periphery," and it is this asymmetry that traditional theory is accused of having overlooked.

1. In the first place, the gains from trade are not equally divided between the center and the periphery; the terms of trade are constantly moving against the primary producing countries. The empirical basis for this statement was a 1949 United Nations study of Britain's terms of trade between 1876 and 1946; an explanation of the phenomenon was sought in the alleged tendency of productivity advances to lead to wage and other factor price increases (and, therefore, constant commodity prices) in the "center," but, largely because of disguised unemployment, to commodity price declines in the periphery. This so-called Prebisch-Singer[21] thesis about the unequal distribution of productivity gains between the industrial and underdeveloped countries and the secular tendency towards a worsening of the latter's terms of trade has been hotly contested and the empirical data which the theory invoked were certainly insufficient to support so broad a generalization. Nevertheless, international price developments of recent years have given fresh support to the Prebisch-Singer views. In any event, what is important for our purposes is that ECLA found a fairly persuasive way of propounding a modern sophisticated version of the old idea that trade can be a vehicle for exploitation rather than a means of increasing welfare all-round.

2. Subsequent ECLA publications have made less of the unequal division of productivity gains and have rather directed attention to another asymmetry: that between the income elasticity of demand for imports of the center compared to that of the periphery. The former was seen as continually declining, largely

21. H. W. Singer proposed the same idea in his article, "The Distribution of Gains between Investing and Borrowing Countries," *American Economic Review* 40 (May 1950): 472–99.

because of Engel's Law,[22] whereas the latter was believed to be potentially extremely large because of the high import content of new investments and because of the demonstration effect. Thus, as income rises in the center, the percentage expenditure on imports from the periphery declines. As income rises in the periphery, however, the percentage of income that goes for imports from the center increases. This discrepancy is held to cause a recurrent tendency toward balance of payments difficulties and, therefore, once more toward a deterioration of the terms of trade for Latin America, at least in the absence of substantial capital imports.

3. Protection plays a different role in developed and underdeveloped countries. In the developed center it interferes with the optimal allocation of resources; but in the periphery, because of disguised unemployment in agriculture and a natural increase in population that cannot be absorbed there, protection of industry is required from the very point of view of resource allocation: within rather wide limits any increase in industrial output is a net addition to the total product. This argument, which has been presented in theoretically precise form by Arthur Lewis, goes considerably beyond the infant industry case for protection.

4. A corollary on which ECLA has frequently insisted is that in the periphery the impact of import restrictions is different from that in the center. In the latter, such restrictions will lead to a shrinkage of total trade, whereas in the periphery they will merely lead to a redirection of total imports, since (a) exports are what they are—the periphery exerts a negligible influence by its own purchases in the center on what the center will buy abroad; and (b) given the high and eternally unsatisfied demand for imports, the holding-back of some imports will only lead to their substitution by some others.

The preceding propositions share two characteristics. In the first place, they supply an answer to the fundamental question about the reason for Latin America's backwardness: it lies with

22. Engel's Law states that percentage expenditure on food is on the average a decreasing function of income.

the international trading system with which Latin America has become involved, and with the misleading free trade doctrines insofar as they have been applied. Secondly, they all point to the need for public policies designed to correct the faults of that international system through deliberate intervention: The need is for the promotion of industrialization through systematic interference with the balance of payments, i.e., through protection and import controls. Moreover, since exports cannot be relied on to provide the Latin American economies with the "engine for growth," it is necessary actively to plan and accelerate the process of import substitution, since otherwise continued economic development will run into a rigid foreign exchange barrier.

These tenets have remained deeply ingrained in all the important ECLA pronouncements. Logically enough, ECLA conceived its mission as a dual one: to alert the Latin American countries to the precariousness of their position, and to appeal for outside help to an area which was being buffeted and victimized by forces beyond its control. These preoccupations are reflected in ECLA's annual surveys, which consistently point to the dark spots in the economic picture. Even though numerous Latin American countries achieved considerable economic progress during the postwar period, the successive annual reports frequently read as though things were tolerable enough until a few months ago, but have *now* started to take a definite turn for the worse. In this fashion, Latin America's situation was dramatized with the aim of stimulating both national and international action.[23] In the latter respect, ECLA documents stressed the inadequacy and unreliability of foreign capital inflow, criticized certain of the lending policies of international institutions such as the World Bank, and proposed additional international financial facilities and agencies.[24] In 1954 a special committee appointed by the Secretariat pro-

23. For further remarks along these lines, see the discussion of the "action-arousing gloomy vision" in chap. 16, pp. 350–53.

24. See in particular ECLA, *International Cooperation in a Latin American Development Policy* (New York: United Nations, 1954).

posed an annual foreign aid and investment target for Latin America of one billion dollars for at least ten years.[25]

The Programming Technique

While ECLA was in these various fashions acquiring a distinct and militant personality, the organization felt that it had to undertake something practical if it were to acquire a more direct influence. For this purpose, ECLA chose to interest individual Latin American governments in the detailed programming of economic development and to lend them a helping hand in this unfamiliar task. This work marks the second major phase of ECLA activity. As with the first, it also has its basic document, namely, the brochure *An Introduction to the Technique of Programming,* which was presented at the fifth session at Rio in 1953; a revised version was printed in 1955.

This brochure represents an attempt to provide guidance in the drawing up of medium- and long-term aggregate and sectoral projections of economic growth on the basis of empirical knowledge and various theories that were then being rapidly accumulated by economists concerned with development problems: the projection of domestic demand in accordance with consumer budget studies; the projection of the capacity to import on the basis of an estimate of foreign markets; estimates of savings and capital-output ratios; and the application of various investment criteria and of input-output analysis. In conjunction with the setting of a certain growth target, say a 2 per cent annual increase in per capita income, these techniques, if combined with adequate statistical information (admittedly a large "if"), can be made to trace out in detail the path which the economy appears likely to follow.

The brochure is at pains to point out that the technique does

25. Contemptuously dismissed at the time in the United States as a hare-brained scheme (see Introduction above, p. 29), this was the precise figure that was picked eight years (and one revolution) later as the goal for the annual United States contribution to the Alliance for Progress during its first decade!

not imply anything with respect to the extent of "rigid state control of the economy." It does imply, however, that without state action to call forth the correct amount of investment and to direct it into the proper channels, the Latin American economies would make numerous wrong decisions; they would choose too much consumption and too little investment, too much export promotion and too little import substitution, too much investment in secondary industry and not enough in basic power and transportation facilities, too much capital-intensive technology, etc.

The "technique" has been applied by ECLA to a number of countries: Brazil, Colombia, Bolivia, Argentina, Panama and Peru. In the process, ECLA has learned much about the real conditions and problems of these countries and has contributed to the economic education of those in the countries who collaborated with the ECLA team; but in terms of actually influencing national economic development policies, this activity has been less rewarding.

At first, ECLA's studies were acquiesced in rather than actively promoted by the national governments; under these conditions and since the development programs drawn up by even the most highly placed official bodies have frequently remained "on paper," it is not surprising that this very fate has befallen most of the ECLA-sponsored programs. In the most recent country studies, those of Panama and Peru, local governmental agencies have cooperated more intimately with the ECLA teams, and ECLA is now also extending some direct technical assistance to governmental planning agencies, as recently in Colombia, Bolivia and Cuba. But the fundamental problem which faced ECLA in this phase of its effort was not so much that of cooperation with the governmental agencies in charge of development planning, but the question whether development planning of the kind pursued by ECLA was felt to be a compelling need by the principal policy-making officials. ECLA itself expressed some doubts on the subject in a study on Bolivia:

> Programming is not entirely the task of experts in the central organizations; it also requires the collaboration of

public and private technical and economic offices. . . . without energetic support of the highest policy circles . . . it is difficult for the programming authorities to carry out their work. This is not only a question of status. In Bolivia, as well as in other countries, the National Commission for Coordination and Planning or its equivalent is placed at the highest level, but it still cannot be said to have received wholehearted official support. What is chiefly required is the "will to plan" on the part of the supreme political authorities. . . . Certain factors appear to have militated against this spirit.[26]

Thus, the "programming" activity of ECLA was not without its frustrations, and it is probably being pursued at the present time with a somewhat diminished ardor, the more so since a new and powerful interest has arisen for ECLA: the Latin American Common Market.

The Latin American Common Market

As early as in his 1949 "manifesto," Prebisch pointed out that one limitation to industrial growth was "the present division of markets, with its consequent inefficiency" and that this obstacle "could be overcome by the combined efforts" of the Latin American countries.[27] In the early fifties ECLA compiled a study of inter-Latin American trade, and its Mexico branch was entrusted with technical assistance for the economic integration program which was being undertaken by the five Central American republics. The fairly satisfactory experience with this program was one of the elements that in 1958 rather suddenly moved the Common Market into the forefront of ECLA's activities. Other factors were: perhaps, as already mentioned, some feeling of frustration over what was being achieved with "programming"; certainly the establishment of the European Economic Community, with the example it provided and the threat it posed for some of Latin America's export products; and the fact that even in

26. "The Economic Development of Bolivia," *Economic Bulletin for Latin America* (October 1957), p. 44.
27. Prebisch, *Economic Development,* p. 47.

some of the bigger countries industrialization was reaching a stage at which a fairly large number of industries could best be established if they could count, at least initially, on some export markets.

In making the case for closer economic integration in Latin America, ECLA relied on some of its earlier analyses. According to its projections, so it argued, Latin American exports could not possibly expand as fast in the next fifteen years as would be required to maintain the present ratio of imports to national income; and the only way, therefore, in which economic progress could be maintained would be by intensifying the import substitution process. Given the industries which have to be developed, primarily in capital goods, such an expansion can only be achieved if industrialization is no longer pursued and "duplicated" within twenty "watertight compartments."[28]

In ECLA's thinking the Common Market is thus primarily required to avert a disastrous slowdown in Latin America's economic growth rather than as a means to improve economic efficiency, organization and policy; among the possible arguments in favor of the Common Market, little attention is given to the advantages of continent-wide competition for some of Latin America's young, yet already run-down or poorly run industries, or of the check which economic integration might constitute for unwise national economic policies.

The Direction of ECLA Influence

The foregoing summary makes it clear that ECLA, while it has transferred the principal center of its activity from one area to another as it ran into difficulties or decreasing returns, has maintained the identity of its personality throughout these shifts.

The "ECLA doctrine" has essentially consisted in assuming a critical and militant attitude toward the industrial "center" on behalf of the underdeveloped "periphery" and in calling upon the governments of the latter to undertake new responsibilities in the promotion of economic development. In doing so ECLA gave ex-

28. *The Influence of the Common Market on the Economic Development of Latin America* (April 1959), E/CN.12/C.1/13.

pression and direction to feelings that are diffuse among important intellectual and middle-class circles in Latin America: first, to various resentments against the United States and in particular to the suspicion of exploitation; and, second, to the idea that the cure for society's ills lies in empowering the state to deal with them. But while ECLA has mirrored these basic emotions, it has also controlled them, and has progressively turned them to increasingly constructive tasks, such as the detailed study of national economic structures and inter-Latin American economic cooperation.

To perceive the specific direction in which ECLA has exercised its influence, it is useful to realize which are the areas where ECLA has not brought a particularly intensive effort to bear. Thus, while the need for import substitution has been a constant theme, the possibilities of promoting new or traditional exports have not received similar emphasis. Industries which are to be established or substantially expanded, such as iron and steel, or pulp and paper, have been intensively studied, but the efficiency of industries which already exist has received scant attention, except for an excellent but isolated early report on the productivity of the textile industry in four Latin American countries. Problems such as those of agrarian reform and social security (not to speak of excessive military expenditures) have been shunned, partly because ECLA could not afford to prod and antagonize its members in these highly sensitive areas; partly, perhaps, because they were felt to be in the area of competence of other international agencies: the Food and Agriculture Organization and United Nations headquarters for agrarian reform[29] and the International Labor Office and the Organization of American States for social security.

In discussing the problem of inflation, ECLA has stressed various "structural" factors responsible for inflationary pressures, and has been skeptical of the "orthodox" remedies of fiscal-monetary retrenchments and realistic exchange adjustments advocated by

29. ECLA's 1959 *Economic Survey of Latin America* (New York: United Nations, 1960) carries for the first time a short chapter on "Recent Developments in Latin American Land Reform."

the International Monetary Fund. With respect to the analysis of the growth process in general, ECLA is rather firmly committed to the notion that development depends primarily on the generation of an adequate supply of capital, domestic and foreign. In this connection, the International Bank has on occasion been criticized for inadequate lending and overrestrictive criteria. But ECLA has not only been a claimant for new resources; it has also attempted to instruct Latin American governments and planning agencies in the best use of whatever funds they have at their disposal; the programming technique has been communicated through seminars held in all major Latin American countries to a large number of economic policy-making officials.

ECLA has undoubtedly advocated the assumption of larger economic responsibilities on the part of the national states, and eventually, perhaps, on the part of regional authorities in a variety of fields. But the principal task of government is, in ECLA's view, to give long-range direction to economic development by means of detailed plans which must be carefully laid and observed. Formulated in this way, ECLA's design has a utopian ring for societies where simple ministerial changes frequently mean total reversals of policies and where the policy makers themselves take pride in being unpredictable. But it is this very situation that permits us better to understand ECLA's intent. Its programming activities can perhaps be interpreted as an attempt to "reform" certain inveterate traits such as the propensity to improvise, the lack of foresight, the failure ever to see the handwriting on the wall. ECLA's detailed projections where all economic sectors are made to mesh harmoniously are in a sense the twentieth-century equivalent of Latin America's nineteenth-century constitutions—and are as far removed from the real world. They are a protest, both pathetic and subtle, against a reality where politicians relying on brilliant or disastrous improvisations hold sway, where decisions are taken under multiple pressures rather than in advance of a crisis and emergency situations, and where conflicts are resolved on the basis of personal considerations after the contending parties have revealed their strength in more or less open battle rather than in accordance with objective principles and scientific criteria.

Some years ago, an impressive amount of evidence was marshalled to show that the movement and style of the Bolsheviks was born out of a protest against, and a determined negation of, the Russian character and "soul" that had been popularized by the great Russian novelists of the nineteenth century.[30] Similarly the style that ECLA would like to implant in Latin America is perhaps born from the desire to stamp out those traditional traits which are felt to be hindrances and handicaps on the road to economic progress. Here ECLA rejoins essentially those earlier analysts of Latin American backwardness who had concluded that the Latin American character has to be thoroughly remolded before anything useful can be achieved. ECLA never says so; on the contrary, as we have seen, it has devised new arguments in support of the idea that the "periphery's difficulties are to be blamed on the "center"—but these difficulties being taken for granted, ECLA's prescriptions are nevertheless implicitly premised on a revolutionary overhauling of the basic realities of economic policy making in the continent.

ECLA's CRITICS

ECLA's voice is, no doubt, the one that is heard loudest today in the debate on Latin America's economic problems, and there is little doubt that its views are representative of a large section of the new middle class. But it would be a mistake to think that its doctrines are unquestioningly accepted by all influential economic circles in Latin America. The opposition comes essentially from two different sectors: in the first place, from those who are highly skeptical of the ability of the state in Latin America to operate competently in the field of economic policy and planning; and, secondly, from those who simply dissent in various other ways from ECLA's diagnosis and emphasis.

Distrust of the State's Capabilities

For many Latin Americans, the state has so thoroughly demonstrated its total ineptness in the discharge of economic functions that the idea of entrusting it with some sort of general staff func-

30. Nathan Leites, *A Study of Bolshevism* (Glencoe, Ill.: The Free Press, 1953).

tions in the direction of the national economy seems utterly ludicrous to them. Their "ideological vision" is similar to that of Adam Smith, who, as Schumpeter said, felt nothing but "disgust . . . at the inefficiency of the English bureaucracy and at the corruption of the politicians."[31] This kind of feeling is far more widespread in Latin America than might be supposed from a perusal of current Latin American economic writings.

It has been said, and perhaps with good reason, that the private entrepreneur does not command nearly as much prestige in underdeveloped countries where he merely "imitates" as he once enjoyed in the pioneer industrial countries where he truly innovated. But that does not mean that correspondingly more prestige is held by the state. Long experience with official corruption and incompetence has led to an attitude of distrust and contempt toward the state and a bureaucracy which has no civil service tradition and where all major as well as most minor appointments are political. Frequently the state is compared to the organized bandits of the backlands exacting their tribute and leading a purely parasitic existence. The idea that economic development takes place in spite of, rather than because of, state action is well expressed in the Brazilian saying "Our country grows by night when the politicians sleep." Even those who are anxious to have the state carry out important new functions and tasks for economic development show occasionally an awareness of the considerable difficulties of such an undertaking, difficulties arising from the bureaucratic, parasitic and "clientelistic" traditions of what is known in Brazil as the *"Cartorial* (paper-shuffling or notarial) State."[32] The violent desire to put an end to the *"Cartorial* State" and to start afresh in an atmosphere dedicated to economic and social progress and uncontaminated by old-time *clientelismo* goes far toward explaining the move of Brazil's capital from Rio to Brasília.

The lengthy period of civil war and virtual anarchy punctu-

31. Joseph Schumpeter, "Science and Ideology," *American Economic Review* 39 (March 1949): 353.
32. Cf. Helio Jaguaribe, *O Nacionalismo na atualidade brasileira* (Rio de Janeiro: Instituto Superior de Estudos Brasileiros, 1958), pp. 41, 44.

ated by military dictatorship through which most of Latin America passed in the nineteenth century was ill-suited to create in the Latin American mind a very respectful picture of the state. During that period, a particularly confusing stretch of Colombia's history is known as the time of the *"patria boba,"* the "stupid fatherland"; and *"hacer patria,"* "to make (or build) the fatherland," denotes there typically the activity not of agents of the state, but of farmers who are settling virgin territories or of engineers and entrepreneurs building new plants and factories. In all countries many tales are current about the utter incompetence of the state as an entrepreneur; some draw the conclusion that "better planning" is needed, but others are convinced that state-run enterprises are necessarily stillborn.

These diffuse feelings of skepticism about the state's entrepreneurial and planning abilities found, of course, particularly vigorous spokesmen in the nineteenth century. Thus, most of Alberdi's economic essays lead up to the moral that "there is no better or safer way to impoverish a country than to entrust its government with the task to enrich it."[33]

The depression of the thirties and the rise of Soviet power have made it impossible for the contemporary observer to be quite so trenchant, but Latin American experiences of recent years with their widespread and often misguided interventionism has nevertheless permitted some strong critics to appear on the scene, the best known of whom is perhaps Professor Eugenio Gudin of Brazil. In a discussion of the ECLA programming technique, after enumerating all the factors of uncertainty (particularly irrational governmental policies) to which economic life in Latin America is subject, Gudin writes:

> Considering all these factors . . . , to pretend to frame quantitative estimates of demand, supplies, savings, investments, sounds like discussing the sex of the angels in the midst of a serious battle. . . . What the governments of these countries can do for their economic development is not programming: it is simply *not to disturb or prevent it* by in-

33. Alberdi, *Escritos póstumos,* p. 544.

dulging in such evils as political warfare, demagogy, inflation, hostility . . . to foreign capital, unbalanced or excessive
protection to industry and/or agriculture, etc. If these evils
can be avoided, then economic development is almost
automatic; if they cannot, then economic development is
doomed.[34]

We are almost back here to Adam Smith, who said: "Little else
is requisite to carry a state to the highest degree of opulence from
the lowest barbarism, but peace, easy taxes, and a tolerable administration of justice." However, in the positive part of his paper
and in other writings,[35] Professor Gudin has principally stressed
the importance of agriculture (where foreign techniques cannot
simply be copied), of the export sector (where underdeveloped
countries are under compulsion to turn out a quality product),
and of education (because of the cessation of large-scale immi-
gration Latin America must devote more resources to education
than did the United States at a corresponding stage of its history).
Sentiments similar to those of Gudin are also expressed in a
recent "primer" on Colombian economic problems, written by a
prominent Colombian industrialist:

> In the Latin American countries there exists an important
> school which maintains that economic progress must neces-
> sarily be directed by the State. . . . What foundation is there
> for such a statement? None.

> The public should not accept blindly development plans.
> It must recall that bureaucracy is always interested in elabo-
> rating such plans, since they give it economic power and ad-
> vantages.

> The paperwork imposed by public agencies is one of the
> biggest obstacles to production in Latin America. . . . the
> state complicates the life of the citizens and it doesn't care if

34. Discussion paper presented at the Rio roundtable of the International Economic Association, 1957.
35. E.g., *Inflação,* 2d ed. (Rio de Janeiro: AGIR, 1959).

it makes them lose their time. It behaves with an unshakable indifference, like an occupation army in a defeated country.

In Colombia the state has invested huge sums to build low-cost houses, but has accomplished nothing in spite of the money that has been spent. The reason of this failure is that the state is a very poor manager. This goes for every state and particularly the Colombian one. Now, of all economic activities the one most difficult to manage and where opportunities for thievery are greatest is that of construction. As was to be expected, the building of low-cost houses by the state has resulted in a huge destruction of national wealth.[36]

Seldom does one find these ideas expressed so openly and candidly; their most vocal advocates are businessmen ordinarily not given to putting their opinions on paper.[37] Nevertheless, it is useful to realize the strength of these feelings of distrust toward the state's actions and capabilities; periodically they gain the upper hand in one or the other of the Latin American countries and we find ourselves surprised to deal with a minister of finance whose enthusiasm for the dismantling of all controls and whose aversion to public investment in industry and to development planning seem a bit hysterical and old-fashioned to us!

Policy vs. Projections

Apart from the groups which are out of sympathy with ECLA simply because its view implies what they deem to be an excessive degree of governmental intervention in the economy, there are those who oppose or criticize ECLA because they disagree with

36. Hernán Echavarría Olózaga, *El sentido común en la economía colombiana* (Bogotá: Imprenta Nacional, 1958), pp. 176–77, 230, 301.

37. In a survey among large Colombian corporations on artificial barriers to private domestic investment, the instability of governmental economic policies was mentioned most frequently by the respondents, ahead of such other factors as lack of bank credit, high taxes, etc. Cf. Eduardo Wiesner Durán, "Barreras artificiales a la inversión doméstica en la industria nacional," *Revista del Banco de la República* (September 1959).

parts of the ECLA analysis and with some of its policy implications. Perhaps the most outspoken of this group of ECLA's critics is the Brazilian economist, Roberto de Oliveira Campos, who, as director of the Brazilian National Bank for Economic Development from 1955 to 1959, frequently came into close contact with ECLA. The following account of Campos's views is based on several of his papers, primarily on a memorandum he prepared for the Seventh Session of ECLA at La Paz in 1957.[38] In this memorandum Campos does not criticize ECLA directly, but his emphasis is markedly different.

Campos pays the compliment to Prebisch that he has been a "creator of enthusiasms and a destroyer of illusions, tasks which are not always easy to reconcile." Evidently, he believes that Prebisch has been more successful in the former role than in the latter, for he devotes most of his paper to an analysis of the illusions which the Latin American countries still have to overcome:

1. the illusion that inflation can be used, except for brief and intermittent periods, as an instrument to increase capital formation;
2. the illusion that merely by substituting state for private management (e.g., in public utilities) new economic resources are being created;
3. the illusion that social progress and redistribution of income can be legislated regardless and ahead of output and productivity gains;
4. a "mechanistic" illusion which consists in giving undue priority to industrial development in comparison with agriculture, and to physical capital in comparison with investment in education and technical skills.

In listing and commenting on these illusions, Campos probably intended to prod ECLA into giving more attention to influencing the current economic policies of Latin American governments. In general, his principal point of difference with ECLA appears to

38. As published in *El Trimestre Económico* 24 (April-June 1957): 214–24.

consist in the position that many more economic variables are subject to change through policy than ECLA's projections would lead one to believe. In analyzing shortages in power and transportation, he focuses less on inadequate capital formation and faulty programming than on more proximate factors such as utility and railway rate fixing policies. If export receipts are inadequate he does not proclaim an inevitable tendency toward low price and income elasticities of demand for Brazil's export products, but suggests to his own country the adoption of a realistic exchange rate and to Brazil's customers a reduction in their revenue duties and excise taxes.[39]

Campos thus is concerned with present and pressing dangers, and appears to look at problems in a pragmatic or, to use Lindblom's term, "incrementalist" way.[40] Several other Latin American economists could be similarly characterized. For the time being, they are clearly an exception on the emotion-ridden Latin American scene. But the exception is significant for it appears among those who have been wrestling with the real problems faced by economies in the process of rapid growth.

ACCOUNTING FOR RECENT GROWTH: MEXICO AND BRAZIL

Here we come to a strange gap in Latin America's economic literature: few analyses are available of the very substantial economic progress that has actually taken place in a number of Latin American countries over the past twenty years.[41] ECLA, as we have seen, has minimized this progress by stressing its precarious-

39. As one of the four experts who wrote the report *Trends in International Trade* for GATT in 1958, Campos was particularly responsible for the sections dealing with these taxes and their effect on the exports of underdeveloped countries.

40. C. E. Lindblom, "Policy Analysis," *American Economic Review* (June 1958).

41. Mexico and Brazil should clearly be moved up into Rostow's take-off column. The "take-off" concept, however, runs into some trouble when one tries to apply it to Latin American countries; some of them, like Argentina, appear to behave like helicopters with their ability to hover and come right down again after take-off, rather than like the conventional planes of Rostow's metaphor.

ness and its dependence on nonrecurrent windfall gains, such as the postwar improvement in Latin America's terms of trade. Actually, however, the exceptionally favorable factors appear frequently to be more than offset by such unfavorable contingencies as civil war in Colombia and inflation in Brazil. Where growth has taken place it is therefore a rather sturdy reality begging for an explanation.

On the whole, the experience of economic growth has not yet profoundly affected attitudes and certainly has not yet led to a climate in which hope and confidence have a secure place. Development is still discussed as something to be miraculously "launched" rather than something whose momentum is to be maintained. It is hard to break with the habit of fault-finding and self-recrimination. The question asked is hardly ever: How can we build on our achievements of the last ten or twenty years?[42]

The only two countries where an intellectual effort has been made to come to grips with the phenomenon of growth appear to be Mexico and Brazil. The economic development of these countries has been sufficiently sustained and conspicuous in recent decades that notice had to be taken by intellectuals, novelists, and even by economists.

To start with the latter and with Mexico, we find an interesting account of the process in a series of articles by Edmundo Flores, an agricultural economist.

According to Flores, the basis of Mexico's development is the agrarian reform. It led to the

> unchaining of creative forces to which we must largely attribute the development of modern Mexico. . . . The Conquest submerged the power and creative genius of the extraordinary civilizations of pre-Columbian America. The technological superiority . . . of the Conquerors dislocated

42. An exception is supplied by an essay of Víctor Urquidi which discusses the tasks ahead for the Mexican economy against the backdrop of what the author calls and convincingly documents as the Mexican economic "miracle" of the last twenty years. See his "Problemas fundamentales de la economía mexicana," *Cuadernos Americanos,* no. 1 (1961): 69–103.

violently the world of the Indian, destroyed his religion and institutions and caused a cultural and social trauma. The Indian . . . withdrew within himself and assumed an attitude of passivity and despair and retrogressed to primitive forms of living. But when he once more came to own land and to occupy a position of the first rank in national politics, the rupture healed rapidly. Within a few decades, the heritage of the Indian became an active factor in the formation of new institutions and in economic progress.[43]

In a more recent article, he returns to this theme of tracing Mexico's development almost exclusively to the revolution and land reform.

The Revolution . . . opened the country to overwhelming innovational forces. Mexico shed the inertia of the colonial period to enter the cosmopolitan stream of the twentieth century . . . Unwittingly the conditions for the industrial revolution had been fulfilled. The barriers to economic growth were shattered. Technological progress became a condition for survival.[44]

Later he describes the regrouping of forces that resulted from the social mobility which the revolution brought in its wake:

A middle class and new elite emerged. The latter was formed by the coalescence of the first and second generation of the *revolucionarios* with the avowedly conservative, but adaptable, remains of the aristocracy. As a further proof of the newly acquired social fluidity the *revolucionarios* now appear in the guise of elder statesmen, bankers, industrialists, top bureaucrats and intellectuals while the old aristocracy that salvaged and later increased its urban estate wealth has merged with the newer families bringing to them the patina of old family names.[45]

43. Edmundo Flores, "Un año de reforma agraria en Bolivia," *El Trimestre Económico* 23 (April–June 1956): 260.

44. Flores, "The Significance of Land-Use Changes in the Economic Development of Mexico," *Land Economics,* 35 (May 1959): 115.

45. Ibid., p. 117.

This view of the revolution as the agent of economic transformation and of circulation of the elites is also powerfully expressed in a remarkable novel by Carlos Fuentes, *La región más transparente*. There, a successful banker-businessman, son of a peon, tells a young intellectual, after admitting that there is still much poverty and injustice in Mexico:

> But there are also millions who could go to the schools which we, the Revolution, built for them, millions who found jobs in urban industries, millions who without 1910 would have been peons and now are skilled workers, who would have been domestic servants and now are typists with good salaries, millions who in twenty years have passed from the lower to the middle class, who have cars and use toothpaste and spend five days a year in Tecolutla or Acapulco. . . . These people are the only concrete achievement of the Revolution and this was our achievement. We laid the bases of Mexican capitalism.[46]

Very similar ideas are expressed by Octavio Paz in *El laberinto de la soledad:*

> Without the Revolution and its government we would not even have Mexican capitalists. In truth national capitalism is not only the natural consequence of the Revolution, but in good part it is the child and offspring of the revolutionary state. Without the distribution of land, the great public works, the state enterprises and those with "state participation," the policy of public investment, the direct and indirect subsidies to industry, and in general without the intervention of the state in the economy, our bankers and businessmen would have no opportunity to carry on their activities or perhaps they would be part of the native personnel of some foreign company.[47]

This unanimous testimony about the social mobility and general vitality imparted by the 1910 Revolution and the agrarian

46. Carlos Fuentes, *La región más transparente* (Mexico: Fondo de Cultura Económica, 1958), p. 110.
47. Paz, *El laberinto,* pp. 161–62.

reform to Mexico's society and economy is impressive and it contributes much to our understanding of the climate of opinion in that country. The stress on the continued creativity of the revolution makes for the acceptance and even amused expectation of advances by trial and error, and for readiness to experiment in social and economic policy.

Periodically, of course, the question is being raised whether the revolution is being betrayed, as in the following outburst of another character in Fuentes' novel: "I cannot bring myself to think that the only concrete result of the Mexican revolution is the formation of a new privileged class, the economic hegemony of the United States, and the paralysis of all domestic political life."[48]

Nevertheless, one senses a basic confidence that the country will be able to overcome the new problems it is encountering. This confidence is enhanced by the idea that growth has become possible because of the reactivation of long-dormant indigenous forces and energies. In this manner, economic development itself appears as a realistic way, not of returning to the past, but of resuming contact with it and of thereby overcoming the traumas of conquest and imperialism.[49]

Naturally, the Flores-Paz-Fuentes view of Mexico's economic growth leaves unanswered our question about the mainsprings of the development process in other countries which have moved forward in the absence of any Mexican-type revolution. Flores resolves the problem rather too simply when he writes:

> Without the agrarian revolution Mexico would probably be today in a similar situation to that of contemporary Colombia, Peru or Venezuela. There would be good roads leading from ports to mines, oil wells and plantations: Industry and farming would show development along a few specific lines. One would find urban expansion, Hilton hotels, air conditioning, supermarkets, funiculars, submarines and

48. Fuentes, *La región más transparente*, p. 273.

49. The tension between archaism and modernism in the ideologies of developing countries such as China, India, Turkey and Egypt is well documented in the article by Matossian cited in n. 2.

other conspicuous innovations. Subject to distortions and with considerable lag, the economy would display in spots a semblance of technological sophistication but there would be little or no evidence of the social fluidity that accompanied the industrial growth of the advanced nations. Mexico avoided this chromium-plated dead-end because, irrespective of the deficiencies of the *ejido* and of the small-holding, massive land redistribution forced the way for concurrent social and economic improvement.[50]

However well written, this statement is really an exercise in formal, and rather dogmatic, logic. Major premise: to have "genuine" economic development, a country must go through an agrarian revolution. Minor premise: certain Latin American countries have not had an agrarian revolution. Conclusion: any development experienced by these countries must be "artificial." The validity of this verdict may be doubted. Causal sequences in economic development do not necessarily run one way only, i.e., in some situations land reform could be the result rather than the cause of industrialization and urbanization.[51] Moreover, in some conditions a postponement of land reform combined with a "squeeze" on rural groups through tax, tariff or exchange rate policies may be a more effective way of mobilizing capital for industrialization than the creation of an independent peasantry which it would be politically impossible to squeeze in the same fashion.[52]

50. Flores, *Land-Use Changes,* p. 116.

51. In another article Flores shows himself well aware of this possibility. Analyzing the recent growth of Mexico City, he shows that urbanization and industrialization are not only induced by agrarian reform but can in turn act as powerful agents of agricultural change and progress. See Flores, "El crecimiento de la ciudad de México: Causas y efectos económicos," *Investigación Económica* (1959): 247–81.

52. An active and instructive discussion on virtually the same point, namely, whether agrarian reform is a "prerequisite" to successful economic development, has taken place in Italy. The absence of agrarian reform during the Risorgimento has frequently been cited as the principal reason for the retardation of the country's industrialization as compared to that of other European powers; however, this viewpoint, which was originally

We may note that Flores does not mention Brazil, which has not had an agrarian revolution either, but where economic growth is far too impressive a reality to be dismissed as a "chromium-plated dead-end."

In fact, another remarkable note of confidence in the economic prospects of Latin America has recently been sounded by the Brazilian economist Celso Furtado, who had long been associated with ECLA and was one of its principal theoreticians. Returning to Brazil and entrusted with important policy-making responsibilities there,[53] he now finds that his country is in the process of escaping from some of the dilemmas and vicious circles of underdevelopment. In an impressively optimistic paper, Furtado describes how Brazil, through its industrial development in basic iron and steel, petroleum and capital goods, has "conquered decision centers" that previously were located abroad. Hence the economy's capacity to grow is no longer rigidly limited by the availability of foreign exchange, so that "the flexibility of the whole economic system shall be augmented." Similarly, "there will be no longer the dichotomy between growth with inflation or stagnation, since the two vectors in the process of capital formation—savings and investment—will be subjected to the discipline of internal decisions." The Brazilian economy, in other words, is in the process of shedding its "peripheral" character and stands a good chance of becoming a "center" in its own right.[54]

---

put forward by Gramsci, has recently been attacked by Romeo, who argues, on the contrary, that the feudal organization of Italy's agriculture was of considerable help in raising the capital needed for railroad and similar basic investments in the twenty years following unification. Cf. Rosario Romeo, *Risorgimento e capitalismo* (Bari: Laterza, 1959), and Alexander Gerschenkron, "Rosario Romeo e l'accumulazione primitiva del capitale," *Rivista Storica Italiana* 71 (December 1959): 557–86.

53. He has been a director of the National Bank for Economic Development in 1958–59, and was named early in 1960 to head a newly created and powerful agency for the development of the northeastern region (SUDENE).

54. Celso Furtado, "The Brazilian Economy in the Mid-Twentieth Century," paper prepared for the International Conference on Science in the Advancement of New States, Israel, 1960 (mimeographed). Some of the

With his assertion of confidence in Brazil's growth, Furtado complements in the important area of economics the work of Gilberto Freyre, who, almost a generation earlier, had made Brazilians aware of their unique contribution to the relations among races and social classes.[55]

As in the Mexican literature previously quoted, it becomes clear in the writings of Furtado and of other commentators on Brazil's economic, social and political problems that the aim of economic development is far more than an increase in per capita incomes: it is also, and most importantly, this "conquest of decision centers," which were previously in foreign hands, and a new ability to strike out on one's own, economically, politically and intellectually. For this reason, the quest for development is also a quest for self-discovery and self-affirmation and thus comes to be indissolubly tied to a new nationalism which is so noticeable a feature of the intellectual scene in Latin America. This is particularly true in such countries as Mexico and Brazil whose pace of development has been fastest. One may almost say that the more these countries begin to resemble economically the older established industrial communities, the more they differentiate themselves from them ideologically.

CONCLUDING REMARKS

The search of Latin Americans for the cause of their continent's economic backwardness has focused successively on a number of possible explanations: on the supposedly intrinsic defects of the Latin American character, on imperialist exploitation and on being subjected to false economic doctrines, on the lack of pur-

---

ideas contained in this paper are foreshadowed in the last chapter of Furtado's outstanding book, *Formação econômica do Brasil*. The events of the 1960s radically changed Furtado's views. See chap. 3, p. 88.

55. Frank Tannenbaum singles out Mexico and Brazil as the two Latin American countries that have achieved "self-discovery," Mexico through its revolution, Brazil as a result of Freyre's classic, *Masters and Slaves* (1933). See Tannenbaum, "Toward an Appreciation of Latin America," in *The United States and Latin America* (New York: American Assembly, 1959), pp. 52–53.

poseful action by the state or alternatively on excessive and arbitrary state intervention, on the deadening rigidity of the social and economic structure inherited from the Spanish Conquest, or on a combination of several of these factors. Every one of these explanations then leads naturally and logically to the espousal of certain policies and positions over a wide range of social and economic issues: in other words, each determines a "system," is part of an ideology.

With increasing frequency, we are told these days that in the West ideology is dead, that "the old passions are exhausted,"[56] that we no longer are in the "disposition to approach policy as though great ideological issues were to be decided."[57] We are no longer ready to become partisans of systems, spoiling for a fight with our opponent over the minutest issue; rather, we are now picturing ourselves as reasonable, sophisticated "incrementalists" bored with yesterday's ideological bouts.

If this is so, then we are seriously out of phase with the mood prevailing in Latin America. For, there, ideologies are in their accustomed roles, holding men in their grip, pushing them into actions that have important effects, both positive and negative, on economic growth.

Part of the mutual difficulties between Latin America and the United States may derive from this disparity. Given our present distaste for ideology, we are unwilling to grant that certain convictions which may seem naïve to us can be held with the utmost sincerity and intensity. We are unable to understand that certain propositions which we feel have long turned into half-truths are essential ingredients of the intellectual atmosphere elsewhere. In general, we are annoyed by the doctrinaires of Right and Left, and a few traces of such annoyance may well be found in this essay.

Latin Americans, on the other hand, frequently misinterpret our actions. They look for the "system" behind our policies and

56. Daniel Bell, *The End of Ideology* (Glencoe, Ill.: The Free Press, 1960).

57. Lindblom, *Policy Analysis*, p. 301.

impute to us rigid principles which we have long decisively qualified or given up.

Mutual awareness of the disparity in intellectual climate should
be helpful in mitigating such misunderstanding and frictions. This
paper, incomplete and exploratory as it is, also has attempted to
show that the ideologies which hold sway in Latin America frequently have considerable originality, are usually less rigid than
may at first appear, and are themselves in a continuing process of
adaptation to the fast changing reality. The scene we have surveyed is varied and vigorous; it is part of the vitality which today
characterizes the Latin American economy and society.

APPENDIX: UNITED STATES VIEWS ON LATIN AMERICAN ECONOMIC DEVELOPMENT

How have economists and social scientists from the industrial
countries reacted to the protracted difficulties of economic advance in Latin America? To ask this question is virtually to put in
an order for a survey of the history of Western thought on the economic development of underdeveloped areas. We shall attempt a
less ambitious task and limit this note to a few contributions which
represent reactions to the Latin American views previously discussed or deal otherwise specifically or preferentially with Latin
America.

The militancy of ECLA's writings and its proudly proclaimed
intent to demolish "traditional" economic theory could produce
the impression that it was setting out on a lonely mission. Actually,
as has already been said, ECLA found itself during the past decade in the company of a large number of Western economists who
were then evolving what has recently been called the "new orthodoxy" in development economics. Thus ECLA has incorporated into its writings the arguments for protection and industrialization which are easily derived from the late Ragnar Nurkse's
writings on "disguised unemployment," on the "demonstration
effect," and from his pessimistic outlook on future world demand
for primary products. Variations on one of the most famous
Prebisch themes, namely, the unequal division of the gains from
trade between the center and the periphery, are found in articles

and books of Hans Singer, Arthur Lewis and Gunnar Myrdal. The inadequacy of the market mechanism in allocating resources for development has been explained to us at length by Rosenstein-Rodan, Scitovsky and Tinbergen. In brief, a substantial and perhaps dominant group of Western economists shares some of ECLA's most characteristic points of view.

Naturally, the "traditional" economists, whose theories have been attacked by ECLA as wholly inapplicable to Latin American reality and as development-retarding in their policy implications, have replied to these accusations with their usual forthrightness and unshakable confidence in the fundamental correctness of the classical tradition. In a series of lectures at Rio, Jacob Viner vigorously contradicted the thesis of the intrinsic superiority of industry over agriculture which he held to be the basis of the Prebisch-ECLA doctrine as expressed in its 1949 "manifesto." He did not counsel against industrialization but he opposed the notion that Latin America's concentration on primary production was responsible for its backwardness. Rather he said: "The real problem in poor countries is not agriculture as such, or the absence of manufacturers as such, but poverty and backwardness, poor agriculture, or poor agriculture and poor manufacturing."[58] Consequently, Viner warns against the misallocation of resources which would result from state action designed to "exploit" a systematic difference in productivity between agriculture and industry which, according to him, is purely imaginary. According to ECLA and the "new orthodoxy," such a difference is caused by the existence of disguised unemployment in agriculture; consistently enough, Viner later devoted an article to a refutation of this concept.

The Prebisch-Singer thesis on the unequal division of the gains from trade between the industrial and underdeveloped countries and on the tendency of the latter's terms of trade to deteriorate has also come under considerable attack by "traditional" economists. An early critique of these theories and of the empirical evidence that was supposed to support them is in Buch-

58. Jacob Viner, *International Trade and Economic Development* (Glencoe, Ill.: The Free Press, 1952), p. 71.

anan and Ellis, *Approaches to Economic Development.*[59] Detailed rebuttals can be found in the writings of Gottfried Haberler.[60]

But apart from such counterattacks on the ECLA doctrine, what specific views have been put forward by parties outside of Latin America on the continent's development problems? The list we have to present here is surprisingly short.

1. *The U.S. government.* The U.S. position on Latin American economic affairs has been undergoing a rapid and radical change since 1958. Up to that year it could be held that the U.S. government had a fairly consistent view of Latin America's best development strategy: while technical assistance was extended in such fields as health, education and agriculture and while the Export-Import Bank and the International Bank were both active in Latin America, the principal development job was expected to be done by private capital, both domestic and foreign. To stimulate the generation of domestic capital and the inflow of foreign capital, the principal task was to maintain or restore a monetary stability and a favorable investment climate; and the often-used phrase "put your house in order" referred primarily to measures that were held to be required in these two fields.[61]

Under the impact of the Nixon trip first and then of the Cuban revolution, the U.S. position on Latin American economic development has undergone a series of fundamental changes which are likely to be carried further by the new Democratic administration. The role of public lending was given enhanced recognition with the creation of the Development Loan Fund and the Inter-American Development Bank; within public lending a place was made for "soft" loans, repayable in local currencies. The

59. New York: Twentieth Century Fund, 1955, pp. 261 ff.

60. "International Trade and Economic Development" (Cairo: National Bank of Egypt, 1959); and "Terms of Trade and Economic Development," in Howard S. Ellis, ed., *Economic Development for Latin America* (New York: St. Martin's Press, 1961), pp. 275–307.

61. It may be remarked that formally the Communist therapy is similar: The command is still "Put your house in order," but its meaning is: "Throw out the Yankee imperialists and their allies!" instead of "Stop the inflation and welcome private capital!"

United States moved cautiously in the direction of participating in agreements to stabilize prices of some of Latin America's principal export commodities. Most important, it was realized that in Latin America's "house" many elements of "disorder" were even more fundamental than price instability: there were abject living conditions in city slums, maldistribution of land, illiteracy, etc., etc. Thus a "social development" program was suddenly proposed to attack some of these social evils directly rather than rely on the general process of economic development stimulated primarily by private capital to take care of them in good time. The new U.S. position is thus remarkably eclectic; for the time being it expresses essentially a retreat from a previously held view, and a search for a new one.

2. Among individual commentators mention should perhaps be made first of Simon G. Hanson, long-time editor of the journal *Inter-American Economic Affairs* and author of a book, published in 1951, *Economic Development in Latin America*. Hanson has wide experience and knowledge of the Latin American economy, but both he and some of the principal contributors to his journal seem to have become increasingly skeptical about the possibilities of economic improvement of the area in general and of the justification of U.S. aid for this end in particular. This point of view is already in evidence in Hanson's book, whose principal thesis (pp. 4–5) is that "great economic advances can be effected in Latin America without assistance or leadership or pressure from the United States." His frequently incisive description of the shortcomings of Latin American social structure, business practices and economic policies makes his book a lineal descendant of the literature of self-incrimination, so popular at one time in Latin America, except that such a book comes, of course, with much less grace from an outsider. Hanson, like those earlier writers we mentioned, seems to be convinced that the basic failings in the Latin American social and economic structure are deeply ingrained; it is a pity that a person who clearly has a lively empathy with the reality of Latin America did not have sufficient sympathy for that continent to explore possible avenues toward change.

3. An interesting contribution to the debate on Latin America

was made in 1956 by Theodore W. Schultz in a brochure, *The Economic Test in Latin America*.[62] After criticizing the concept of disguised unemployment and the idea that industrialization is necessarily the road to riches, he suggests that far too little attention has been paid to what he calls "non-conventional inputs," namely, the improvement in the quality of people as productive agents and in technical and managerial knowledge. Schultz thus deflects the emphasis from physical capital to "plans and budgets for education at all levels and for skills and technical competence, for study abroad, for research centers and institutes and experiment stations" (p. 74). The stress on these activities is motivated by recent research findings on the inability of the conventional, quantifiable inputs (labor, capital and land) to account for the output increases in both developed and underdeveloped countries. To Latin Americans the stress on education should not come as a great novelty: as we have seen, at one point the only hope that Latin American observers saw for their continent was a thorough change in the character of its inhabitants through education. To some extent it is the rejection of this earlier notion which has produced the present commitment of Latin Americans to models where capital accumulation is cast in the role of prime mover.

4. The reasoning of my own book, *The Strategy of Economic Development*,[63] is cast in general terms, but it has grown almost entirely out of my Latin American experience as I stated in the preface. I do not wish to repeat here my principal arguments, but it may be useful to explain what I conceive to be the direction of whatever influence my views may be able to exert.

Some of my main contentions could serve to reconcile the Latin Americans with their reality, to assure them that certain ubiquitous phenomena such as bottlenecks and imbalances in which they see the constantly renewed proof of their ineptness and inferiority are on the contrary inevitable concomitants and sometimes even

62. New York State School of Industrial and Labor Relations Bulletin no. 35 (Ithaca, N.Y.).
63. New Haven: Yale University Press, 1958.

useful stimulants of development.[64] It seems to me that Latin Americans still have not fully emerged from the stage of self-denigration; they are far too ready to issue blanket condemnations of their own ways and to escape to a dream world of ever-new laws, perfectly designed institutions or scientifically calculated plans. Frequently they do not realize how much they could learn if only they scrutinized the growth that is already taking hold here and there.[65] Instead of yearning for an unattainable simultaneous solution of their problems, they should, in my opinion, train themselves to perceive and evaluate the various possibilities of sequential decision making and problem solving. The Latin American reality itself suggests the sequences which are more efficient, i.e., less likely to be abortive, than others; and it points toward the technical tasks which these societies are likely to perform best and which induce learning about other, more difficult tasks. This view of economic development may enhance Latin America's confidence in its own creativity and in its ability to handle successfully its development problems.

64. In discussing controversies on Brazilian monetary policy, Celso Furtado puts in a similar plea for probing into the hidden rationality of practices that are perpetually at odds with established doctrine: "Any historian of economic ideas in Brazil will not fail to be surprised by the monotonous insistence with which one tags as an aberration and abnormality everything that happens in the country: inconvertibility, deficit financing, issuing of paper money. This secular abnormality is never studied systematically. In effect, no serious effort is ever made to understand this abnormality which, after all, was the reality within which one lived" (Formação econômica do Brasil, p. 190).

65. The need for such learning has also been noted in other developing countries, as appears from the following quotation: "There is little inclination to test against the realities of the Indian economic and social scene the basic assumptions . . . which are implicit in the present models of growth underlying India's development program. Nor is there any great pressure to bring to light the many revealing insights that can be found in recent years of actual development effort" (Wilfred Malenbaum, East and West in India's Development [Washington: National Planning Association, 1959], pp. 36–37).

14. Obstacles to Development: A Classification and a Quasi-Vanishing Act

One could think of several ways of classifying obstacles: natural (lack of resources) and man-made (lack of law and order, lack of capital), objective (lack of resources or of capital) and subjective (lack of entrepreneurship and risk-taking, lack of a desire for change, contempt for material success), internal (all the factors so far named) and external (exploitation by a foreign power), etc.

I find it useful, however, to adopt a classification which is grounded in the concept of "obstacle" itself and which, in the process, questions its solidity from the outset. It is a principal contention of this note that the concept is far from solid, that it is not possible to identify either a finite number of "reliable" obstacles to development or a hierarchy among these obstacles which would permit us to arrange them neatly into boxes marked "basic," "important," "secondary," etc.

The traditional method of identifying an obstacle to development points immediately to the conceptual weakness we have in mind. The method consists in looking up the history of one or several economically advanced countries, noting certain situations that were present at about the time when development was brought actively under way in one or several of these countries (a temperate climate, a population belonging to the white race, "primitive" accumulation of capital, coal deposits, law and order, widespread literacy, a group of Schumpeterian entrepreneurs, a fairly efficient and honest civil service, agrarian reform, the Protestant ethic, etc., etc.), and then construing the absence of any of these situations as an obstacle to development. This procedure could lead one to conclude that the more countries develop, the more difficult does it appear for the remainder to do the same, for each successfully developing country does so under

Reprinted by permission from *Economic Development and Cultural Change* 13 (July 1965): 385–93. © 1965 by the University of Chicago.

a set of special conditions, thus lengthening the list of obstacles (i.e., the absence of these conditions) which have to be "overcome."

Fortunately, this conclusion is as implausible as it is dismal. The usual way of escaping from it is by the successive substitution of a newly discovered fundamental obstacle for those that held sway before the latest theoretical or historical insight. In this paper we shall proceed in a more empirical vein and attempt to classify obstacles in the order of their greater or smaller reliability as obstacles, on the basis of what evidence we have been able to collect.

Suppose some specific situation or condition can be shown to have been essential for the development of country X at time t; in other words, the absence of this condition performed as an insuperable barrier to the development of X. Now it is possible that the development experience of other countries confirms that of X; on the other hand, one can think of the following ways in which the barrier or obstacle would fail to perform as such in other countries:

1. The obstacle does not constitute an absolute barrier in the case of country Y; certain forward moves are available to this country, and the obstacle, while still exerting a negative influence on development, can be dealt with, perhaps more easily, at a later time.

2. The alleged obstacle, in view of another set of circumstances, turns out not to be an obstacle at all and therefore does not need to be removed, either now or later.

3. The alleged obstacle, in view of yet other circumstances, turns into a positive advantage and asset for development.

In justifying each of these possibilities—and, in the process, discovering several other variants—we shall invert the order in which they have been cited and thus start with the extreme case.

AMBIVALENCE: ALLEGED OBSTACLES THAT TURN INTO ASSETS

How difficult it is to classify certain concrete situations as unequivocally hostile or favorable to economic development is well illustrated by the institution of the extended or joint family.[1] Several Western economists belonging to quite different schools of thought have taken the position that the extended family dilutes individual incentives and that its demise and replacement by the nuclear family is required for dynamic development to occur.[2] This is, of course, a highly ethnocentric argument. Westerners who hold this view find it difficult to imagine that any one would want to exert himself if the fruits of his labors accrue largely to what they consider as distant relatives; implicit in the idea that the extended family is a bar to economic progress is therefore the judgment that no one in his right mind can really care for the welfare of his third cousin.

But suppose "they" do? In that case the argument against the extended family not only falls to the ground, but one can immediately conceive of several advantages in an arrangement in which the basic economic decision making unit is not the nuclear family, but a wider grouping. For one, the special relationship existing among the members permits them to undertake new tasks requiring cooperation without prior mastery of such complications as hiring labor and keeping accounts.[3] Furthermore, the members may pool their resources not only for consumption, but equally for investment purposes; and thus it may be possible for

1. For points similar to those made in this and the following section and for illustrations from India and Nigeria, respectively, see Lloyd I. Rudolph and Suzanne Hoeber Rudolph, *The Modernity of Tradition: Political Development in India* (Chicago: University of Chicago Press, 1967); and C. S. Whitaker, Jr., "A Dysrhythmic Process of Political Change," *World Politics* 19 (January 1967): 190–217.

2. P. T. Bauer and B. S. Yamey, *The Economics of Under-Developed Countries* (Chicago: University of Chicago Press, 1957), p. 66; and Benjamin Higgins, *Economic Development* (New York: Norton, 1959), p. 256.

3. C. S. Belshaw, *In Search of Wealth: A Study of the Emergence of Commercial Operations in the Melanesian Society of South-Eastern Papua* (Menasha, Wis.: American Anthropological Association, 1955), chaps. 5 and 7.

them to finance business ventures as well as advanced education for the more gifted among them.[4]

Can we save the proposition for the rather special situation where the extended family still exists as a formal behavior code but can no longer command the full loyalty of the individual member of the society and is perhaps actively resented by him? In that case the strictures of our economists would seem to apply fully. Yet, such is the variety of possible situations that even here we must tread with care. For example, the very desire to withhold extra earnings from one's family may deflect the more enterprising members of the family from a bureaucratic career (where earnings are fixed and a matter of public knowledge) into a business career (where earnings are uncertain and can be concealed).[5] Moreover, if there is any time lag between the newly won affluence of the individual and the famous moving-in of all the relatives to share in his newly won riches, then the institution of the extended family combined with the desire to escape from it provides a stimulus to ever new spurts of temporarily relative-exempt entrepreneurial activity.[6] Hence, even if the sharing implicit in the extended family system is resented, the obligation to share may act like those taxes that stimulate individuals to greater effort at securing nontaxable gains (and at tax evasion).

Our point is strengthened by the observation that, just as the extended family cannot be held to stunt growth under all circumstances, so the nuclear family will not always promote development. If the economic operator perceives no possibility of com-

4. Peter Marris, *Family and Social Change in an African City* (London: Routledge, 1961), p. 138. The importance of kinship ties in the early spread of banking and mercantile enterprise in the West is of course well established.

5. Ibid., p. 139.

6. "The fact that, under the customary rules of inheritance, individual property was always in process of conversion to family property provided individuals with a great incentive to acquire additional lands, over which they had, for some time at least, unlimited control." Polly Hill, *The Migrant Cocoa-Farmers of Southern Ghana* (Cambridge: Cambridge University Press, 1963), p. 16.

mon interest, action, or gain with anyone outside his immediate blood relatives, then economic advance is likely to be severely hamstrung, as I have explained elsewhere and as has been documented by several empirical studies.[7]

A more general remark is in order at this point. We have said that an obstacle to development may usually be defined as the absence of a condition that was found to be present in a country which subsequently developed. But in many cases the question that ought to have been asked is how much of this condition was present. Too much may be just as deleterious as too little. It is too much rather than too little individualism and entrepreneurship and too little willingness to work with discipline in a hierarchical organization that plagues much of Southeast Asia and also other underdeveloped lands.[8] Too much law and order may be as stifling as too little is disruptive. Let us arrange the possible states of society along a horizontal scale with two such extremes at opposite ends. Suppose we measure the chances for development along the vertical scale. In most cases, then, these chances will seriously drop off at both ends of the scale, but they may well be tolerably good during a wide stretch in the middle. In other words, societies that are all individualistic entrepreneurship or that are all hierarchical discipline will both be hard put to develop, but in the real world we are likely to encounter predominantly individualistic and predominantly hierarchical societies that contain some, perhaps well hidden, ingredients of discipline and of entrepreneurship, respectively; hence, they may both be capable of development, even though the paths on which they will set out toward this goal are likely to be very different.

We have dwelt at some length on the extended family, since it illustrates well our notion of ambivalence of alleged obstacles. We

7. A. O. Hirschman, *The Strategy of Economic Development* (New Haven: Yale University Press, 1958), pp. 14–20; Edward C. Banfield, *The Moral Basis of a Backward Society* (Glencoe, Ill.: The Free Press, 1958); Clifford Geertz, *Peddlers and Princes* (Chicago: University of Chicago Press, 1963), pp. 42–47, 73 ff., 122 ff.

8. "Malaya probably suffers from an excess of enterprise, since this is a factor which tends to disintegrate existing business." T. H. Silcock, *The Economy of Malaya* (Singapore: Moore, 1956), p. 44.

shall now give a few more examples, rapidly and at random, to suggest the wide spectrum of situations to which the notion applies.

In Europe the tradition of very high craftsmanship was initially most helpful in the development of new mechanical methods. But the rapid pace of development in the United States in the nineteenth century has been explained in part by the absence of such a tradition in the new continent and by the relative scarcity of skilled labor which stimulated the introduction of capital-intensive, skilled-labor-saving techniques.[9]

Lack of social mobility ranks high as an impediment to economic progress because it sets limits to individual achievement and prevents the best utilization of manpower resources. In Japan, however, the rigid social barriers which kept the merchants and their sons from joining the bureaucracy or from becoming landlords have been hailed as one of the sources of private entrepreneurship and have been contrasted with the harmful effects of the ease with which such transitions were effected by the successful merchants of China.[10]

What could be more inimical to the accumulation of material wealth than the ascetic ideal? Yet, as soon as this ideal extends to combating indulgence in leisure (in addition to indulgence in food, drink, and sex), capital accumulation through self-denying work is a likely, if surprising, result.[11]

Law and order and the absence of civil strife seem to be obvious preconditions for the gradual and patient accumulation of skills, capital, and investors' confidence that must be the foundation for economic progress. We are now told, however, that the presence of war-like Indians in North America and the permanent conflict between them and the Anglo-Saxon settlers was a great

9. H. J. Habakkuk, *American and British Technology in the 19th Century* (Cambridge: Cambridge University Press, 1962), pp. 116, 128–29.

10. M. J. Levy, Jr., "Contrasting Factors in the Modernization of China and Japan," in S. Kuznets et al., eds., *Economic Growth: Brazil, India, Japan* (Durham, N. C.: Duke University Press, 1955), pp. 496–536.

11. Karl F. Helleiner, "Moral Conditions of Economic Growth," *Journal of Economic History* 11 (Spring 1951): 97–116.

317

advantage, because it made necessary methodical, well-planned, and gradual advances toward an interior which always remained in close logistic and cultural contact with the established communities to the East. In Brazil, on the contrary, the backlands were open and virtually uncontested; the result was that once an excessively vast area had been occupied in an incredibly brief time span the pioneers became isolated and regressed economically and culturally. Jacques Lambert, author of this observation, sums up his remarks in the following sentence: "In contradiction to a deeply entrenched legend, which paints the Anglo-Saxon colonizers as individualists and adventurers and the Iberians as colonial functionaries without initiative, Brazil is now paying dearly for the taste of adventure of the Portuguese and for their excess of initiative."[12]

ALLEGED OBSTACLES WHOSE ELIMINATION TURNS
OUT TO BE UNNECESSARY

We turn now to a somewhat less paradoxical type of situation: the presumed obstacle no longer changes colors and becomes a blessing in disguise; its existence simply leads to the charting of a hitherto unfamiliar path to economic progress, and the resulting, economically more advanced society exhibits a profile that is "different" because of the survival of certain institutions, attitudes, etc., which were originally thought to be incompatible with development. These situations can be difficult to distinguish clearly from the preceding ones; for if the presumed obstacle has at all survived, then one can frequently show that it is not only tolerated, but actually lends strength to the new state of affairs. Nevertheless, there is a difference, at least initially, between an obstacle that is being turned or neutralized and one that turns out not to be an obstacle at all, but a factor that promotes and propels development.

The confusion on this score is due to the somewhat shapeless notion of "challenge." Any difficulty or obstacle can be transmuted by a sort of semantic hocus pocus into a challenge which

12. Jacques Lambert, *Os dois Brasís* (Rio: Ministerio da Educação, 1959), pp. 116–17.

evokes a response. But these Toynbeean terms are not helpful, for they dissolve the concepts of difficulty and obstacle altogether, instead of permitting the differentiated analysis we are aiming at here. To recall an example from our preceding section, it is incorrect to say that the existence of the extended family is a "challenge" to developers; it is rather a real troublemaker in some respects and some situations and a valuable asset in others, as we have shown. The notion of challenge is similarly ineffectual in the case, now under consideration, of obstacles which have no positive dimension, but which do not preclude development via some "alternate route" (alternate to the removal of the obstacle). Let us take a country which lacks an important natural resource such as coal or whose history has not permitted any sizeable "primitive accumulation of capital"; when such countries substitute hydroelectric energy for coal, or bank credit and state finance for private equity capital,[13] they are not "responding" to a "challenge." They are merely encountering a different way of achieving growth which, of course, they might never have discovered had they been more "normally" endowed. "Believe me," says the Marquise de Merteuil in Laclos's *Les Liaisons Dangereuses,* "one rarely acquires the qualities he can do without." Yet, to acquire these very qualities is less a matter of responding to a challenge than of discovering one's comparative advantage. In doing so a country may not even have been aware of the fact that the lack of a certain natural resource, institution, or attitudinal endowment constituted a special difficulty, an obstacle, or much less, a "challenge."

If a country lacks one of the conventional "prerequisites," it can overcome this lack in two distinct ways. One consists in inventing its own substitute for the prerequisite; as just mentioned, Gerschenkron has given us an exceptionally rich and convincing account of such substitution processes for the Marxian prerequisite of primitive accumulation of capital. The other possibility is that the purported "prerequisite" turns out to be not only sub-

13. Alexander Gerschenkron, *Economic Backwardness in Historical Perspective* (Cambridge, Mass.: Harvard University Press, 1962), chaps. 1 and 2.

stitutable, but outright dispensable; nothing in particular needs to take its place, and we are simply proven wrong in our belief that a certain resource, institution, or attitude needed to be created or eradicated for development to be possible. In other words, the requirements of development turn out to be more tolerant of cultural and institutional variety than we thought on the basis of our limited prior experience. Recent research shows this to be the case in various parts of the world. A revealing study of the Japanese factory by Abegglen has shown in considerable detail how "rationalization and impersonalization are not necessary to the adoption from the West of an industrial economy."[14] Here we are admittedly only one step away from our previous category, where the negative factor is transmuted into a positive one. A study of Argentine entrepreneurship takes this step explicitly.

> Analysts of entrepreneurship hold certain of the Latin American characteristics to be deterrents to success in the development of industry. Granting that [Di Tella, the founder of the firm under study] neither could nor wanted to break the emotional patterns of an inward-looking individualism, a reliance on *personalismo,* or the claims of the family . . . he skillfully neutralized these assumed deterrents or turned them into positive assets. He used themes and relationships such as *personalismo, dignidad, simpatia, confianza,* and the *patrón*-client relation for the development of [his firm].[15]

In a somewhat different vein, a study of Indian village life has

14. James G. Abeggjen, *The Japanese Factory* (Glencoe, Ill.: The Free Press, 1958), p. 141.

15. Thomas C. Cochran and Reuben E. Reina, *Entrepreneurship in Argentine Culture: Torcuato Di Tella and S. I. A. M.* (Philadelphia: University of Pennsylvania Press, 1962), pp. 262–63. Abegglen also occasionally takes this step, arguing that certain elements of traditional Japanese culture are not only compatible with the new order, but actually lend strength to it: "the principle of family loyalty and cohesion, when successfully symbolized and incorporated into military, industrial and financial organizations, may have become an important source of energy and motivation for the transition to industrialization" (*Japanese Factory,* pp. 136–37).

shown that the social, political, and cultural changes that come with development may be of sharply different dimensions depending on the precise way in which economic opportunities arise. The study deals with two villages and the way in which they have taken advantage of irrigation. Change is shown to be more extensive and comprehensive in the dry village whose lands are close to, but not right in, the irrigation district than in the wet village. In a perceptive introduction, Sir Arthur Lewis remarks: "What we need to know is just how powerful a solvent the love of money is. The answer seems to be that it dissolves what stands in its way, but nothing more. How much is changed depends partly on how much is compatible, and partly on how closely interrelated the various institutions are."[16] It appears from the studies here surveyed that a variety of non-Western institutions are either more compatible with economic development (Sir Arthur's "love of money") or less interrelated with those that are incompatible than has been believed by those who look at each social situation as an "interrelated whole."[17]

OBSTACLES WHOSE ELIMINATION IS POSTPONABLE

We are now ready for those obstacles which we come closest to recognizing as such, those that refuse to turn mysteriously into assets or to be accommodated in an unexpected fashion within an economically progressive society. They stubbornly remain factors detrimental to development which ought to be eliminated. In

16. T. S. Epstein, *Economic Development and Social Change in Southern India* (Manchester: Manchester University Press, 1962), p. x.

17. ". . . [various] studies suggest that the impact of economic modernization upon the total social system is not necessarily as revolutionary and all-embracing as it has sometimes been described; or, put somewhat differently, a modern economic system may be compatible with a wider range of non-economic cultural patterns and social structures than has often been thought." Geertz, *Peddlers and Princes,* p. 144. For an interesting essay on the compatibility of certain traditional values (as distinct from "traditionalism") with progressive economic development, see Bert F. Hoselitz, "Tradition and Economic Growth," in Braibanti and Spengler, eds., *Tradition, Values and Socio-Economic Development* (Durham, N. C.: Duke University Press, 1961), pp. 83–113.

many cases, however,—and this is the point of the present section —the priority which this task commands can be shown to be less rigidly defined than had been thought.

I am returning here to a theme which I have set forth at length in my previous writings. I have drawn attention to "inverted" or "disorderly" or "cart-before-the-horse" sequences that are apt to occur in the process of economic and social development; and I have argued that, under certain circumstances, these sequences could be "efficient" in the sense of making possible the achievement of stated goals of economic expansion within a briefer time period or at a smaller social cost than would be possible if the more orderly sequence were adhered to.[18]

The implication of this approach for the notion of barrier and obstacle is evident. While it grants that insufficient electric power, inadequate education, or the absence of agrarian reform are serious defects, it is suspicious of theories that erect the elimination of such defects into prerequisites for any forward movement; in addition to the head-on assault on these defects, it will evaluate, look for, and scrutinize ways in which the economy can be moved forward elsewhere and how thereby additional pressure can be brought to bear on the acknowledged obstacles. If they are truly hindrances, then any forward move that can be instigated in spite of them is going to make it even more imperative than before to get rid of them; if, on the other hand, this additional pressure is not generated, then perhaps these obstacles are not to be taken quite so seriously, and they belong, at least in part, in our second category (alleged obstacles that, as it turns out, can be accommodated into an economically progressive society).

Rather than repeat my earlier argument and cite a series of examples to which it applies, I shall limit myself here to one particular type of inverted sequence which seems to me of considerable interest and with which I have not dealt before.

As the search for the conditions of economic development has been unremittingly pursued by social scientists over the past years, increasing attention has been given to the role of attitudes,

18. See Hirschman, *Strategy,* pp. 80–81, 93–94, 154–55; and *Journeys Toward Progress,* p. 260.

beliefs, and basic personality characteristics favorable to the emergence of innovation, entrepreneurship, and the like. While these theories, with their expeditions into psychology and psychiatry, are frequently fascinating, the message they leave behind is almost as dismal as that of the very first theories of development which attributed a decisive role to such unalterable factors as race, climate, and natural resources. Rooted, as they are purported to be, in childhood experiences and transmitted unfailingly from one generation to the next, the deplored attitudes or personality structure appear to be similarly refractory to any but the most radical treatment.

We have already seen, in our first two sections, that a good many attitudes which, on the basis of some previous experiences, had been believed to be detrimental to development can, in different settings, be neutralized or even be put to positive use, as the case may be. But let us accept now the premise that some residual attitudes, beliefs, and personality characteristics are really and truly incompatible with sustained economic advance—must we then accept the conclusion that *all* our efforts should be concentrated on extirpating them, and that no other road to progress is available?

Fortunately, while the behavioral scientists have become depth psychologists, the psychologists have come up with the discovery that attitudinal change can be a *consequence* of behavioral change, rather than its precondition! From a variety of approaches exploring this nexus, I shall single out the *Theory of Cognitive Dissonance,* which was originated in 1957 by Leon Festinger in a book bearing that title. Since then the theory has been widely investigated, tested, and discussed; much of the empirical evidence which has been gathered, together with a chapter on the applicability of the theory to problems of social change, can be found in a volume by Jack W. Brehm and the late Arthur R. Cohen, *Explorations in Cognitive Dissonance.*[19]

19. It should be pointed out that the theory is by no means universally accepted. For a highly critical appraisal, see N. P. Chapanis and A. Chapanis, "Cognitive Dissonance: Five Years Later," *Psychological Bulletin* (January 1964): 1–22.

Briefly and in nontechnical language, the theory states that a person who, for some reason, commits himself to act in a manner contrary to his beliefs, or to what he believes to be his beliefs, is in a state of dissonance. Such a state is unpleasant, and the person will attempt to reduce dissonance. Since the "discrepant behavior" has already taken place and cannot be undone, while the belief can be changed, reduction of dissonance can be achieved principally by changing one's beliefs in the direction of greater harmony with the action.

The theory thus predicts significant shifts in attitude consequent upon commitment to discrepant behavior, and its predictions have been verified empirically. In a classic experiment, for example, college students are asked to write an essay supporting the side opposite to their private view on a current issue. It turns out that after writing the essay (and to some extent even right after committing themselves to write it and before actually writing it), the students' attitude shifts away from what they used to consider their position on the issue. An interesting refinement of the experiment consists in varying the reward given to the students for writing the essay: it then appears that, in contrast to the usual ideas about reinforcement, highly rewarded students change their opinion much less than the lowly rewarded ones, the reason being that dissonance and hence the extent of the shift is highest when the discrepant behavior cannot be explained away and dismissed by the ego as having at least some pleasurable result.

This theory has been of practical use in helping us understand the processes of "thought reform" or "brainwashing" as applied, for example, to U.S. prisoners of war by their Chinese captors during the Korean War; in a more constructive vein, the theory has contributed to illuminate the psychological processes leading to acceptance of racial integration. A further fruitful field of application of the theory may be the process of attitude change which is required in the course of economic development. The following quotations from the Brehm-Cohen volume are suggestive:

> The theory is different in its essential nature than most other theoretical models in psychology. Where the major concern

> in other theories has been largely with the guidance of be-
> havior—that is, with what leads to a given behavior or com-
> mitment—dissonance theory deals, at least in part, with the
> *consequences* of a given behavior or commitment.[20]

> Dissonance theory attempts to understand the conditions
> under which behavioral commitments produce cognitive and
> attitudinal realignments in persons.[21]

In other words, dissonance theory deals with the possibility of
replacing the "orderly" sequence, where attitude change is conceived as the prerequisite to behavioral change, by a "disorderly"
one, where modern attitudes are acquired ex post, as a consequence of the dissonance aroused by "modern" type of behavior
which happens to be engaged in by people with nonmodern attitudes. One question will, of course, be asked, namely: how can a
commitment to "modern" behavior be obtained from people
whose values and attitudes preclude in principle such behavior?
Actually, however, this is not much of a problem among latecoming societies surrounded by modernity and by opportunities to transgress into or try out modern behavior; at one time
or another, it is likely that the latecomer will stumble more or less
absentmindedly into such behavior as pursuit of individual profit,
entrepreneurial risk-taking, promotion according to merit, long-
term planning, holding of democratic elections, etc.; dissonance
will thus arise and will then gradually lead to those changes in
attitude and basic beliefs which were thought to be prerequisites
to the just-mentioned modes of behavior. The art of promoting
development may therefore consist primarily in multiplying the
opportunities to engage in these dissonance-arousing actions and
in inducing an initial commitment to them.[22]

20. Jack W. Brehm and Arthur R. Cohen, *Explorations in Cognitive
Dissonance* (New York: John Wiley & Sons, 1962), p. 299.

21. Ibid., p. 271.

22. If one were to extend the above-mentioned "refinement" of the
theory to the development context, one would conclude that the conditioning of foreign aid on internal reform can do positive harm at the
stage when an underdeveloped country is about to commit itself to new
types of "modern" or reform actions; to reward such perhaps partly dis-

One observation will conclude this section. A country which achieves economic advance and modernization through the process just described, i.e., where behavioral change paces attitudinal change, is likely to exhibit a personality rather different from the country whose elite right at the outset of the development journey is imbued with the Protestant ethic and saturated with achievement motivation. Because, in the case of the former country these motivations are being laboriously acquired ex post and en route, its path will be more halting and circuitous and its typical personality may well be subject to particularly strong tension between traditional and modern values.[23] While a country can well develop without being endowed at the outset with all the "right" values and attitudes, its development profile and experience cannot but bear the marks of the order and manner in which it accomplishes its various tasks.

This is the end of our exercise in classification. It goes without saying that its purpose was not to destroy entirely the notion of barrier, obstacle, or prerequisite. In the first place, the classification was not meant to be exhaustive, and there may well exist a

---

sonant behavior would lead to less cumulative change than if the behavior could not be dismissed by the actors as something they did just to get hold of the aid funds. In this way, the theory throws some light on the difficulties of using aid as a means of promoting internal reform which have beset the Alliance for Progress since its inception. Besides many other constructive uses, foreign aid may be helpful in promoting reform and will serve as a reinforcing agent when it is conceived and presented as a means of reducing the cost of a reform to which the policy makers in the recipient country are already firmly committed; but it is cast in a self-defeating role if it is proffered as a quid pro quo for the reform commitment itself. See also chap. 10, p. 206.

23. In *Journeys Toward Progress,* pp. 235 ff., I have drawn a related difference by distinguishing between societies which, in the process of tackling their problems, let motivation to solve problems outrun their understanding, and those that do not usually tackle problems unless the means to solve them are close at hand. Here also the two styles of problem solving are shown to result in sharply differing development experiences.

residual category of obstacles which by no stretch of the imagination can be considered as assets, which cannot be accommodated or neutralized, and whose removal must be accomplished before any other forward step can be usefully attempted. Secondly, if certain alleged obstacles turn out to be blessings in disguise, quite a few factors, hitherto considered as wholly favorable to development, are likely to function in some situations as *curses* in disguise.

Finally, and most important, while our exercise points to many ways in which obstacles can be made into assets or lived with or turned, it says nothing about the ability to perceive these possibilities on the part of the policy makers in developing countries. If this ability is strictly limited, as is often the case, then this very limitation emerges as a superobstacle, which commands and conditions the existence and seriousness of the more conventional obstacles. And it can now be told that the survey here presented was really aimed at loosening the grip of this central difficulty.

15. Underdevelopment, Obstacles to the Perception of Change, and Leadership

During a recent visit to a Latin American capital, I wished to resume contact with X, an economic historian who had returned there some time ago after spending several years in Europe. I had been invited for dinner by a sociologist whom I asked whether he knew X; he did indeed, quite well, but did not have X's telephone number; no doubt, however, he could find it by calling a common friend. Unfortunately the friend was not home. I asked whether there might be a chance that X would be listed in the telephone directory; this suggestion was shrugged off with the remark that the directory makes a point of listing only people who have either emigrated or died. After a while, the other dinner guests, an economist and his wife, appeared. They were asked about X's telephone number. The economist said that X must be both much in demand and hard to reach, as several people had inquired about how to get in touch with him within the past few days. The subject was dropped as hopeless, and everybody spent a pleasant evening.

Upon waking up the next morning in my hotel room, I noticed the telephone directory on the night table. I could not resist opening it to look for a listing under X's name. I found it immediately and dialed the number, still sure that it must be the one he owned five years ago before leaving for Europe. But the familiar voice answered my call from the other end of the line.

The first part of this paper was written immediately after a trip to Brazil, Chile, and Colombia in the summer of 1967. The second part was added later, as a result of discussions during a *Daedalus* symposium on political leadership. Reprinted by permission from *Daedalus* (Journal of the American Academy of Arts and Sciences) 97, no. 3 (Summer 1968): 925–37.

SPECIAL OBSTACLES TO THE PERCEPTION OF CHANGE IN UNDERDEVELOPED COUNTRIES

It so happens that X is Claudio Véliz, at present the director of a new Institute of International Studies in Santiago and editor of the recent volume *Obstacles to Change in Latin America*.[1] In the course of our conversation, he asked me to give a talk at his institute. Since the episode I had just lived through confirmed my longstanding suspicion that obstacles to change are intertwined in Latin America and in other less developed areas with considerable obstacles to the perception of change, I suggested that an exploration of these obstacles might be an interesting, if somewhat disrespectful, topic. The observations in this section are based on the talk that ensued and also owe much to the lively discussion it provoked.

To a considerable extent, the difficulties of perceiving change are universal. At all stages of development, men are loath to abandon the old clichés and stereotypes that have served them so well, for they make the world around them intelligible, comfortable, and meaningful—or, as in our episode, almost endearingly absurd. Historians and psychologists have documented the difficulties of perceiving what, on the basis of previous experience, is felt to be incongruous as well as the reluctance to absorb new information that conflicts with established beliefs or is otherwise unpleasant.[2] Here, however, I am not so much interested in the general phenomenon as in the possible existence of special or additional obstacles to the perception of change in countries where economic and social development has been laggard.

1. Claudio Véliz, *Obstacles to Change in Latin America* (London: Oxford University Press, 1965).

2. Some basic references from the psychological literature are Jerome S. Bruner and Leo Postman, "On the Perception of Incongruity: A Paradigm," *Journal of Personality* 18 (1949): 206–23; and Leon Festinger, *A Theory of Cognitive Dissonance* (Stanford: Stanford University Press, 1957). For a remarkable historical case study of blocks to perception in a highly developed country, see Roberta Wohlstetter, *Pearl Harbor: Warning and Decision* (Stanford: Stanford University Press, 1962).

As a preliminary, a not quite terminological point must be briefly discussed. A distinction is often made between "real" and "apparent" or between "fundamental" and "superficial" changes: this device permits one to categorize as superficial a great number of changes that have, in effect, taken place and to assert in consequence that there has not yet been any real change. The decision to assert that *real change* has occurred is made to hinge on one or several tests. For example, it is often affirmed that there has been "no real change" unless the absolute distance which separates the per capita income of the underdeveloped countries from that of the developed has been substantially narrowed or unless there has been the kind of radical and sudden redistribution of wealth and power which comes as the result of a socialist revolution. But to set up such demanding tests is in itself an indication of a special difficulty and reluctance to concede change except when it simply can no longer be denied. It is precisely our task to explain this reluctance and this difficulty.

Persistence of the "Little Tradition"

A first, still rather general obstacle to the perception of change derives from the persistence of traits which are related to what Robert Redfield has called the "little tradition." An example: I land at the Bogotá airport after a five-year absence, and the first thing I notice on leaving the plane is the characteristic manner in which several of my fellow passengers are folding handkerchiefs around their noses; having long known this to be a strange custom of the Bogotanos as they emerge from their homes, movie theaters, or bordellos into the dangerous open air, I immediately whisper to myself: "Nothing has changed here!"

Numerous traits of this kind are both harmless and perfectly compatible with the highest levels of economic and political development. Since they were first encountered at a time when the country was backward, however, they have taken on an aroma of backwardness, and the impression is created—by no means only among foreign visitors—that modernization requires a surrender of these traits.

Clearly the observer is in error when he decides that nothing has changed because a number of traits of the "little tradition" are still extant. But the error is not only pardonable, it is almost inevitable. When backwardness is pervasive, it is easy to overestimate the interrelatedness of its components and correspondingly difficult to diagnose correctly which traits will and must be changed in the course of modernization and which ones may be—and perhaps should be—safely kept.[3]

The Bias in the Perception of Cumulative Change

Our next obstacle to the perception of change depends more critically on the division of the world into advanced and less developed countries and is, therefore, central to our argument. It arises because what leads to cumulative change in one country does not necessarily do so in another. In other words, the extent to which a given social event or innovation—industrialization, agrarian reform, the achievement of mass literacy, and so forth—involves a society in further important social and political changes varies considerably from country to country and from period to period. A fundamental transformation of the sociopolitical structure accompanied the coming of industry to England and France; for Germany, Russia, and Japan, the transformation was less radical or more delayed; and for the "late-late-comers" of Latin America, industrialization has ordinarily brought even less immediate and fundamental sociopolitical changes. Somehow the existing structures in these countries seem to be better at absorbing and accommodating the new industries and their promoters, technicians, and labor force than was the case in those societies where industry first raised its head.[4]

A similar development may be in the making within Latin

3. See chap. 14 above. It can be argued that keeping some seemingly backward traits is essential if modernization is to be successful since one element of success is the maintenance of a separate identity on the part of the modernizing society.

4. "Latin American politics is something of a 'living museum' in which all the forms of political authority of the Western historic experience continue to exist and operate, interacting one with another in a pageant that seems to violate all the rules of sequence and change involved in our understanding of the growth of Western civilization." Charles W. Anderson, *Politics and Economic Change in Latin America* (Princeton: Van Nostrand, 1967), p. 104. See also chap. 3 above.

America with respect to agrarian reform. Whereas the elimination of the *latifundio* in Mexico, Bolivia, and Cuba required nothing less than a revolution, a number of countries (Chile, Venezuela, Colombia, and perhaps even Peru) seem to be able to achieve substantial progress in land tenure conditions without a concomitant or prior drastic change in the sociopolitical environment.

Marx said that when history repeats itself, it reproduces in the form of comedy what first appeared as tragedy. The preceding situations suggest a slight variant: it looks as though a given change or innovation appears for the first time with revolutionary, history-making force, but tends to be reported the next time in the "News-in-Brief" column. If we had put our finger on a historical law here, we would then have encountered a reason why fundamental change is less easy to come by in countries which introduce the "revolutionary" innovations of the advanced countries after a substantial time lag.

The matter is not settled so easily, however, for our historical law breaks down as soon as we consider some additional examples. While some innovations cause less cumulative change among the latecomers than they did among the pioneers, the opposite relationship can be shown to hold for others. Take, as a striking example, the transistor radio; its impact is far more revolutionary in countries where a large part of the population had previously been wholly out of touch with national and international events than in countries where, as a result of fairly universal literacy and electrification, the transistor radio is merely one additional medium for the transmission of information.

Another example is the truck (or bus), which has become an important medium of not only geographical, but social mobility in some African and Latin American countries. While social mobility had long been a feature of the societies which invented the truck, the possibility of achieving truck ownership opened up an important new avenue toward social improvement in more rigidly stratified societies. In a similar vein, I have related recently how the telephone led to the replacement of cash by credit operations in Ethiopia;[5] such a revolutionary role was obviously denied the telephone in North America and Europe, where credit instruments had been perfected for several centuries prior to Bell's invention.

Objectively, therefore, it is hardly possible to assert that cumulative change is more difficult to ignite in underdeveloped countries than in advanced ones. But subjectively the situation looks quite different, for observers in the less developed countries will expect a cumulative change to be connected with those processes which had a revolutionary function in the advanced countries. When these processes fail to perform in this way in their own countries, the observers will disappointedly conclude that "nothing ever changes here." Instances of the opposite relation—namely, that some innovations which were easily accommodated by the existing sociopolitical structure of the advanced countries will cause considerable ferment when transplanted to the less advanced—are not likely to occur to these observers since they always expect changes to take place in accordance with the patterns of the "leading" countries which they emulate and with which they attempt to catch up. This expectation, then, induces a bias in perception—that is, an emphasis on those processes which wrought considerable change in the advanced countries, but are easily domesticated when they are transplanted, while the opposite situations are ignored.

Styles of Change in Dependent and Leading Countries

The less developed countries are usually *dependent* countries: They have considerably less freedom of movement than the leading or more nearly independent countries.[6] This situation is likely to have important consequences for the manner in which change is typically brought about in each kind of country, and it turns out

5. See my *Development Projects Observed* (Washington: Brookings Institution, 1967), pp. 151–52.

6. The term "dependent," in lieu of underdeveloped, less developed, and so forth, is beginning to have currency in Latin America. See, for example, Osvaldo Sunkel, "Politica nacional de desarrollo y dependencia externa," *Estudios Internacionales* 1 (Santiago, Chile; April, 1967).

that such differences in styles of change once again create special difficulties for the perception of change in the dependent countries.

In its extreme form, dependence of a formally independent underdeveloped country is revealed through military intervention of a leading power. But, operating as it does in an open international economic system, the dependent country is also subject to a whole range of intermediate pressures and potential threats: denial of international financing, domestic capital flight, diversion of purchases of goods for export and of tourist services to alternative suppliers, and so forth. Some of these potential threats are likely to become actual not only when the interests of a dominant foreign country are under direct attack, but even when a determined attempt is made to change the domestic social and economic structure. Often there is considerable uncertainty about the international repercussions of internal reform moves. Leading countries are subject neither to such threats nor to such uncertainties.

The consequence for the style of change of the two kinds of countries is obvious: the leading countries can afford to place all their cards on the table and to shout about their achievements in change from the rooftops. When, on the other hand, the desire for change comes to the fore in a dependent country, and as long as dependent status is accepted as a datum and a constraint, there will be an instinctive tendency to play it safe by introducing change in small doses so that each individual unit of change will either not be noticed at all or will remain below some "foreign repercussion threshold." The dependent country, thus, will endeavor to dissimulate change by making it as gradual and nonspectacular as possible. Brazil's well-known record of gradual and comparatively nonviolent transitions may be an example of this *stealthy* style of change, and Colombia supplies us once again with an illustrative story. A Polish mission recently visited Colombia and found out all at once about the many basic and not-so-basic economic activities which are at present in the hands of the government, the Central Bank, or other public bodies; not realizing that this state of affairs is the end result of a gradual process which had extended over a period of many years, the

Poles are reported to have asked: "Excuse our ignorance, but in which year did you make The Revolution?"

The nonspectacular, stealthy style of change is a defense mechanism used by political leadership in the dependent countries, and in many ways it is admirably clever. Like any human institution, moreover, the style has a tendency to perpetuate itself even when the circumstances which have given rise to it no longer prevail. There is something to be said for turning necessity into virtue and for celebrating the style, as has often been done in Brazil, as a genuine invention and contribution to the art of history making.

The trouble is that the style is too clever. It may fool the intervention-prone foreigner or the traditional domestic power holder whose position it slowly erodes. But the general public and, even more, the intellectuals also fail frequently to recognize that change is being achieved. The reason is clear: because of the overriding prestige of the dominant countries, change is widely equated with that particular "loud" *style* of change which these countries can so well afford; thus, change is denied to have occurred at all until and unless it takes the particular shape—violent revolution, civil war, and so forth—which is familiar to us from the history of change in the leading countries. A country that is not taking this particular road to change is considered by its own countrymen as too "lazy to make history" or as a country of "ambiguity and half tones."[7] Thus, once again, fascination with the patterns of change characteristic of the leading, dominant countries makes it difficult to perceive processes of change actively at work among latecoming and dependent countries.

The Special Misfit and Durability of Imported Ideologies

In addition to the biases in perception already described, observers in less developed countries can be affected by a special difficulty in detecting changes in their own societies, regardless of any comparison with what happens or has happened elsewhere. A reason for this difficulty can be found in the image which these

7. The first term is used by Antonio Callado in *Tempo di Arraes* (Rio de Janeiro: José Alvaro, 1965), p. 16; the other by Fernando Pedreira in the *Correo da Manha,* 16 July 1967.

observers have of their own societies, in the lenses they use to look at them, or, for short, in their ideologies. It is probably a principal characteristic of less developed, dependent countries that they *import* their ideologies, both those that are apologetic and those that are subversive of the status quo. There always exists a considerable distance between variegated and ever-changing reality, on the one hand, and the rigid mold of ideology, on the other. The distance and the misfit, however, are likely to be much more extensive when the ideology is imported than when it is homegrown. In the latter case, an important social change which is not accounted for by the prevailing ideology will soon be noted and the ideology will be criticized and either adapted to the new situation or exchanged for a new one. A good example is the revisionist criticism of orthodox Marxism which appeared even during the lifetime of Engels as a result of certain developments in German society which were hard to fit into Marxist doctrine.

When the ideology is imported, on the other hand, the extent to which it fits the reality of the importing country is usually quite poor from the start. Given this initial disparity, additional changes in the country's social, economic, or political structure that contradict the ideology do not really worsen the fit substantially and are therefore ignored or else easily rationalized. The free trade doctrine imported from England into Latin America in the nineteenth century and so poorly adapted to the needs of that continent was fully routed there only as a result of the two world wars and the depression.[8] The long life of the oft refuted explanation of Latin American societies in terms of the dichotomy between oligarchy and mass may be another case in point. On the North American Left, the notion, imported by Marxist thought, that the white working class is the "natural ally" of the oppressed Negro masses also held sway for an extraordinarily long period, considering the overwhelming and cumulative evidence to the contrary.[9]

8. See, for example, Nicia Vilela Luz, *A luta pela industrialização do Brasil* (São Paulo: Difusão Européia do Livro, 1961).

9. See Harold Cruse, *The Crisis of the Negro Intellectual* (New York: William Morrow, 1967), pp. 174–75, 262–63 and passim.

Thus, an ideology can draw strength from the very fact that it does so poorly at taking the basic features of socioeconomic structure into account. Among ideologies, in other words, it is the least fit that have the greatest chance of survival! And as long as the misfit ideology survives, perception of change—and of reality in general—is held back.

To illustrate the point further, I must tell one last story. A man approaches another exclaiming: "Hello, Paul. It's good to see you after so many years, but you have changed so much! You used to be fat, now you are quite thin; you used to be tall, now you are rather short. What happened, Paul?" 'Paul' rather timidly replies: "But my name is not Paul." Whereupon the other retorts, quite pleased with his interpretation of reality: "You see how much you have changed! Even your name has changed!"

In sum, our search for obstacles to the perception of change specific to underdeveloped countries has been surprisingly successful.[10] This success will give us pause and concern: when there are special difficulties in perceiving ongoing change, many opportunities for accelerating that change and taking advantage of newly arising openings for change will surely be missed. The obstacles to the perception of change thus turn into an important obstacle to change itself. The matter can also be put in the form of a vicious circle: to the extent that a country is underdeveloped, it will experience special difficulties in perceiving changes within its own society; hence, it will not notice resulting opportunities for even larger and more decisive changes. A country that fails to perceive these opportunities is likely to remain underdeveloped.

PERCEPTION OF CHANGE AND LEADERSHIP: CHARISMA VS. SKILL

Is it not possible, one might ask, to break out of this vicious circle by the right kind of change-perceiving leadership? To link in this way the problem of perception of change to that of leadership may seem farfetched; yet these problems are so difficult that

10. A further obstacle of this kind is discussed in chap. 16, pp. 352–53.

roundabout approaches are worth trying. One useful indirect approach to the leadership problem would consist in first ascertaining, as I have just done, some average beliefs, attitudes, and perceptions that prevail not only in the community at large, but also among its elites. One could then inquire whether and how leaders are liable to deviate from these averages and try to define leadership in terms of such deviations.

The trouble with such a definition (but also its interest) is that deviations from average attitudes and perceptions can take several contrasting forms. In the first place, leadership may be achieved by those who hold to the average perceptions with an uncommon degree of "passionate intensity," who articulate them most forcefully, and who best reflect and express what is in everybody's heart and mind. Average *mis*perceptions, such as those we have reviewed, are of course also reflected and accentuated by this sort of leader, and his ability to empathize with them or his blindness to ongoing change may be an important part of his appeal. Robert Tucker observes that charismatic leadership rests to a considerable extent on the leader's ability "to accentuate the sense of being in a desperate predicament,"[11] presumably regardless of whether this sense is justified by actual events.

Yet, accentuation, exaggeration, and forceful articulation of prevailing attitudes and perceptions cannot be the only basis for leadership. Another is surely the ability to overcome and transcend some of these attitudes. In our case, it is precisely the ability to perceive change when most of one's contemporaries are still unable to do so that would enable a leader to take advantage of new opportunities as soon as they arise; in this situation, a leader often appears to *create* such opportunities singlehandedly.

An illustration of this sort of leadership which is based on the perception rather than the denial of opportunity was recently supplied by Carlos Lleras Restrepo, whose masterful "reform-mongering" performance in initiating agrarian reform legislation and then seeing it through the Colombian Congress I reported a few

11. Robert C. Tucker, "The Theory of Charismatic Leadership," *Daedalus* (Summer 1968): 751.

years ago.[12] Elected president in 1966, but lacking the two-thirds majority in Parliament that is required for passing all legislation of any importance, he and his administration seemed condemned to even more immobilism than had plagued earlier governments elected under the "National Front" arrangement in which Conservatives and Liberals shared the responsibilities and privileges of power. But in the first year of his administration, Lleras had given so many tokens of a determination to push for socioeconomic reforms that he was able to attract votes from the opposition which included a left-wing Liberal group that had split from the main Liberal party in the late fifties. Eventually, this group decided to rejoin the main party in August 1967, thereby enabling the administration to muster the needed two-thirds majority. Commenting on these developments in a televised speech, Lleras exclaimed:

> [There are those] who took pleasure in predicting difficulties, who were sure that we would never be able to resolve our problems. . . . [They said that] because we did not have the two-thirds majority, the whole life of the country was threatened and that the future was somber. *As though there were not the art of politics! As though all situations were unchangeable! As though there were no possibilities of achieving agreements!* The truth is that all these predictions came to naught—in fact, even *before* the Liberal union was sealed and *before* the two-thirds majority was secure, several important laws had been passed.[13]

Here is a leader who excels at perceiving opportunities, takes great pleasure in his special powers of perception, acts successfully on what he perceives, and strengthens his claims to leadership as a result.

Through our indirect approach—ascertaining first some "average" attitudes and perceptions and then defining leadership in terms of deviations from the norm—we have, in fact, come upon

12. See my *Journeys Toward Progress* (New York: Twentieth Century Fund, 1963), chap. 2.

13. *El Tiempo* (Bogotá), 14 September 1967.

two contrasting components of leadership: skill, on the one hand, and charisma, on the other. Skill requires a stronger-than-average ability to perceive change, while charisma is based in part on a stronger-than-average refusal to do so. The charisma and the skill requirements of leadership, thus, are often at loggerheads, and the most effective leaders are likely to be those who can somehow accommodate both. Lenin with his extraordinary powers to rouse people to action *and* the "infinite fertility of his tactical imagination"[14] is a particularly fascinating example.

But such an even blend of charisma and skill is most uncommon. Usually any one leader is likely to be better either at charisma or at skill, precisely because these two qualities are in part based on opposite deviations from the norm. Once in a while, one encounters a "division of labor" between leaders working in informal concert toward the same goal, as in the remarkable case of the charismatic Garibaldi and the skilled Cavour. Again, however, such an arrangement is not easy to come by.

Finally, the contradiction between the two ingredients of leadership may be attenuated because one ingredient, usually charisma, can be allowed to predominate in the first period of struggle and mobilization, while the skill requirements are more needed in the next stage, when the leader moves closer to or actually into power. That leadership often requires this successive display of contrasting characteristics by the same person has been noted by several authors.[15] It is indeed a fundamental point about

14. Tucker, "Charismatic Leadership," p. 751.

15. "The talents of the founder of a state are different from those of the ruler of an established one" (Dankwart A. Rustow, "Ataturk as Founder of a State," *Daedalus* [Summer 1968]: 821). "The qualities necessary for a charismatic . . . leader's coming to power are not those that he needs in order to stay in power or to protect his work" (Stanley and Inge Hoffmann, "de Gaulle as Political Artist," *Daedalus* [Summer 1960]: 869). I would add that, in many cases, the required switch from one set of qualities to another must take place not after the conquest of power, but at some point prior to it, when agitation and mobilization give place to negotiation with and partial winning over of the existing powerholders. In the course of the Mexican Revolution, such a change in leadership style came about fortuitously through the death of Zapata and the subsequent emergence of Magaña as commander-in-chief of the Morelos revolutionaries. See chap. 16 below, pp. 347–49.

the difficulty of securing continuity in effective leadership. As such, the point was unlikely to escape Machiavelli who made it while discussing the chances that violent seizure of power might change a corrupt republic for the better:

> The project to reform the state presupposes a generous and upright citizen. To become sovereign by force . . . presupposes, on the contrary, an ambitious and evil citizen. Hence it will be difficult to find a person who would wish to use reprehensible means to achieve a just end, or an evil man who will suddenly act like a fine citizen and make virtuous use of an ill-gotten authority.[16]

However the conflict between the skill and charisma requirements may be resolved, a minimum of skill will have to be forthcoming in almost any conceivable situation if leadership is to be at all successful. In recent theorizing on leadership, we probably have had an overemphasis on the charisma component—and in recent practice, we certainly have had an overdose of it and a corresponding underdose of skill, particularly in the Third World. Names of highly charismatic leaders who failed because they were short on skill come to mind only too readily.

What has been said applies to both revolutionary leaders and "reform-mongers." Both need a minimum of skill—or, in terms of our preceding analysis, both would do a better job if they trained themselves to overcome the obstacles to the perception of change and to recognize change when it happens. Only in this way can they do better for the communities which they pretend to lead than these communities would be expected to do if one were to predict their future on the basis of their average attitudes, perceptions, and misperceptions. This is the ultimate function and justification of the leader: to improve on the average prospects for advance of those whom he leads, to raise the expected value of their future.

16. *Discorsi,* bk. 1, chap. 18.

16. The Search for Paradigms as a Hindrance to Understanding

A recent journal article argued forcefully against the "collection of empirical materials as an end in itself and without sufficient theoretical analysis to determine appropriate criteria of selection."[1] The present essay presents a complementary critique of the opposite failing. Its target is the tendency toward compulsive and mindless theorizing—a disease at least as prevalent and debilitating, so it seems to me, as the spread of mindless number work in the social sciences.

While the latter phenomenon has been caused largely by the availability of the computer, several factors are responsible for the compulsion to theorize, which is often so strong as to induce mindlessness. In the academy, the prestige of the theorist is towering. Further, extravagant use of language intimates that theorizing can rival sensuous delights: what used to be called an interesting or valuable theoretical point is commonly referred to today as a "stimulating" or even "exciting" theoretical "insight." Moreover, in so far as the social sciences in the United States are concerned, an important role has no doubt been played by the desperate need, on the part of the hegemonic power, for shortcuts to the understanding of multifarious reality that must be coped with and controlled and therefore be understood at once. Interestingly enough, revolutionaries experience the same compulsion: while they are fond of quoting Marx to the approximate effect that interpreting the world is not nearly as important as changing it, they are well aware of the enormous strength that is imparted to revolutionary determination by the conviction that one has indeed fully understood social reality and its "laws of

Reprinted by permission from *World Politics* 22, no. 3 (March 1970): 329–43. © 1970 by Princeton University Press.

1. Oran R. Young, "Professor Russett: Industrious Tailor to a Naked Emperor," *World Politics* 21 (April 1969): 489–90.

change." As a result of these various factors, the quick theoretical fix has taken its place in our culture alongside the quick technical fix.

In the following pages, I do not have a central epistemological theorem to offer that would permit us to differentiate between good and bad theorizing, or between fruitful and sterile paradigmatic thinking. My accent throughout is on the kind of *cognitive style* that hinders, or promotes, understanding. I introduce the topic by a critical look at two books that exemplify opposite styles. Subsequently, I make an attempt to delineate various areas in which an impatience for theoretical formulation leads to serious pitfalls. Theorizing about Latin American society and economy, on the part of both Latin Americans and outside observers, receives special attention because it has been particularly marked by the cognitive style I find unfortunate.

I

John Womack's *Zapata and the Mexican Revolution*[2] and James L. Payne's *Patterns of Conflict in Colombia*[3] are the two books I shall use to open the argument. They have in common that they are both by young North American scholars; both, in fact, were originally written as doctoral dissertations; and they both reached my desk early in 1969. But this is where any possible resemblance ends. At this point I should state that both books aroused in me unusually strong feelings: I found Womack's way of telling the Zapata story extraordinarily appealing, while I was strongly repelled by Payne's book in spite of its crispness, cleverness, and occasional flashes of wit. There are of course many striking contrasts between the two books that can account for these opposite reactions, not the least perhaps being that Womack obviously fell in love with revolutionary Mexico and the Zapatistas whereas Payne's treatment exudes dislike and contempt for Colombians in general, and for Colombian politicians in particular. But the more important, and not necessarily related, difference is in the cognitive styles of the two authors. Within the

2. New York: Knopf, 1969.
3. New Haven: Yale University Press, 1968.

first few pages of his book Payne presents us triumphantly with the key to the full and complete understanding of the Colombian political system. The rest of the book is a demonstration that the key indeed unlocks all conceivable doors of Colombian political life, past, present, and future. Womack, on the other hand, abjures any pretense at full understanding right in the preface, where he says that his book "is not an analysis but a story because the truth of the revolution in Morelos is in the feeling of it which I could not convey through defining its factors but only through telling of it." "The analysis that I could do," he continues, "and that I thought pertinent I have tried to weave into the narrative, so that it would issue at the moment right for understanding it."[4] And indeed what is remarkable about the book is the continuity of the narrative and the almost complete, one might say Flaubertian, absence from its pages of the author who could have explained, commented, moralized, or drawn conclusions. Yet whoever reads through the book will have gained immeasurably in his understanding not only of the Mexican Revolution, but of peasant revolutions everywhere, and Womack's very reticence and self-effacement stimulate the reader's curiosity and imagination. Payne's book, on the contrary, obviously explains far too much and thereby succeeds only in provoking the reader's resistance and incredulity; the only curiosity it provokes is about the kind of social science that made an obviously gifted young man go so wrong.

Here, then, is the experience behind the title of this essay: understanding as a result of one book without the shadow of a paradigm; and frustration as a result of another in which one paradigm is made to spawn thirty-four hypotheses (reproduced, for the convenience of the reader, in the book's appendix) covering all aspects of political behavior in Colombia and, incidentally, the United States as well.

Perhaps I should explain briefly what Mr. Payne's basic "insight" or paradigm consists in: politicians in Colombia, he has found out through questionnaires, interviews, and similar devices,

4. Womack, *Zapata*, p. x.

are motivated primarily by status considerations rather than by genuine interest in programs and policies, as is predominantly and fortunately the case in the United States. He uses the neutral-sounding terms "status incentive" and "program incentive"; the former characteristically motivates Colombian political leaders whereas the latter animates their North American counterparts. In plain language, occasionally used by the author, Colombian politicians are selfish,[5] ambitious, unscrupulous, unprincipled, exceedingly demagogic—interested exclusively in increasing their own power, always ready to betray yesterday's friends and allies, and, to top it all, incapable of having friendly personal relations with anyone because they feel comfortable only with abject supplicants.[6] On the other hand, there is the politician with a program incentive whose preferred habitat is the United States of America. *He* enjoys working on concrete policies and achieving a stated goal; hence he is principled, willing to defend unpopular causes, always ready to come to constructive agreements, hard-working, and generally lovable.

For a North American to contrast Colombian and United States politicians in terms of such invidious stereotypes is, to say the least, a distasteful spectacle. We must of course allow for the possibility that truth, as unearthed by the scholar, turns out to be distasteful. But Payne does not betray any sense of realizing the unpleasantness of his discovery. On the contrary, he evidently draws much satisfaction from the edifice he has built and takes good care to make sure that there will be no escape from it. At various points he assures us that Colombians are like that; that, as he put it in a subtitle, they are not "on the brink of anything"; that it is futile to expect any change in the pattern of Colombian politics from such incidental happenings as industrialization or urbanization or agrarian reforms: like the three characters in Sartre's *Huis Clos,* the twenty million Colombians will just have to go on living in their self-made hell while Mr. Payne, after his seven-month diagnostic visit (from February to September, 1965,

5. Payne, *Patterns,* p. 70.
6. Ibid., p. 12.

as he informs us in the preface), has returned to his own, so much more fortunate section of the hemisphere.

It is easy to show that the Payne model is as wrong as it is outrageous. In the first place, it is unable to explain the very wide swings of Colombian politics; after all, during almost all of the first half of the twentieth century Colombia stood out as a "stable" democracy with peaceful transfers of power from one party to another; throughout the Great Depression of the thirties when almost all other Latin American countries experienced violent political convulsions, constitutional government continued in spite of much social unrest.

This experience is hard to explain by a theory that holds that vicious political infighting, untrammeled by any concern with programs or loyalty, holds continuous sway throughout the body politic. Moreover, such a theory ought to take a good look at—and give a special weight to—the body's head: if Payne had done that he might have noticed that his stereotype, the politician with a status incentive, simply does not apply to a number of the most outstanding leaders and recent presidents of Colombia—there is no need to mention names, but it is amusing to quote, in contrast, from a recent portrait of a contemporary president of the United States: "His preoccupation seems to have been success—in this case the achievement of power rather than its use for political purposes."[7]

Supposing even that the diagnosis is essentially correct and that politicians in Colombia are more interested in the quest for power per se than in the use of this power for the carrying out of specific programs—what does this "insight" explain? Suppose that we find, as Payne indeed does, that those self-seeking politicians frequently switched sides or vote for demagogic measures, does this finding teach us anything fundamental about the political system, its ability to accommodate change, to solve newly arising problems, to assure peace, justice, and development? It does nothing of the sort, but at best leaves us with the proposition, which inci-

7. Nora Beloff and Michael Davie, "Getting to Know Mr. Nixon," *The Observer*, 23 February 1969.

dentally is both platitudinous and wrong, that if the politicians are vicious, the ensuing politics are likely to be vicious too!

Let us pass now from the paradigms of James Payne to John Womack, who has rigorously excluded from his universe any semblance of a paradigm. It is of course impossible to do justice to his narrative. I shall refer here only to one particular turn of the events he describes in order to show how he invites speculation and thereby contributes to the possibility of understanding.

It has perhaps not been sufficiently remarked that the book has *two* protagonists: Zapata dominates the action during the first nine chapters, but in the important last two chapters (eighty pages) the leading figure is Gildardo Magaña who became Zapata's ranking secretary after mid-1917 and, after a brief fight for the succession, the chief of the Zapatista movement following Zapata's death in April, 1919. Womack honors Magaña with one of his too-rare character portraits: "From these stresses [of his youth] Gildardo Magaña somehow emerged strong and whole. What he had learned was to mediate: not to compromise, to surrender principle and to trade concessions, but to detect reason in all claims in conflict, to recognize the particular legitimacy of each, to sense where the grounds of concord were, and to bring contestants into harmony there. Instinctively he thrived on arguments, which he entered not to win but to conciliate."[8]

Womack then relates the exploits of Magaña as a resourceful negotiator of ever new alliances and contrasts him with the rigid and sectarian Palafox, Zapata's earlier principal secretary, who "seemed in retrospect the individual responsible for the Zapatistas' present plight—the man they could blame for their disastrous involvement with Villa in 1914, their alienation of worthy chiefs in the constitutionalist party, and their abiding reputation as the most intransigent group in the revolutionary movement."[9]

After the murder of Zapata, Magaña maneuvered tactfully and successfully among the various chiefs. After six months, the succession crisis was over and Magaña was recognized as commander-in-chief, with the movement virtually intact. Womack

8. Womack, *Zapata*, p. 290.
9. Ibid., p. 306.

347

then traces the complex events through which the Zapatistas, as he puts it in the title of his last chapter, "Inherit Morelos"—that is, how they manage, by alternately fighting and negotiating and by backing Obregón at the right moment, to pass from outlaws into local administrators and members of a national coalition. "So ended the year 1920, in peace, with populist agrarian reform instituted as a national policy, and with the Zapatista movement established in Morelos politics. In the future through thick and thin these achievements would last. This was the claim Zapata, his chiefs, and their volunteers had forced, *and Magaña had won and secured.*"[10]

Twice Womack implies that this outcome was due not only to the presence of Magaña, but perhaps also to the absence of Zapata from the scene. There is first the "extraordinary maneuver" by which Magaña offered the Carranza government the Zapatistas' support when United States intervention threatened in the Jenkins case in 1919. Womack says here flatly, "Had Zapata lived, Zapatista strategy could not have been so flexible."[11] Then again at the celebration of Obregón's victory, on 2 June 1920,

> twenty thousand Agua Prieta partisans marched in review through the Zócalo, among them the forces from Morelos. And watching with the honored new leaders from a balcony of the Palacio National . . . stood the squat, swarthy de la O, frowning into the sun. From an angle he looked almost like Zapata, dead now for over a year. (If de la O had been killed and Zapata had lived, Zapata would probably have been there in his place, with the same uncomfortable frown, persuaded by Magaña to join the boom for Obregón but probably worrying, as Magaña was not, about when he might have to revolt again.)[12]

Out of these bits and pieces, there emerges a proposition or hypothesis that must have been on Womack's mind, but that he allows the reader to formulate: did the comparative success of the

10. Ibid., p. 369; my italics.
11. Ibid., p. 348.
12. Ibid., p. 365.

348

Morelos uprising within the Mexican Revolution rest on the *alternating* leadership, first of the charismatic, revolutionary Zapata and then of the skillful, though highly principled, negotiator Magaña?[13] And what are the "lessons" of this story for other revolutions and, in particular, for revolutionary movements that are confined to a limited portion or sector of a nation-state?

The historian is probably ambivalent about such questions. He revels in the uniqueness of the historical event, yet he constantly intimates that history holds the most precious lessons. And I believe he is right on both counts! Perhaps the rest of this essay will show why this is not a self-contradictory position.

II

First let me return briefly to the comparison of Payne and Womack. What strikes the reader of the two books most is, as I said before, the difference in cognitive style: Payne, from the first page to the last, breathes brash confidence that he has achieved complete understanding of his subject, whereas Womack draws conclusions with the utmost diffidence and circumspection. His respect for the autonomy of the actors whose deeds he recounts is what gives his book its special appeal and probably contributed to the spectacular accolade he received from Carlos Fuentes in the *New York Review of Books*.[14] For it is today a most unusual restraint. I believe that the countries of the Third World have become fair game for the model builders and paradigm molders, to an intolerable degree. During the nineteenth century several "laws" were laid down for the leading industrial countries whose rapid development was disconcerting to numerous thinkers who were strongly affected by what Flaubert called "la rage de vouloir conclure."[15] Having been proven wrong by the unfolding events

13. The need for combining or alternating charisma and skill if leadership for social and political change is to be effective, and the difficulties in meeting this need are discussed in chap. 15 above, pp. 337–41.

14. 13 March 1969.

15. I have long looked for a good translation of this key concept into English. It now strikes me that an apt, if free, rendering of Flaubert's meaning would be "the compulsion to theorize"—which is the subject and might have been the title of the present essay.

in almost every instance, the lawmakers then migrated to warmer climes, that is, to the less developed countries. And here they really came into their own. For the less developed, dependent countries had long been objects of history—so that to treat them as objects of iron laws or rigid models from whose working there is no escape came naturally to scholars who turned their attention to them. Soon we were witnesses to a veritable deluge of paradigms and models, from the vicious circle of poverty, low-level equilibrium traps, and uniform stage sequences of the economist, to the traditional or non-achievement-oriented or status-hungry personality of the sociologist, psychologist, or political scientist. A psychologist may find it interesting some day to inquire whether these theories were inspired primarily by compassion or by contempt for the underdeveloped world. The result, in any case, is that the countries of Latin America, for example, appear to any contemporary, well-read observer far more constrained than, say, the United States or France or the USSR.[16] Latin American societies seem somehow less complex and their "laws of movement" more intelligible, their medium-term future more predictable or at least formulable in terms of clearcut simple alternatives (such as "reform or revolution?"), and their average citizens more reducible to one or a very few stereotypes. Of course, all of this is so exclusively because our paradigmatic thinking makes it so. Mr. Payne is merely the latest in a long line of "law" makers, model builders, and paradigm molders who have vied with one another in getting an iron grip on Latin American reality. And it must now be said that Latin American social scientists have themselves made an important contribution to this headlong rush toward the all-revealing paradigm.

Elsewhere in this volume I have described as "the age of self-incrimination" one phase of the efforts of Latin Americans at understanding their own reality and the lag of their countries

16. Lévi-Strauss's structuralist anthropology has had a similar effect, as it "has on the whole refrained from attempting to impose totalizing structures on the so-called higher civilizations" (Benjamin I. Schwartz, "A Brief Defense of Political and Intellectual History with Particular Reference to Non-Western Cultures," *Daedalus* [Winter 1971]: 110).

behind Europe and the United States.[17] Incidentally, traces of this phase can be found in a few contemporary Latin American intellectuals, and they, jointly with their bygone confrères, provide Payne with some telling quotations about the despicable character of Colombian politicians and politics. By and large, the phase has fortunately passed; it has, however, been replaced by a somewhat related phase that might be called the age of the *action-arousing gloomy vision:* on the basis of some model or paradigm, the economic and social reality of Latin America is explained and the laws of movement of economy and society are formulated in such a way that current trends (of terms of trade, or of income distribution, or of population growth) are shown to produce either stagnation or, more usually, deterioration and disaster. The art of statistical projection has made a potent contribution to this type of forecast, which is then supposed to galvanize men into action designed to avert the threatened disaster through some fairly fundamental "structural changes."

Now I believe that this strategy for socioeconomic change has sometimes been and can on occasion again be extremely useful in just this way. But for several reasons I would caution against the exclusive reliance on it that has recently characterized Latin American social and economic thought.

There is a world of difference, by the way, between this action-arousing gloomy vision and the Marxian perspective on capitalist evolution. In the Marxian perspective, events in the absence of revolution were not at all supposed to move steadily downhill. On the contrary, capitalist development, while punctuated by crises and accompanied by increasing misery of the proletariat, was nevertheless expected to be going forward apace. It was in fact the genius of Marxism—which explains a large part of its appeal —that it was able to view both the advances and the setbacks of economic development under the capitalist system as helping toward its eventual overthrow.

My first criticism of the vision ties in directly with my dislike of paradigms laying down excessive constraints on the conceivable

17. See chap. 13, above.

351

moves of individuals and societies. Why should all of Latin America find itself constantly impaled on the horns of some fateful and unescapable dilemma? Even if one is prepared to accept Goldenweiser's "principle of limited possibilities" in a given environment, any theory or model or paradigm propounding that there are only two possibilities—disaster or one particular road to salvation—should be prima facie suspect. After all, there *is,* at least temporarily, such a place as purgatory!

The second reason for which I would advocate a deemphasis of the action-arousing gloomy vision is that it creates more gloom than action. The spread of gloom is certain and pervasive, but the call to action may or may not be heard. And since the theory teaches that in the normal course of events things will be increasingly unsatisfactory, it is an invitation *not* to watch out for possible positive developments. On the contrary, those imbued with the gloomy vision will attempt to prove year by year that Latin America is going from bad to worse; a year like 1968—and this may hold for 1969 as well—when the economic performance of the three large and of several small countries was little short of brilliant, will come as a distinct embarrassment.

Frequently, of course, the theories I am criticizing are the result of wishful thinking: wouldn't it be reassuring if a society that has been unable to meet some standard of social justice or if an oppressive political regime were ipso facto condemned to economic stagnation and deterioration? For that very reason we should be rather on our guard against any theory purporting to prove what would be so reassuring.

But the propensity to see gloom and failure everywhere is not engendered only by the desire to reprove further an oppressive regime or an unjust society. It may also be rooted in the fact that one has come to expect his country to perform poorly because of its long history of backwardness and dependence; hence any evidence that the country may possibly be doing better or may be emerging from its backwardness is going to be dissonant with previous cognitions and is therefore likely to be suppressed; on the contrary, evidence that nothing at all has changed will be picked up, underlined, and even greeted, for it does not necessitate any change in the preexisting cognitions to which one has become comfortably adjusted. This is so because people who have a low self-concept and expect failure apparently feel some discomfort when they suddenly perform well, as psychologists have shown.[18] In this manner, social psychology provides a clue to a Latin American phenomenon that has long puzzled me, yet has struck me with such force that I have invented a name for it—the "failure complex" or "fracasomania."

Finally the paradigm-based gloomy vision can be positively harmful. When it prevails, hopeful developments either will be not perceived at all or will be considered exceptional and purely temporary. In these circumstances, they will not be taken advantage of as elements on which to build. To give an example: the rise of the fishmeal industry in Peru and the similarly spectacular growth of banana planting in Ecuador from about 1950 to the mid-sixties contradicted the doctrine that the era of export-promoted growth had ended in Latin America. As a result, economists first ignored these booms, then from year to year predicted their imminent collapse. It is quite possible that particularly the latter attitude held down the portion of the bonanza that the two countries might otherwise have set aside for longer-term economic and social capital formation; for why bother to exert oneself and, in the process, antagonize powerful interests if the payoff is expected to be so limited and short-lived? More recently, another theory of gloom has been widely propagated: it seems that now the opportunities for import-substituting industrialization have also become "exhausted" even though it can be argued that, just as life left in *desarrollo hacia adentro*.[19] Again, if the exhaustion earlier in the case of *desarrollo hacia afuera,* there is still much

18. Elliott Aronson, "Dissonance Theory: Progress and Problems," in R. P. Abelson et al., eds., *Theories of Cognitive Consistency: A Source Book* (Chicago: Rand McNally, 1968), p. 24. I have just presented a general reason why obstacles to the perception of change and of forward movement are likely to be particularly strong in countries with a history of backwardness. See chap. 15 for other observations on this theme.

19. See chap. 3, above. The Spanish terms *desarrollo hacia afuera* and *desarrollo hacia adentro* are convenient shorthand expressions for growth through the expansion of exports and of the domestic market, respectively.

thesis is wholly accepted it may weaken the search for and prevent the discovery of new industrial opportunities.

In all these matters I would suggest a little more "reverence for life," a little less straitjacketing of the future, a little more allowance for the unexpected—and a little less wishful thinking. This is simply a matter, once again, of cognitive style. With respect to actual socioeconomic analysis, I am of course not unaware that without models, paradigms, ideal types, and similar abstractions we cannot even start to think. But cognitive style, that is, the kind of paradigms we search out, the way we put them together, and the ambitions we nurture for their powers—all this can make a great deal of difference.

III

In trying to spell out these notions in greater detail I shall make three principal points. In the first place, I shall explain why the gloomy vision is in a sense the first stage of any reflections about a backward reality, and shall make a plea for not getting stuck in that stage. I shall then attempt to show that in evaluating the broader social and political consequences of some ongoing event we must be suspicious of paradigms that pretend to give a clearcut answer about the desirable or undesirable nature of these consequences. And finally, I shall suggest that large-scale social change typically occurs as a result of a unique constellation of highly disparate events and is therefore amenable to paradigmatic thinking only in a very special sense.

The initial effort to understand reality will almost inevitably make it appear more solidly entrenched than before. The immediate effect of social analysis is therefore to convert the real into the rational or the contingent into the necessary. Herein, rather than in any conservatism of "bourgeois" social scientists, probably lies the principal explanation of that much commented-upon phenomenon—the conservative bias of social science in general, and of functional analysis in particular. This very conservatism takes, however, a strange turn when the target of the social scientist is a society that is viewed from the outset as backward or unjust or oppressive. For analysis will then make it appear, at least to start with, that the backwardness, injustice and oppression are in reality far more deep-rooted than had been suspected. This is the origin of all the vicious circle and vicious personality theories that seem to make any change impossible in the absence of either revolution, highly competent central planning with massive injection of foreign aid, or massive abduction of the young generation so that it may be steeped elsewhere in creativity and achievement motivation.[20] Interestingly enough, enough, then, the same analytical turn of mind that leads to a conservative bias in the case of a society that we approach without a strong initial commitment to change, leads to a revolutionary or quasi-revolutionary stance in the case of societies that are viewed from the outset as unsatisfactory. In the case of the former, the analyst, like the ecologist, often becomes enamored of all the fine latent functions he uncovers, whereas in the latter case he despairs of the possibility of change (except for the most massive and revolutionary varieties) because of all the interlocking vicious circles he has come upon.

Fortunately these initial effects of social science analysis wear off after a while. In the case of the backward countries, the realization will dawn that certain so-called attributes of backwardness are not necessarily obstacles, but can be lived with and sometimes can be turned into positive assets. I have elsewhere attempted to bring together the accumulating evidence for this sort of phenomenon.[21] This evidence, then, should make us a bit wary when new vicious circles or new development-obstructing personality types or new deadends are being discovered. Though such discoveries are bound to occur and can be real contributions to understanding, they carry an obligation to look for ways in which they may play not a reinforcing but a neutral or de-

20. It is only fair to note that, in his more recent work on achievement motivation, David McClelland has changed his earlier views on these matters. Thus he writes (after having given cogent reasons for doing so): "To us it is no longer a self-evident truth that it is easier to produce long-range personality transformations in young children than it is in adults" (David C. McClelland and David G. Winter, *Motivating Economic Achievement* (New York: Free Press, 1969), p. 356.

21. See chap. 14, above.

bilitating role in so far as system maintenance is concerned. Perhaps social scientists could pass a rule, such as has long existed in the British Parliament, by which an M.P. proposing a new item of public expenditure must also indicate the additional revenue through which he expects the nation to finance it. Similarly it might be legislated by an assembly of social scientists that anyone who believes he has discovered a new obstacle to development is under an obligation to look for ways in which this obstacle can be overcome or can possibly be lived with or can, in certain circumstances, be transformed into a blessing in disguise.

IV

A related element of the cognitive style I am advocating derives from the recognition of one aspect of the unfolding of social events that makes prediction exceedingly difficult and contributes to that peculiar open-endedness of history that is the despair of the paradigm-obsessed social scientist. Situations in which the expertise of the social scientist is solicited frequently have the following structure: some new event or bundle of events such as industrialization, urbanization, rapid population growth, etc., has happened or is happening before our eyes, and we would like to know what its consequences are for a number of social and political system characteristics, such as integration of marginal or oppressed groups, loss of authority on the part of traditional elites, political stability or crisis, likely level of violence or of cultural achievement, and so on. Faced with the seemingly reasonable demand for enlightenment on the part of the layman and the policy maker, and propelled also by his own curiosity, the social scientist now opens his paradigm box to see how best to handle the job at hand. To his dismay, he then finds, provided he looks carefully, that he is faced with an embarrassment of riches: various available paradigms will produce radically different answers. The situation can be compared, in a rough way, with the quandary the forecasting economist has long experienced: the magnitudes that are of most interest to the policy makers, such as the prospective deficit or surplus in the balance of payments or the budget, or the inflationary or deflationary gap, or the rate of unemployment, are usually—and maddeningly—differences between gross magnitudes. Hence even if the gross magnitudes are estimated with an acceptable margin of error, the estimate of the difference may be off by a very large percentage and may easily be even of the wrong sign. The hazards in forecasting qualitative social events on the basis of perfectly respectable and reliable paradigms can be rather similar. Take the question: what is the effect of industrialization and economic development on a society's propensity for civil war, or for external adventure, or for genocide, or for democracy? As with the effect, say, of accelerated growth on the balance of payments, the answer must be: it depends on the balance of the contending forces that are set in motion. Industrialization creates new tensions, but may allay old ones; it may divert the minds of the elite from external adventure while creating new capabilities for such adventure, and so forth. Thus the outcome is here also a difference whose estimate is necessarily subject to a particularly high degree of error. This ambiguous situation, incidentally, characterizes also less crucial, more "middle-range" causal relationships. An example is the effect of bigness and diversity of an organization on innovation. As James Q. Wilson has argued, bigness and diversity increase the probability that members will conceive of and propose major innovations; but they also increase the probability that any one innovation that is proposed will be turned down. Again the net effect is in doubt.[22]

Wilson's dilemma is the sort of cognitive style in paradigmatic thinking that is not often met with; ordinarily social scientists are happy enough when they have gotten hold of one paradigm or line of causation. As a result, their guesses are often farther off the mark than those of the experienced politician whose intuition is more likely to take a variety of forces into account.

V

Finally, the ability of paradigmatic thinking to illuminate the

22. James Q. Wilson, "Innovation in Organization: Notes Toward a Theory," in James D. Thompson, ed., *Approaches to Organizational Design* (Pittsburgh: University of Pittsburgh Press, 1966), pp. 193–218.

paths of change is limited in yet another, perhaps more fundamental way. In the context of most Latin American societies, many of us are concerned with the bringing about of large-scale change to be carried through in a fairly brief period of time. But ordinarily the cards are stacked so much against the accomplishment of large-scale change that when it happens, be it a result of revolution or reform or some intermediate process, it is bound to be an unpredictable and nonrepeatable event, unpredictable because it took the very actors by surprise and nonrepeatable because once the event has happened everybody is put on notice and precautions will be taken by various parties so that it won't happen again. The uniqueness and scientific opaqueness of the large-scale changes that occur when history "suddenly accelerates" have often been remarked upon. Womack brings this out as well as anyone in his narrative of the Mexican Revolution. I shall invoke the authority of two recent commentators belonging to rather different camps. The first is the anthropologist Max Gluckman, who addresses himself to "radical change" after having defended anthropology against the charge that it is not interested in change. He writes, "The source of radical change escapes these analyses [of other kinds of change]. Perhaps this is inevitable because social anthropology aims to be scientific. Scientific method cannot deal with unique complexes of many events. The accounts of the actual course of events which produce change therefore necessarily remain historical narrative."[23]

Perhaps a more significant witness, because as a Marxist he should be an inveterate paradigm-lover, is Louis Althusser. In his remarkable essay, "Contradiction and Over-determination," Althusser makes much of some striking statements of Lenin's about the unique constellation of events that made possible the Russian Revolution of 1917. The key passage from Lenin is: "If the revolution has triumphed so rapidly it is exclusively because, as a result of a historical situation of extreme originality, a number of completely distinct currents, a number of totally heterogeneous class interests, and a number of completely op-

23. *Politics, Law and Ritual in Tribal Society* (Chicago: Aldine, 1965), p. 286.

posite social and political tendencies have become fused with remarkable coherence."[24]

On the basis of Lenin's testimony Althusser then proceeds to explain that revolutions never arise purely out of the basic economic contradictions that Marx stressed, but only when these contradictions are "fused" in some unique manner with a number of other determinants. This fusion or embedding is the phenomenon he calls "overdetermination" of revolutions. Actually this is a poor term (as he himself recognizes) for it could imply that, had one of the many circumstantial factors not been present, the revolution would still have taken place. But the whole context of the essay, and certainly the quotations from Lenin, exclude this interpretation. On the contrary, it is quite clear that even with all these converging elements the revolution won by an exceedingly narrow margin. Thus, while a surprising number of heterogeneous elements almost miraculously conspired to bring the revolution about, every single one of them was still absolutely indispensable to its success. Uniqueness seems a better term for this phenomenon than overdetermination.

Incidentally, this interpretation of revolutions undermines the revolutionary's usual critique of the advocacy of reform. This critique is generally based on the high degree of improbability that a ruling group will ever tolerate or even connive at the elimination or destruction of its own privileges; the only way to achieve this end is by smashing the "system" through revolutionary assault. But with the view of revolutions as overdetermined or unique events, it turns out to be a toss-up which form of large-scale change is more unlikely—so we may as well be on the lookout for whatever rare openings in either direction appear on the horizon.

In sum, he who looks for large-scale social change must be possessed, with Kierkegaard, by "the passion for what is possible" rather than rely on what has been certified as probable by factor analysis.

This view of large-scale social change as a unique, nonrepeat-

24. As quoted in Althusser, *Pour Marx* (Paris: S. Maspero, 1966), p. 98.

able, and *ex ante* highly improbable complex of events is obviously damaging to the aspirations of anyone who would explain and predict these events through "laws of change." Once again, there is no denying that such "laws" or paradigms can have considerable utility. They are useful for the apprehending of many elements of the complex and often are stimuli to action before the event and indispensable devices for achieving a beginning of understanding after the event has happened. That is much, but that is all. The architect of social change can never have a reliable blueprint. Not only is each house he builds different from any other that was built before, but it also necessarily uses new construction materials and even experiments with untested principles of stress and structure. Therefore what can be most usefully conveyed by the builders of one house is an understanding of the experience that made it at all possible to build under these trying circumstances. It is, I believe, in this spirit that Womack makes that, at first sight rather shocking, statement, "the truth of the revolution in Morelos is in the feeling of it." Perhaps he means not only the truth, but also the principal lesson.

Index

Abegglen, James G., 320
Abelson, R. P., 353*n*
Abramovitz, Moses, 70*n*
Abrazo, 171, 172–73
Achievement motivation, 326, 355
Action-arousing gloomy vision, 284*n*, 351–54. See also *Fracasomania*
Adam, 7*n*
ADELA (Atlantic Community Development Group for Latin America), 221, 251
Adler, John H., 228*n*
Africa, cleavages in, 14
Aggregative analysis, value of, 42–44
Agrarian reform, 312, 345; in Peru, 31; in Colombia, 180, 332, 338–39; as prerequisite to U.S. foreign aid, 184; as result of unsuccessful land tax, 186; and ECLA, 289; in Mexico, 298–99, 301–02, 348; virtues of postponement of, 302; in Bolivia, 332; in Venezuela, 332; through reform-mongering, 332, 338; through revolution, 332, 348. *See also* Change
Agriculture, 42, 43, 294
AID (Agency for International Development), 251
Airlines, 58
Alagoas, Brazil, 145
Alberdi, Juan Bautista, 275, 276, 293
Alianza vs. *Progreso,* 182. See also *Abrazo;* Alliance for Progress
Alliance for Progress, 175–82, 199, 232, 285*n*, 326*n*

Alternation: of policies, 25–26, 255–69; of charisma and skill, 340–41, 349
Althusser, Louis, 358–59
Amazonas region, Brazil, 128
American Challenge, The (Servan-Schreiber), 227
Anaconda Corporation, 251
Anderson, Charles W., 331*n*
An Introduction to the Technique of Programming (ECLA document), 285
Anti-imperialism, 276–79
Approaches to Economic Development (Buchanan and Ellis), 308
Aprismo, Aprista. See Haya de la Torre
Argentina, 12, 114, 234, 250, 286, 320
Arguedas, Alcides, 274*n*
Aronson, Elliot, 353*n*
Article 34/18, 124–58. *See also* Northeast Brazil; Tax credit system
Ascetic ideal, 317
Ascher, Robert, 35*n*, 183*n*
Asia, 14. *See also* Southeast Asia

Backward linkage, 59–62, 66, 90–92, 121; resistances to, 101–04, 106–08, 118, 123; importance of market size, 104–05; political economy of process, 106–13; and "technological strangeness," 114
Baer, Werner, 98*n*
Bahia, Brazil, 142, 145
Balanced development (or growth), 49, 63; of industry and agriculture, 42, 61; definition of, 64,

66n. *See also* Development plans and programs

Balance of payments, 43. *See also* Exchange rates and controls

Banfield, Edward C., 316n

Bauer, P. T., 161, 163, 314n

Bay of Pigs, 175

Bekker, Konrad, 55n

Bell, Daniel, 305n

Beloff, Nora, 346n

Belshaw, C. S., 314n

Bird, Richard M., 197, 198n

Blessing in disguise, 313–18; and economics-cum-politics, 13; and possibilism, 29–30; in Peru, 33; and industrialization, 108, 113; in Argentina, 320. *See also* Curse in disguise; Obstacles

BNB (Bank of the Northeast of Brazil), 125, 126, 128, 134–36 passim, 142, 147

Bolívar, Simón, 275

Bolivia, 286, 332

Bomfim, Manoel, 274

Bonilla, Frank, 96n

Boserup, Esther, 36n

Bottleneck Industry, 105

Bottlenecks, 310–11. *See also* Imbalances; Shortages; Unbalanced Growth

Braibanti, Ralph, 321n

Branco, Humberto Castello, 151

Brasilia, 292

Brazil, 87–88, 250, 297n, 298, 311n; characteristics of, 14, 185; and industrialization, 95–96, 114; and nineteenth-century domestic entrepreneurship, 97; and backward linkage, 108; economy of, 184, 298, 303–04, 318; and attitude toward foreign trade, 202, 232; and move to neutralism, 208; stealthy change in, 235, 334; and ECLA, 286; pessimism in, 292. *See also* Northeast Brazil

Brehm, Jack W., 323, 324, 325n

Brown, Murray, 104n

Bruner, Jerome S., 329n

Buchanan, James M., 4n

Buchanan, Norman, 307–08

Budget, 264, 265

Bunge, C. O., 273n, 274

Burke, Edmund, 46, 76

Burma, 202

Burns, Arthur F., 99n

Cairncross, A. K., 229n

Callado, Antonio, 335n

Campos, Roberto de Oliveira, 296, 297n

Capital: and investment planning, 48, 57, 278; use of in developing countries, 54–55, 57; private, as road to development, 308. *See also* Investment, domestic

Capital intensity, 48, 54–57, 62, 93

Capitalist development, 351

Capital market, captive, 128, 130–33

Capital movements. *See* Foreign aid; Foreign investment

Capital-output ratio, 42–43, 285

Cardoso, Fernando Henrique, 109n

Caribbean, 276

Carranza, Venustiano, 348

Cartorial State, 292

Castro, Fidel, 177

Caves, Richard E., 90n

Cavour, Camillo Benso, Count of, 340

Ceará, Brazil, 145

Center-South, Brazil, 129, 131, 134, 147, 153, 157. *See also* Article 34/18; Brazil; Northeast Brazil; Rio de Janeiro; São Paulo

Central America, 88

Central Planning, 80, 355

Centro de Altos Estudios Militares (CAEM), 32–33, 34

Challenge and response, 20, 318–19

Change, 1; political, 16–19, 22; agents of, 20–21, 22; in U.S., 22, 180–81; paradigms and laws of, 27–28, 342–43, 357–58; forces opposed to, 28; large-scale, 28, 358, 359–60; possibilistic outlook of, 29, 31; unintended, 31, 34–37; obstacles to the perception of, 328–41; recognition of, 330, 338, 339; types, 330; cumulative, 331, 332, 333; fundamental, 332; and dependent countries, 333–35; loud vs. stealthy, 334, 335; as result of projected disaster, 351; despair over possibility of, 355. *See also* Leadership; Obstacles; Reform-mongering; Revolution

Chapanis, N. P. and A., 323*n*

Charisma. *See* Leadership

Chase International Investment Corporation, 221

Chile, 280; and industrialization, 113; and foreign investors, 232; inadequate economic progress in, 274; agrarian reform in, 332

China, 317

CIA (Central Intelligence Agency), 175

Circular causation, 33–34. *See also* Cumulative disequilibrium

Citizens, role of in public affairs, 5–7

Cleavages, 14

Cochran, Thomas C., 320*n*

Coexistence vs. *abrazo,* 170–74

Coffee: price fluctuations, 11, 13, 15; and politics, 11–12, 13; and economic policy, 11–12, 15; and industrial expansion, 97. *See also* Brazil; Colombia

Cognitive dissonance, 206, 324–25; foundation for possibilism, 30; deficiencies of theory, 31, 33; in foreign aid recipient, 206; and inverted sequences, 323–25; and *fracasomania,* 352–53

Cognitive style, 343–44, 349

Cohen, Arthur R., 323, 324, 325

Cohen, R., 63*n*

Colombia: characteristics of, 14, 52*n*, 343–50 passim; agriculture, 43; "poor planning," 46; and foreign aid, 49, 50; stresses and shortages, 51; maintenance of public transportation system, 58; inverted development, 59–60, 61; nineteenth-century history, 97, 293; industrialization, 114; agrarian reform, 180, 332, 338–39; politics, 184, 344–45, 346; and ECLA, 286; inefficiency of state, 295, 298; stealthy change, 334

Commodity prices, fluctuations of, 11, 161–62, 163–64, 173, 175

Commodity Trade and Economic Development (U.N. publication), 167

Common Market, in Latin America, 122, 173–74, 241, 281, 287–88

Community ownership, 252

Comprehensive planning. *See* Development plans and programs

Conceição Tavares, Maria de, 88

Constitutions, in Latin America, 47*n*, 272–73, 290

Consumer surplus, 8

Corden, W. M., 111*n*

Cosío Villegas, Daniel, 270

Costa, Rubens, 136*n*

Cruse, Harold, 336*n*

Cuba, 175, 185, 286, 308, 332

Cumulative change. *See* Change

Cumulative disequilibrium, 13. *See also* Circular causation

Curse in disguise, 13, 29–30, 327. *See also* Blessing in disguise

Customs Unions, 8

Da Cunha, Euclides, 274*n*

Davie, Michael, 346*n*

Dean, Warren, 97*n*

Debray, Régis, 37

Decision making, 63, 70, 72, 78

Decreasing returns, in politics, 20, 21, 22

Demand, faulty estimates of, 48, 99*n*

Democracy, democratic governments: and consensus, 30; and public spending patterns, 51

Demonstration effect, 56*n*, 257, 275*n*, 283, 306

Devaluation, of exchange rate, 265

Development: destabilizing effects of, 16; and unbalanced growth, 63–66; circumstances favorable to, 66, 79, 186, 250–51, 292; and loss of autonomy, 171, 181–82, 231, 304, 331*n;* ideologies of, 270–311; tied to nationalism, 304; obstacles to, 312–27; and non-Western institution, 321; obstacles to the perception of, 328–37, 352–53. *See also* Backward linkage; Change; Industrialization

"Developmentalist" ideology, in Brazil, 95–96

Development decisions, 69*n;* and linkages, 81

Development Loan Fund, 308

Development plans and programs, 42–44; criticisms of, 45–48, 77, 257–58; as prerequisite to foreign aid, 173, 177, 183–87, 199; func-

tions of, 256–57; and ECLA, 285–87, 290–91. *See also* Balanced development (or growth); Program aid

Development Projects Observed (Hirschman), 14*n*, 82*n*, 333*n*

Development sequences. *See* Sequences

Dialectical process *vs.* cumulative social process, 34

Díaz, Porfirio, 273

Direct investment, 234, 237. *See also* Portfolio investment

Disequilibrium. *See* Imbalances; Unbalanced growth

Disguised unemployment, 306, 307, 310

Disjointed incrementalism, 71–72

Divestment, 29, 181; built-in, 221, 243–48; difficulties with, 239–40, 244–45, 249; Corporation, 240–43; and coproduction agreements, 251

"Domophobia," 61

Dorfman, Adolfo, 89*n*

Dorfman, Robert, 4*n*

Downs, Anthony, 3, 4

Earmarking of fiscal revenues, 264–66

Echavarría Olózaga, Hernán, 295*n*

ECLA (Economic Commission for Latin America), 42, 55, 55*n*, 86*n*, 175, 280–97 passim, 303. *See also* Prebisch, Raúl

Economic advisers, 19*n*, 184, 255–56, *See also* Economists; Technical assistance

Economic development. *See* Development

Economic Development in Latin America (Hanson), 309

Economic Development of Latin America and Its Principal Problems, The (Prebisch, ECLA), 280

Economic policy: role in ISI process, 114; sequences of, 184; and foreign aid negotiations, 203–07; and government behavior, 255, 264–65; irrational, 256; method in madness of, 256, 264, 268–69; and ECLA, 296. *See also* Development; Policy making

Economic programming. *See* Development plans and programs

Economics, 3–4, 54, 57

Economics-cum-politics, 2–3, 7–17, 20, 26. *See also* Political economy

Economic Test in Latin America, The (Schultz), 310

Economic Theory of Democracy, An (Downs), 3

Economies of scale, 101–05

Economists, 1, 161; and free rider problem, 5; neglect of politics by, 6–7, 20, 255; concepts of applied to politics, 13; expertise of, 41; methods criticized, 41–62 passim, 256–57; as planners, 43, 49–50, 52; as scarce resource, 46–47; "traditional," 307. *See also* Economic advisers

Ecuador, 88, 353

Edge Act financial corporations, 221

Education, 52, 294

Effective protection, 107, 110*n*

Eisenhower, Milton, 172*n*

Eisenhower Administration, 175, 177

Electric power, 46*n*, 47–48, 51, 52, 54

El laberinto de la soledad (Paz), 272, 300

Ellis, Howard S., 117*n*, 307, 308

Encina, Francisco, 274, 275*n*

Engel, Ernst, 336, 383, 383*n*

England, 14, 92

"Entrained wants," 79–80

Entrepreneurs, entrepreneurship, 317, 323; as profit maximizers, 4; misperceptions of, 24; and hostile environment, 60; and sectoral imbalances, 64–65; foreign vs. indigenous, 96; in late late industrializing countries, 96–97; lack of prestige of, 97, 292; type desirable in Latin America, 109; lack of, 275*n;* state as, 293. *See also* Industrialists

Epstein, T. S., 321*n*

Equilibrium growth models, 15

Erikson, Erik, 26*n*

Ethiopia, 333

European Economic Community, 287

Exchange rates and controls, 117, 264, 297

"Exhaustion" thesis, in ISI process, 101–02, 103. *See also* Import-substituting industrialization

Exit, 9

Exit, Voice, and Loyalty (Hirschman), 4*n*, 6*n*, 26*n*, 31*n*

Experts. *See* Economic advisers; *Técnicos*

Explorations in Cognitive Dissonance (Brehm and Cohen), 323

Export-Import Bank, 175, 308

Export of capital, 228

Export-propelled growth, 88, 281, 353

Exports: of primary products, 98*n*, 281, 353; of manufacturers, 115–17, 119–22

Expropriation, 31, 225

Extended family, 314–15

Factors of production, specialization in, 228–29, 230

Failure complex. See *Fracasomania*

Feis, Herbert, 235*n*

Felix, David, 98*n*

Festinger, Leon, 30, 323, 329*n*
Fidelismo, 180
Final demand linkage, 90
Fiscal policy, 260–65. *See also* Tax credit system
Flores, Edmundo, 298–99, 301–02, 303
Foreign aid: and political influence, 10–11, 186, 187, 188, 325*n;* calculations of need, 42; misconceived as catalyst, 179, 183, 204; prerequisites to, 183–84; criticism of, 183–87; and tax reform, 184; crises as part of, 186; nonexistence of one best policy of, 187; maximization of, 189; plus independence, 190–95; plus commitment, 191–93; characteristics of, 197; 1960 changes in approach to, 199; and cognitive dissonance, 206, 325–26*n;* recipients' resistance to, 207; diplomacy of, 208–10; and donor's claim to superiority, 209; new technique proposed, 211–12; contribution to by individual taxpayer, 212; imperialist nature of, 213; alleged need for, 355. *See also* Program aid; Project aid
Foreign investment: political implications of, 10–11; negative effects of, 50, 226–30, 232; in course of ISI, 96, 101; and Article 34/18, 130–31*n;* and gradual withdrawal, 181, 225–51. *See also* Divestment; Portfolio investment
Foreign investor: mousiness of, 231; crises due to presence of, 232; and divestment, 240–41; keeping him interested, 247, 248
Foresight, 77, 78
Fortaleza, Brazil, 145
Forward linkage, 90

Fracasomania, 85, 88–89, 353. *See also* Self-deprecation
Frank, Andre Gunder, 63*n*
Free Rider problem, 4, 5, 7*n*
Free trade, 228, 275, 284, 336
French Revolution, 20
Frey, Bruno S., 3*n*
Freyre, Gilberto, 185, 304
Fuentes, Carlos, 300, 301, 349
Furtado, Celso, 87–88, 87*n*, 117*n*, 118*n*, 276, 303, 304, 311*n*

Gain, from trade, 13, 282, 307
Galbraith, John Kenneth, 22*n*, 183, 185
Garibaldi, Giuseppe, 340
Geertz, Clifford, 316*n*, 321*n*
Germany, 92, 97*n*, 184
Gerschenkron, Alexander, 94, 95, 96*n*, 120, 184, 271, 303*n*, 319
Getulio Vargas Foundation, 141*n*
Gloomy vision. *See* Action-arousing gloomy vision
Gluckman, Max, 358
Goals, 67, 69*n*, 75, 76
Goldenweiser, Alexander, 352
Gordon, Lincoln, 171*n*
Governments: action in economic field, 23; responses to sectoral imbalances, 64–65; behavior required for aid, 183; improvisation of, 259–60; principal tasks of (ECLA), 290
Gramsci, Antonio, 303*n*
"Great spurt," 95
Greece, 220
Green, Forrest, 59
Gudin, Eugenio, 293–94
Guerilla warfare: in Peru, 32–34; and foreign aid, 186, 187
Guitton, Henri, 4*n*

Habakkuk, H. J., 317*n*
Haberler, Gottfried, 90*n*, 308
Hanson, Simon G., 309

Haya de la Torre, Víctor, 277–78, 278n, 279
Hayek, Friedrich von, 2, 161
Health, 52
Heilbroner, Robert, 22n, 185
Helleiner, Karl F., 317n
Higgins, Benjamin, 314n
Hill, Polly, 315n
Hindu life style, 26n
Hirschman, Albert O., 63, 75, 78, 79, 80–82
Hockett, Charles F., 35n
Hoffmann, Stanley and Inge, 340n
Holt, Robert T., 2
Hoselitz, Bert F., 55n, 321n
Huis Clos (Sartre), 345
Human capital, 51. See also Education; Health
Huntington, Samuel P., 2n

Ideologies, 29, 270–311; imported, 4, 335–37; vs. reality, 47, 272–73, 336, 337; commitment to, 192; defined, 270n; end of, 305
Imbalances, 17, 19, 20, 21, 68, 83; usefulness of, 69, 73; in systems, 73, 74; limits to, 83; as stimulant to development, 310–11. See also Sectoral imbalances; Unbalanced growth
Imperialism, 214, 277, 278, 301. See also Foreign aid; Foreign investment
Import restrictions, 283
Import-substituting industrialization (ISI), 18, 21, 86–123, 284, 289; principal characteristics of, 89–94; diverse origins of, 90–91; phases and processes of, 90–91, 99, 100; initial phase of, 91–94, 103, 112; sequential nature of, 92; consequences of in late late industrializers, 97, 98; psycho-political consequences of, 99–100; seen as fracaso, 100–01; "exhaustion" thesis, 101–02, 353; and backward linkage effects, 102; and high levels of protection, 107; sequentiality in, 123. See also Industrialists; Industrialization
Improvisation, 47
Inauguration, of projects, 51
Income elasticity, of demand for imports, 42, 282–83
"Incrementalists," 305
India, 89, 199, 208, 220
Indian past, of Latin America, 279, 299
Indifference curves, map, 4, 189–92
Industrialists: options open to, 21; resistance to backward linkage, 106–07, 108–11; lack of political influence, 119–20; noninvolvement of foreign, 230–31; and divestment, 240
Industrialization, 18, 42, 60, 183, 345; effect of in developing countries, 11, 331; in postwar Argentina, 12; as unintended side effect, 36, 91; in Northeast Brazil, 124–57; national vs. regional, 146–47; in Cuba, 178; coolness of nineteenth-century writers to, 276; call for, 281; priority of over agriculture, 296; and agrarian reform, 302. See also Article 34/18; Backward linkage; Import-substituting industrialization
Infant industry. See Protection
Inflation: and overevaluation, 117–18, 146; explanation for recurrence of, 260–66; uses of, 262–63; as analyzed by ECLA, 289–90; and capital formation, 296
Information, imperfect, 78–79
Innovations, revolutionary effect of, 332

Instability: of political alignment, 193; of economic policies, 256–68. *See also* Commodity prices, fluctuations of

Institutional inertia, 24–25, 225, 250–51

Integrated Development Program. *See* Development plans and programs

Inter-American Development Bank, 216, 221, 238, 308

Inter-American Divestment Corporation, 237–43. *See also* Divestment

Interest groups, 18

Intermediate goods, 91–92, 105

Internal rate of return, 246

International Bank for Reconstruction and Development, 49, 50, 198, 210, 213, 216, 221, 278, 284, 290, 308

International Finance Corporation, 219, 221, 238, 239, 251

International Monetary Fund, 203, 208, 290

International Petroleum Company, Peru, 31, 225

Inverted sequences, 59–60, 66, 184, 322–25. *See also* Cognitive Dissonance; Democracy

Investment, domestic: size vs. composition of, 43; patterns of, 44–45, 258; sector, 45; in electric power, 48; demonstration effect, 56*n;* under Article 34/18 in Brazil, 126–28, 139, 141; industrial, 149; decisions activated, 152; as condition for aid, 198; and development programs, 258; public vs. private, in inflation, 261; role of state in, 286

Investment, foreign. *See* Foreign investment

Investment opportunities, 23, 131, 133

Investment planning: difficulties of, 45; biases, 51–52. *See also* Development plans and programs

Investment projects, 49–53

ISI. *See* Import-substituting industrialization

Italy, 184, 303*n,* 340

Jaguaribe, Helio, 292

Japan, 317, 320

Jesus, 7*n*

Jordan, 220

Journeys Toward Progress (Hirschman), 13*n,* 19*n,* 116*n,* 124*n,* 147*n,* 184*n,* 322*n,* 326*n,* 339*n*

Judean-Christian thought, 26*n*

Kafka, Alexandre, 117*n*

Kennecott Corporation, 251

Kennedy, John F., 175, 176, 198

Kerstenetzky, Isaac, 98*n*

Keynes, John Maynard, 161, 270

Kierkegaard, Soren, 359

Klein, Burton, 63, 66*n,* 66–69, 75, 76, 79, 82

Knapp, J., 228*n*

Korea, 220

Kubitschek, Juscelino, 100, 108

Kuznets, Simon S., 99*n,* 317*n*

Labor mobility, 167–68

Laclos, Choderlos de, 319

Laissez-faire, 25*n,* 275, 276. *See also* Free trade

Lambert, Jacques, 318

Land reform. *See* Agrarian reform

La región más transparente (Fuentes), 300

Latecomers 184, 271, 276; and social leapfrogging, 240; and cognitive dissonance, 325; and sociopolitical change, 331. *See also* Late industrialization

Late industrialization: examples of, 94; aspects of, 94–95; vs. late

late, 94–96, 116–17. *See also* Import-substituting industrialization; Late late industrialization

Late late industrialization, 92–96; unspectacular aspect of, 95. *See also* Import-substituting industrialization; Industrialization; Latecomers; Late industrialization

Latifundio, 279, 332

Law and order, 317–18

Leadership, 6; change-perceiving, 337–38, 339–40; charisma and skill in, 337–41, 349; definition of, 338; ultimate function of, 341; in Colombia, 346

Leites, Nathan, 291*n*

Lenin, Nikolai, 107, 340, 358–59

Les Liaisons Dangereuses (Laclos), 319

"Leverage." *See* Program aid

Lévi-Strauss, Claude, 350*n*

Levy, Marion, J., Jr., 317*n*

Lewis, Sir Arthur, 283, 307, 321

Lindblom, Charles E., 63, 70, 75, 76, 78–79, 80–82, 297, 305*n*

Linder, S. B., 116*n*

Linkage effects, 80–82, 142. *See also* Backward linkage; Forward linkage

Lipset, S. M., 109*n*

Liquidation of foreign investment: past mechanisms of, 233–36; as occasion for social change, 240. *See also* Divestment; Portfolio investment

"Little tradition," 330

Lleras Restrepo, Carlos, 338–39

Logic of Collective Action, The (Olson), 3

Low-level-equilibrium trap, 16

Lungfish, 35–36

Luz, Nicia Vilela, 336*n*

Macario, Santiago, 88, 107*n*

Machiavelli, Niccoló, 30*n*, 341

Machinery, secondhand, 152–53

McClelland, David, 355*n*

Magaña, Gildardo, 340*n*, 347–49

Maginot Line, 73, 74*n*

Maintenance: of capital, 51, 57; as criterion for investment planning, 57–59, 62

Malenbaum, Wilfred, 311*n*

Mandeville, Bernard de, 34

Margolis, Julius, 4*n*

Mariátegui, José Carlos, 277, 279

Market and nonmarket forces, 17

Market size, 104, 107, 109

Marris, Peter, 315*n*

Marshall, H., 234*n*

Marx, Karl, 342, 359; on history, 16–18, 332, 351; on capital goods, 93

Marxism, 20, 22, 336

Masters and Slaves (Freyre), 185

Matossian, Mary, 271*n*, 301*n*

Meckling, William, 63, 66–69, 75, 76, 79, 82

Medellín, Colombia, 113

Merton, Robert K., 33

Mexico, 250, 297*n*, 343; and backward linkage, 108; industrialization in, 114; and feelings of pride, 185; *ejido*, 240, 279; and Porfirio Díaz, 273–74; and U.S. intervention, 276; its Revolution, 276, 277, 300, 340*n*; economic "miracle" in, 298*n*; perception of development in, 298–303; and agrarian reform, 299, 332

Military: in Peru, 31–33; outside intervention, 276, 334

Misperceptions of opportunities, 22–26

Mixed blessing. *See* Curse in disguise

Monetary stability: maintenance of, 50; as prerequisite for capital

inflow, 177, 183–84; in developing nations vs. advanced, 261–63
Monod, Jacques, 27
Monterrey, Mexico, 113
Montesquieu, Charles de, 2
Moore, Barrington, Jr., 10n
Morelos, Mexico, 340n, 344
Morley, Samuel A., 99n
Multilateral aid, 195–96
Multinational corporations, 241, 249
Multiple exchange rates, 264–66
Myint, H., 169n
Myrdal, Gunnar, 13, 33, 34, 161, 168, 307

Napoleon, Louis, 185, 277
Nationalism, 15, 25, 304
Nationalization, 225, 277. See also Divestment
National Power and the Structure of Foreign Trade (Hirschman), 9n
Neglect, "wise and salutary," 46, 68, 76, 251
Neutralism, 4, 188–96; stability of, 3; and aid-giving patterns, 189; nonpenalization of, 189, 191
Nigeria, 14
Nixon, Richard M., 172, 175, 308
Normano, J. F., 235n, 272n, 275n
Northeast Brazil, 124–58, 180, 216. See also Article 34/18; Tax credit system
Northrop, F. S. C., 273n
Nuestra América (Bunge), 274
Nuestra inferioridad económica (Encina), 274
Nun, José, 32n
Nurkse, Ragnar, 56n, 161n, 162, 163, 306

OAS (Organization of American States), 280
Obregón, Alvaro, 348

Obstacles: exaggerated notions of, 29; as blessings in disguise, 29–30, 313–18, 355–56; overcoming of, 52n, 185; in underdeveloped regions, 153; needed action upon discovery of, 184; to production, 294; classification of, 312; that can be lived with, 318–21, 355–56; postponable type, 321–26; to the perception of change, 329, 333, 353. See also Blessing in disguise
Obstacles to Change in Latin America (Véliz), 329
Olson, Mancur Jr., 3, 6n
O parasitismo social (Bomfim), 274
Opportunity set. See Transformation curve
Optimal policies, 25, 26
Ospina Vásquez, Luis, 97n
Overdetermination, 359. See also Uniqueness

Paish, Frank W., 163
Pakistan, 14, 89, 208, 220
Palafox, Manuel, 347
Panama, 276, 286
Panama Canal, 181, 277
Paradigms, 342–60; absence of, in Womack, 347; fascination with, 350; usefulness of, 354, 360. See also Possibilism; Uniqueness
Parker, William N., 97n
"Participation Explosion," 5, 6
Partisan mutual adjustment, 72, 80
Pascal, Blaise de, 7n, 30n
Patch, Richard W., 279n
Patterns of Conflict in Colombia (Payne), 343
Paul (Apostle), 7n
Payne, James L., 343–50 passim
Paz, Octavio, 272, 300, 301
Paz de Rio steel mill, 49
Pazos, Felipe, 228n, 229

Pedreira, Fernando, 335n
Perception of change. See Change
Pérez Jiménez, Marcos, 100
Pernambuco, Brazil, 142, 145
Perón, Juan Domingo, 12, 100, 234
Peru, 31–33, 34, 88; and IPC, 225; and foreign investors, 232; and revolutionary theories, 277; and ECLA, 286; agrarian reform in, 332; fishmeal industry in, 353. See also Military
Pike, F. B., 171n
Pinto Santa Cruz, Aníbal, 85
Policy makers, 231, 327
Policy making, 81–83; rationality affected by foreign investment, 231. See also Economic policy
Political change. See Change
Political economy. See Economics-cum-politics
Political scientists, 1–2, 5, 14
Politicians, Colombia vs. U.S., 345–46
"Poor planning," 46
Portfolio investment, 10; modified revival of, 221; advantages of, over direct, 234–36
Possibilism, 28–29, 35–37. See also Change; Paradigms; Uniqueness
Postman, Leo, 329n
Power, John H., 107n
Prebisch, Raúl, 86, 88, 238, 280, 281n, 282, 287, 296, 306
Prebisch-Singer thesis, 307
Prerequisites (or preconditions), 183–84; to development, 319–20. See also Obstacles
Primary production, 60, 61, 62, 162, 281, 282, 307. See also Backward linkage
Product convergence, 104–05
Production-possibility set. See Transformation curve

Production techniques, used by late-comers. See Capital intensity
Program aid, 10, 183–84; criticisms of, 198–211; definition of, 199; political implications of, 200; hidden costs of, 208; donor's claim to superior knowledge, 209; colonial situation created by, 210; positive aspects of, 210; recommendations for improvement of, 211. See also Alliance for Progress; Foreign aid; Project aid
"Program incentive," 345–46
Project aid, 10; vs. program aid, 198–211; deals with peripheral decisions, 198, 200; pure, 200–01; donor's superior knowledge, 209. See also Foreign aid; Program aid
Protection (tariff), 86, 90, 283–84; effective, 107, 110–11n
Protestant ethic, 30, 109, 326
Public administration, 266–67
Public goods, 4–7
Public policies: as public good, 5; need for, to change perceptions, 24; and backward linkage, 108; and foreign aid, 204; needed to change international trading system, 284. See also Economic policy; Policy making
Public utilities: shortages in, 48; expansion of, 51; during inflation, 265; transferred from private to public sector, 296. See also Electric power
Puerto Rico, 148, 173

Quadros, Janio, 208

Railroads, in Colombia, 50, 58; vs. roads, 54
Recife, Brazil, 145

Redfield, Robert, 330
Reform, 28–29, 186, 359. *See also* Agrarian reform; Change; Social development
Reform-mongering, 338
Regional integration, in Latin America, 122, 249–50, 277–78, 287–88
Reina, Reuben E., 320*n*
Research and development, 66–69, 82–83
Revolution: Marxian concept of, 17, 18, 20; in hegemonic and dependent countries, 19; and vanguard group, 22; as only one avenue to change, 33, 186, 330, 355; remaking the last, 37; overdetermination of, 358–59. *See also* Cuba; French Revolution; Mexico, its Revolution; Russian Revolution
Revolutionaries, 20, 342–43, 358, 359
Ricardo, David, 228
Rio de Janeiro, 131, 133, 225
Roads: in Colombia, 50, 58; as shortcut to development, 52; and railroads, 54; and maintenance, 58–59. *See also* Maintenance
Rogers, Carl, 185
Rojas Pinilla, Gustavo, 100
Romeo, Rosario, 303*n*
Romer, A. S., 35
Roosevelt, Franklin D., 225
Rosenberg, Nathan, 93, 104*n*
Rosenstein-Rodan, Paul N., 244, 307
Rostow, W. W., 297*n*
Rousseau, Jean-Jacques, 2, 6
Rudolph, Lloyd I. and Suzanne H., 314*n*
Russett, Bruce M., 3*n*
Russian Revolution, 276
Rustow, Dankwart, 30*n*, 340*n*

Salvador, Brazil, 145
São Paulo, 113, 130, 131, 133, 152. *See also* Center-South, Brazil
Sarmiento, Domingo F., 275
Sartre, Jean-Paul, 345
Savings, 260, 261. *See also* Investment, domestic
Schelling, Thomas C., 10*n*
Schmitt, Hans O., 10*n*, 231
Schultz, Theodore W., 310
Schumpeter, Joseph, 292
Schumpeterian entrepreneurs, 24–25*n*, 312
Schwartz, Benjamin I., 350*n*
Scitovsky, Tibor, 307
Sectoral imbalances, 64–66. *See also* Imbalances; Unbalanced growth
Sector projects and planning, 46–51. *See also* Development plans and programs
Self-deprecation, 85, 271–76, 309, 350–51; attempts to correct, 24; consequences of 51–52; persistence of, 298, 311. *See also* Action-arousing gloomy vision; *Fracasomania*
Self-fulfilling prophecy, 33
Sequences: economic-political, 1, 18, 20, 23, 24, 26; in economic policy making, 19, 20, 184; uniform, 27; and laws of change, 28; one-way orderly, 29, 31; inverted, 30, 31, 322; in decision making, 77, 311; permissive and compulsive, 83; variety of, 185. *See also* Cognitive dissonance
Sermon on the Mount, 76*n*
Shortages: and sector planning, 48; in public utilities, 48, 297; as result of economic growth, 51. *See also* Bottlenecks; Imbalances
Siegfried, André, 47
Sierra, Justo, 273

Silcock, T. H., 316*n*

Singer, Hans W., 165, 282*n*, 307

Skill. *See* Leadership

Smith, Adam, 2, 34, 228, 292, 294

Smith, Gordon W., 99*n*

Social change. *See* Change

Social Contract, The (Rousseau), 6

Social development: projects in Alliance for Progress, 176; prerequisite for U.S. foreign aid, 177, 199, 309

Social mobility: lack of, as blessing in disguise, 113, 317; in Mexico, as result of revolution, 299; via trucks, 332

Social science: general laws vs. search for uniqueness, 27–28; conservative bias of, 354; paradigm-obsessed, 356–57. *See also* Economics-cum-politics

Solari, Aldo, 109*n*

Soligo, R., 107*n*

Southard, F. A., Jr., 234*n*

Southeast Asia, 316

Soviet Union, 197

Special Drawing Rights, 243

Spengler, J. J., 321*n*

Stability: of neutralism, 188–96; of economic policies, 268. *See also* Instability

Stabilization. *See* Commodity prices, fluctuations of

State, economic capabilities of, 291–95. *See also* Public policies

"Status incentive," 345–46

Stern, J. J., 107*n*

Stigler, George, 93*n*

Strategy of Economic Development, The (Hirschman), 17, 20, 21*n*, 26*n*, 30*n*, 41*n*, 63–66, 76*n*, 81, 82*n*, 90*n*, 106, 107*n*, 147*n*, 310, 316*n*, 322*n*

Streeten, Paul, 244

Structuralist strategy of problem solving, 116

Substitutes, synthetics, 165–69

SUDENE (development agency for Northeast Brazil), 125, 128, 155, 156, 303*n*; definition of, 124; administration of 34/18 funds, 128–30; bias against second-hand machinery, 152. *See also* Article 34/18; Center-South, Brazil; Northeast Brazil

Sunkel, Osvaldo, 116*n*, 333*n*

Synoptic problem solving, 70–71

Taiwan, 220

"Take-off," 297*n*

Tannenbaum, Frank, 185, 304*n*

Tariffs. *See* Protection

Tax credit system: of Article 34/18, 124–58; advantages of, 148–50, 222–24; compared to customs duties, 150–51; problems with, 152; where suitable, 157–58; on international scale, 158, 212–14. *See also* Article 34/18; Foreign aid

Taylor, V. W., 234*n*

Technical assistance, 265, 308; disillusionment with, 183; Point Four 198; analyzing failure of, 255–56. *See also* Foreign aid

Technological progress; need for control of, 167–69

Technology: adaptation in developing countries, 55–56, 92–94; research, 249–50; revolutionary impact of, 332–33

Técnicos (planner-technicians), 108, 130

Tendler, Judith, 139*n*

Teodori, Massimo, 22*n*

Theory of Cognitive Dissonance, The (Festinger), 323

Thompson, James D., 357*n*

Tinbergen, Jan, 307

Tolstoy, Leo, 273
Toynbee, Arnold, 20
Trade creation, 9–10
Trade diversion, 9–10
Transformation curve, 3, 4, 189–95
Transistor radio, 332
Trucks, 332
Tucker, Robert C., 338, 338n, 340n
Turner, John E., 2

Umschlagen, 33. See also Dialectical process
Unbalanced growth: argument for, 64–66, 70; to bring pressure on obstacles, 157, 184. See also Bottlenecks; Imbalances; Shortages
Unintended side effects: in Peru, 34, 37; and change, 34–37; of wars and depressions, 36, 89, 233–34
Uniqueness: and social science, 27–28, 37; of large-scale changes, 349, 358–60
United Nations Conference on Trade and Development (UNCTAD), 121
United Nations Economic Commission for Latin America. See ECLA
Urbanization, 302, 345
Urquidi, Victor, 298n

Vargas, Getulio, 225
Véliz, Claudio, 32n, 329
Venezuela, 88, 332

Vernon, Raymond, 122n, 244, 249
Vico, Giambattista, 34
Viña del Mar Conference, 251
Viner, Jacob, 9, 307
Voice, 6n, 9

Wallich, Henry C., 166
Watkins, Melville H., 90n
Weffort, Francisco C., 98n
Whitaker, C. S., Jr., 314n
Wiesner Durán, Eduardo, 295n
Wilson, James Q., 357
Winter, David G., 355n
Wohlstetter, Roberta, 329n
Womack, John, 343–50 passim, 358, 360
Wood, Bryce, 225
World Bank. See International Bank for Reconstruction and Development
World Development Funds, 212, 215–21

Yamey, B. S., 314n
Young, Oran R., 342
Ypsilon, 171n

Zapata, 340n, 347–49
Zapata and the Mexican Revolution (Womack), 343
Zea, Leopoldo, 273n
Zona da mata (Northeast Brazil), 157